"This book is a tour de force within the school counseling literature. *Introduction to School Counseling* provides a reader-friendly blueprint for conceptualizing, planning, and delivering comprehensive school counseling programs within complex twenty-first-century school contexts. This book strikes an important balance between theory, research, and practice; situates school counseling prominently within school reform initiatives; provides concrete strategies and recommendations for school counseling programs; and recognizes diversity and social justice as an indispensable component of school counseling."

Norma L. Day-Vines, *PhD, Associate Dean for Diversity and Faculty Development, Professor of Counseling and Human Development, Johns Hopkins University*

"I will gladly use this textbook with our students. It is current, comprehensive, well-written, thoroughly researched, and exceedingly accessible. Even though I am deeply familiar with the content, I found myself reading with great interest and enthusiasm. I highly recommend this textbook for all who wish to learn about the past, the present, and the future of the school counseling profession. The authors have constructed an engaging textbook for graduate students and practicing professionals alike."

Kevin Wilkerson, *PhD, NCC, ACS, Associate Professor, Department of Counseling and Human Services, University of Scranton*

"This book does an outstanding job establishing the modern-day context of school counseling both by reviewing the evolution of the field with compelling analysis of diverse perspectives on important trends and developments and by featuring impressive use of data and research to separate opinions from facts. Great examples to illustrate sometimes-vague concepts abound, as do concrete and practical suggestions for both novice and seasoned school counselors. Throughout, the writing is clear, crisp, and learner-friendly."

Johnston M. Brendel, *EdD, LPC, LMFT, Clinical Associate Professor, the College of William and Mary*

Introduction to School Counseling

This book is a comprehensive introduction to the profession for school counselors in training, providing special focus on the topics most relevant to the school counselor's role, and offers specific strategies for practical application and implementation.

In addition to the thorough coverage of the fourth edition of the *ASCA National Model*, readers will find thoughtful discussions of the effects of trends and legislation, including the Every Student Succeeds Act (ESSA), multitiered systems of support (MTSS), and school-wide positive behavioral interventions and supports (SWPBIS). The text also provides readers with understanding of how school counselors assume a counseling orientation within the specific context of an educational setting. Each chapter is application-oriented, with an equal emphasis both on research and on using data to design and improve school counselors' functioning in school systems. Complementing this book is the companion website, which includes PowerPoints, templates and handouts, annotated website links and video links for students, and a test bank and discussion questions for instructors.

This book is essential reading for all school counselors in training as it provides a comprehensive look at the profession and explores topics that are most relevant to the role of school counselor.

Jered B. Kolbert, PhD, is a professor of counselor education at Duquesne University. He obtained his doctorate in counseling from the College of William and Mary.

Laura M. Crothers, DEd, is a professor of school psychology at Duquesne University. Her doctorate in school psychology is from Indiana University of Pennsylvania.

Tammy L. Hughes, PhD, is a professor of school psychology at Duquesne University. Her doctorate in school psychology is from Arizona State University.

Introduction to School Counseling

Theory, Research, and Practice

Second Edition

Jered B. Kolbert, Laura M. Crothers, and Tammy L. Hughes

Routledge
Taylor & Francis Group

NEW YORK AND LONDON

Designed cover image: Getty Images

Second edition published 2023
by Routledge
605 Third Avenue, New York, NY 10158

and by Routledge
4 Park Square, Milton Park, Abingdon, Oxon, OX14 4RN

Routledge is an imprint of the Taylor & Francis Group, an informa business

© 2023 Jered B. Kolbert, Laura M. Crothers, and Tammy L. Hughes

First edition published by Routledge 2016

Library of Congress Cataloging-in-Publication Data
Names: Kolbert, Jered B., author. | Crothers, Laura M., author. | Hughes,
    Tammy L., 1977– author.
Title: Introduction to school counseling : theory, research, and practice /
    by Jered B. Kolbert, Laura M. Crothers, and Tammy L. Hughes.
    Other titles: Introduction to professional school counseling
Description: Second Edition. | New York : Routledge, 2023. | "First edition
    published by Routledge 2016"—Copyright page. | Includes bibliographical
    references and index.
Identifiers: LCCN 2022027795 (print) | LCCN 2022027796 (ebook) |
    ISBN 9780367766108 (Hardback) | ISBN 9780367766092 (Paperback) |
    ISBN 9781003167730 (eBook)
Subjects: LCSH: Educational counseling—United States. | Student counselors—
    In-service training—United States.
Classification: LCC LB1027.5 .K5968 2023 (print) | LCC LB1027.5 (ebook) |
    DDC 371.4—dc23/eng/20220812
LC record available at https://lccn.loc.gov/2022027795
LC ebook record available at https://lccn.loc.gov/2022027796

ISBN: 978-0-367-76610-8 (hbk)
ISBN: 978-0-367-76609-2 (pbk)
ISBN: 978-1-003-16773-0 (ebk)

DOI: 10.4324/9781003167730

Typeset in Sabon
by Apex CoVantage, LLC

Access the companion website: www.routledge.com/cw/kolbert

Dedicated to

Jered B. Kolbert: To my children, Kennedy Isabel and Karlena Swanhild.

Laura M. Crothers: To my children, Meredith Julia Lipinski, Samuel Conrad Lipinski, and Caroline Susan Lipinski.

Tammy L. Hughes: I would like to thank my husband, Dr. Jeff Miller, and son, Mason, for always giving me the time to work and write. I am also thankful for the opportunity to work with youth and systems that serve them during trying times.

Contents

Author Biographies

Jered B. Kolbert, PhD, is a professor and the school counseling program coordinator in the Department of Counselor Education and School Psychology at Duquesne University. Dr. Kolbert has worked as a school counselor and mental health counselor. He obtained his doctorate in counseling from the College of William and Mary. Dr. Kolbert has coauthored books regarding bullying, school-based consultation, and approaches to educating children with psychological disorders. His research interests include issues related to the school counseling profession, bullying, relational aggression, and gender and sexual orientation. He is on the editorial board of *Professional School Counseling* and the *Journal of School Counseling*.

Laura M. Crothers, DEd, is a professor in the Department of Counselor Education and School Psychology at Duquesne University. Her doctorate in school psychology is from Indiana University of Pennsylvania. She has worked as a school psychologist and a school consultant. Dr. Crothers has been recognized as a national expert in childhood bullying by the National Association of School Psychologists. Dr. Crothers has written both journal articles and books on the topics of bullying, relational aggression, and professional issues in school psychology.

Tammy L. Hughes, PhD, ABPP, is a professor of School Psychology at Duquesne University. She is a school psychologist, is a licensed psychologist, and is board-certified in School Psychology. She is a past president of the Division of School Psychology (16) of the American Psychological Association (APA) and Trainers of School Psychologists (TSP). She is a fellow of the American Psychological Association. Her writing focuses on marginalized youth and the inequities they experience, particularly those who are at high risk for disciplinary actions that result in juvenile or criminal justice contact.

Chapter 1

History and Trends in the School Counseling Profession

Box 1.1 2016 Council for the Accreditation of Counseling and Related Educational Programs (CACREP, n.d.) School Counseling Specialty Area Standards

1.a History and development of school counseling
2.a School counselor roles as leaders, advocates, and systems change agencies in P-12 schools
2.m Legislation and government policy relevant to school counseling

---

Box 1.2 ASCA (2019a) Standards for School Counselor Preparation Programs (ASCA CAEP SPA)

1.1 Describe the organizational structure, governance, and evolution of the American education system, as well as cultural, political, and social influences on current educational practices and on individual and collective learning environments.
1.2 Describe the evolution of the school counseling profession, the basis for a comprehensive school counseling program, and the school counselor's role in supporting growth and learning for students.
7.2 Describe the impact of federal and state laws and regulations, as well as district policies, on schools, students, families, and the school counseling practice.

The school counseling profession continues to pursue the long-sought objective of achieving a consistent identity. The role of the school counselor (SC) often varies between districts and even schools within the same district (ASCA, 2019b; Gysbers & Stanley, 2014). In some schools, SCs function in a manner similar to mental health therapists, providing individual counseling to at-risk students. In other schools, SCs are heavily burdened with clerical duties, which may include registering and scheduling new students, coordinating standardized test administrations, coordinating student study teams, maintaining attendance records, completing college applications, etc. Role confusion appears to be prevalent among school counselors and is associated with a lack of self-efficacy (Jellison, 2013).

A new elementary SC once complained to one of the authors that each principal of the three schools in which she worked had an entirely different view of her role. One principal wanted her to function as a crisis counselor, expecting her to constantly be on call to assist with students who had been removed from class for disciplinary reasons. Another principal requested that the SC primarily organize the administration of various standardized tests. Finally, her remaining principal wanted her to establish a comprehensive school counseling program, including the development of a school counseling curriculum; however, she found that her duties at her other schools interfered with her ability to implement such a program.

Many SCs in training enter the profession with the expectation that they will essentially entail providing individual counseling to students. While individual is certainly an important aspect of the role of SCs, school counselors in training are often to surprised to learn, and maybe a bit intimidated as well, that the role of the SC is much more encompassing with best practice (Cinotti, 2014) considered to entail the provision of comprehensive programming in which SCs provide a variety of direct and indirect services. Direct services that SCs are expected to provide include instruction, appraisal, and advisement, and indirect services involve collaboration, consultation, and referrals, and the collection and analysis of data to evaluate the effectiveness of the school counseling program (ASCA, 2019b). Readers of this chapter are encouraged to be mindful of their experience in learning about the multifaceted role of SCs. Most likely, SCs in training are likely to feel more comfortable with some aspects of functioning as SCs and less comfortable with others. For example, SCs in training tend to be attracted to those aspects of the position that involve working closely with students and more anxious about collaborating with teachers, consulting with parents, or using data to analyze the effectiveness of school counseling activities. The role of SCs can be thought of as encompassing the merging of both the education and the counseling professions. Learning to become an expert educator and counselor requires considerable training and experience, which is a challenging but highly worthy objective. Readers of this book are encouraged to adopt a long-term perspective, viewing the role of becoming SCs as a long-term process in which the SCs must regularly assess their strengths and areas for improvement.

Chandler et al. (2018) assert that there are two prominent reasons for role ambiguity among SCs. First, many stakeholders, including administrators, teachers, and parents, misunderstand the role of SCs. For example, SCs' responsibilities may be largely influenced by established traditions or customary roles from the past. Recently, an SC informed one of the authors that upon assuming a new elementary school counseling position, she was informed by the principal that she was in charge of conducting student lice checks because that was what the previous SC did. The other prominent reason for role confusion is that administrators often assign SCs noncounseling duties to meet the needs of the school. It is not unusual for SCs to be assigned to cover classrooms for absent teachers, because substitute teachers are lacking. The authors of a study published as recently as 2018 concluded that role confusion among SCs persists (Chandler et al., 2018). In order to understand the current state of the profession, it is essential to understand its history.

Origins of the Profession

The Industrial Revolution during the turn of the twentieth century changed the United States from an agrarian to an industrial economy, resulting in a large immigration of both Americans and European immigrants to cities attracted to manufacturing and industrial jobs (Savickas, 2009). The rise of factories also spurred an increase in the use of child labor, with children as young as eight not attending school in order to work in coal mines and factories (Erford, 2018). Due to the large increase of newcomers to the cities and concerns about the use of child labor, "social reformers began to call for vocational guidance"

(Savickas, 2009, p. 194) to be provided by professionals, whereas previously such efforts had been conducted by charity workers. The efforts to provide vocational guidance to the immigrants to American cities are considered to be the origins of what is now referred to as the school counseling profession (Slaten et al., 2019). Erford (2018) points out that many of the societal issues that contributed to the rise of the school counseling profession at the turn of the century, namely, economic and technological challenges and social justice issues, are similar to the challenges currently facing today's society.

Frank Parsons, a trained civil engineer and lawyer, was a social activist who sought to improve the lives of the underprivileged who were being exploited by the new industries (Gysbers, 2010). Parsons, who has been given the title the "Father of Guidance," promoted the use of a more formal, scientific approach to career decision-making, recognizing this process as one of life's most important decisions, second only to choosing a spouse to replace the haphazard manner in which youth typically at that time entered the workforce (Gysbers, 2010). Parsons (1909) criticized public schools for being overly focused on book learning, recommending that schools emphasize industrial education. He advocated for a formal approach to guidance, referred to as Parsons's trait and factor, which involves a three-step approach to vocational guidance: (1) finding your aptitudes, strengths, and interests; (2) developing a knowledge of the career choice and conditions for success; and (3) understanding the relationship between the first two steps. Within a few years of the publication of Parsons's book *Choosing a Vocation*, more than 900 high schools in the United States included vocational guidance (Geisler, 1990).

Box 1.3

Did You Know?

Parsons's trait and factor theory was originally developed as the talent-matching approach, which later became the trait and factor theory of occupational choice. The premise of this theory is to match people's individual talents to the attributes required in particular jobs (careers.govt.nz, n.d.).

While Parsons has been given the moniker of the "Father of Guidance," Jesse B. Davis, a principal, is often regarded at the "first school counselor" through his efforts to create a systematic guidance program in Michigan public schools (Pope, 2009). Davis (1956) argued that "students should be respected for their own abilities, interests, ideas, individual differences and cultural identity" (Davis, 1956, p. 176) in an effort to support all the students within the school setting. In order to incorporate classroom guidance into the general curriculum, Davis encouraged English teachers to take on the role of teaching guidance, representing the first time that teachers were encouraged to assume a counseling role (Thompson, 2012).

The advocacy of Parsons, Davis, and other early pioneers in vocational guidance resulted in the establishment of a national professional organization, the National Vocational Guidance Association (NVGA), in 1913 (Wilson, 2013). The initial objectives of the NVGA included decreasing the large number of adolescents who were leaving school for manufacturing jobs through the incorporation of vocational guidance within the educational system and providing training for vocational counselors. Up until the 1940s, the primary role of vocational counselors was to help students in preparing for the world of work. Most of the counseling services provided within the schools were practiced by teachers, administrators, and deans of students, who often received no additional pay or little guidance, with few full-time school counselors in existence (Gysbers, 2010).

The emphasis on vocational guidance was reinforced by the federal government's efforts to respond to the decline of the economy during the Great Depression (Erford, 2018). To address the need for a national occupational classification system, the first edition of the *Dictionary of Occupational Titles* was published in 1938, and the Bureau of Labor Statistics was created in 1940. The US Employment Service was created in 1933, and several laws during the 1930s provided funding for vocational guidance activities.

The emergence of humanism in the 1940s moved the profession toward a more person-centered approach, emphasizing personal growth and one-on-one support (Slaten et al., 2019). Although Carl Rogers was not directly involved in advocating for the profession of school counseling, Rogers's concepts of unconditional positive regard and his nondirective, client-centered approach have become foundational competencies for school counselors in training (Thompson, 2012). Rogers's theoretical premise of the self-determination of the client was extended by school counselors to students and resulted in SCs seeing themselves as child and adolescent specialists. Training programs de-emphasized the traditional trait and factor theory in favor of approaches that emphasized the promotion of students' self-concept and social adjustment. This new movement pushed the topics of self-esteem and personality into the forefront of training, with the adjustment of the individual becoming the new goal of guidance and counseling. This shift moved the profession from its vocational focus to the mental hygiene model for school counseling. With that shift came another change in title and function from guidance to pupil personnel services.

In 1957, the Russians' launch of the first space satellite during the height of the Cold War led many Americans to perceive the nation to be at risk of falling behind the Russians in terms of technological and scientific proficiency. The National Defense Education Act (NDEA), passed in 1958, greatly increased the funding for the hiring and training of secondary SCs, resulting in a tripling in the number of SCs nationwide between 1958 and 1967 (Thompson, 2012). Secondary SCs were tasked with using standardized tests to identify exceptional students and encourage them to pursue careers in the sciences, engineering, and mathematics (Baskin & Slaten, 2014). Whereas the NDEA encouraged SCs to attend to the academic and career needs of exceptional students, the Elementary and Secondary Education Act (ESEA, 1965) promulgated a different role for SCs, as the act provided grants to local school districts to establish programs to prevent school dropout, particularly among the economically disadvantaged and students with disabilities (Erford, 2018).

The ESEA also increased the number of elementary SCs (Gysbers, 2010). While elementary SCs were in existence as early as the 1920s, during the first several decades of their professional functioning, their positions were primarily viewed as educational and not therapeutic. Furthermore, the foundational guidance provided by elementary SCs was seen as a vital component to the education of all students. However, gradually, there was increasing overlap in the duties of school psychologists, school social workers, and SCs. There was also debate regarding the relationship between elementary and secondary SCs, with some arguing that elementary SCs should seek to see themselves as distinct and separate from secondary SCs. Dinkmeyer was a strong advocate for elementary SCs at this time, asserting that the roles and functions of elementary SCs should include consultation, counseling, classroom guidance, group guidance, and coordination of services. Both NDEA and ESEA resulted in a significant increase in the number of SCs and in college and universities providing preparation programs. In addition, the combined effects of the legislative acts also resulted in the elimination of the counselor-teacher position that was prevalent in the beginning of the century and the hiring of many full-time counselors (Baskin & Slaten, 2014). SCs were categorized under pupil personnel services, which usually included a school psychologist, a social worker, a nurse or health officer, and an attendance officer (Cinotti, 2014).

Box 1.4

Did You Know?

There is a substantial overlap between the roles of a mental health counselor and a clinical social worker—both perform psychotherapy—but social workers tend to be more focused on modifying the environment to accommodate their clients, while counselors are more strongly oriented toward helping their clients adapt to the environments in which they function (OnlineEducation, n.d.).

Governmental legislation influenced by the civil rights and women's liberation movements during 1960s and 1970s impacted the school counseling profession, often in a contradictory manner. The Vocational Education Act of 1963, the Vocational Education Amendments of 1968, and the Career Education Incentive Act of 1976 sought to address inequities in employment and poverty and redirected the profession's focus back to its origins of career awareness and career decision-making (Gysbers & Henderson, 2006). In contrast, the Elementary and Secondary Education Act of 1965 encouraged school counselors to address social issues, as the act provided grants to local school districts to establish programs to prevent school dropout, particularly among the economically disadvantaged and students with disabilities (Erford, 2018). These acts, along with legislation resulting in the mainstreaming of special education students, increased SCs' focus on diversity and the needs of special populations.

The 1970s witnessed a major shift in the profession as school counseling was defined as involving the provision of a comprehensive, developmental program (Baskin & Slaten, 2014; Cinotti, 2014). The redefinition involved developing comprehensive approaches consisting of using planned developmentally appropriate, measurable student outcomes (Cinotti, 2014). This movement toward a comprehensive approach was not largely realized, as budgetary reductions in the 1970s led to the reduction of SCs. In order to create more visibility and ensure the continuance of the profession, SCs' role and identities shifted to more administrative tasks and responsibilities. These new responsibilities were often what today are considered noncounseling roles, such as scheduling, recess duty, clerical duties, etc. (Baskin & Slaten, 2014).

There were also internal divisions with the school counseling profession during the 1960s and 1970s that contributed to role ambiguity (Gysbers, 2010). Some sought to adhere to a psychologist modeling of counseling, which emphasized using individual counseling to meet the needs of at-risk students, whereas others preferred a guidance educational model, which emphasized prevention through the provision of comprehensive services. Because many graduate programs in school counseling at that time emphasized a psychological orientation, many states began to eliminate the requirement of teaching experience for school counseling certification. As of 2021, only Kansas, Kentucky, Louisiana, Nebraska, North Dakota, Oregon, and Texas still required teaching experience as requirement to become a school counselor (ASCA, n.d.A). Studies have consistently demonstrated that having prior teaching experience is not an indicator of perceived effectiveness for SCs (e.g., Moyer & Yu, 2012).

Comprehensive Developmental Guidance Programs (CDGPs)

The pupil personnel services model of the 1960s and 1970s included the provision of direct services, primarily provided to at-risk students, but lacked a systemic approach for promoting student development, often resulting in school counselors being assigned to administrative or clerical tasks (Slaten et al., 2019). SCs were encouraged to develop and define their own roles and responsibilities based on the needs of each school. This individualized movement added fuel to the fire of the role confusion in the field of school counseling.

In the 1970s and 1980s, the concept of a comprehensive program was developed to address the profession's lack of clarity and focused on the school counseling program versus the role of the school counselor (Baskin & Slaten, 2014). Comprehensive school counseling programs were based upon five foundational premises (Gysbers & Henderson, 2006). First, school counseling is a program that, similar to other educational programs, has standards, activities, and interventions to enable students to achieve the standards; the activities and the interventions are provided by certified personnel and use accountability measures to determine students' acquisition of the standards. The second premise is that school counseling programs are developmental and comprehensive. School counseling programs are developmental in that they seek to promote students' growth in three areas of student development: academic, career, and social/emotional. They are also developmental in that they are guided by developmental theories that indicate what most students need at that stage/period of development. For example, in a CDGP program, elementary students are exposed to the world of work by learning the various types of careers, middle school students are assisted in exploring the world of work, examining how their abilities and interests apply to specific careers, and high school students are supported in developing career plans. They are comprehensive in that they seek to impact the entire student population through the provision of a range of services rather than merely focusing upon at-risk students or students with whom SCs meet individually. Third, school counseling programs use a team approach in which while the SC is the leader of the team, the entire school staff is expected to be involved in the delivery of the program. Fourth, school counseling programs are created and maintained through a process of systematic planning, designing, implementing, and evaluating. The fifth premise is that school counseling programs include leadership and advocacy to promote systemic change. Unfortunately, the adoption of Gysbers and Henderson's CDGP was slow and inconsistent (Hatch & Chen-Hayes, 2008). Federal funding to support the profession's movement toward the implementation of a comprehensive, standards-based curriculum was provided through the Elementary School Counseling Demonstration Act of 1995 and the Carl D. Perkins Vocational and Applied Technology Act of 1990 (Erford, 2018).

Current Challenges to the School Counseling Profession

The continued need of the school counseling profession to achieve a consistent identity is currently affected by declining education budgets and the considerable emphasis on accountability for educational institutions. Although ASCA (2019b) recommends a ratio of one school counselor per 250 students, there is no federal requirement for a particular ratio and states vary widely in their school counselor ratios, with some states not even mandating school counselors (Ohrtman et al., 2016). As of 2019, the national average was 455 students per counselor (Tate, 2019). Sometimes, school counselors are among the first school personnel to be eliminated due to budget reductions. The increasing expectation that schools and educators should be accountable for students' achievement or lack thereof, an expectation which is significantly represented in the No Child Left Behind (NCLB) Act (2002) and Every Student Succeeds Act (ESSA; US Department of Education, n.d.) of 2015, has exerted pressure on the profession to identify how school counselors contribute to the academic mission of schools and to measure the impact of these contributions.

The school counseling profession must not only establish a niche within the education professions but also help the public understand their role and the positive impact of school counseling–related programs in order to counter some of the common negative perceptions of school counselors. School counseling students may find that they receive interesting reactions when they reveal what they are studying to laypeople, and it is common for such individuals to complain that their school counselor only helped them with scheduling, claimed that they would not amount to anything, etc. A national survey of recent high school graduates conducted in 2009 revealed that the students primarily gave their high school SCs a fair or poor rating and viewed them as less helpful than teachers in providing career development (Johnson et al., 2010). Moreover, 67% of respondents rated their school counselor as fair or poor for the assistance they provided in selecting a college, and 55% rated their school counselor as fair or poor in the assistance they provided with the college application process. In China, where there has been a rapid increase in the number of SCs in the past several decades, high school students generally had positive perceptions of the services they received from SCs, but they reported that they wanted more vocational guidance and more knowledge of achievement tests from their SCs (Shi et al., 2014).

The ASCA National Model

The ASCA published the *National Model* in 2003 to increase unity within the profession and hasten the profession's adoption of comprehensive programming. The *ASCA National Model*, which was subsequently revised in 2005, 2012, and 2019, is the form of comprehensive school counseling that is most utilized across the country (Dahir et al., 2009) and is considered best practice for SCs (Cinotti, 2014). The *ASCA National Model* integrated three widely used comprehensive programs, i.e., the comprehensive (Gysbers & Henderson, 2006), developmental (Myrick, 2003), and results-based approached created by Johnson and Johnson (2003). The objective of the *National Model* is to integrate CDGPs (Dahir et al., 2009) into the academic mission of schools to ensure that SCs support the mission of the school and are perceived as integral members of the school. The focus shifted from the services provided by SCs to viewing school counseling as an integral program that supports but is also distinct from the school's academic curriculum. Organizations which collaborated with ASCA in the creation of the ASCA Model include the College Board and Education Trust (Gysbers, 2010), more about which will be discussed later.

The *ASCA National Model* (2019b) consists of four components that are considered necessary to create and maintain effective comprehensive programming. The four components are *define*, which includes the standards that are used to promote student development and assess the effectiveness of the school counseling program; *manage*, which consists of the program focus and planning tools to guide the development and implementation of a school counseling program; *deliver*, which identifies the direct and indirect student services school counselors use in providing the school counseling program; and *assess*, which includes the methods SCs use to determine the effectiveness of the school counseling program. Furthermore, the four themes of leadership, advocacy, collaboration, and systemic change are interwoven throughout the *ASCA National Model*. The *ASCA National Model* emphasizes that SCs use education-based approaches to promoting student development and do not function as mental health therapists. A study published in 2017 estimated that, on average, school counseling programs have implemented the *ASCA National Model* at about a three-quarter level (Fye et al., 2017).

The components and various aspects of each component of the *ASCA National Model* are a major focus of this textbook and will be discussed in greater depth in each chapter.

ASCA has established standards, referred to the ASCA Student Standards (2021), which students should be able to exhibit as a result of the school counseling program. The ASCA Student Standards indicate the knowledge, skills, and attitudes needed to achieve academically, to be college and career ready, and for social/emotional development. SCs operationalize these standards by selecting "competencies that align with the specific standards and become the foundation for classroom lessons, small groups, and activities addressing student developmental needs."

Recognized ASCA Model Program (RAMP)

Shortly after the publication of the first edition of the *ASCA National Model*, ASCA established the RAMP designation. To receive the RAMP designation, SCs must submit an extensive application to ASCA which is reviewed by an independent panel of SCs using a rubric that is available on ASCA's website (ASCA, n.d.B). The RAMP designation indicates that the school's counseling program is consistent with *the model* and is recognized by the professional community as following best practice. The application requires a narrative documenting the efforts in ten components, including the activities in developing the school counseling program's vision and mission statements, annual student outcome goals, classroom and group mindsets and behaviors action plan, annual administrative conference, calendars (annual and weekly), lesson plans (classroom and group), classroom instruction results report, small-group results report, and closing-the-gap action plan/results report. Schools receiving the distinction are allowed to identify themselves as a RAMP-designated school, which is often appealing to school administrators as it is an indication of excellence. RAMP status is maintained for five years, and schools may reapply for RAMP status at the end of the term, a process which is referred to as re-RAMPing. As of April 2022, ASCA's website lists 425 schools which at that time have received the RAMP designation (ASCA, n.d.C).

Education Trust's Transforming School Counseling Initiative (TSCI)

One of the organizations that ASCA partnered with to reform the school counseling profession is Education Trust (n.d.), which is a national nonprofit organization that seeks to reform education for the purposes of eliminating the opportunity gap that affects students of color and low-income families. Education Trust formed a subgroup in 1995 called the National Center for Transforming School Counseling (NCTSC), which seeks to ensure that school counselors are capable of helping all groups of students reach high academic standards by serving as an advocate, leader, team member, and consultant in removing barriers to students' high achievement. Education Trust's Transforming School Counseling Initiative (TSCI) has primarily focused upon modifying the way in which school counselors are educated in graduate schools, providing grants to select universities to train students in a transformed model of school counseling and encouraging state departments of education to adopt new standards for school counselor preparation (Perkins et al., 2010). The TSCI vision for school counselors involves the following: (1) de-emphasizing a mental health perspective in favor of an academic/student achievement focus, (2) adopting a whole school or systems perspective vs. focusing on individual student issues, (3) using data to effect change as opposed to school counselors simply being involved with data as part of record-keeping, and (4) serving as change agents to promote educational equity (Education Trust, 2009).

No Child Left Behind Act (NCBL) and Every Student Succeeds Act (ESSA)

The NCLB Act of 2001 (2002) and the Every Student Succeeds Act (ESSA; US Department of Education, n.d.), which replaced NCLB in 2015, are probably the most significant pieces of educational legislation in the past several decades, and both have had a profound impact upon the school counseling profession. A primary aim of the NCLB Act was to increase schools' accountability for ensuring student achievement through the administration of statewide standardized tests. The NCLB also strove to reduce the achievement gap between White and Asian students and historically disadvantaged groups, including Latin@ American, Black, and Native American students; economically disadvantaged students; students with disabilities; and students with limited English proficiency. NCLB mandated that states require school districts to collect "disaggregated data" of subgroups (defined by gender, race, ethnicity, disability status, low-income status, English-language proficiency, and migrant status) and implement corrective actions to address the needs of these subgroups. Whereas in the past, students were held liable for a lack of academic achievement, now teachers and school personnel were also deemed as accountable for student achievement.

Although the NCLB Act emphasized the need for schools to provide programs for issues typically associated with school counseling, including dropout prevention, career counseling, substance abuse counseling, safe and drug-free schools, etc., a major concern for the profession was that SCs were not involved in the educational reform initiated with NCLB, nor were they explicitly identified in this legislation. This spurred the school counseling profession to undergo modifications in order to be perceived as integral members of the academic mission of schools and educational reform through closer collaboration with other education professions and contributed to the ASCA's creation of the *National Model*.

While NCLB (2002) did not explicitly identify the role of SCs, the act impacted the profession. The NCLB Act's (2002) emphasis on accountability resulted in a renewed commitment to accountability for SCs (Dahir, 2004). The NCLB Act required schools to use empirically supported teaching methods. Likewise, the school counseling profession sought to increase the rigor of studies evaluating the impact of school counseling–related programs and interventions. Prior to NCLB, evaluation studies yielded support for the effectiveness of a variety of school counseling interventions, including providing group, peer, and individual counseling and conducting classroom lessons (McGannon et al., 2005). However, much of this research did not employ an experimental design and thus did not qualify as scientifically based according to the definitions used by the NCLB Act. Consequently, the Center for School Counseling Outcome Research and Evaluation (CSCORE) was established to develop the research base required for evidence-based practice (Carey et al., 2008).

The NCLB Act (2002) was comprehensive and was designed to impact various aspects of education, including activities that historically have been associated with the role of school counselors. For example, the NCLB Act mandated that schools regularly provide parents and the public data regarding students' achievement and to create programs that involve parents in meaningful ways. The "safe and drug-free schools" provision of NCLB required that state departments of education identify schools that are unsafe. Schools that had consistently high levels of violent behavior for two years could be designated "persistently dangerous" and suffer penalties, such as voluntary student transfers.

A national survey of SCs revealed that while 2.3% of the participants identified positive effects of NCLB upon the school counseling program's delivery system, 33.6% of the study participants identified negative impacts, including teachers being hesitant to yield class time for counseling or the developmental curriculum, testing responsibilities interfering with counseling students, and a decreased focus on the social and emotional needs of students (Dollarhide & Lemberger, 2006). Although 25.1% of the SCs indicated that they were engaging in activities related to the testing process that are considered to be appropriate within the *ASCA National Model*, such as interpreting tests and counseling students about test anxiety, majority of SCs identified they had to engage in testing activities that are not considered appropriate by ASCA. Inappropriate activities included functioning as the building test coordinator, proctoring tests and conducting makeup tests, ensuring the implementation of test accommodations for students with disabilities, and providing academic remediation. Dollarhide and Lemberger (2006) concluded that the high-stakes testing ushered by the NCLB Act reinforced the perception that SCs function as test administrators. In order to counter this perception, these authors recommend that SCs use data to advocate the need for students' holistic development.

In 2015, the NCLB Act was replaced by the Every Student Succeeds Act (ESSA; US Department of Education, n.d.), which continued the emphasis on the accountability of school personnel for student achievement and establishing high standards for educating all students (Brown et al., 2019). However, ESSA provides more flexibility to states and districts for establishing standards and determining how growth will be measured, including nonacademic factors, and identify the consequence for insufficient performance. School districts are still required to assess students' learning in the form of standardized testing in reading and math in grades 3–8 and once in high school, but ESSA reduces the emphasis on standardized testing in several major respects, which are listed as follows (National Education Association [NEA], 2015):

- The NCLB requirement that schools demonstrate adequate yearly progress (AYP) toward achieving 100% proficiency in reading and math was replaced with the requirement that states must establish long-term achievement goals with measures of interim progress.
- Federal funding is provided to states to develop alternative assessments that will reduce duplication of assessments.
- High schools may apply to use another nationally recognized assessment, such as the ACT (2016), instead of the state assessment test.
- States may establish a cap limiting the amount of time students engage in test-taking.
- Parents have the right to opt children out of state assessments where local and state policies allow them to do so.
- Elementary and middle schools may provide a measure of student growth or another academic indicator to assess differences among student groups.

The ESSA maintains the NCLB Act's emphasis on reducing the achievement gap but uses different indicators to identify struggling schools and different interventions to support those schools (NEA, 2015). Whereas NCLB required that all schools which failed to meet AYP for several years provide students the option of transferring to other schools and restructuring of the school's leadership and staff, ESSA uses different indicators to identify struggling schools. In ESSA, states would have to identify and provide assistance to schools which are the bottom 5% of performers, schools which have a graduation rate below 67%, and schools which have subgroups (e.g., race, gender, special education) which are struggling. Under ESSA, schools identified in need of support must implement evidence-based, locally determined interventions, and for schools which have a low-performing subgroup, the school must identify in their improvement plan resource inequities that likely contribute to the underperformance of the subgroup. ESSA indicates that schools may, but are not required to, permit students to transfer to another school. SCs were explicitly identified as professionals who should contribute input to the required improvement plan for struggling schools (ASCA, 2015).

ESSA increased emphasis on students' college and career readiness in a number of ways (Malin et al., 2017). Federal funds from ESSA can be used to encourage students' participation in dual-enrollment programs and career and technical education (CTE) to encourage cross-sector partnerships with higher education institutions and to prepare educators to integrate academic and CTE strategies, including funds to train SCs regarding use of labor market information and financial literacy. Furthermore, ESSA granted states the right to use students' postsecondary readiness and completion of advanced coursework as indicators of school performance.

ASCA (2015) issued a statement in support of ESSA, citing the legislation's emphasis on academic and career counseling, importance of providing students with a well-rounded education, and improving the safety and health of school environments. In ESSA, the Elementary and Secondary School Counseling Program (ESSCP) was incorporated into a large block grant along with many other programs. This large block grant now explicitly lists school counselors as being eligible for federal professional development monies, which could result in increased funding for school counselors.

Brown et al. (2019) identified three aspects of ESSA that are very relevant to the role of SCs: whole-child education, college and career readiness, and home-school-community partnerships. Whereas NCLB emphasized academic outcomes content areas, ESSA places greater emphasis on preparing students for their futures with technology, innovation, and career and life skills. More funding is available for programs that promote a well-rounded education and which "may be conducted in partnership with an institution of higher education, business," etc. (US Department of Education, n.d., pp. 176–177). Such plans may include

> college and career guidance and counseling programs, such as postsecondary education and career awareness and exploration activities; training for counselors to effectively use labor market information in assisting students with post-secondary education and career planning; and financial literacy and federal financial aid awareness activities.
>
> (p. 176)

SCs are uniquely positioned to assume leadership on ESSA's emphasis on college readiness, given that they are the only professionals within the school who receive formal training in providing college guidance. SCs can enhance the program's capacity to educate all families on the costs of college attendance (Bryan et al., 2011). Most high school students overestimate the cost of university tuition (Nienhusser & Oshio, 2017). Large percentages of high school students and their parents lack awareness of financial aid sources (Montalto et al., 2019) or underestimate the amount of aid available (George-Jackson & Gast, 2015). Students with lower levels of information about college are less likely to intend to attend college (Dynarski & Scott-Clayton, 2013), apply to college (Roderick et al., 2011), or enroll in college (Bryan et al., 2011). Students from urban schools and low-income families have less information about the cost of tuition and sources of financial aid (George-Jackson & Gast, 2015). Although students in urban high schools are provided by SCs with considerable information about college entrance process and requirements, students are often not informed regarding how to determine whether their current performance would make them competitive college applicants (Shamsuddin, 2016). Students of color and low income receive less information about attending college from family members who are less likely than nondisadvantaged parents to have attended college themselves (Welton & Martinez, 2013).

SCs must collaborate with others in increasing students' college access. In the ASCA's position statement on college access professionals, the role of the SC is distinguished from a college access professional who serves to assist students in navigating pathways to college (ASCA, 2016). SCs enhance graduation rates through career planning and increasing financial literacy and facilitate a culture of college and career readiness.

ESSA permits educational agencies to use funds to "develop, implement, and evaluate comprehensive programs and activities that . . . foster and support, safe, healthy, supportive, and drug free-environments that support academic achievement; [and] promote the involvement of parents in the activity of the program" (p. 178). Some of the programs identified in ESSA include programs designed to prevent drug use, bullying, violence, and harassment, school-based mental health services, and programs that promote relationship-building skills. It is hoped that the explicit identification of these programs in ESSA will result in increased funding opportunities and opportunities for SCs to implement such programs (Brown et al., 2019). Brown et al. (2019) points out that implementing prevention programs requires that SCs collaborate with other school-based professionals and community members. The ASCA (2019c) position statement regarding promoting safe schools states that "school counselors collaborate with teachers, administrators, parents/guardians, and the community to deliver prevention programs encouraging student growth and achievement and ensuring a safe school climate." Although SCs are trained in providing mental health services, their primary role is not to provide individual counseling (Brown et al., 2019). ESSA's support of supplemental programs for mental health services in schools through schools' collaboration with outside entities means that SCs need to collaborate with other mental health professionals in providing school-based mental health services.

The inclusion of school-based mental health services reflects the trend within the past several decades of schools serving as the site for mental health services for children which are often provided by community health professionals rather than school-based mental health providers, such as SCs or school psychologists. It has been estimated that 70–80% of youth behavioral health services are delivered in the schools (Merikangas et al., 2010). Training programs have emerged to cater to this trend. For example, Penn State's counselor education program offers a master's degree in clinical mental health counseling in schools and communities (Penn State University, n.d.). Often, school-based mental health services involve a team approach in which a team of involved "stakeholders," such as the child's teachers, administrators, mental health professionals, and the child's parents/

caregivers collaborate in devising interventions to address a child's personal/social needs (Messina et al., 2015). Although the role of SCs in such teams appears to be evolving, it is possible the SCs' primary role on such teams may be to serve as the liaison between both families, the mental health system, and the educational system, given that they are one of the few professionals who have received training in both the educational and mental health systems.

Brown et al. (2019) assert that ESSA offers increased opportunities to SCs to collaborate with parents and families. Under the NCLB Act, funds for professional development were limited to teachers and administrators, but ESSA explicitly states that funds may be used for the professional development of SCs. Brown et al. (2019) encourage that these funds be used to train SCs to enhance their collaboration with the families of socially and economically disadvantaged youth, as Brown et al. (2019) suggest that revisions of ESSA emphasize that schools seek to develop socially just partnerships with parents and families.

The increased flexibility within ESSA for defining accountability may result in an expanded role for SCs. Whereas NCLB focused primarily on defining accountability in terms of academic achievement indicators, ESSA grants states the right to allow school districts to use such indicators as student and teacher engagement, postsecondary readiness, and school climate/safety (Education Week, 2015). The opportunity to use more varied forms of indicators may lead to an increased emphasis on career and personal/social development, which have been traditionally associated with the school counseling program.

Some have argued that one of the reasons the school counseling profession has lacked a consistent identity is related to its little to no involvement in educational reform movements. As school districts look to eliminate personnel, the profession no longer has the luxury of watching educational reform from the sidelines. The American School Counselors Association (ASCA) has sought to be actively involved in the educational reforms that have had considerable impact on school operations within the past two decades.

Common Core State Standards

The Common Core State Standards (CCSS) are an initiative by states to use universal standards in English and mathematics (ACA School Counseling Task Force, 2013) in order to ensure that graduating students are college- and career-ready. The CCSS were developed by the states to address some of the perceived limitations of the NCLB Act (2002). The NCLB Act sought to increase standardization within education by requiring states to establish academic standards and corresponding assessments (National Governors Association and Council of Chief State School Officers (n.d.). The NCLB Act left it up to the individual states to define proficiency, and research indicated that the states' definition of *proficiency* vary widely. Another common concern is that the NCLB Act's focus on proficiency meant that state assessments were designed to measure a low to moderate level of knowledge and skills. The CCSS Initiative seeks to develop a higher level of standards that are based on skills necessary for postsecondary success. Students would be required to understand content at a deep level and be able to apply the content to problem-solving and reason from evidence, as these skills were deemed to be required to succeed in college. It has been hypothesized that student outcomes on the CCSS would be used as an early identifier of student performance; therefore, SCs would need to use this data in scheduling and student placement, in college and career selection, and for identifying remedial services for students (ACA School Counseling Task Force, 2013). Although most states had indicated a commitment to adopt the CCSS, many states have rescinded their commitment. ESSA requires that states adopt "challenging" academic standards but explicitly states that states do not have to adopt the CCSS (Education Week, 2015). In summary, initially it looked as if the CCSS could have had a major impact upon the profession; as of late, there has not been much discussion in the professional literature regarding the need for SCs to focus upon the CCSS.

Professional Associations and the School Counseling Profession

The Occupational Information and Guidance Service (OIGS) of the late 1930s may have been the first official voice for the school counseling profession (Gysbers, 2010). This organization eventually became the National Association of Guidance Supervision and Counselor Trainers, currently known as the Association of Counselor Education and Supervision (ACES). Concerned with the lack of consistency in the education and training of the school counselors, the OIGS collaborated with the Division of Higher Education of the US Office of Education. The American Personnel and Guidance (APGA) grew out of the NVGA, and eventually the APGA became the American Counseling Association (ACA). In 1952, the APGA (which is now ACA) created the American School Counselor Association (ASCA) division, which was the first organization specific to SCs.

Initially, the focus of APGA (now ASCA) was influenced by the profession's origins in providing vocational guidance. The term *guidance* rather than *counseling* was used to refer to what all counselors did (Sweeney, 2001). *Guidance* implied that the SC used a directive form in advising students and maintained student records about their schedules and progress. In the 1989, ASCA adopted the term *school counselor*, as the term *guidance counselor* was seen as no longer being reflective of the profession (ASCA, n.d.D). The term *guidance counselor* was perceived as being reactive, involving the provision of services to some students, lacking the use of standardized measurements of effectiveness, an ancillary role within the school, and not being an integral member of the school's academic mission. In contrast, ASCA intended the term *school counselor* to be associated with data-driven decision-making, meeting the needs of all students, use of achievement, attendance, and behavior data to measure effectiveness, involving a commitment to school improvement, leadership, and a planned program versus the role of providing services.

ASCA, from its inception, has sought to define, unify, and promote the school counseling profession. The mission of ASCA (n.d.E) is to "represent school counselors and to promote professionalism and ethical practices." The organization provides professional developmental opportunities, including holding an annual conference and offering online specialty certificates; seeks to influence legislation relevant to the profession; initiates and supports research and evaluation on school counselors; and publishes ethical standards. There is an affiliated organization within each state.

The ASCA separated from the ACA in 2018. There was contention between ACA and ASCA regarding the professional identity of school counselors. The ASCA's perspective is that SCs' primary professional identification should be as educators. The former director of the Education Trust's Transforming School Counseling Initiative, Dr. Peggy Hines, believes that one of the primary obstacles to the school counseling reform concerns the training of school counselors (Hines et al., 2011). She argues that SCs are unprepared to implement comprehensive programs to promote students' college and career readiness because their master's-level training focuses upon providing mental health therapy to individual clients and their professors often lack an understanding of the school context.

The separation of ASCA and ACA will likely have implications on the preparation of SCs that are difficult to forecast at this time. The Council for the Accreditation of Counseling and Related Educational Programs (CACREP), which was formed in 1981 for the purpose of developing standards of preparation for all types of counseling professionals, has been the primary organization for issuing standards regarding the preparation of SCs since the 1980s (Gysbers, 2010). The National Board for Certified Counselors (NBCC), which was created in 1982 for the purpose of developing a national credentialing that assesses students' mastery of CACREP's eight knowledge areas, issues a National Certified Counselor (NCC) certificate and also issues certificates for the specific types of counseling professionals, including the National Certified School Counselor (NCSC) designation. Some states and school systems offer increased salaries for NCSCs. In 2019, the ASCA worked with the Council for the Accreditation of Educator Preparation (CAEP) in issuing separate standards for school counselor preparation (ASCA, 2019a). The ASCA's expressed rationale for issuing new standards is that the CACREP standards "do not address the critical role of a comprehensive school counseling program for all students, nor do they fully address the unique role of school counselors district from the roles of clinical counselors."

Summary

The evolution of school counseling has been more cyclical than linear. Initially, the profession's focus was upon vocational education. However, school counseling now emphasizes a more holistic view of students, as reflected in the *ASCA National Model*'s prioritization of the academic, career, and social/emotional domains. The original focus of "guidance counseling" involved assessments for career decision-making; however, educators often presumed that the role of an SC was coordinator of assessments related to learning. Ironically, this controversy continues to concern the profession, as the coordination of testing is a time-consuming responsibility of many SCs. Although SCs are trained in test preparation, the distribution, scheduling, and proctoring of tests is not considered by ASCA to be effective use of the professional school counselor's time. The movement in the 1980s and 1990s toward a comprehensive, standards-based approach to school counseling is regarded as a turning point in the effort to establish legitimacy for the school counseling profession. The *ASCA National Model* seeks to align school counseling with the mission of schools, ensure that school counselors devote 80% of their time to provision of direct and indirect services to students, and promote the utilization of strategies for management and accountability to ensure that school counselors impact the entire student population. Perhaps more importantly, the school counseling profession's commitment to a comprehensive, standards-based system of service delivery renders it less vulnerable to the reactionary responses of prevailing political and social issues.

The paradigm of the profession has been changed through viewing school counseling as an integral component in the education system and not merely as that which is provided by or to a few lone individuals within the school or district. In embracing this shift, the school counseling profession has taken the next step in its evolution. With legislative advocacy and proactive behaviors exhibited on the part of individual SCs, state school counseling organizations, and national professional organizations, school counseling is poised to no longer be viewed as ancillary to the educational system but rather as a program that ensures the holistic development of all students.

The profession seems to have recognized that a reactive mode in which we attend to students' crises limits SCs ability to impact the entire student population and is not likely to yield the type of impact that is readily recognized by teachers, parents, and administrators. An SC had told one of the authors that her role was to help students in any way possible. The SC provided an example in which she had assisted a student by looking through the garbage in the cafeteria to help the student locate his retainer. The problem with this example is that the SC did not feel that it was necessary to use comprehensive services, such as classroom or small-group instruction, or data to evaluate the impact of her school counseling program, as she was confident that others would perceive her caring. Thus, the SC most likely missed opportunities to help students in meaningful ways, such as enabling students to think about their life purpose or learn how to more effectively relate to others or motivate themselves to pursue their life goals.

The challenge facing the profession is how to use systematic and comprehensive approaches to impact the entire student population. Ideally, school counseling programs should be driven by students' developmental needs, providing students with the knowledge, attitudes, and skills they need to negotiate changes in their lives. Thankfully, within the last several decades, there has been the development of a consistent and unique professional identity for SCs, and the emergence of frameworks such as the *ASCA National Model*, that can enable SCs to assume a proactive approach.

References

American Counseling Association (ACA) School Counseling Task Force. (2013). *Common core state standards: Essential information for school counselors.* Author. www.counseling.org/docs/resources-school-counselors/common-core-state-standards.pdf?sfvrsn=2

American School Counselor Association. (2015). *American school counselor association endorses every student succeeds act.* Author. www.schoolcounselor.org/asca/media/asca/Press%20releases/ESSA.pdf

American School Counselor Association. (2016). *The school counselor and college access professionals.* Author.

American School Counselor Association. (2019a). *ASCA standards for school counselor preparation programs.* Author. www.schoolcounselor.org/getmedia/573d7c2c-1622-4d25-a5ac-ac74d2e614ca/ASCA-Standards-for-School-Counselor-Preparation-Programs.pdf

American School Counselor Association. (2019b). *The ASCA national model: A framework for school counseling programs* (4th ed.). Author.

American School Counselor Association. (2019c). *The school counseling and safe schools and crisis response.* Author.

American School Counselor Association. (2021). *ASCA student standards: Mindsets & behaviors for student success.* Author. www.schoolcounselor.org/Standards-Positions/Standards/ASCA-Mindsets-Behaviors-for-Student-Success

American School Counselor Association. (2022). *ASCA standards-aligned school counseling curriculum.* Author.

American School Counselor Association. (n.d.A). *State certification requirements.* Author. www.schoolcounselor.org/school-counselors-members/careers-roles/state-certification-requirements

American School Counselor Association. (n.d.B). *Thinking about RAMP.* Author. www.schoolcounselor.org/school-counselors/recognized-asca-model-program-(ramp)/thinking-about-ramp

American School Counselor Association. (n.d.C). *Current RAMP schools by state.* Author. www.schoolcounselor.org/school-counselors/recognized-asca-model-program(ramp)/current-ramp-schools

American School Counselor Association. (n.d.D). *Guidance counselor vs. school counselor.* Author. www.schoolcounselor.org/asca/media/asca/Careers-Roles/GuidanceCounselorvsSchoolCounselor.pdf

American School Counselor Association. (n.d.E). *About ASCA.* Author. www.schoolcounselor.org/school-counselors-members/about-asca-(1)

Baskin, T. W., & Slaten, C. D. (2014). Contextual school counseling approach: Linking contextual psychotherapy with the school environment. *The Counseling Psychologist, 42*(1), 73–96. https://doi.org/10.1177/0011000012473664

Brown, M. H., & Lenares-Solomon, D., & Deaner, R. G. (2019). Every student succeeds act: A call to action for school counselors. *Journal of Counselor Leadership and Advocacy, 6*(1), 86096. https://doi.org/1080/2326716X.2018.1557574

Bryan, J., Moore-Thomas, C., Day-Vines, N. L., & Holcomb-McCoy, C. (2011). School counselors as social capital: The effects of high school college counseling on college application rates. *Journal of Counseling & Development, 89*(2), 190–199. https://doi.org/10.1002/j.1556-6678.2011.tb00077.x

careers.govt.nz. (n.d.). *Parson's theory.* www.careers.govt.nz/resources/career-practice/career-theory-models/parsons-theory/

Carey, J. C., Dimmitt, C., Hatch, T. A., Lapan, R. T., & Whiston, S. C. (2008). Report of the national panel for evidence-based school counseling: Outcome research coding protocol and evaluation of Student Success Skills and Second Step. *Professional School Counseling, 11*(3), 197–206. https://doi.org/10.1177/2156759X0801100306

Chandler, J. W., Burnham, J. J., Kiper Riechel., M. E., Dahir, C. A., Stone, C. B., Oliver, D. F., Davis, A. P., & Bledsoe, K. G. (2018). Assessing the counseling and non-counseling roles of school counselors. *Journal of School Counseling, 16*(7). www.jsc.montana.edu/articles/v16n7.pdf

Cinotti, D. (2014). Competing professional identity models in school counseling: A historical perspective and commentary. *The Professional Counselor, 4*(5), 417–425. https://doi.org/10.15241/dc.4.5417

Council for the Accreditation of Counseling and Related Educational Programs. (n.d.). *2016 CACREP standards.* www.cacrep.org/for-programs/2016-cacrep-standards/

Dahir, C. A. (2004). Supporting a nation of learners: The role of school counseling in educational reform. *Journal of Counseling and Development, 82*(3), 344–353. https://doi.org/10.1002/j.1556-6678.2004.tb00320.x

Dahir, C. A., Burnham, J. J., & Stone, C. (2009). Listen to the voices: School counselors and comprehensive school counseling programs. *Professional School Counseling, 12*(3), 182–192. https://doi.org/10.1177/2156759X0901200304

Davis, F. G. (1956). *The saga of a school master.* Boston University Press.

Dollarhide, C. T., & Lemberger, M. E. (2006). "No child left behind": Implications for school counselors. *Professional School Counseling, 9*(4), 295–304.

Dynarski, S., & Scott-Clayton, J. (2013). *Financial aid policy: Lessons from research* (No. w18710). National Bureau of Economic Research.

Education Trust. (2009, January 1). *The new vision for school counselors: Scope of the work.* Author. https://edtrust.org/resource/the-new-vision-for-school-counselors-scope-of-thework/#:~:text=The%20National%20Center%20for%20Transforming,academic%20success%20for%20all%20students

Education Trust. (n.d.). *Who we are.* Author. https://edtrust.org/who-we-are/

Education Week. (2015, December 9). *The every student succeeds act: Explained.* Author.

Elementary and Secondary Education Act, Pub. L. No. 89-10, 79 Stat. 27, 20 U.S.C.ch. 70 (1965).

Erford, B. T. (2018). Becoming a professional school counselor: Current perspectives, historical roots, and future challenges. In B. T. Erford (Ed.), *Transforming the school counseling profession* (5th ed., pp. 1–25). Pearson.

Fye, H. J., Miller, L. G., & Rainey, S. J. (2017). Predicting school counselors' supports and challenges when implementing the ASCA National Model. *Professional School Counseling, 21*(1). https://doi.org/10.1177/2156759X18777671

Geisler, J. S. (1990). *A history of the Michigan Association for Counseling and Development: The silver anniversary.* The Association.

George-Jackson, C., & Gast, M. J. (2015). Addressing information gaps: Disparities in financial awareness and preparedness on the road to college. *Journal of Student Financial Aid, 44*(3), 3. https://ir.library.louisville.edu/jsfa/vol44/iss3/3

Gysbers, N. C. (2010). *School counseling principles: Remembering the past, shaping the future: A history of school counseling.* American School Counseling Association.

Gysbers, N. C., & Henderson, P. (2006). *Developing and managing your school guidance program* (4th ed.). American Counseling Association.

Gysbers, N. C., & Stanley, B. (2014, January/February). From position to program. *ASCA School Counselor, 51,* 22–27.

Hatch, T., & Chen-Hayes, S. (2008). School counselor beliefs about the ASCA National Model school counseling program components using the SCPCS. *Professional School Counseling, 12*(1), 34–42. https://doi.org/10.1177/2156759X0801200104

Hines, P. L., Lemons, R. W., & Education Trust. (2011). *Poised to lead: How school counselors can drive college and career readiness: K-12 practice.* MetLife Foundation.

Jellison, V. D. (2013). *High school counselors' perceived self-efficacy and relationships with actual and preferred job activities* (Doctoral dissertation). Retrieved from ProQuest LLC. (Accession No. ED561452).

Johnson, J., Rochkind, J., & Public Agenda. (2010). *Can I get a little advice here? How an over-stretched high school guidance system is undermining students' college aspirations.* https://files.eric.ed.gov/fulltext/ED508672.pdf

Johnson, S. K., & Johnson, C. D. (2003). Results-based guidance: A systems approach to student support programs. *Professional School Counseling, 6*(3), 180–184. www.jstor.org/stable/42732427

Malin, J. R., Bragg, D. D., & Hackmann, D. G. (2017). College and career readiness and the every student succeeds act. *Education Administration Quarterly, 53*(5), 809–838. https://doi.org/10.1177/0013161X17714845

McGannon, W., Carey, J., & Dimmitt, C. (2005). *The current status of school counseling outcome research* (Research Monograph No. 2). University of Massachusetts, School of Education.

Merikangas, K. R., He, J., Burstein, M., Swanson, S. A., Avenevoli, S., Cui, L., Benjet, C., Georgiades, K., & Swendsen, J. (2010). Lifetime prevalence of mental disorders in U.S. adolescents: Results from the National Comorbidity Survey Replication-Adolescent Supplement (NCS-A). *Journal of the American Academy of Child & Adolescent Psychiatry, 49*(10), 980–989. https://doi.org/10.1016/j.jaac.2010.05.017

Messina, K. C., Kolbert, J. B., Hyatt-Burkhart, D., & Crothers, L. M. (2015). The role of mental health counselors in promoting school-family collaboration within the tiered school-wide positive behavioral intervention and support (SWPBIS) model. *The Family Journal: Counseling and Therapy for Couples and Families, 23*(3), 277–285. https://doi.org/10.1177/1066480715574471

Montalto, C. P., Phillips, E. L., McDaniel, A., & Baker, A. R. (2019). College student financial wellness: Student loans and beyond. *Journal of Family and Economic Issues, 40*(1), 3–21. https://doi.org/10.1007/s10834-018-9593-4

Moyer, M. S., & Yu, K. (2012). Factors influencing school counselors' perceived effectiveness. *Journal of School Counseling, 10*(6). www.jsc.montana.edu/articles/v10n6.pdf

Myrick, R. D. (2003). *Developmental guidance and counseling: A practical handbook* (5th ed.). Educational Media Corporation.

National Education Association. (2015). *Important changes from No Child Left Behind (NCLB) Act introduced by Every Student Succeeds Act (ESSA).* http://neatoday.org/wp-content/uploads/2015/12/Every-Student-Succeeds-Act-and-Testing.png

National Governors Association and Council of Chief State School Officers. (n.d.). *Common core state standards initiative.* www.corestandards.org

Nienhusser, H. K., & Oshio, T. (2017). *Research in Higher Education, 58*(7), 723–745. https://doi.org/10.1007/s11162-017-9447-1

No Child Left Behind Act of 2001, Pub. L. No. 107–110 (2002).

Ohrtman, M., Cronin, S., Torgerson, E., Thuen, M., & Colton, E. (2016). Perceptions of effectiveness of school counselors with former graduates in a TRIO college program. *Journal of Applied Research on Children: Informing Policy for Children at Risk, 7*(1), 1–6. https://eric.ed.gov/contentdelivery/servlet/ERICServlet?accno=EJ1188513

OnlineEducation. (n.d.). *What are main differences between mental health counseling and clinical social work?* Author. www.onlineeducation.com/counseling/faqs/counseling-lpc-versus-social-work-lcsw#:~:text=Answer%3A%20Counseling%20and%20social%20work%20are%20distinct%20but,mental%20health%20services%20to%20individuals%2C%20groups%2C%20and%20communities

Parsons, F. (1909). *Choosing a vocation.* Houghton Mifflin.

Penn State University. (n.d.). *Clinical mental health counseling in schools and communities emphasis.* Author. https://ed.psu.edu/epcse/counselor-education/masters-program-1/mentalhealthcounseling

Perkins, G., Oescher, J., & Ballard, M. B. (2010). The evolving identity of school counselors as defined by stakeholders. *Journal of School Counseling, 8*(31). https://files.eric.ed.gov/fulltext/EJ895917.pdf

Pope, M. (2009). Jesse Buttrick Davis (1871–1955): Pioneer of vocational guidance in the schools. *Career Development Quarterly, 57*(3), 248–258. https://doi.org/10.1002/j.2161-0045.2009.tb00110.x

Roderick, M., Coca, V., & Nagaoka, J. (2011). Potholes on the road to college: High school effects in shaping urban students' participation in college application, four-year college enrollment, and college match. *Sociology of Education, 84*(3), 178–211. https://doi.org/10.1177/0038040711411280

Savickas, M. L. (2009). Pioneers of the vocational guidance movement: A centennial celebration. *The Career Development Quarterly, 57*(3), 194–198.

Shamsuddin, S. (2016). Taken out of context: Piecing together college guidance information in urban high schools. *Urban Review, 48*(1), 101–122. https://doi:10.1007/s11256-015-0347-4

Shi, Q., Liu, X., & Leuwerke, W. (2014). Students' perceptions of school counselors: An investigation of two high schools in Beijing, China. *The Professional Counselor, 4*(5), 519–530. https://eric.ed.gov/?id=EJ1063208

Slaten, C., Verriden, A. W., & Baskin, T. W. (2019). General history and conceptual frameworks of school counseling. In C. T. Dollarhide & M. E. Lemberger-Truelove (Eds.), *Theories of school counseling for the 21st century* (pp. 13–24). Oxford University Press.

Sweeney, T. J. (2001). Counseling: Historical origins and philosophical roots. In D. C. Locke, J. Myers, & E. L. Herr (Eds.), *The handbook of counseling* (pp. 1–13). Sage.

Tate, E. (2019, September). *Student-to-counselor ratios are dangerously high. Here's how two districts are tackling it.* EdSurge. www.edsurge.com/news/2019-09-19-counselor-to-student-ratios-are-dangerously-high-here-s-how-two-districts-are-tackling-it

Thompson, R. A. (2012). *Professional school counseling: Best practices for working in the schools* (3rd ed.). Routledge.

US Department of Education. (n.d.). *Every student succeeds act (ESSA).* Author. www.ed.gov/essa?src%3Drn

Welton, A. D., & Martinez, M. A. (2013). Coloring the college pathway: A more culturally responsive approach to college readiness and access for students of color in secondary schools. *Urban Review, 46*(2), 197–223. https://doi.org/10.1007/s11256-013-0252-7

Wilson, F. (2013, May). *The creation of the National Vocational Guidance Association.* www.ncda.org/aws/NCDA/pt/sd/news_article/74076/_PARENT/CC_layout_details/false

Professional Identity of School Counselors and the *American School Counselor Association National Model* (2019)

Box 2.1 2016 Council for the Accreditation of Counseling and Related Educational Programs (CACREP, n.d.) School Counseling Specialty Area Standards

1.a History and development of school counseling
1.b Models of school counseling programs
2.a School counselor roles as leaders, advocates, and systems change agencies in P-12 schools
2.c School counselor roles in relation to college and career readiness
2.d School counselor roles in school leadership and multidisciplinary teams
2.f Competencies to advocate for school counseling roles
2.l Professional organizations, preparation standards, and credentials relevant to the practice of school counseling
3.a Development of school counseling program mission statements and objectives

---

Box 2.2 ASCA (2019a) Standards for School Counselor Preparation Programs (ASCA CAEP SPA)

1.2 Describe the evolution of the school counseling profession, the basis for a comprehensive school counseling program, and the school counselor's role in supporting growth and learning for all students.
4.1 Plan, organize, and implement a variety of instructional and counseling strategies as part of a comprehensive school counseling program (direct and indirect student services) to improve pre-K–12 student attitudes, knowledge, and skills.
5.1 Use data and student standards, such as the ASCA Mindsets and Behaviors for Student Success and appropriate state standards, to create school counseling program goals and action plans aligned with school improvement plans.
6.1 Explain appropriate scope of practice for school counselors defined as the overall delivery of the comprehensive school counseling program, providing education, prevention, intervention, and referral services to students and their families.

DOI: 10.4324/9781003167730-2

This chapter explores the professional identity of the SC. An overview of the four components of the *ASCA National Model: A Framework for School Counseling Programs* (ASCA, 2019b), which include foundation, management, delivery, and accountability, is provided, and much of the content of this chapter specifically, and this book generally, are informed by the content of the *ASCA National Model*. The Education Trust's (2009) Transforming School Counseling Initiative (TSCA) and the partnership between ASCA and the Education Trust are discussed. The role of SCs within the various essential educational frameworks, including multitiered systems of support (MTSS), response to intervention (RtI), and school-wide positive behavioral interventions and supports (SWPBIS), is reviewed. The chapter includes an overview of systems-ecological theory, which is either implicitly or explicitly identified in the various educational reforms previously referenced and efforts to transform the profession of school counseling. Finally, a discussion of McMahon et al.'s (2014) ecological school counseling model (ESCM) is provided as a specific example of how SCs can use a systems framework.

Professional Identity of School Counselors

The school counseling profession continues to pursue the long-sought objective of achieving a consistent identity. As an example of this problem, the role of the SC often varies between districts and even schools within the same district. In some schools, SCs function in a manner similar to mental health therapists, providing individual counseling to at-risk students. In other schools, SCs are heavily burdened with clerical duties, which may include registering and scheduling new students, coordinating the standardized test administrations, coordinating student study teams, maintaining attendance records, completing college applications, etc.

The effort to achieve a consistent identity is currently affected by overburdened education budgets and the considerable emphasis on accountability for educational institutions. SCs are not mandated by law in many states and sometimes are among the first school personnel to be eliminated due to budget reductions. The increasing expectation that schools and educators should be accountable for students' achievement or lack thereof, an expectation which is significantly represented in the No Child Left Behind (NCLB) Act (2002) and the Every Student Succeeds Act (ESSA; US Department of Education, n.d.) of 2015, has exerted pressure on the profession to identify how SCs contribute to the academic mission of schools and measure the impact of these contributions.

The school counseling profession must not only establish a niche within the education professions but also help the public understand their role and the positive impact of school counseling–related programs in order to counter some of the common negative perceptions of school counselors. School counseling students may find that they receive interesting reactions when they reveal what they are studying to laypeople, and it is common for such individuals to complain that their school counselor only helped them with scheduling, claimed that they would not amount to anything, etc. A national survey of recent high school graduates conducted in 2009 revealed that the students primarily gave their high school SCs a fair or poor rating and viewed them as less helpful than teachers in providing career development (Johnson et al., 2010). Moreover, 67% of respondents rated their school counselor as fair or poor for the assistance they provided in selecting a college, and 55% rated their school SC as fair or poor in the assistance they provided with the college application process.

The *ASCA National Model* (2019b) and Comprehensive School Counseling Programs

Thankfully, there appears to be progress in the development of a consistent and unique professional identity for SCs. During the last several decades, the American School Counselors Association (ASCA) and prominent SC educators have encouraged SCs to work systematically and collaboratively to meet the developmental needs of all students through the design and implementation of what are referred to as comprehensive school counseling programs. A comprehensive school counseling program includes a guidance curriculum that proactively addresses the academic, career, and social/emotional needs of students. The curriculum is distinct from but supports the school's academic curriculum. Whereas in previous decades, the profession focused upon the role of the SC and the services he or she provided, in the comprehensive school counseling program model, the emphasis is on the effectiveness of the program as opposed to the services conducted by the SC. In this model, the SC is regarded as a coordinator or leader of the program and works collaboratively with other school personnel, including teachers and administrators, in delivering the curriculum. The curriculum is delivered through a variety of program components, including classroom lessons, appraisal and advising, individual and group counseling, crisis response, referrals, consultation, and collaboration.

The *ASCA National Model* (2019b) is the predominant comprehensive school counseling program, and several chapters of the book are devoted to this model in significant detail. The *ASCA National Model* is comprised of four interrelated components: assess, deliver, define, and manage (see Figure 2.1). The foundation concerns

Figure 2.1 The *ASCA National Model* diamond graphic.

Source: Reprinted with permission, American School Counselor Association, www.schoolcounselor.org.

what the program is about—student knowledge, attitudes, and skills that the program seeks to promote—and the beliefs that will influence the program's activities used to facilitate the identified student competencies.

Define

ASCA Student Standards: Mindsets and Behaviors for Student Success (ASCA, 2021a)

The ASCA Student Standards (2021), which are available on ASCA's website, "describe the knowledge, skills and attitudes students need to achieve academic success, college and career readiness, and social/emotional development" (p. 1). They were developed based upon a review of the literature conducted by the University of Chicago Consortium on Chicago School Research concerning five categories of noncognitive factors that are associated with student achievement (Farrington et al., 2012). The 36 mindset and behavior standards identify the expected outcomes for the school counseling program (ASCA, 2021a). SCs identify the standards and behaviors that are addressed in classroom lessons and small groups. The ASCA Student Standards are comprised of three domains of academic, career, and social/emotional development, and each of the 36 standards may be applied to any of the three domains. The Mindset Standards are comprised of six psychosocial attitudes students have about themselves regarding their learning. The behavior standards are grouped into three subcategories: learning strategies, self-management skills, and social skills. For example, the first mindset is "Belief in development of whole self, including a healthy balance of mental, social/emotional, and physical well-being" (p. 2). Each of the subcategories of behavior standards has ten more specific behaviors. For example, the behavior standard for learning strategies is "Critical-thinking skills to make informed decisions" (p. 2).

ASCA School Counselor Competencies (ASCA, 2019c)

The ASCA School Counselor Competencies (2019c) identify the knowledge, skills, and attitudes that are regarded as necessary for implementing a comprehensive school counseling program. SCs may use the ASCA School Counselor Competencies for self-evaluation and identify potential areas for professional development.

Manage

The manage component of the ASCA National Model (2019b) is comprised of both organizational tools and assessments. The tools of the management component include (1) an advisory council that coordinates the school counseling program, (2) annual administrative conferences between the SC(s) and administration concerning the structure and goals of the school counseling programs, (3) classroom and ASCA Student Standards and closing-the-gap action plans that identify the objectives for these activities and specify how they are measured, and (4) annual and weekly calendars to inform stakeholders of program activities.

Vision Statement

The define component of the ASCA National Model includes a vision statement that is compatible with the school's and district's vision and that reveals what the SCs ideally wish for the students and school community to attain or achieve in the future. The vision statement should indicate the best but also achievable outcomes for students within the next 5–15 years and depicts a future in which the school counseling program's goals are being realized.

Box 2.3 Sample Vision Statement

The School Counseling Department of Propel McKeesport envisions students as lifelong learners and critical thinkers. Students will fulfill their post–secondary education aspirations by embracing diversity, acting as advocates for themselves and others, and contributing to the overall mission of global citizenship.

Reproduced with permission from Carley Kaercher, Hayley King, and Nadene Santelli, Propel Charter Schools, McKeesport (RAMP certified), Pennsylvania.

Mission Statement

The mission statement is also more concise than the vision statement and identifies the specifics for achieving the depiction provided in the vision statement. The mission statement should be compatible with the school's and district's missions, have students as the primary focus, advocate for equity and success for all students, and indicate the long-range goals for students.

Box 2.4 Sample School Counseling Mission Statement

The mission of the Propel McKeesport Counseling Department is to provide a comprehensive, developmental school counseling program that addresses the academic, career, social, and emotional needs of all students. Through collaboration with students, teachers, administrators, parents, and community members, we will facilitate a positive, supportive, and culturally sensitive program that will ensure our school communities are safe, healthy, and nurturing. We will create a college-bound and career-readiness culture that promotes academic excellence, self-efficacy, and lifelong learning.

Reproduced with permission from Carley Kaercher, Hayley King, and Nadene Santelli, Propel Charter Schools, McKeesport (RAMP certified), Pennsylvania.

Annual Student Outcome Goals

Annual student outcome goals reflect how the vision and mission statement will be achieved and direct the development of curriculum, small-group, and closing-the-gap action plans. The program goals identify specific, measurable student outcomes in the domains of academic, career, and social/emotional development. School data are used to identify the particular needs of the school and often seek to address gaps between educational access, equity, and achievement between White students and typically disadvantaged groups of students. School data that is reviewed for disparities include the frequency of discipline referrals, enrollment patterns in rigorous courses, and student absences (e.g., Dimmitt et al., 2007). There is more discussion of the process of using data in the goal-setting process in the chapter on management and accountability. Examples of specific, measurable, and attainable goals may include the following:

- A 20% increase in attendance for the students who had ten more absences the previous year.
- A 20% increase in the number of Black students enrolled in Advanced Placement (AP) courses.
- Within two years, Latin@ American students' average gain in reaching achievement, as indicated by the state achievement test, will be 20% greater than the White students' gain scores.

Deliver

The delivery system involves both direct and indirect student services. Direct services are comprised of the school counseling curriculum, which includes both classroom and group activities that support the school counseling program's curriculum, appraisal and advising, and responsive services, which are defined as individual and group counseling and crisis response. The delivery system also involves indirect services that may consist of providing referrals and consulting and collaborating with parents, school personnel, and community organizations. The deliver component of the *ASCA National Model* is reviewed in extensive depth in several chapters of this book.

Assess

The last component of the model, assess, refers to the need to use data to assess the impact of the school counseling program upon student achievement and inform revisions to the program. The assess component of the *ASCA National Model* (2019b) is reviewed in great detail in various chapters of the book. Using data is an explicit assess component and is an integral aspect of each of the organizational assessments that consist of school counselor competency and school counseling program assessments developed by ASCA.

Box 2.5

Did You Know?

California, Georgia, Indiana, North Carolina, and Virginia have a large number of schools with RAMP status (ASCA, n.d.B).

Education Trust's Transforming School Counseling Initiative (TSCI)

Education Trust (2009) is a nonprofit organization that seeks to reform education consistent with the primary aims of NCLB and ESSA, namely, promoting high levels of academic achievement for all students and closing the achievement gaps between Asian and White students and typically disadvantaged students, including low-income students and students of color. Education Trust formed a subgroup, called the National Center for Transforming School Counseling (NCTSC), which seeks to "prepare graduates [of school counseling programs] to serve as student advocates and academic advisors who demonstrate the belief that all students can achieve high levels on rigorous, challenging academic course content" (Martin, 2002, p. 148).

ASCA and NCTSC have worked to position the school counseling profession as a significant contributor to educational reform. ASCA developed the National Model (2019b) and ASCA Student Standards (2021) to influence currently practicing school counselors. Education Trust's Transforming School Counseling Initiative (TSCI) has primarily focused upon modifying the way in which SCs are educated in graduate schools, providing grants to select universities to train students in a transformed model of school counseling, and encouraging state departments of education to adopt new standards for school counselor preparation (Perkins et al., 2010). The TSCI vision for school counselors involves the following: (1) de-emphasizing a mental health perspective in favor of an academic/student achievement focus, (2) adopting a whole school or systems perspective vs. focusing on individual student issues, (3) using data to effect change as opposed to school counselors simply being involved with data as part of record-keeping, and (4) serving as change students to promote educational equity (Education Trust, 2009).

ASCA and TSCI have much provided a framework for unifying the school counseling profession, but debate continues regarding the role of SCs. A 2010 survey of elementary SCs, elementary principals, elementary teachers, and SC educators revealed that each group identified the social/emotional domain as being a more important focus for elementary SCs than the academic and career domains (Perkins et al., 2010). This finding may indicate that elementary SCs and their stakeholders may not have accepted the Education Trust's encouragement of school counselors to primarily adopt an academic focus in their role functioning.

The ASCA National Model (2019b) Themes

The close partnership between ASCA and NCTSC is reflected in the *ASCA National Model*'s (2019b) four themes, leadership, advocacy, collaboration, and systemic change, which were part of the initial TSCI efforts. SCs function as leaders in coordinating the school counseling program and promote systemic change by removing barriers and implementing programs that facilitate high levels of academic achievement for all students. TSCI and ASCA agree that SCs must use data in advocating for the rights of all students to be taught at a high level. SCs collaborate with other stakeholders, including administrators, teachers, parents, students, and community members, in order to effect systemic change. Subsequent chapters of this book will explore the model themes in greater detail.

Empirical Support for Comprehensive School Counseling Programs

Studies investigating the effectiveness of comprehensive school counseling programs have compared schools with more fully developed comprehensive school counseling programs to those with less-developed comprehensive school counseling programs or have compared schools which have Recognized ASCA Model Programs (RAMP; ASCA, n.d.A) to schools which have similar demographic characteristics that lack RAMP status. Studies of state-based school counseling programs have revealed positive aspects of student outcomes in schools with comprehensive programs. Investigations of students' achievement in Nebraska

(Carey et al., 2012a) and Utah (Carey et al., 2012b) revealed that, after controlling from demographic differences, specific components of a CSCP were associated with positive student outcomes, including in regards to attendance, behavior, achievement test scores, and graduation rates. In Missouri, middle school students with fully implemented CSCPs, in comparison to students attending schools with lower implementation fidelity, reported less conflict with peers, improved relationships with their teachers, and were more likely to believe that their education was applicable to their future (Lapan et al., 2001). In Washington, elementary (Sink & Stroh, 2003) and middle school students (Sink et al., 2008) who attended schools with more fully implemented CSCPs had higher state assessment scores in comparison to students who attended schools without fully implemented CSCPs.

There is less efficacy research regarding RAMP programs. Ward (2009) found that elementary students who attended RAMP schools had higher attendance rates and achievement test scores than elementary students who attended non-RAMP schools. In Indiana, elementary students who attended in RAMP schools had higher pass rates on state achievement tests than students who attended non-RAMP schools, but there were no significant differences for middle or high school students (Wilkerson et al., 2013). In comparing elementary students from RAMP schools to non-RAMP schools within a large school district, Milsom and Morey (2019) found that students from non-RAMP schools actually had higher attendance rates and course grades than students who attended RAMP schools. Goodman-Scott et al. (2020) found that a comparison of schools with a RAMP in Georgia and Virginia to matched schools which lacked RAMP revealed that there is no difference in terms of student achievement and suspension and attendance rates. Milsom and Morey (2019) concluded that additional research is necessary to understand the impact of RAMP.

Multitiered Systems of Support (MTSS)

Another major trend impacting education and school counseling programs has been the emergence of multitiered systems of support (MTSS). MTSS is an overarching term that is used to refer to the academically focused response to intervention (RtI) and the behaviorally focused school-wide positive behavioral interventions and support (SWPBIS). A school-based leadership team coordinates the MTSS implementation, seeking to enhance student outcomes through the use of data (e.g., at the student and school level), systems (e.g., school policies and procedures), and tiered interventions (e.g., tier one prevention for all students, and tier two and tier three interventions for students who have more significant needs (Goodman-Scott & Ziomek-Daigle, 2021). MTSS is associated with a number of positive student outcomes, including lower discipline referral, suspension, and truancy rates and academic achievement and attendance (e.g., Pas et al., 2019).

ASCA's (2021b) position statement regarding MTSS is that SCs, using their collaboration, coordination, and leadership skills, align their work within an MTSS framework to meet the holistic needs of students, which include students' academic, career, and social/emotional needs (Shepard et al., 2013). In tier one, SCs support MTSS by providing classroom instruction, collaborating for the implementation of school-wide programming, and collecting and analyzing data, including data from universal screening, to identify students who are at risk for mental health, academic, and behavioral concerns (Donohue et al., 2016). In tier two, SCs conduct such direct services as targeted group counseling and individualized interventions, which include brief individual counseling and implementation of behavioral modification plans. At the tier three level, SCs typically only conduct indirect services, providing support through the form of consultation, collaboration, and referrals as members of the MTSS team (Goodman-Scott et al., 2020). Ockerman et al. (2012) note that MTSS and comprehensive school counseling programs have important similarities in that they can be characterized as collaborative, proactive, data-driven, multitiered, and involve in advocating for holistic development and educational equity.

Both MTSS and comprehensive school counseling programs emphasize increased attention to tier one interventions, given that they are the most efficient way to serve the majority of students. Tier one or school-wide interventions within the comprehensive school counseling programs could be considered to include lessons that support the school counseling curriculum; substance abuse prevention activities; career development events, such as career days; and academic incentive programs. Tier two interventions could involve group counseling and peer support services, such as peer mentoring or tutoring. Tier three interventions represent the most intensive and individualized level of service, which for school counselors could involve individual counseling, behavior or academic improvement plans, repeated parent consultation, or community referral.

Response to Intervention (RtI)

RtI uses data-driven decision-making and a multitiered approach for the dual purposes of reforming general education and assisting struggling learners (Buffum et al., 2009). The reauthorization of the Individuals with Disabilities Education Improvement Act (IDEA, 2004) allowed schools to use RtI as an alternative to the traditional discrepancy model for determining whether a child has a specific learning disability (PL No 108–446). The federal government permitted this alternative for identification of a learning disability partly as a means to address the overrepresentation of minority students in special education (Buffum et al., 2009). RtI is also designed to improve the core curriculum and provide a framework for providing increasing levels of differentiation to students within the regulation education setting in order to reduce inappropriate referrals to special education.

RtI emphasizes the need to ensure the effectiveness of the tier one core curriculum through the use of empirically supported practices that are implemented with treatment fidelity, which means that the practice was applied in a manner that is consistent with the protocol. The model expects that 80–85% of students will respond positively to the core curriculum. Failure of more than 20% of the students to achieve benchmarks results in a review and possible modification of the core curriculum. The 15–20% of students who fail to demonstrate expected levels of progress receive tier two intervention, which consists of small-group intervention, typically involving three to five group sessions of up to 30 minutes per week. Lack of response to tier two intervention results in the application of tier three intervention, which often consists of individualized instruction. It is estimated that 3–5% of students may require tier three intervention if the model is being effectively implemented. In some states, failure of a student to respond to tier three intervention automatically results in assessment for special education services, whereas in others the student would automatically receive special education services without a disability assessment.

RtI uses data-driven decision-making, which involves "a continuous process of regularly collecting, summarizing, and analyzing information to guide development, implementation, and evaluation" (Buffum et al., 2009, p. 206). Universal screens are typically used at the beginning, middle, and end of each academic year to assess student performance in comparison to benchmarks and learning standards. With each level of instruction, there is an increase in how frequently student performance is assessed. For example, at tier two, progress monitoring of students' reading achievement may occur twice a month. At tier three, a student's progress may be assessed on a weekly or even daily basis.

The limited research available concerning school counselors' involvement with RtI indicates that some SCs coordinate the student support team, which may also be called the child study team, behavior intervention team, or RtI team (Ockerman et al., 2012). In their role as team coordinator, some SCs monitor and analyze the data for both academic and behavioral interventions for each tier of RtI. Ockerman et al. (2012) recommend that SCs seek to achieve a balance between serving a supportive role as an RtI team member and an active role as an intervention provider. SCs can make significant contributions to the RtI team, sharing their knowledge of the connections between the academic, social/emotional, and career development of students and expertise in the use of data, knowledge, and prevention and intervention strategies, and facilitating constructive collaboration between school personnel and family members. However, they should avoid serving as the RtI team coordinator as the considerable coordination duties may interfere with their ability to coordinate the comprehensive school counseling program. Ryan et al. (2011) provide an example in which an SC coordinated the screening and placement of students within the tiers and evaluated the impact of the RtI program on student achievement but also infused social/emotional and career objectives into the academic curriculum objectives. A survey of teachers revealed that they positively viewed the SC's contributions to the program.

School-Wide Positive Behavioral Interventions and Supports (SWPBIS)

SWPBIS is a universal, behavioral theory–based prevention and intervention program that is employed by many schools that use RtI to focus specifically upon students who exhibit behavioral and mental health issues. SWPBIS, encouraged by the US Department of Education and several state departments of education, similar to RtI, uses a three-tiered model to address disruptive behavior (Bradshaw et al., 2010). Whereas traditionally, school-based behavioral interventions primarily focused upon the individual student, SWPBIS and other types of "proactive classroom management" programs seek to alter the school environment through the universal application of principles of behavioral theory. At the tier one level, students are taught and positively reinforced for demonstrating school-wide behavioral expectations. Data are used at all levels to establish the behavioral expectations, evaluate the effectiveness of tiered interventions, and identify students in need of an increased intensity of intervention. Research suggests that when it is implemented with fidelity, 80–85% of students positively respond to Tier 1 interventions.

Tier two is intended to assist the 10–15% of students who tend to not positively respond to tier one interventions. Common tier two interventions include social skill and academic instruction groups and check-in/check-out. Tier three interventions are individualized for the 3–5% of students who fail to respond to both tier one and tier two interventions. Common tier three interventions include use of functional behavior analysis and assisting the family members in obtaining mental health services that might be provided in the school or community setting. A meta-analytic survey found that SWPBIS yielded statistically significant improvements, resulting in small to moderate reductions in school discipline and small to moderate increases in academic achievement (Lee & Gage, 2020).

Data-driven decision-making is used within the various tiers of SWPBIS. There are a variety of universal screening instruments used to identity students at risk for emotional and behavioral difficulties, including the Systematic Screening for Behavioral Disorders (Albers et al., 2007), the Student Risk Screening Scale (Drummond, 1994), the Behavioral Assessment for Children-2 (BASC-2) (Reynolds & Kamphaus, 2004), and the Strengths and Difficulties Questionnaire (SDQ: Goodman et al., 1998). The universal screening instruments use a multiple-gating procedure which typically involves having teachers rank in order which students they consider to be at risk as indicated by observable behaviors, followed by the teacher completing a standardized assessment for the identified students. Students who are identified as at risk through both procedures are referred to tier two intervention. Other forms of data used to identify behaviorally and emotionally at-risk students include office discipline referrals (ODR) and the students' attendance/tardy rates. The effectiveness of tier two interventions may be assessed through a daily progress report that indicates students' progress in meeting individualized behavioral expectations. At tier three, a functional behavioral assessment (FBA) and functional assessment interview are often conducted to identify hypotheses regarding the function of the students' behavior and develop a more comprehensive behavioral modification plan. Some states use universal screens to identify students who are at risk for mental health issues, including depression and suicide among adolescents. Students who are identified as having an elevated risk for depression and suicide may receive services from mental health professionals in the community or within the schools. Clearly, SCs are likely to play a significant role in administering and interpreting data concerning behavioral and emotional functioning, providing services to such students, and collaborating with mental health professionals for students receiving tier three interventions.

SCs are likely to be an integral member, but not leader, of the school committee coordinating SWPBIS, given their background in data-driven decision-making and the fact that students who require increased levels of support are more likely to qualify for a mental health diagnosis (Martens & Andreen, 2013). Martens and Andreen (2013) encourage SCs to collaborate with other school staff in implementing check-in/check-out (CICO). CICO uses a structured routine in which an identified student meets with a school staff member to review the student's progress in meeting targeted behavioral expectations. Students carry a daily report card throughout the school day on which teachers rate students' exhibition of targeted behaviors using a Likert-type scale. In demonstrating progress, students receive positive reinforcement that is uniquely developed for the individual child, and students' progress is regularly shared with both the students' teachers and parents/guardian. A meta-analytic study revealed that CICO is effective in reducing problematic behavior (Drevon et al., 2019). Martens and Andreen (2013) believe that CICO enables SCs to positively impact a group of students through individualized interventions and is consistent with the *ASCA National Model*'s (2019b) emphasis on data-driven decision-making. SCs can use their knowledge of mental health issues and principles of behavioral modification in constructing students' behavioral expectations and in consulting with school personnel who are involved in the CICO process.

Systems-Ecological Theory

A prevailing theme found within recent educational reforms and efforts to transform the school counseling profession is the need for school personnel to adopt a broader, comprehensive perspective of students. The following statement by Dr. Peggy Hines, who has served as Director of TSCI, succinctly states the need for systemic change:

> The idea is that it's not always the students that are broken; sometimes it's the system or the school that is broken. If school counselors can get schools to change policy and practice, and support those kinds of systemic interventions for students, then that's going to be a lot more effective than trying to change kids one at a time.
>
> (Perusse & Colbert, 2007, p. 478)

Much of ASCA's efforts in the past several decades emphasize the need for SCs to implement and support programs that promote all students' achievement by enhancing the environments in which students function. The trends in educational reform and, as a consequence, the transformation of the school counseling profession are reflective of the emergence of an ecological perspective of student achievement.

The systems-ecological framework represents an alternative scheme for understanding children's behavior in contrast to the traditional linear model of cause and effect. We are using the term "systems-ecological" to refer to two similar theories: general systems theory (von Bertalanffy, 1968) and social ecology theory (Bronfenbrenner, 1979). The main assumption of the systems-ecological framework is that children's functioning and development is the result of the interaction between the child and the environment. General systems theory represents a paradigm shift in that it rejects the traditional linear causal perspective of Western science and the medical model, which conceptualizes behavior as being the result of a single cause or chain of causes that occur within the child. In contrast, general systems theory posits a circular causal perspective in which a child's behavior instead is believed to be a function of numerous interacting variables that reciprocally influence each other.

Parents, teachers, and peers are seen as potentially impacting a child's behavior and, in turn, being impacted by the child in question. No one person or environmental context is regarded as causative; persons and contexts are seen as potential contributors to children's development. Bronfenbrenner's (1979) theory of social ecology shares some of the basic principles of systems theory, including the importance of reciprocal interaction, but is broader in scope than systems theory. Whereas systems theory tends to focus upon the interactions within a system, particularly the family system, Bronfenbrenner claimed that the multiple embedded systems in which the child exists, which include the peer, family, school, community, and cultural environments, may be equally as important in promoting children's development. Children do not develop in isolation but instead are influenced by various contexts (e.g., society, peers, family, etc.) in which they interact. Although not as intensely researched as traditional, linear behavioral models, some studies have directly evaluated systems-ecological models for childhood issues, providing empirical support for the model's application to school violence (Khoury-Kassabri et al., 2004) and bullying (Espelage et al., 2013). Indeed, Henggeler et al.'s (1996) review of the research literature revealed that "serious antisocial behavior is multidetermined by the reciprocal interplay of characteristics of the individual youth and the key social systems in which youths are embedded (i.e., family, peer, social, neighborhood, and community)" (p. 6–7).

Systems-ecological theory offers significant advantages over the traditional, linear model for identifying implications for intervention and prevention with children. In the traditional, linear model, school personnel have a tendency to become overly focused upon the individual child, often resulting in thinking about the child's deficits and their cause, such as biological deficiencies, lack of student motivation, etc. This tends to lead to what has been referred as a "blame game," in which teachers overly focus upon the deficiencies of the student, parents, or previous teachers, and parents focus on the school's inadequacies. The systems-ecological theory provides practitioners with a framework that is more complex, in the encouragement to think about various variables and their interactions, which most likely is a more realistic view of behavior and child development, and more conductive to self-reflection by school personnel. School personnel can consider the school- and community-based factors that may contribute to a student's lack of achievement, implications for modifying the larger environment, or what might be referred to as prevention. In terms of intervention, school personnel can examine how their instruction of a child or their relationship with a child may possibly contribute to the issue, or how family factors may contribute, or even how the relationship between the family and the school could be enhanced. It can be argued that NCLB, RtI, and SWPBS were instituted in order to create such a paradigm shift in encouraging school personnel to assume more ownership for student achievement.

Ecological School Counseling Model (ESCM)

McMahon et al. (2014) presented an ecological model of school counseling (ESCM) which they developed to support the *ASCA National Model* (2019b) by providing a theoretical/ conceptual foundation for the atheoretical structural model of the *ASCA National Model*. This model was also developed as a framework for guiding comprehensive interventions, in contrast to the more individualistic counseling theories that have traditionally informed the work of school counselors. McMahon et al. (2014) present a number of basic assumptions for ESCM. The core assumption from which all their other assumptions derive is that schools are ecosystems. As ecosystems, schools are comprised of numerous subsystems (e.g., classrooms, grade level, clubs, cliques) and are part of larger systems, or "suprasystem" (e.g., school districts, community, state). The school, its subsystems, and the suprasystems in which the school is embedded are interconnected in various ways, and changes within any of these levels can affect each other.

Another principle of ESCM is that well-functioning schools are dynamic, balanced, and flexible. Schools function as a network of interdependently related components that are continually undergoing change but also strive to achieve a healthy balance within the face of change. They require semipermeable boundaries that permit the distinction of clear subgroups (e.g., teachers, students, administrators) but are also flexible enough to allow for healthy connection between the groups. In schools that achieve this balance, members comprehend the roles and expectations to be part of the system and any subsystems with which they might identify. Well-functioning schools are also more likely to be diverse. A diverse faculty can promote academic achievement, as students are more likely to identify with school personnel who are similar to them in terms of race and/or ethnicity. A diverse peer group provides students with enhanced perspective taking by being exposed to different forms and styles of communication. Exposure to such diversity increase the likelihood that graduates will more readily adapt to the changes within the larger society.

Similar to a family system, schools use feedback to identify and manage emerging issues (McMahon et al., 2014). Ecosystems must have mechanisms, referred to as feedback loops, to address imbalances in the system. When ecosystems become unbalanced either toward too much structure, meaning, they are rigid in the face of change, or too much change, in which members lack clear expectations regarding their roles and the rules of the organization, new structures or patterns will spontaneously develop within the ecosystem in an effort to find order within the system. Intentional feedback loops used in the schools include the use of data for decision-making and strategic planning. However, as with all ecosystems, schools also have feedback loops that emerge spontaneously, often among students who have less officially sanctioned power. McMahon et al. (2014) present the examples of absenteeism and gangs as indicators that the ecosystem is not addressing the needs of the members but which are often perceived by school personnel as problems that must be eradicated as opposed to a need for redress of the ecosystem.

McMahon and colleagues' (2014) ESCM postulates that meaning is both constructed and experienced within schools and their subsystems. Meaning-making is an essential aspect of the human condition, and people constantly make meaning of their experiences that occur within an environmental context. McMahon et al. (2014) identify two main implications of the meaning-making process. One is that the school must provide a process for which members of both the school and its various subsystems define the identity and purpose of the respective systems for that particular time. The other implication is that meaning-making is derived from feedback that is received by the school-as-system. The feedback is received through both formal processes, such as school outcome data, and informal processes, such as offhand complaints by parents about teachers. These data do not reveal objective truth; rather, they are interpreted differently based on the unique perspectives of the viewer and his or her context.

The final principle of McMahon et al.'s (2014) ESCM is that healthy schools are sustainable. The organisms and subsystems contribute in their unique way to the functioning of the system, and the school has a reciprocal relationship with the community in which it is embedded. An effective reciprocal relationship between the school and community involves the production of graduates who are to fulfill the various jobs and functions of the community, including the teaching, parenting, and mentoring of the new generation of students who will comprise the school community. The implication is that schools should keep at the forefront its mission of preparing graduates to meet the needs of the community.

ASCA and TSCI urge SCs to adopt such a systems-ecological perspective. ASCA incorporated TSCI's emphasis on systemic change, which is one of four themes within the *ASCA National Model*. The description of systemic change within the *ASCA National model* indicates that a school functions much like a family system in that the various components or members reciprocally influence each other. The *ASCA National Model* and the ASCA Student Standards (2021) provide SCs with models to promote all students' academic, social/emotional, and career development, thus providing students with the skills to negotiate developmental challenges, as opposed to school counselors primarily focusing upon remediating the problems of at-risk students. TSCI calls for SCs to contribute to increases in the rigor and effectiveness of the academic curriculum in promoting college and career readiness. The systems-ecological perspective has significant implications for the way in which SCs intervene with individual students and expands intervention options. SCs can conduct brief individual counseling with students but can also consider consulting with teachers and parents to assist them in more effectively responding to a student's needs. SCs need to consider what intervention with whom is most likely to be successful and which is the most time-efficient. Talking with a teacher or parent for 20 minutes may be more effective than conducting three individual sessions with a child. In consulting with parents and teachers, SCs can use a systems-ecological perspective to identify how the patterns between the child and the teacher or parent may contribute to the respective issue, or even how the relationship between the parents and the teacher may be modified.

The phenomenon of bullying can be used as a case illustration of the systems-ecological approach. Espelage et al.'s (2013) review of the literature found support for the contention that bullying behaviors are influenced by characteristics of the individual, family, and school environments. In terms of individual characteristics, perpetrators of bullying are more likely to be male, physically larger than their peers, and be enrolled in special education. Victims tend to be less popular and have lower social status than their peers. The parents of perpetrators are more likely than the parents of nonperpetrators to provide inadequate supervision, be less involved in their children's lives, and encourage aggression and retaliation. The parents of victims of bullying are more likely than the parents of nonvictims to be abusive or inconsistent, while victims of bullying who have nurturing relationships with their families have more positive outcomes. Classrooms that are less democratic and have larger disparities in social power are associated with greater bullying.

In schools which have higher rates of bullying, students are less likely to seek assistance from teachers and staff, and perpetrators are more likely than victims to have high social status.

The complex nature of bullying and the fact that it is influenced by contextual variables appear to be recognized in the comprehensive approach used by many bullying prevention programs. For example, Olweus's bullying prevention program (Olweus & Limber, 2010) seeks to modify the school's culture through the implementation of rules and sanctions for bullying, increased supervision of identified high-frequency areas for bullying, and classroom lessons that define bullying and provide bystanders and victims with strategies to address bullying. A meta-analytic study, which involves aggregating the results of various studies, revealed that bullying prevention programs reduce school-bullying perpetration by about 19–20% and school-bullying victimization by approximately 15–16% (Gaffney et al., 2019). Gaffney et al.'s (2021) meta-analytic study found that various approaches, including social-ecological approaches which seek to alter environmental conditions that support aggression among youth, are effective in reducing school bullying. Activities that involve informal peer involvement, which typically include whole-class or small-group discussions, cooperative group work, or other types of activities that promote peer interaction, are associated with greater reductions in school bullying than other types of bullying activities. Such informal peer involvement activities do not directly target perpetrators, victims, or bystanders of bullying but appear to be effective in promoting a prosocial classroom and school ethos. The presence of classroom rules and a whole-school approach is more effective than programs which do not include these approaches. Nonpunitive disciplinary methods are associated with greater reductions in bullying. Providing information to parents via leaflets/letters is associated with reductions in bullying, whereas more formal involvement of parents, such as encouraging parents to attend information evenings, is not associated with reductions in bullying.

These findings have implications for SCs' roles in bullying prevention and illustrate the need for school counselors to think comprehensively. Within the mental health model, in which SCs were trained in previous decades, the SC might tend to focus upon providing individual counseling to victims and perpetrators of bullying. However, the data do not appear to support such an approach. Certainly, SCs should consider providing counseling to students in need, but they should simultaneously consider programmatic/systemic interventions that seek to alter the school and community environment that supports bullying behaviors. SCs can advocate for the need for a bullying prevention program and lobby the state and federal government for legislation and funding for bullying prevention programs. SCs can collaborate with teachers, administrators, and parents in creating and coordinating a bullying prevention program. SCs can lead trainings for parents and teachers. For individual victims and perpetrators, SCs might most effectively intervene by consulting with their parents. SCs have erroneously equated systems theory with conducting family counseling; rather, systems-ecological theory provides a way of thinking about issues that enables practitioners to consider the larger framework of contextual variables and their implications for working with the specific needs of an individual student.

Summary

SCs must understand the reforms that are reshaping the US educational system in order to remain relevant in an era of accountability and shrinking budgets. ASCA and TSCI provide SCs with a framework for contributing to the academic mission of schools while simultaneously developing a distinct identity. SCs are encouraged to understand systems-ecological theory and the implications it has for prevention and intervention at multiple levels. The chapters that follow will examine many of these issues in greater depth and provide applied examples.

References

Albers, C. A., Glover, T. A., & Kratochwill, T. R. (2007). Where are we, and where do we go now? Universal screening for enhanced educational and mental health outcomes. *Journal of School Psychology, 45*(2), 257–263. https://doi.org/10.1016/j.jsp.2006.12.003

American School Counselor Association. (2019a). *ASCA standards for school counselor preparation programs.* Author. www.schoolcounselor.org/getmedia/573d7c2c-1622-4d25-a5ac-ac74d2e614ca/ASCA-Standards-for-School-Counselor-Preparation-Programs.pdf

American School Counselor Association. (2019b). *The ASCA national model: A framework for school counseling programs* (4th ed.). Author.

American School Counselor Association. (2019c). *ASCA school counselor professional standards & competencies.* Author. www.schoolcounselor.org/asca/media/asca/home/SCCompetencies.pdf

American School Counselor Association. (2021a). *ASCA student standards: Mindsets & behaviors for student success.* Author. www.schoolcounselor.org/Standards-Positions/Standards/ASCA-Mindsets-Behaviors-for-Student-Success

American School Counselor Association. (2021b). *The school counselor and multitiered systems of supports.* Author.

American School Counselor Association. (n.d.A). *Recognized ASCA model program.* Author. www.schoolcounselor.org/Recognition/RAMP

American School Counselor Association. (n.d.B). *Current RAMP schools.* Author. https://www.schoolcounselor.org/Recognition/RAMP/Current-RAMP-Schools

Bradshaw, C. P., Mitchell, M. M., & Leaf, P. J. (2010). Examining the effects of schoolwide positive behavioral interventions and supports on student outcomes: Results from a randomized controlled effectiveness trial in elementary schools. *Journal of Positive Behavioral Interventions, 12*(3), 133–148. https://doi.org/10.1177/1098300709334798

Bronfenbrenner, U. (1979). *The ecology of human development: Experiments by nature and design.* Harvard University Press.

Buffum, A., Mattos, M., & Weber, C. (2009). *Pyramid response to intervention: RTI, professional learning communities, and how to respond when kids don't learn.* Solution Tree Press.

Carey, J., Harrington, K., Martin, I., & Hoffman, D. (2012a). A statewide evaluation of the outcomes of implementation of the ASCA National Model school counseling programs in rural and suburban Nebraska high schools. *Professional School Counseling, 16*(2), 100–107. https://doi.org/10.1177/2156759X0001600203

Carey, J., Harrington, K., Martin, I., & Stevenson, D. (2012b). Implementation of ASCA National Model counseling programs in Utah high schools. *Professional School Counseling, 16*(2), 89–99. https://doi.org/10.1177/2156759X0001600203

Council for the Accreditation of Counseling and Related Educational Programs. (n.d.). *2016 CACREP standards.* www.cacrep.org/for-programs/2016-cacrep-standards/

Dimmitt, C., Carey, J. C., & Hatch, T. (2007). *Evidence-based school counseling: Making a difference with data-driven practices.* Corwin Press.

Donohue, P., Goodman-Scott, E., & Betters-Bubon, J. (2016). Universal screening for early identification of students at risk: A case example from the field. *Professional School Counseling, 19*(1), 133–143. https://doi.org/10.5330/1096-2409-19.1.133

Drevon, D. D., Hixson, M. D., & Wyse, R. D. (2019). A meta-analytic review of the evidence for check-in check out. *Psychology in the Schools, 56*(3), 393–412. https://doi.org/10.1002/pits.22195

Drummond, T. (1994). *The Student Risk Screening Scale (SRSS).* Josephine County Mental Health Program.

Education Trust. (2009, January 1). *The new vision for school counselors: Scope of the work.* Author. https://edtrust.org/resource/the-new-vision-for-school-counselors-scope-of-thework/#:~:text=The%20 National%20Center%20for%20Transforming,academic%20success%20for%20all%20students

Espelage, D. L., Rao, M. A., & De La Rue, L. (2013). Current research on school-based bullying: A social-ecological perspective. *Journal of Social Distress and the Homeless, 22*(1), 7–21. https://doi.org/10.1179/1053078913Z.0000000002

Farrington, C. A., Roderick, M., Allensworth, E., Nagaoka, J., Keyes, T. S., Johnson, D. W., & Beechum, N. O. (2012). *Teaching adolescents to become learners: The role of noncognitive factors in shaping school performance-A critical literature review.* Consortium on Chicago School Research.

Gaffney, H., Ttofi, M. M., & Farrington, D. P. (2019). Evaluating the effectiveness of school bullying prevention programs: An updated meta-analytical review. *Aggression and Violent Behavior, 45*, 111–133. https://doi.org/10.1016/j.avb.2018.07.001

Gaffney, H., Ttofi, M. M., & Farrington, D. P. (2021). What works in anti-bullying programs? Analysis of effective intervention components. *Journal of School Psychology, 85*, 37–56. https://doi.org/10.1016/j.jsp.2020.12.002

Goodman, R., Meltzer, H., & Bailey, V. (1998). The strengths and difficulties questionnaire: A pilot study on the validity of the self-report version. *European Child & Adolescent Psychiatry, 7*, 125–130. https://doi.org/10.1007/s007870050057

Goodman-Scott, E., Betters-Bugon, J., Olsen, J., & Donohue, P. (2020). *Making MTSS work.* American School Counselor Association.

Goodman-Scott, E., Taylor, J. V., Kalkbrenner, M. T., Darsie, J., Barbosa, R., Walsh, K., & Worth, A. (2020). A multivariate analysis of variance investigation of school-level RAMP status across two states. *Counseling Outcome Research and Evaluation, 11*(1), 31–44. https://doi.org/10.108 0/21501378.2019.1575696

Goodman-Scott, E., & Ziomek-Daigle, J. (2021). School counselors' leadership experiences in multi-tiered systems of support: Prioritizing relationships and shaping school climate. *Journal of Counseling & Development*, 1–12. https://doi.org/10.1002/jcad.12426

Henggeler, S. W., Schoenwald, S. K., Borduin, C. M., Rowland, M. D., & Cunningham, P. B. (1996). *Multisystemic treatment of antisocial behavior in children and adolescents.* Guilford Press.

Individuals with Disabilities Education Improvement Act (2004). Public Law 108–446 (20 U.S.C 1400 *et seq.*)

Johnson, J., Rochkind, J., Ott, A. N., & DuPont, S. (2010). *Can get a little advice here? How an overstretched high school guidance system is undermining students' college aspirations.* Public Agenda. https://files.eric.ed.gov/fulltext/ED508672.pdf

Khoury-Kassabri, M., Benbenishty, R., Astor, R. A., & Zeira, A. (2004). The contributions of community, family, and school variables to student victimization. *American Journal of Community Psychology, 34*(3–4), 187–204. https://doi.org/10.1007/s10464-004-7414-4

Lapan, R. T., Gysbers, N. C., & Petroski, G. F. (2001). Helping seventh graders be safe and successful: A statewide study of the impact of comprehensive guidance and counseling programs. *Journal of Counseling & Development, 79*(3), 320–330. https://doi.org/10.1002/j.1556-6676.2001. tb01977.x

Lee, A., & Gage, N. A. (2020). Updating and expanding systematic reviews and meta-analyses on the effects of school-wide positive behavior interventions and supports. *Psychology in the Schools, 57*(5), 783–804. https://doi.org/10.1002/pits.22336

Martens, K., & Andreen, K. (2013). School counselors' involvement with a school-wide positive behavior support intervention: Addressing student behavior issues in a proactive and positive manner. *Professional School Counseling, 16*(5), 313–322. https://doi.org/10.1177/21567 59X1201600504

Martin, P. (2002). Transforming school counseling: A national perspective. *Theory Into Practice, 41*(3), 148–155. https://doi.org/10.1207/s15430421tip4103_2

McMahon, H. G., Mason, E. C. M., Daluga-Guenther, N., & Ruiz, A. (2014). An ecological model of professional school counseling. *Journal of Counseling & Development, 92*(4), 459–471. https://doi.org/10.1002/j.1556-6676.2014.00172.x

Milsom, A., & Morey, M. (2019). Does RAMP matter? Comparing elementary student grades and absences in one district. *Professional School Counseling, 22*(1), 1–8. https://doi.org/10.1177/2156759X19847977

No Child Left Behind Act of 2001, Pub. L. No. 107–110 (2002).

Ockerman, M. S., Mason, E. C. M., & Feiker, A. (2012). Integrating RTI with school counseling programs: Being a proactive professional school counselor. *Journal of School Counseling, 10*(15), 1–37. https://jsc.montana.edu/articles/v10n15.pdf

Olweus, D., & Limber, S. P. (2010). Bullying in school: Evaluation and dissemination of the Olweus Bullying Prevention Program. *American Journal of Orthopsychiatry, 80*(1), 124–134. https://doi.org/10.1111/j.1939-0025.2010.01015.x

Pas, E. T., Ryoo, J. H., Musci, R. J., & Bradshaw, C. P. (2019). A statewide quasi-experimental effectiveness study of the scale-up of school-wide positive behavioral interventions and supports. *Journal of School Psychology, 73*, 41–55. https://doi.org/10.1016/j.jsp.2019.03.001

Perkins, G., Oescher, J., & Ballard, M. B. (2010). The evolving identity of school counselors as defined by the stakeholders. *Journal of School Counseling, 8*(31), 1–28. https://jsc.montana.edu/articles/v8n31.pdf

Perusse, R., & Colbert, R. D. (2007). The last word: An interview with Peggy Hines, director of the education trust's national center for transforming school counseling. *Journal of Advanced Academics, 18*(3), 477–487. https://doi.org/10.4219/jaa-2007-493

Reynolds, C. R., & Kamphaus, R. W. (2004). *Behavior assessment for children* (2nd ed.). AGS Publishing.

Ryan, T., Kaffenberger, C. J., & Carroll, A. G. (2011). Response to intervention: An opportunity for school counselor leadership. *Professional School Counseling, 14*(3), 211–221. https://doi.org/10.1177/2156759X1101400305

Shepard, J. M., Shahidullah, J. D., & Carlson, J. S. (2013). *Counseling students in levels 2 and 3: A PBIS/RTI guide*. Sage.

Sink, C. A., Akos, P., Turnbull, R. J., & Mvududu, N. (2008). An investigation of comprehensive school counseling programs and academic achievement in Washington state middle schools. *Professional School Counseling, 12*(1), 43–53. https://doi.org/10.1177/2156759X0801200105

Sink, C. A., & Stroh, H. R. (2003). Raising achievement test scores of early elementary school students through comprehensive school counseling programs. *Professional School Counseling, 6*(5), 350–364. www.jstor.org/stable/42732452

US Department of Education. (n.d.). *Every student succeeds act (ESSA)*. Author. www.ed.gov/essa?src%3Drn

Von Bertalanffy, L. (1968). *General systems theory: Foundation, development, applications*. Braziller.

Ward, C. A. (2009). An examination of the impact of the ASCA National Model on student Achievement at Recognized ASCA Model Program (RAMP) elementary schools. *Dissertation Abstracts International*, Proquest, LLC. UMI #3401416. Texas A&M University.

Wilkerson, K., Perusse, R., & Hughes, A. (2013). Comprehensive school counseling programs and student achievement outcomes: A comparative analysis of RAMP vs. non-RAMP schools. *Professional School Counseling, 16*(3), 172–184. https://doi.org/10.1177/2156759X1701600302

Chapter 3

Social Justice, Advocacy, Collaboration, Leadership, and Systemic Change

---

Box 3.1   2016 Council for the Acreditation of Counseling and Related Educational Programs (CACREP, n.d.) School Counseling Specialty Area Standards

1.d   Models of school-based collaboration and consultation
2.a   School counselor roles as leaders, advocates, and systems change agents in P-12 schools
2.d   School counselor roles in school leadership and multidisciplinary teams
2.f   Competencies to advocate for school counseling roles
2.j   Qualities and styles of effective leadership in schools
3.k   Strategies to promote equity in student achievement and college success

---

Box 3.2   ASCA (2019a) Standards for School Counselor Preparation Programs (ASCA CAEP SPA)

1.3   Describe aspects of human development, such as cognitive, language, social/emotional, and physical development, as well as the impact of environmental stressors and social inequities on learning and life outcomes.
2.1   Describe established and emerging counseling and educational methods, including but not limited to child and adolescent development, learning theories, behavior modification and classroom management, social justice, multiculturalism, group counseling, college/career readiness, and crisis response.
2.2   Demonstrate strengths-based counseling and relationship-building skills to support student growth and promote equity and inclusion.
4.2   Collaborate with stakeholders, such as families, teachers, support personnel, administrators, and community partners, to create learning environments that promote educational equity and support success and well-being for every student.

The *American School Counselor Association's Ethical Standards for School Counselors* (2022) requires that SCs function as change agents by advocating, assuming leadership, and collaborating in order to provide "equitable educational access and success" (p. 1).

DOI: 10.4324/9781003167730-3

We provide practical examples of the way in which school counselors use the *ASCA National Model*'s (2019b) themes of advocacy, collaboration, and leadership toward systemic change to promote minority students' achievement. We will also identify school counselors' use of direct services, including small- and large-group instruction and counseling, which incorporate a social justice focus.

Achievement Gap

The two primary objectives of the No Child Left Behind (NCLB, 2002) Act and the Every Student Succeeds Act (ESSA; US Department of Education, n.d.), which replaced NCLB in 2015, are to raise academic achievement for all students and to address achievement gaps between affluent students and students from poor families and the racial achievement gap, which is defined as the gap in academic performance between Asian and White students on one hand and Latin@ and Black students on the other hand. Despite the implementation of these educational reform legislative acts, there remain considerable racial disparities in educational achievement.

Box 3.3

Achievement gap—term used to describe the sizable differences between Black and White, Latin@ and White, and recent immigrant and White students on both standardized testing scores and overall academic achievement nationwide (Ladson-Billings, 2006).

In 2016, the school dropout rate for Asians was 2.2%, 3.9% for Whites, 7.0% for Blacks, and 9.1% for Latin@s (National Center for Education Statistics, 2019). Among high school seniors for 2013, the White-Black gap in math and reading scores was 30 points, and the White-Latin@ gap was 22 points in reading and 21 points in math (National Assessment for Educational Progress, 2013). Among high school students, 59% of the variance in math and 52% in language test scores are accounted for by socioeconomic status (SES) and racial factors (White et al., 2016). For 2019, the average SAT scores for Asian students was 1,223, 1,114 for White students, 978 for Latin@ students, and 933 for Black students (The College Board, n.d.). Black and Latin@ students are underrepresented in gifted and talented education programs (Ford, 2013). Despite federal and state efforts to increase minority students' participation and achievement in classes in science, technology, engineering, and mathematics, or what is commonly referred as STEM subjects, in 2013, Black and Latin@ students were significantly less likely than Whites and Asians to both take and pass STEM-related AP tests (The College Board, 2013). Although the gap in college enrollment rates between White and minority students declined between 1985 and 2012, the decline was primarily due to increased enrollment of minority students in nondegree and two-year colleges, and there remains significant disparities between White and minority student enrollment in four-year colleges (Baker et al., 2016) (see Figure 3.1).

Figure 3.1 Picture of four children holding the American flag.

Source: Copyright: www.istockphoto.com.

Critical Race Theory

The critical race theory (CRT) acknowledges that race is a pervasive aspect of our society which impacts many components of an individual's life (Carter, 2008). The premise of critical race theory is that there is a racial hierarchy in which members of the dominant racial group are empowered at the expense of racial minority groups (Hylton, 2012). Carter (2008) asserts that Black adolescents are more likely than their White peers to face additional burdens that hamper their success, such as having to be vigilant for overt and covert racial discrimination. Furthermore, Black adolescents' achievement is also hampered by a lack of academic resources (e.g., Muller et al., 2010).

Causes of the Achievement Gap

According to Chambers (2009), initiatives in the 1960s and 1970s to reduce the racial achievement gap primarily focused on addressing the perceived cultural deficits and intrapsychic issues of Black and Latin@ persons, which implied that the problem resided within minority students' ability to achieve. It is now commonly understood that the issue of racial disparities in education is complex and multifaceted and cannot be explained in terms of individual deficits of minority students. Researchers have identified a number of environmental variables that are associated with the racial achievement gap, although the research literature is not always conclusive regarding which variables are most strongly related to the racial achievement gap. For example, the extant literature base concerning whether teacher-student ratios are associated with the racial achievement gap is mixed (Rowley & Wright, 2011).

Box 3.4

Historically, there have been two patterns of theories as to what has caused the achievement gap (McKown, 2013):

- **Cultural or intrapsychic deficit**—minority groups have some internal issue or inherent skill deficit that causes them to be less likely to achieve.
- **Environmental deficit**—problems with the environment that minority students are more likely to be exposed to cause them to be less likely to achieve.

McKown's (2013) review of the research literature identified a number of factors that appear to contribute to the White-Black achievement gap. Racial-ethnic differences in parenting practices appear to account for a substantial portion of White-Black achievement gap even after controlling for SES. This is demonstrated through findings suggesting that White parents are more likely than Black parents to engage in practices that are associated with academic achievement, including such practices as warmth, sensitivity, involvement in school activities, monitoring, and involving children in decision-making. White students are also more likely than Black students to receive high-quality instruction in that they often are taught by better teachers, are exposed to a more challenging curriculum, and have better relationships with teachers than their Black peers with comparable records of achievement.

McKown concluded that the extant research supports the contention that racism contributes to the racial achievement gap as Black students receive direct and indirect messages from society and teachers that their race is considered inadequate in comparison to Whites. For example, Black students are likely to interpret lower teacher expectations as an indicator of being less competent than White students. Similarly, studies have found that higher rates of disciplinary referrals for Black and Latin@ students are associated with minority students perceiving school personnel as unfair and may be interpreted by minority students that they are less valued, which likely negatively impacts their academic achievement.

Peer and neighborhood influences are also likely to partially explain the White-Black achievement gap, although McKown indicated that the empirical support for their role is not as strong as it is for family factors and high-quality instruction. Some studies have found that the stigma related with academic achievement and its association with White culture, which has been referred to as stereotype threat, contributes to the underachievement of Black students. The level of cohesion and social support within a community, which may be considered as protective factors when strong, also may contribute to the academic achievement of Black students when lacking.

Segregation and tracking, such as scheduling students in classes with fewer academic demands, also appear to contribute to the racial achievement gap. Despite the fact that the Supreme Court segregated schools to be unconstitutional in 1954, Black children, in comparison to White youth, are five times more likely to attend schools that are highly segregated by race and ethnicity and twice as likely to attend high-poverty schools (Garcia, 2020). Racial school segregation is strongly associated with achievement gaps in third grade between White and minority students, and with increases in the gaps from third to eighth grade (Reardon et al., 2019). Increases in exposure of Black to White students resulted in small but statistically significant reductions in the achievement gaps (Condron et al., 2013). Also, segregation within schools also appears to contribute to the racial achievement gap. Black and Latin@ students are more likely than White students within the same schools to be assigned teachers with less years of experience (Benson et al., 2020). Berends et al. (2008) found that the percentage of Black students who reported being enrolled in a college track placement in high school increased between 1972 and 2004 and that this increase was associated with a considerable decrease in the White-Black gap in mathematics test scores during this time period.

Despite the increase in the number of Black students who reported being in a college track placement, many minority students appear to believe that postsecondary degrees are not within their reach, which is thought to lead them to disengage from an educational setting that they do not perceive to be encouraging their aspirations (Herring & Salazar, 2002). It has been proposed that between-school segregation and within-school segregation, or tracking, increase racial stratification by creating richer educational environments for White students, which further exacerbates the unequal access to resources that Whites have outside of schools (Condron et al., 2013). It appears that nonschool factors (e.g., parenting practices, socioeconomic status, neighborhood cohesion), between-school factors (e.g., racial segregation), and within-school factors (e.g., curriculum differentiation/ tracking) all contribute to the racial achievement gap. In summary, the research literature appears to support the contention of CRT (Carter, 2008) that Black students' achievement is limited by both the psychological costs of being minority in the United States and lacking access to academic resources.

Another contributor to the racial achievement gap that received increased attention in the past decade is the prejudicial use of school discipline practices. Black students represent 15% of K–12 students, yet they comprise 39% of the population with at least one suspension (Children's Equity Project & Bipartisan Policy Center, 2020). A recent nationwide review of school district policies indicated that majority of policies do not include most of the evidence-based recommendations for preventing the overuse of exclusionary discipline practices (Green et al., 2021). Although school-wide positive behavioral interventions and supports (SWPBIS) frameworks have been promulgated as a potentially effective approach to reducing disproportionality in school discipline practices, a recent study found that tier one implementation of SWPBIS in urban schools sustained and, in some cases, exacerbated disproportionality for Black and Latin@ students in comparison to White students (Zakszeski et al., 2021). Exclusionary discipline has been associated with a number of negative outcomes, including school disengagement, lower academic achievement, and future involvement in the juvenile justice system (Cartledge & Kourea, 2008).

Educators' Negative Contributions to the Achievement Gap

As mentioned earlier, McKown's (2013) review of the research literature indicated that teachers' racism and differential approaches of teachers toward White and Black students appear to contribute to the White-Black achievement gap. McKown (2013) concluded that the racial achievement gap is likely to be reduced by emphasizing strong instruction for all students, promoting positive teacher-child relationships, and training school personnel to reduce stereotyping of students. Many educational experts have written about the need for training to help school personnel learn about how their frequently unconscious assumptions about minority students and their learning negatively impact minority students.

Stephens and Lindsey (2011) assert that education is permeated by the values and assumptions of the dominant White majority culture, with the simultaneous denial that culture and heritage are not an inherent part of the learning process. They argue that teachers who identify with the dominant-group perspective merely tolerate minority students, whom they regard as problematic because of their underperformance.

Stephens and Lindsey (2011) have several terms to characterize such educators. *Cultural destructiveness* is defined as the desire to eliminate any mention of cultures other than the dominant, majority culture within the school setting. Educators who are culturally destructive might issue such statements as, "I don't see why we have to have Black History Month, we don't have a White History Month," or "I am here to teach students math, I'm not here to babysit."

Cultural incapacity involves demeaning other cultures and persons from lower socioeconomic statuses, often characterizing them as deficient. Educators who are culturally incapable might make such statements as, "They just need to pull themselves by their bootstraps," "I don't see why they keep bringing up slavery, I never owned slaves," or "Their problem is that they don't care about education."

Cultural blindness refers to the failure to recognize the culture and socioeconomic status of others. Educators with such a perspective might be heard to utter, "I don't see color, I only see individuals," or such teachers might assert that the racial achievement gap is about socioeconomic status rather than race or ethnicity, implying that a student's cultural background is not important to consider in relating to and teaching students. Stephens and Lindsey (2011) assert that some educators are resistant to change, believing that persons from other cultures should change by adapting to the dominant, majority culture. Some educators even deny the existence of both oppression and the privileges enjoyed by the White middle class that are not available to members of traditionally disadvantaged groups.

Box 3.5

Cultural destructiveness—the desire to eliminate any mention of culture other than the dominant culture.

Cultural incapacity—demeaning persons from other cultures or socioeconomic statuses as deficient.

Cultural blindness—the failure to recognize the culture and/or socioeconomic status of others.

(Stephens & Lindsey, 2011)

Stephens and Lindsey (2011) also identify several types of barriers to cultural proficiency that are often displayed by educators. One barrier is being resistant to change. Educators may believe that others, but not them, are responsible for making changes. Another barrier is failing to acknowledge that systems of oppression, including classism, racism, sexism, and ethnocentrism, are real. Finally, Stephens and Lindsey (2011) state that educators may deny the notion of privilege, meaning, that they fail to recognize that certain groups receive more benefits than others simply because of their race, gender, sexual orientation, or socioeconomic status.

Social Justice and School Counselors

The disparities in achievement between racial groups and the role of the environment in contributing to the gap highlight the need for SCs to demonstrate a commitment to social justice. Social justice counseling has been defined as intentional efforts to remove systems of oppression, inequity, inequality, or exploitation of traditionally marginalized groups in order to promote equity and participation (Constantine et al., 2007). During the past decade, the school counseling literature has increasingly focused upon the need for SCs to engage in advocacy and leadership in order to address educational inequalities by removing institutional barriers to student achievement. It has been argued that SCs, for a variety of reasons, are in a unique position to assume a leadership position to advocate for persons from marginalized groups in order to promote systemic change and, thereby, social justice.

First of all, SCs have traditionally been expected to fix the "underachieving students," who Stephens and Lindsey (2011) argue should more rightly be referred to as "underserved students." In contrast, as the school counseling profession seeks to move away from primarily being identified as working with solely at-risk students, they have the challenge articulated in the *ASCA National Model* (2019b) of meeting the needs of the entire student population. Such a commitment requires a broad perspective and a focus on comprehensive interventions. SCs also have unique access to both formal data, such as school-wide data regarding academic achievement, attendance, and disciplinary reports, and informal data, in the way of their interactions with the diverse array of students and parents. Additionally, SCs' training in multiculturalism, human relations, change processes, group work, learning theories, and program evaluation sets them apart from other school personnel, providing SCs with the skills to promote collaboration among school personnel and to serve as the liaison between families and the school (Borders & Shoffner, 2003).

The school counseling profession rightly recognizes that the achievement gap should not be conceptualized merely from an intrapsychic model, which emphasizes individual student deficits. The *ASCA National Model* emphasizes the need for school counselors to think comprehensively to promote equity and educational achievement for all students. As discussed in depth in Chapter 1, the systems-ecological perspective provides SCs with a framework for thinking comprehensively in regards to addressing environmental issues that have contributed to the achievement gap. The recognition that social justice is a moral imperative is also reflected in the *ASCA's Ethical Standards for School Counselors* (2022). SCs are called on to be advocates, leaders, collaborators, and consultants in creating an equitable educational environment that promotes access and success for all students.

The school counseling profession appears to be in the process of developing evidence-based approaches that require SCs to play a significant role in reducing the racial achievement gap. Therefore, the remainder of this chapter examines models and interventions available in literature that concern school counselors' role in this process. Research clearly indicates that the racial achievement gap is related to factors that are embedded within society, communities, and the culture of the school. Thus, SCs must have a broad perspective for implementing interventions that impact the larger systems, as well as thinking about how to help individual teachers, students, and parents.

Identifying Systemic Barriers and Closing-the-Gap Action Plans

One of the first steps for SCs in facilitating systemic change is to identify inequities through the disaggregation of data (ASCA, 2019b). As part of the ASCA's (2019b) annual data review, SCs are required to identify gaps between various student groups in terms of achievement, attendance, and discipline. For the closing-the-gap action plan, created by ASCA as a template for social justice advocacy, SCs identify targeted disparities, identify the selected interventions, and monitor the effectiveness of the implemented interventions. Hartline and Cobia's (2012) analysis of SCs' closing-the-gap action plans revealed that a majority of the plans resulted in increases in student achievement. Atkins and Oglesby (2019) recommend that SCs identify such possible inequities as whether students of color, in comparison to White peers, have more office referrals, are more likely to be suspended or recommended for Advanced Placement or honors courses, or express a lack of belonging on climate surveys. Do students of color, in comparison to White students, have lower rates of attendance, or are they less likely to be on cohort for graduation?

Davis et al. (2013) present an excellent example of how SCs can assume leadership in identifying and implementing a program to reduce an achievement gap. An SC, an SC intern, and an Advanced Placement (AP) teacher collaborated to increase Black students' enrollment in AP courses in a suburban high school in the Southeast, which was lower than that of White or of other minority student groups. The first step involved recruitment to identify Black students with potential for AP success and to encourage their participation. A school-based team examined the educational records of rising junior and senior Black students, selecting students who had an overall grade point average of 3.0 or above, who had never been identified as gifted or recommended for the gifted program, or who had never scored at or above the 85th percentile or any standardized measure. Furthermore, the team had academic teachers identify their top three Black students in terms of academic potential. The second step was encouraging identified Black students to enroll in the school's AP psychology course and to participate in a support program. The SC and the AP teacher met individually with each student and contacted each student's parent or guardian. The students and families were invited to a dinner to learn more about the program and meet with Black students currently enrolled in AP courses.

Of the 35 Black students recruited to participate in the program, 12 completed the support program, while 10 enrolled in the AP course but did not participate in the support program (Davis et al., 2013). Students participated in a two-week program primarily conducted by the AP psychology teacher and SC intern with supervision from university faculty. The two-week program sought to promote a sense of group cohesion among the students and adult participants and help students understand their potential to reduce the AP equity gap. The objectives of the group counseling sessions were to cultivate a community of achievement, increase students' perceptions of themselves as scholars, and facilitate students' awareness of their fears and goals. Students participated in trust-building activities that included a ropes course, established group and personal achievement goals, interacted with Black professionals, and toured the campus of a historically black college and university (HBCU). The participating students were placed as a cohort in a one of the four sections of the school's AP psychology course. The SC or SC intern met with the cohort 30 minutes each week, discussing such topics as overcoming obstacles, problem-solving, resilience, and fostering students' identity as academics. The Black students who participated in the program performed better than the Black students who did not and the national norms for Black students who took the national AP exam. Qualitative data confirmed the investigators' perceptions that the program promoted a sense of cohesion between the participant students and the investigators.

School Counselors Advocating for Social Justice

Singh et al. (2010) identified seven overarching strategies used by 16 SCs who identity as social justice change agents. *Political savvy* refers to knowing how to intervene in a manner that strikes an appropriate balance between being a supportive counselor and an aggressive change agent by delivering information that can be heard and knowing when or with whom to intervene. In other words, the SC must understand who has power in particular situations, or who are the key players, and how to communicate in a way that is likely to influence the persons with power. *Consciousness raising* is defined as the intent of advocacy conducted by SCs, meaning, that SCs' use of advocacy is a tactic of increasing educational personnel's understanding of the needs of diverse students. *Initiating difficult dialogues* refers to the fact that school counselors who are identified as social change agents typically feel discomfort in discussing topics that they recognize will likely result in other school personnel feeling defensive. *Building intentional relationships* is indicative of nearly all the SCs who are identified as change agents indicating that they intentionally sought to develop allies from various groups, including students, parents, administrators, teachers, and school support staff (e.g., custodians), in order to create broad coalitions. Each of the participating SCs identified the importance of *teaching students self-advocacy skills*. Examples of this skill include teaching low-income students how to use the internet to identify college scholarships, how to navigate the college admissions process, and providing students with the vocabulary and skills necessary to understand complex situations. *Using data for marketing* refers to all but one of the school counselors who claimed to be a social justice change agent asserting that they used data to increase the consciousness of their school-based colleagues. *Educating others about school counselors' role as advocate* reflects that most of the SCs identified the importance of educating others about their specific social justice interventions.

Box 3.6

School counselors who desire to be social justice change agents should be able to (Singh et al., 2010):

- Demonstrate political savvy
- Raise consciousness
- Initiate difficult dialogues
- Build intentional relationships
- Teach students self-advocacy skills
- Use data for marketing
- Educate others about school counselors' role as advocate

Antibias Social Emotional Learning for Students

Atkins and Oglesby (2019) recommend that SCs use the Teaching Tolerance Social Justice standards (Southern Poverty Law Center, 2018) to provide students with instruction regarding race and equity. The Teaching Tolerance standards, along with suggested classroom activities, are available for free at www.learningforjustice.org/sites/default/files/2018-11/TT-Social-Justice-Standards-Facilitator-Guide-WEB_0.pdf. The Teaching Tolerance standards are comprised of four domains: identity, diversity, justice, and action. The objectives of the identity domain are for students to demonstrate self-awareness, confidence, pride in one's family, and positive social identities. At the elementary level, children are taught to identify their own strengths and the positive characteristics of their cultural identities. For example, a Hindu girl whose female family members place a bindi on their forehead is taught about the cultural significance of the bindi and to communicate pride in their social identity as a Hindu. As adolescents develop the capacity for abstract reasoning, the antibias curriculum can help students reflect upon their multiple identities along with the common challenge of learning to balance multiple identities. The goal of the diversity domain is to ensure that children appreciate diversity and genuine relationships. Younger students learn about different types of families and individuals, including the recognition that such diversity contributes to our communities. Adolescents are taught how to actively engage in learning about the beliefs and values of others in a respectful manner. The goal of the justice domain is to provide students with the skills to identify and discuss unfairness and understand its impact on victims. Younger students are presented with stories of unfairness and persons who have worked to address unfairness. Adolescent students are exposed to examples of injustice beyond their experiences and learn about the complex processes for addressing injustices. The goal of the action domain is that students acquire the skills, either individually or in concert with others, to challenge prejudice and discrimination. Younger students are taught how to take action within their classroom or school building, being taught to support such initiatives as building a buddy bench or engaging in a food drive. Adolescent students can be taught to engage in action within their schools, and even at the state and national level.

Stereotype Threat Interruption Model (STIM)

The *ASCA Ethical Standard for School Counselors* (2022) require that SCs provide leadership to create systemic change, a role which often requires SCs to collaborate with stakeholders to address barriers that impede students' opportunities for achievement. Edwards's et al. (2019) presents a systematic model to reduce stereotype threat that requires such systemic leadership in providing school-based consultation. The stereotype threat interruption model (STIM) integrates multicultural consultation and a problem-solving model (i.e., problem identification and definition, problem analysis, plan design and implementation, and intervention evaluation).

Stereotype threat represents a social premise for a psychological threat in which someone from a stigmatized group fears that they will underperform on a task, such as a test, and, in doing so, confirms a negative stereotype about the identity of the group (Steele & Aronson, 1995). Much evidence in the social psychological literature has attested to the negative effects of stereotype threat in testing and nontesting situations in which an authority figure is in a position to evaluate a person of a stigmatized cultural group (e.g., Lamont et al., 2015). However, a meta-analytic study has revealed that interventions to counter stereotype threat may yield moderate benefits (Liu et al., 2021).

An example of an intervention to ward against the negative effects of stereotype threat is STIM, a student-centered, teacher-focused, environmentally relevant sequential, multiphase approach (Edwards et al., 2019). Preventive psychoeducation with teachers comprises the initial phase of STIM and explores the characteristics and negative impact of stereotype threat. Reception of a referral initiates the next phase of STIM through case conceptualization, which involves use of problem-identification processes to determine whether stereotype threat is a contributing factor to a student's difficulty. The consultant evaluates potential biases through journaling thoughts and beliefs about the course and using other resources to understand possible cultural factors. For example, if the referral involves a female student of color who has an anger outburst, the consultant may provide materials that help the consultee understand the emotional and environmental experiences of female students of color.

The third phase of STIM is structural analysis, in which the consultant conducts interviews and formal classroom observations to assess teacher and student behaviors and their interactions. The consultation explores such questions as how students are placed in specific groups and if there are similarities or differences of the students in the assigned groups. The consultant may use surveys and checklists to identify how teachers assist students who are struggling and how students problem-solve in school subjects where they are experiencing difficulty.

The fourth phase of STIM, intentional application, is similar to the plan design and implementation of the problem-solving phase (Edwards et al., 2019). In this phase, the consultant works to support teachers by collaboratively considering modifications to their instructional and behavioral practices by engaging in reflective teaching, which involves an intentional evaluation of the effectiveness of a teacher's classroom practices (Larrivee, 2008). For example, consultants can work to sensitively identify potential evidence of differential treatment of students from stigmatized cultural groups (Edwards et al., 2019). Consultants may highlight steps to engage in the implementation of equitable instruction, behavioral interaction, and curricula. For example, if a teacher tends to ask question and receive answers from boys, the teacher can be directed to establish a target number of responses from girls each day.

Consultants may also call teachers' attention to the tendency to use common phrases that suggest differential treatment of students of a stigmatized cultural group (Steele & Cohn-Vargas, 2013), including such statements as "Those kids" or "Students like that" (Edwards et al., 2019, p. 10). One common recommended instructional strategy to combat stereotype threat is the use of positive role models, as students who are anxious about confirming a negative stereotype tend to perform better when they identify with a positive role model of their stigmatized group (Steele & Cohn-Vargas, 2013). Consultants can assist teachers with identifying role models of the students' stigmatized group for the respective academic discipline. Teachers will also use student-centered STIM strategies, which will be discussed in a later section.

The final teacher phase of STIM, akin to the plan evaluation phase of problem-solving consultation, involves assessing whether teacher practices change and students' work or behaviors improve (Edwards et al., 2019). Baseline performance is compared to postintervention implementation. With regard to stereotype threat, examples of measurable objectives may include reductions in grouping students by performance and using stereotypic speech patterns.

The STIM model includes student-centered strategies, such as encouraging teachers to share examples of members of students' stigmatized group performing successfully, an empirically supported strategy. For example, when math students are informed that their tests do not reveal gender differences, women's test performance substantially improved, with women scoring higher than the men in the course (Good et al., 2008). It is important for teachers to emphasize that tests are a method to improve learning rather than a means to diagnose disabilities or problems (Edwards et al., 2019). Indeed, studies have revealed that Black students who understand that intelligence and academic achievement are able to be altered exhibit greater appreciation for school and better grades than do comparison groups (Suzuki & Aronson, 2005).

Another student-centered strategy is to teach stigmatized students cognitive behavioral strategies to reduce anxiety (Edwards et al., 2019). Students are taught to recognize that their anxiety comes from self-doubting thoughts, which impair performance (Johns et al., 2008). The specific strategies that are taught to students include thought stopping (Logel et al., 2009), which involves recognizing dysfunctional thoughts and replacing them with self-affirming thoughts regarding their abilities and previous successes (Edwards et al., 2019), strategies in reducing stereotype threat, including writing reflective essays about their goals and desired legacy (Bowen et al., 2013), writing about people they see as aspirational (Miyake et al., 2010), and values-affirmation writing exercises (Sherman et al., 2013). Other empirically supported strategies include helping stigmatized students to realize that stereotyping is illegitimate and that they are alike members of the majority group (Spencer et al., 2016).

The third student-centered strategy involves modifying the environment to eliminate stereotype threat (Edwards et al., 2019), which is establishing identity-safe schools and classrooms (Steele & Cohn-Vargas, 2013). Identity-safe schools establish conditions for students to enhance their identities and their individuality (Davies et al., 2005). Such schools also use such student-centered teaching strategies as teamwork, resourcefulness, and student participation in decision-making (Steele & Cohn-Vargas, 2013).

Diversity is encouraged through varied methods of instruction, classroom activities, and learning materials, as well as a diverse faculty. Role-playing and skills training are used to teach and then practice socioemotional learning. Consultants may help schools promote identity safety by encouraging schools to hold school assemblies renouncing stereotyping (Edwards et al., 2019) and teaching staff to quickly address name-calling, derogatory statements, and acceptance of negative stereotypes (Spencer et al., 2016). Schools' appreciation of diversity can be observed through wall decorations, public announcements, and school newsletters (Steele & Cohn-Vargas, 2013).

Schulz et al.'s (2014) Collaborative Strategies for Promoting Cultural Responsiveness

Educators have been urged to adopt culturally responsive teaching (CRT) strategies as a means to reduce the achievement gap. Gay (2018) asserts that CRT teaches to and through the strengths of diverse students by using the strengths of their culture, their prior experiences, and their performance styles to make learning more relevant and interesting for them, thereby establishing a bridge between diverse students' home and school lives.

Box 3.7

Culturally responsive teaching (CRT)—teachers utilizing the strengths of diverse students' cultures, prior experiences, and performance styles to make learning more relevant and interesting (Gay, 2018).

Schultz et al. uses this bridge metaphor, asserting that SCs' role in cultural responsiveness is to create a bridge between teachers and students. Table 3.1 identifies Schulz et al.'s model of how SCs can collaborate with teachers and other adults in order to promote cultural responsiveness within schools. The examples of collaboration are divided into three levels of intervention. The first level, *faculty development*, includes strategies that can be implemented with entire faculties. The next level, *small-group development*, provides examples of strategies that can be used with small groups of teachers, administrators, and staff. The

Table 3.1 Culturally Responsive Strategies

Level of Implementation	Examples
1. Faculty Development	a) Workshops focused on building cultural competence and culturally responsive philosophy, teacher characteristics, curriculum, instructional strategies, and assessments b) Guest speakers to address special topics c) Vision/mission-building sessions d) Inventory of current building and classroom practices
2. Small Group Development	a) Departmental task-focused group to build philosophy, curriculum, instructional practices, and assessments b) Interdisciplinary group focused on inter- and intrapersonal skill building c) Focus groups reading a book together to promote cultural responsiveness and discussing relevance to own practice (i.e., Tatum, 1997) d) Peer coaching teams to practice and evaluate culturally responsive approaches
3. Individual Development	a) Counselor/teacher collaboration focused on development of teachers' multicultural awareness b) Regular consultation on implementation and practice c) Team teaching using standards blending approach d) Individual and small-group discussion inclusion interventions (see Clark & Breman, 2009)

Source: Adapted from Schulz et al. (2014). "My name is not Michael: Strategies for promoting cultural responsiveness in schools." *Journal of School Counseling, 12*(2). www.jsc.montana.edu/articles/v12n2.pdf. Reprinted with permission from the *Journal of School Counseling.*

third level, titled *individual development*, is comprised of strategies that can be used with individual adults within the school system.

Faculty Development

SCs can assume a leadership role by collaborating with teachers in planning in-service and professional development opportunities that are already required of teachers by nearly all states. Schulz et al. (2014) recommend that SCs use such workshops to help teachers identify their own cultural backgrounds and how these backgrounds influence their perspectives of diverse students. Ford (2010) asserts that teacher training programs typically do not require future teachers to examine their cultural biases and assumptions, nor do they teach future teachers how to tailor teaching strategies to meet the needs of diverse students.

The multicultural competencies for counselors, which are divided into personal awareness, knowledge of diverse groups, and the acquisition of skills for working with diverse groups, can serve as a framework for training teachers in diversity (Schulz et al., 2014). SCs can use the preparation they received in multiculturalism in training teachers to become aware of their cultural assumptions and biases and to increase teachers' understanding of the strengths and worldview of specific diverse groups.

SCs could teach DuPraw and Axner's (1997) six fundamental ways in which cultures tend to differ from each other, which include communication style, attitude toward conflict, approaches to task completion, decision-making styles, attitudes toward disclosure, and approaches to knowing. Such information can help teachers in empathizing and developing rapport with students from diverse backgrounds, consulting/conferencing with parents of diverse background, and using different ways of knowing in their teaching. For example, Gay (2018) asserts that most teachers use deductive reasoning in the classroom, by focusing on specific details which are then generalized to identify the whole. However, many Black, Latin@, and Asian American students tend to prefer a more constructivist style of learning in which information is related to existing cognitive structures. Teaching methods that are considered to be more compatible with a constructivist approach have been given such titles as inquiry learning, discovery learning, and project-based learning. There is also some research to suggest that while White students tend to prefer independent and competitive forms of learning, in which individual achievement is highlighted, Asian American, Black, and Latin@ students perform better in educational environments that use cooperative and collaborative approaches to learning (e.g., Chizhik, 2001). Training in diversity for teachers can also be enhanced through multimedia exposure utilizing videos, contemporary films for starting conversations about unfamiliar social contexts, and experiences promoting a more personal connection with poverty and diversity have shown to be effective in developing cultural competence (Cholewa & West-Olatunji, 2008). Also, teachers can be asked to participate in cultural events, community meetings, and a variety of religious experiences, which may be helpful in increasing connections with their students.

One form of resistance to cultural proficiency that some teachers will display is overt or covert challenges to the SCs' expertise regarding pedagogy, given that many SCs do not possess teacher certification or are no longer in the role of teacher and thus cannot truly understand what it is like to "be in the trenches" (Stephens & Lindsey, 2011). In such situations, SCs are encouraged to align themselves with influential teachers who can take the lead in helping their colleagues understand how to incorporate the strengths and world-views of diverse groups into the classroom and learn to incorporate more constructivist-style teaching strategies. By teaming with influential teachers to increase the cultural responsiveness of the staff in this manner, the school counselor is using some of the strategies that Singh et al. (2010) found to be used by school counselors who identify as change agents. The SC is being *politically savvy* by recognizing who has power within the school and is *intentionally building relationships* with those who have power in order to *initiate difficult dialogues and raise consciousness*.

Small-Group Development

Schulz et al. (2014) assert that small-group development is sometimes preferable to large-group learning experiences in that small-group development can provide greater depth of exploration. The SC can assist subject departments (e.g., social studies, science) in generating vision and mission statements that incorporate cultural responsiveness. SCs can also help departments identify professional development needs that are specific to their department. Schulz et al. (2014) provide the example of assisting a mathematics department in revising their assessments to be more culturally fair/responsive. Schulz et al. (2014) established voluntary reading groups to discuss chapters of Tatum's (1997) *Why Are All the Black Kids Sitting Together in the Cafeteria: And Other Conversations About Race*, had teachers discuss their personal reactions to the book, followed by an exploration of how their new understandings influenced their approach to teaching diverse students.

Individual Development

SCs can also use consultation to increase teachers' cultural proficiency as, unfortunately, didactic training is not always sufficient to address the barriers to cultural proficiency. Rather, many people also learn cultural proficiency through experience in interacting with people who are different from themselves. SCs often have access to information from various stakeholders, such as students and parents, who approach them with concerns about teachers or administrators and may confide in the school counselor about issues with teachers. It is not unusual for teachers to mistrust SCs because of teachers' awareness that school counselors receive such information. Singh et al. (2010) found that SCs who identify as change agents are very purposeful in how they approach teachers about their potential lack of cultural proficiency in order to increase the likelihood that teachers can hear such messages. This is also related to Singh et al.'s (2010) counselor competency of *initiating difficult dialogues*.

The SC may want to first consult with the teacher alone, sharing that a number of students and/or parents have expressed concern about the teacher's responsiveness. The SC should allow the teacher to defend him- or herself and use active listening skills to indicate that they hear the teacher's perspective. The use of active listening skills typically decreases the teacher's emotional intensity, whereupon the SC can ask questions to increase the teacher's understanding of diverse groups. For example, the SC can ask the teacher about what he or she thinks the student's and/or parent's perspective may be.

A common complaint of less culturally proficient teachers is that minority students and their parents do not value education. As such, teachers can misread the behaviors of minority students. By using questions, the SC can assist such a teacher in understanding that the student and parents indeed value education but that they display this value in a different manner, or that help the teacher to realize that the parent and child value different kinds of learning experiences. This can begin to help such a teacher understand that the student's/ parent's behaviors of concern may reflect a healthy mistrust of the educational system, which historically has been unresponsive to their needs. Through such a manner, the SC is attempting to "normalize" the student's mistrust. The SC can then ask the teacher how he or she might approach the student in a different manner, or ask the teacher about times when he or she has related more effectively to the student in question, or when he or she has related effectively to other minority students. By asking such questions, the SC is "framing" the issue as being about how the teacher relates to minority students. The use of data also serves to help teachers develop a more objective perspective about how they are impacting students from diverse groups.

It is not uncommon for minority students to claim that a teacher is prejudiced, which many teachers vociferously deny. However, SCs can help teachers in consultation and trainings realize their prejudices and stereotypes as products of a prejudiced society. Only by increasing awareness of one's prejudices in a nondefensive manner can a person learn how to not act upon them.

Schulz et al. (2014) provides an example of an SC who, upon noticing that 64% of the freshmen earned either a "D" or an "F" grade in their science class, approached two science teachers separately, offering the teachers her support in her role as counselor. Through multiple discussions focusing upon the teachers' personal world and their classroom management and teaching philosophy, the SC assisted the teachers in developing more effective ways of both relating to and teaching students, which resulted in a significant decrease in the number of students who earned a "D" or "F" in the next academic year.

Dowden's Example of Collaboration and Action Research

Dowden (2010) discusses her experience using collaboration, consultation, and counseling to promote social justice as a high school counselor in a Southeastern college town. She utilized Kolb's (1984) action research model, which involves identifying a problem, collecting and analyzing data to develop a plan, implementing a plan, observing the results of the plan by gathering and interpreting outcome data, and reflecting upon the results. The problem she identified was the apparent existence of a school within a school, where the advanced curriculum courses were comprised mostly of White, middle- and upper-middle-class students, while the Black students were mostly enrolled in "regular"-level courses, and the Latin@ students were mostly enrolled in English-as-a-second-language (ESL) courses. Dowden (2010) reports that administrators and other school counselors were indifferent to this disparity.

The first part of Dowden's plan was to inform parents, students, and school staff about these inequities and how they resulted in unequal educational opportunities. She used individual and group counseling to encourage minority students to challenge themselves by taking more advanced courses, encouraged minority students to assume leadership roles within the school, and prompted these students to join academic organizations, such as the math club. Dowden used the College Board's Advanced Placement (AP) Potential (The College Board, 2010) program, which is a web-based tool that identifies students who have potential to succeed in an AP course based upon Practice Scholastic Assessment Test (PSAT) scores. She supported students who accepted the challenge by assuring them that she would advocate for them if necessary, providing them with a mentor and exposing them to the Advancement Via Individual Determination (AVID, n.d.) program, which offers curriculum instruction and foundational academic skills, such as note-taking. Dowden collaborated with a nearby university to recruit Black male students who exposed their mentees to the college through joint participation in campus events. Dowden also established an after-school program in which student discussion forums were created to provide students who had been successful in overcoming social barriers to share their experiences with their peers. Dowden recruited motivational speakers from the local churches to come and speak to the students in the after-school program about self-determination, motivation, and persistence. Parent meetings were also held to inform parents of their options. Dowden (2010) also directly challenged school personnel whom she believed were serving as barriers to equity. She suggested to an art and band teacher who appeared to discourage minority students from enrolling in their courses through the use of high financial fees for associated activities that the required fees could be raised by a booster club.

In order to evaluate the effectiveness of these efforts on minority student engagement and achievement, Dowden first approached the school's principal about conducting a survey of students' perceptions of the school's level of inequities. Despite all the support Dowden had gained through the implementation of the discussed programs and changes, her request to conduct the survey was denied by the principal. Instead, she collected and disseminated disaggregated data on student test scores, course enrollment, and attendance and suspension rates, and the data revealed that there was a gradual improvement in academic achievement of minority students during her three-year tenure at the school.

School Counseling Collaborative Teams

Young et al. (2013) recommend the formation of school counseling collaborative teams (SCCT) to serve as a structure through which school counselors may collaborate and provide instructional leadership. Members of the SCCT share a goal or vision, are committed to the use of collective inquiry and a results orientation, meaning, that there is a continuous cycle of questioning the status, strategy experimentation, and use of data. The initial meetings seek to achieve a consensus regarding the team's goals, which can use the SMART goal practice, meaning, that the goals are specific, measurable, attainable, results-oriented, and time-bound. Once consensus is achieved regarding the goals, members can construct an action plan for each goal. The team engages in inquiry and data collection to determine why students are not achieving the respective goal, and this may involve the formation of a focus group of students and implementation of a needs assessments or surveys to students, parents, and/or teachers. Team members should review the professional literature to identify evidence-based interventions. The concluding step in the process is the evaluation of various types of data to determine whether students have achieved the identified learning outcome.

Young et al. (2013) provide an example of the use of an SCCT to address an achievement gap. After two years of implementation, a middle-school based SCCT had been successful in decreasing the number of students receiving Ds and Fs and increasing the proficiency rates in math and reading. In the third year, the SCCT identified a racial achievement gap in honors courses. The percentage of Black and Latin@ students in honors classes represented the school's composition of minority students, but they were not passing the reading and math state assessment tests at the same rate as White and Asian American students, and they had an average grade of "C" in the honors courses. The SCCT members collaborated with teachers in delivering a Success Prep curriculum, which included fostering healthy relationships, improving organization and study skills, identification of learning styles, self-advocacy, using formative and summative assessment strategies, and setting SMART goals. The intervention resulted in 90% of students passing state assessment tests, and the average grade for Black and Latin@ students increased to a "B."

Small- and Large-Group Interventions to Promote Social Justice

Many of the school counselors that conducted responsive interventions used to reduce the racial achievement gap that can be found in research literature have involved large-group or group counseling interventions seeking to promote the study skills of minority students. Bruce et al. (2009) found that eight sessions of a study-skill counseling group with 15 Black 11th-grade students resulted in a reduction in the gap in the pass rate between White students and Black students, as well as an overall increase in passage rate for Black students on the Georgia High School Graduation Tests. The researchers suggest that a group counseling format may be culturally responsive for Black students as it is consistent with the Black community's shared value on connectedness. A group setting may also provide Black students with an opportunity to bond and discuss personal issues while also working toward a shared goal.

Leon et al. (2011) evaluated the impact of the Spanish Cultural Translation of Student Success Skills (SCT-SSS). Student Success Skills (SSS) is a study skills program, as discussed in previous chapters, that seeks to provide students with cognitive, social, and self-management skills that research literature indicates are associated with increased student achievement (Carey et al., 2008). Studies suggest that SSS promotes students' academic achievement as measured by state achievement tests, but there are questions as to whether students retain the skills promoted within SSS. Five Spanish-speaking SCs from different countries in Latin America adapted the SSS to match both the language and culture of different Latin American nations. Two bilingual SCs implemented the SCT-SSS intervention with 62 fourth- and fifth-grade Latin@ students in two schools, conducting five SCT-SSS 45-minute classroom lessons once per week for five consecutive weeks, followed by three 45-minute booster sessions in three consecutive months. The results revealed that the students who received the treatment had significantly greater increases in math and reading, as measured by Florida's state achievement test, than a comparison group of fourth- and fifth-grade Latin@ students who did not receive the intervention. The effect size for both the math and reading gains was .37, which is generally considered to be a small to moderate intervention impact.

Dowden (2009) used a five-session psychoeducational group to teach self-advocacy skills to six Black adolescents attending a large suburban high school in the Southeast, in order to enhance their self-concept and academic motivation. The second group session sought to enhance students' understanding of cultural power and privilege. Students discussed their reactions to portrayals from the media, which depicted minority populations in a negative fashion, and shared personal experiences of discrimination and received feedback from group members regarding how they managed the discrimination. In the third group session, the group discussed the components of self-determination, including effective and ineffective ways students could demonstrate self-determination. In the fourth group session, members identified examples of social injustice within their school and developed plans for addressing the inequity they identified. Follow-up evaluation of the group members revealed that five of the six students exhibited decreases in truancy and behavior problems, and four of the six students passed all their semester academic classes.

Summary

The school counseling profession has made a clear commitment to advocating for social justice. The examples of social justice interventions involving SCs provided in this chapter indicate that school counselors contribute to systemic change by collaborating with various stakeholders. It is important for SCs to recognize that their training in human relations, multiculturalism, group work, etc. possibly situates them as the educational professional best prepared to invoke such systemic interventions. A consistent theme indicated in the school counseling literature is that school counselors need to recognize that some people will be resistant to such a challenge to the status quo. SCs must understand that social justice advocacy requires a long-term commitment.

References

Advancement Via Individual Determination (AVID). (n.d.). *AVID.* www.avid.org/
American School Counselor Association. (2019a). *ASCA standards for school counselor preparation programs.* Author. www.schoolcounselor.org/getmedia/573d7c2c-1622-4d25-a5ac-ac74d2e614ca/ASCA-Standards-for-School-Counselor-Preparation-Programs.pdf
American School Counselor Association. (2019b). *The ASCA national model: A framework for for school counseling programs* (4th ed.). Author.
American School Counselor Association. (2022). *Ethical standards for school counselors.* Author.
Atkins, R., & Oglesby, A. (2019). *Interrupting racism: Equity and social justice in school counseling.* Routledge.
Baker, R., Klasik, D., & Reardon, F. (2016). *Race and stratification in college enrollment over time.* Center for Education Policy Analysis at Stanford University. https://files.eric.ed.gov/fulltext/EJ1194137.pdf
Benson, T., Bryant, A., & Gezer, T. (2020). Segregation within integrated schools: Racially disproportionate student-teacher assignments in middle school. *Education Policy Analysis Archives, 28*(170). https://eric.ed.gov/?id=EJ1275200
Berends, M., Lucas, S. R., & Penaloza, R. V. (2008). How changes in families and schools are related to trends in black-white test scores. *Sociology of Education, 81*(4), 313–344. https://doi.org/10.1177/003804070808100401

Borders, L. D., & Shoffner, J. F. (2003). School counselors: Leadership opportunities and challenges in the schools. In J. D. West, C. J. Osborn, & D. L. Bubenzer (Eds.), *Leaders and legacies:
Contributions to the profession of counseling* (pp. 51–64). Brunner-Routledge.

Bowen, N. K., Wegmann, K. M., & Webber, K. C. (2013). Enhancing a brief writing intervention
to combat stereotype threat among middle-school students. *Journal of Educational Psychology,
105*(2), 427–435. https://doi.org/10.1037/a0031177

Bruce, A. M., Getch, Y. Q., & Ziomek-Daigle, J. (2009). Closing the gap: A group counseling
approach to improve test performance of African-American students. *Professional School
Counseling, 12*(6), 450–457. https://doi.org/10.1177/2156759X0901200603

Carey, J. C., Dimmitt, C., Hatch, T. A., Lapan, R. T., & Whiston, S. C. (2008). Report of the national
panel for evidence-based school counseling: Outcome research coding protocol and evaluation of
student success skills and second step. *Professional School Counseling, 11*(3), 197–206. https://
doi.org/10.1177/2156759X0801100306

Carter, D. J. (2008). Achievement as resistance: The development of a critical race achievement
ideology among black achievers. *Harvard Educational Review, 78*(3), 466–497. https://doi.
org/10.17763/haer.78.3.83138829847hw844

Cartledge, G., & Kourea, L. (2008). Culturally responsive classrooms for culturally diverse
students with and risk for disabilities. *Exceptional Children, 74*(3), 351–371. https://doi.
org/10.1177/001440290807400305

Chambers, T. V. (2009). The "receivement gap": School tracking policies and the fallacy of the "achievement gap". *Journal of Negro Education, 78*(4), 417–431. www.muse.jhu.edu/article/807007

Children's Equity Project & Bipartisan Policy Center. (2020). *Start with equity: From the early years
to the early grades*. https://childandfamilysuccess.asu.edu/cep/start-with-equity

Chizhik, A. W. (2001). Equity and status in group collaboration: Learning through explanations depends on task characteristics. *Social Psychology of Education, 5*, 179–200. https://doi.
org/10.1023/A:1014405118351

Cholewa, V., & West-Olatunji, C. (2008). Exploring the relationship among cultural discontinu-
ity, psychological distress, and academic achievement outcomes for low-income, culturally
diverse students. *Professional School Counseling, 12*(1), 54–61. https://doi.org/10.1177/21567
59X0801200106

Clark, M. A., & Breman, J. C. (2009). School counselor inclusion: A collaborative model to provide
academic and social-emotional support in the classroom. *Journal of Counseling & Development,
8*(1), 6–11. https://doi.org/10.1002/j.1556-6678.2009.tb00543.x

The College Board. (2010). *AP potential*. Author. https://appotential.collegeboard.com/welcome.do

The College Board. (2013). *Program facts: Overview of the AP program*. Author. http://press.
collegeboard.org/ap/fact-sheet

The College Board. (n.d.). *2019 SAT suite of assessments annual report*. Author. https://reports.
collegeboard.org/pdf/2019-total-group-sat-suite-assessments-annualreport.pdf

Condron, D. J., Tope, D., Steidl, C. R., & Freeman, K. J. (2013). Racial segregation and the black/
white achievement gap, 1992 to 2009. *The Sociological Quarterly, 54*(1), 130–157. https://doi.
org/10.1111/tsq.12010

Constantine, M. G., Hage, S. M., Kindaichi, M. M., & Bryant, R. M. (2007). Social justice and multicultural issues: Implications for the practice and training of counselors and counseling psychologists.
Journal of Counseling & Development, 85(1), 24–29. https://doi.org/10.1002/j.1556-6678.2007.
tb00440.x

Council for the Accreditation of Counseling and Related Educational Programs. (n.d.). *2016
CACREP standards*. www.cacrep.org/for-programs/2016-cacrep-standards/

Davis, P., Davis, M. P., & Mobley, J. A. (2013). The school counselor's role in addressing the
advanced placement equity and excellence gap for African American students. *Professional School
Counseling, 17*(1), 32–39. https://doi.org/10.1177/2156759X0001700104

Davies, P. G., Spencer, S. J., & Steele, C. M. (2005). Clearing the air: Identity safety moderates the
effects of stereotype threat on women's leadership aspirations. *Journal of Personality and Social
Psychology, 88*(2), 276–287. https://doi.org/10.1037/0022-3514.88.2.276

Dowden, A. R. (2009). Implementing self-advocacy training within a brief psychoeducational group to improve the academic motivation of black adolescents. *The Journal for Specialists in Group Work*, 34(2), 118–136. https://doi.org/10.1080/01933920902791937

Dowden, A. R. (2010). A personal journey in promoting social justice as a school counselor: An action research approach. *Journal of School Counseling*, 8(24). https://files.eric.ed.gov/fulltext/EJ895901.pdf

DuPraw, M. E., & Axner, M. (1997). Working on common cross-cultural communication challenges. *Toward a more perfect union in age of diversity: A guide to building stronger communities through public dialog*. Study Circles Resource Center. www.pbs.org/ampu/crosscult.html

Edwards, O. W., Bennett, C. M., & Johnson, B. (2019). School consultation to counter stereotype threat. *Journal of Educational and Psychological Consultation*, 29(2), 188–205. https://doi.org/10.1080/10474412.2018.1482218

Ford, D. Y. (2010). Culturally responsive classrooms: Affirming culturally different gifted students. *Gifted Child Today*, 33(1), 50–53. https://files.eric.ed.gov/fulltext/EJ874024.pdf

Ford, D. Y. (2013). Multicultural issues: Gifted underrepresentation and prejudice: Learning from Allport and Merton. *Gifted Child Today*, 36(1), 62–67. https://doi.org/10.1177/1076217512465285

Garcia, E. (2020). *Schools are still segregated, and black children are paying a price*. Economic Policy Institute. www.epi.org/publication/schools-are-still-segregated-and-black-children-are-paying-a-price/

Gay, G. (2018). *Culturally responsive teaching: Theory, research, and practice* (3rd ed.). Teachers College Press.

Good, C., Aronson, J., & Harder, J. A. (2008). Problems in the pipeline: Stereotype threat and women's achievement in high-level math courses. *Journal of Applied Developmental Psychology*, 29(1), 17–28. https://doi.org/10.1016/j.appdev.2007.10.004

Green, A. L., Hatton, H., Stegenga, S. M., Eliason, B., & Teese, R. N. T. (2021). Examining commitment to prevention, equity, and meaningful engagement: A review of school district discipline policies. *Journal of Positive Behavior Interventions*, 23(3), 137–148. https://doi.org/10.1177/1098300720951940

Hartline, J., & Cobia, D. (2012). School counselors: Closing achievement gaps and writing results report. *Professional School Counseling*, 16(1), 71–79. https://doi.org/10.1177/2156759X1201600109

Herring, R. D., & Salazar, C. (2002). Non-western helping modalities. In J. Trusty, E. J. Looly, & D. S. Sandhu (Eds.), *Multicultural counseling: Context, theory and practice, and competence* (pp. 283–318). NOVA Science Publishers, Inc.

Hylton, K. (2012). Talk the talk, walk the walk: Defining critical race theory in research. *Race, Ethnicity and Education*, 15(1), 23–41. https://doi.org/10.1080/13613324.2012.638862

Johns, M., Inzlicht, M., & Schmader, T. (2008). Stereotype threat and executive resource depletion: Examining the influence of emotional regulation. *Journal of Experimental Psychology: General*, 137(4), 691–705. https://doi.org/10.1037/a0013834

Kolb, D. (1984). *Experiential learning: Experience as the source of learning and development*. Prentice-Hall.

Ladson-Billings, G. (2006). From achievement gap to the education debt: Understanding achievement in US schools. *Educational Researcher*, 35(7), 3–12. https://doi.org/10.3102/0013189X035007003

Lamont, R. A., Swift, H. J., & Abrams, D. (2015). A review and meta-analysis of age-based stereotype threat: Negative stereotypes, not facts, do the damage. *Psychology and Aging*, 30(1), 180–193. https://doi.org/10.1037/a0038586

Larrivee, B. (2008). Development of a tool to assess teachers' level of reflective practice. *Reflective Practice*, 9(3), 341–360. https://doi.org/10.1080/14623940802207451

Leon, A., Villares, E., Brigman, G., Webb, L., & Peluso, P. (2011). Closing the achievement gap of Latina/Latin@ students: A school counseling response. *Counseling Outcome Research and Evaluation*, 2(1), 73–86. https://doi.org/10.1177/2150137811400731

Liu, S., Liu, P., Wang, M., & Zhang, B. (2021). Effectiveness of stereotype threat interventions: A meta-analytic review. *Journal of Applied Psychology*, 106(6), 921–949. https://doi.org/10.1037/apl0000770

Logel, C., Iserman, E. C., Davies, P. G., Quinn, D. M., & Spencer, S. J. (2009). The perils of double consciousness: The role of thought suppression in stereotype threat. *Journal of Experimental Social Psychology*, 45(2), 299–312. https://doi.org/10.1016/j.jesp.2008.07.016

McKown, C. (2013). Social equity theory and racial-ethnic achievement gaps. *Child Development*, 84(4), 1120–1136. https://doi.org/10.1111/cdev.12033

Miyake, A., Kost-Smith, L. E., Finklestein, N. D., Pollock, S. J., Cohen, G., & Ito, T. A. (2010). Reducing the gender achievement gap in college science: A classroom study of values affirmation. *Science*, 330(6008), 1234–1237. https://doi.org/10.1126/science.1195996

Muller, C., Riegle-Crumb, C., Schiller, K. S., Wilkinson, L., & Frank, K. A. (2010). Race and academic achievement in racially diverse high schools: Opportunity and stratification. *Teachers College Record*, 112(4), 1038–1063. https://doi.org/10.1177/016146811011200406

National Assessment of Educational Progress (NAEP). (2013). *The nation's report card: A first look: 2013 mathematics and reading.* http://nces.ed.gov/nationsreportcard/pubs/main2013/2014451. aspx#section3

National Center for Education Statistics. (2019). *Status and trends in the education of racial and ethnic groups.* Author. https://nces.ed.gov/programs/raceindicators/indicator_rdc.asp#:~:text=Based%20 on%20data%20from%20the,%2C%20Black%20(7.0%20percent)%2C

No Child Left Behind Act of 2001, Pub. L. No. 107-110 (2002).

Reardon, S. F., Weathers, E. S., Fahle, E. M., Jang, H., & Kalogrides, D. (2019). *Is separate still unequal? New evidence on school segregation and racial academic achievement gaps.* Stanford Center for Education Policy Analysis. http://cepa.stanford.edu/wp19-06

Rowley, R. L., & Wright, D. W. (2011). No "white" child left behind: The academic achievement gap between Black and White students. *The Journal of Negro Education*, 80(2), 93–107. www. jstor.org/stable/41341113

Schulz, L. L., Hurt, K., & Lindo, N. (2014). My name is not Michael: Strategies for promoting cultural responsiveness in schools. *Journal of School Counseling*, 12(2). www.jsc.montana.edu/ articles/v12n2.pdf

Sherman, D. K., Hartson, K. A., Binning, K. R., Purdie-Vaughns, V., Garcia, J., Taborsky-Barba, S., Tomasetti, S., Nussbaum, A. D., & Cohen, G. L. (2013). Deflecting the trajectory and changing the narrative: How self-affirmation affects academic performance and motivation under identity threat. *Journal of Personality and Social Psychology*, 104(4), 591–618. https://doi.org/10.1037/ a0031495

Singh, A. A., Urbano, A., Haston, M., & McMahon, E. (2010). School counselors' strategies for social justice change: A grounded theory of what works in the real world. *Professional School Counseling*, 13(3), 135–145. https://doi.org/10.1177/2156759X1001300301

Southern Poverty Law Center. (2018). *The teaching tolerance social justice standards: A professional development facilitator guide.* Author. www.learningforjustice.org/sites/default/files/2021- 10/LFJ-Facilitator-Guide-Social-Justice-Standards-Oct-2021-10052021.pdf

Spencer, S. J., Logel, C., & Davies, P. G. (2016). Stereotype threat. *Annual Review of Psychology*, 67, 415–437. https://doi.org/10.1146/annurev-psych-073115-103235

Steele, C. M., & Aronson, J. (1995). Stereotype threat and the intellectual test performance of African Americans. *Journal of Personality and Social Psychology*, 69(5), 797–811. https://doi. org/10.1037/0022-3514.69.5.797

Steele, D. M., & Cohn-Vargas, B. (2013). *Identity safe classrooms: Places to belong and learn.* Corwin Press.

Stephens, D. L., & Lindsey, R. B. (2011). *Culturally proficient collaboration: Use and misuse of school counselors.* Corwin.

Suzuki, L., & Aronson, J. (2005). The cultural malleability of intelligence and its impact on the racial/ethnic hierarchy. *Psychology, Public Policy, and Law*, 11(2), 320–327. https://doi. org/10.1037/1076-8971.11.2.320

Tatum, B. (1997). *Why are all the Black kids sitting together in the cafeteria? And other conversations about race: A psychologist explains the development of racial identity.* Basic Books.

US Department of Education. (n.d.). *Every student succeeds act (ESSA).* Author. www.ed.gov/ essa?src%3Drn

White, G. W., Stepney, C. T., Hatchimonji, D. R., Moceri, D. C., Linsky, A. V., Reyes-Portillo, J. A., & Elias, M. J. (2016). The increasing impact of socioeconomics and race on standardized academic test scores across, elementary, middle, and high school. *American Journal of Orthopsychiatry*, 86(1), 10–23. https://doi.org/10.1037/ort0000122

Young, A. A., Millard, T., & Kneale, M. M. (2013). Enhancing school counselor instructional leadership through collaborative teaming: Implications for principals. *National Association of Secondary School Principals*, 97(3), 253–269. https://doi.org/10.1177/0192636513483356

Zakszeski, B., Rutherford, L., Heidelburg, K., & Thomas, L. (2021). In pursuit of equity: Discipline disproportionality and SWPBIS implementation in urban schools. *School Psychology*, 36(2), 122–130. https://doi.org/10.1037/spq0000428

Chapter 4

Manage and Assess

Box 4.1   2016 Council for the Accreditation of Counseling and Related Educational Programs (CACREP, n.d.) School Counseling Specialty Area Standards

1.d   Models of school-based collaboration and consultation
1.e   Assessment specific to P-12 education
2.a   School counselor roles as leaders, advocates, and system change agents in P-12 schools
2.d   School counselor roles in school leadership and multidisciplinary teams
3.b   Design and evaluation of school counseling programs
3.n   Use of accountability to inform decision-making
3.o   Use of data to advocate for programs and students

Box 4.2   ASCA (2019a) Standards for School Counselor Preparation Programs (ASCA CAEP SPA)

3.1   Use multiple data points, including student interviews, direct observation, educational records, consultation with parents/families/staff, and test results, to systematically identify student needs and collaboratively establish goals.
3.2   Identify research-based individual counseling, group counseling, and classroom instruction techniques to promote academic achievement, college/career readiness, and social/emotional development for every student.
3.3   Demonstrate digital literacy and appropriate use of technology to track student progress, communicate effectively to stakeholders, analyze data, and assess student outcomes.
5.1   Use data and student standards, such as the ASCA Student Standards (ASCA, 2021a) and appropriate state standards, to create school counseling program goals and action plans aligned with school improvement plans.
5.2   Use process, perception, and outcome data, and program and needs assessments, and other survey tools to monitor and refine the school counseling program.
5.3   Use school-wide data to promote systemic change within the school so every student is prepared for postsecondary success.

DOI: 10.4324/9781003167730-4

A criticism of past school counseling practice is that SCs did not measure the impact of their interventions or the school counseling program. Reasons provided as to why SCs historically did not assess the impact of their work include that the nature of counseling is too abstract to be adequately measured, that assessment is too time-consuming and would take away time better spent providing services to children, that SCs lack an understanding of appropriate assessment procedures, and that schools are fearful that the results may indicate that efforts were not impactful (Erford, 2018). The No Child Left Behind (NCLB, 2002) Act introduced an era of accountability in education which was extended by the Every Student Succeeds Act (ESSA; US Department of Education, n.d.). When SCs were not included in the educational reform, introduced NCLB leaders within the school counseling profession began to advocate that SCs should and could seek to enhance their visibility as vital members of the school community by adopting the commitment to accountability and evidence-based practice that was being required of teachers. The American School Counselor Association (ASCA) and Education Trust's Transforming the School Counseling Initiative (TSCI) encourage SCs to collect data that helps answer the question, "How are students different as a result of the school counseling program?" The use of data is an integral component of all four components of the *ASCA National Model* (2019b), and even more so for the manage and assess components of the model.

Scientific-Based Research (SBR)

The expectations of accountability for educators can be divided into two primary types: (1) use of scientific-based research (SBR) practices and the (2) use of evaluation. Obviously, there is overlap between these accountability emphases, but there are some important differences as well. The NCLB Act (2002) requires that schools use SBR methods. Although consensus has not yet been reached regarding the procedure for determining what is considered an SBR method, there appears to be general agreement that the process of identifying an educational intervention as SBR involves the use of either randomized experiments or quasi-experiments (Beghetto, 2003). True experimental designs within an educational context involve randomly assigning students, schools, or districts to a group that receives a particular intervention and to a group that either receives a different intervention (comparison group) or no intervention (control group).

Furthermore, to be considered an SBR method, the practice must be replicated in other settings. The NCLB Act has been criticized as using a narrow definition of SBR, as several forms of qualitative research are not recognized as SBR, including case studies, ethnographies, and action research. Qualitative research methods may be used to develop hypotheses regarding what components of programs are contributing to a program's effectiveness or why a program is working or not working, but they are not considered sufficient for determining whether a program is effective. Other organizations, such as the American Educational Research Association (AERA), have also published descriptions of SBR, which may assist those in interpreting the definition of the term (see Box 4.3).

Box 4.3 Opportunistic Experiment

Did You Know?

An opportunistic experiment is a kind of randomized controlled trial that allows the researcher to study the effects of an intervention or policy change with little additional disruption and cost (Resch et al., 2014).

Experimental research within an educational context seeks to identify a causal relationship, meaning, that an intervention was alone responsible for an increase in student achievement (Carey et al., 2008). This involves ruling out plausible explanations as to why the increase occurred and thus requires "controlling" or keeping constant other variables. There are considerable challenges to conducting experimental research within school settings, as random assignment of subjects to conditions is typically not feasible. Comparison schools/groups will always differ in ways that may potentially impact the outcome measure(s) and also may be reluctant to engage to participate in a research study. Replication is difficult, as teachers and schools are likely to vary in their use of the intervention. It is also cumbersome to use blind conditions, given that use of parent and teacher ratings introduces the potential for subjectivity. Finally, there has been an increased emphasis in the school counseling profession for the use of systemic and comprehensive interventions that seek to impact the school environment as a whole, but it is difficult to control for the variables involved in such all-encompassing interventions.

SBR and School Counseling Interventions

The *ASCA Ethical Standards for School Counselors* (2022) require that SCs use evidenced-based practices (EBP). Unfortunately, some SCs are not aware of current EBPs and often use materials that lack empirical support (Whiston & Quinby, 2009). While the school counseling profession can be considered to be in its infancy in terms of developing EBPs that were created by SCs, there are many EBPs that have been developed by the psychology profession. SCs can learn about EBPs through the repositories provided by the Collaborative for Academic, Social, and Emotional Learning (CASEL) and What Works Clearinghouse (WWC), or though the publishers of manualized curricula.

EBPs includes both programs and practices, and such SC interventions as individual and group counseling are considered EBPs (Brigman et al., 2018). There is empirical support for common SC-led interventions. Whiston et al. (2011) conducted a meta-analytic study of the school counseling intervention literature. Meta-analysis involves aggregating the results of various previous studies by estimating and combining the magnitude of the effect of the intervention, which is referred to as the effect size, in order to identify patterns among study results. The results were that, on average, school counseling interventions produced an effect size of .30, which is considered to be small to moderate. School counseling lessons, responsive services, small-group counseling, and individual planning also yielded small to moderate effect sizes. Parent workshops were found to yield a high effect size, while individual counseling only had a small effect size, but the authors cautioned that there were not enough studies in literature to reach a firm conclusion regarding empirical support for these types of school counseling interventions. School counseling interventions appeared to increase students' problem-solving, attendance, social skills, and result in reduced discipline problems and physical aggression but only had a small impact upon self-esteem. Finally, school counseling interventions yielded a small but significant impact on grade point average and achievement tests, and the authors noted that school counseling interventions are not likely to have a large impact on academic achievement, given the large caseloads of SCs.

A major challenge of the school counseling profession is the need to evaluate the effectiveness of broader, systemic interventions, such as the *ASCA National Model* (2019b).

Most likely, the school counseling profession will never be able to achieve NCLB's definition of SBR, given the near impossibility of using random assignment for school-wide initiatives. Studies investigating the effectiveness of comprehensive school counseling programs have compared schools with more fully developed comprehensive school counseling programs to those with less developed comprehensive school counseling programs, or have compared schools which have Recognized ASCA Model Programs (RAMP) to schools which have similar demographic characteristics that lack RAMP status. Studies of state-based school counseling programs have revealed positive aspects of student outcomes in schools with comprehensive programs. Investigations of students' achievement in Nebraska (Carey et al., 2012a) and Utah (Carey et al., 2012b) revealed that, after controlling from demographic differences, specific components of a CSCP were associated with positive student outcomes, including in regards to attendance, behavior, achievement test scores, and graduation rates. In Missouri, middle school students with fully implemented CSCPs, in comparison to students attending schools with lower implementation fidelity, reported less conflict with peers, improved relationships with their teachers, and were more likely to believe that their education was applicable to their future (Lapan et al., 2001). In Washington, elementary (Sink & Stroh, 2003) and middle school students (Sink et al., 2008) who attended schools with more fully implemented CSCPS had higher state assessment scores in comparison to students who attended schools without fully implemented CSCPs.

There is less efficacy research regarding RAMP programs. Ward (2009) found that elementary students who attended RAMP schools had higher attendance rates and achievement test scores than elementary students who attended non-RAMP schools. In Indiana, elementary students who attended RAMP schools had higher pass rates on state achievement tests than students who attended non-RAMP schools, but there were no significant differences for middle or high school students (Wilkerson et al., 2013). In comparing elementary students from RAMP schools to non-RAMP schools within a large school district, Milsom and Morey (2019) found that students from non-RAMP schools actually had higher attendance rates and course grades than students who attended RAMP schools. Goodman-Scott et al. (2020) found that a comparison of schools with a RAMP in Georgia and Virginia to matched schools which lacked RAMP revealed that there is no difference in terms of student achievement and suspension and attendance rates. Milsom and Morey (2019) concluded that additional research is necessary to understand the impact of RAMP.

Evaluation

Accountability is not only demonstrated through the use of SBR methods but is also demonstrated through the use of evaluation. *Evaluation* has been defined as "the purposeful and systemic collection and analysis of data of information for the purpose of documenting the effectiveness, impact, and outcomes of programs, establishing accountability, and identifying areas needing change and improvement" (Dimmitt, 2009, p. 396). Evaluation and research are similar in that both use the scientific method by establishing a question, developing a hypothesis, analyzing data related to the hypothesis, and forming conclusions from the data. However, evaluation and research differ in terms of the scope of the question being explored and the sophistication of the methods used to answer the question. Research seeks to establish a universal rule, that an intervention would yield similar results if applied to similar children and setting.

Box 4.4   Evaluations Tell You whether the Program or Intervention Worked

Questions Answered by an Impact Evaluation

- Did the program accomplish its goals?
- What are the results?
- Is the program or intervention effective in addressing the problem as intended?
- How did the problem improve?
- How did the program or intervention bring about this improvement? (Paulsen & Dailey, 2002, pp. 2–3).

An example of a research question might be, "Is advisement using Super's (1992) theory of career development effective in increasing career decision self-efficacy?" In contrast, evaluation seeks to assess the impact of a program or intervention on students in a particular setting and is not intended to generalize the findings beyond that setting or group of students. An example of a question used in evaluation might be, "Is an anger management group conducted by the SC in Liberty Middle School effective for a group of six students with externalizing behaviors (e.g., physical and verbal aggression, defiance)?" Because there is no attempt to extend the findings of evaluation beyond the particular setting/population, evaluation typically does not use some of the design methods associated with research, such as random assignment, follow-up testing, numerous measurements of outcomes, and use of valid and reliable measurements. As well-stated by Dimmit (2009), evaluation seeks to answer "Did this program or intervention make a difference for these kids in this setting?" (p. 398).

Data-Driven Decision-Making

Data-driven decision-making is related to the concept of evaluation but also has some important differences. Evaluation, for example, can help determine the impact of an intervention, which is sometimes referred to as summative or outcome evaluation (e.g., Dimmitt, 2009). In contrast, data-driven decision-making encompasses this function of evaluation but also involves the use of data to identify the current and future needs of students, assess the differential impact of interventions on different types of students, and offer possible reasons for the causes of problems. Whereas evaluation provides data regarding the effectiveness of an intervention, data-driven decision-making can be used in the planning stage to make more informed decisions about what types of activities to implement, with whom, and how and also can be used during the process of implementation to make midcourse corrections. Using data to design and modify an intervention during the process of implementing the intervention is commonly referred to as formative evaluation.

The *ASCA National Model* (2019b) and Evaluation

It can be argued that one of the most significant changes in the school counseling profession in the most recent decades is the increased emphasis on using data. All four components of the *ASCA National Model* (2019b) emphasize the use of data. While SC educators have been collaborating with school counseling practitioners in evaluating the empirical support for school counseling–related activities and the *ASCA National Model*, the type of data required of school counseling practitioners following the *ASCA National Model* involves the use of evaluation and data-driven decision-making. While the effort to conduct SBR involves the use of complex research designs and inferential statistics, such as analysis of variance (ANOVA), required for generalization, data-driven decision-making and evaluation conducted by school counseling practitioners is primarily comprised of descriptive data analysis, such as computing averages, frequencies, percentages, etc.

Use of Data

Within the *ASCA National Model*, the use of data is listed as a tool within the manage component. SCs use data for a variety of purposes, including tracking student progress, identifying students who are having academic or behavior difficulties, evaluating the effectiveness of the components of the school counseling program, changing or modifying the services provided to students, informing stakeholders about the effectiveness and potential of the school counseling program, and providing guidance and justification for additional resources.

Following the NCLB Act's (2002) mandate, SCs examine disaggregated data to identify potential barriers to learning, including access and equity issues, and to decrease achievement and opportunity gaps. Disaggregated data involves comparing groups of students on a data indicator. For example, an SC might compare the percentages of students by race, gender, or socioeconomic (SES) status that are enrolled in Advanced Placement (AP) courses to determine if there are inequities in opportunities. SCs may examine state achievement test data to determine if there are achievement gaps by gender, race, SES status, or language spoken at home. SCs may also analyze behavioral data to explore whether there are differences between groups in rates of attendance, suspension, discipline, substance use violations, homework completion, and extracurricular participation.

School Data Summary Template and Annual Data Review

Data collection and analysis reveal students' needs, which serve as the school counseling program's focus and direction. The school data summary template and annual data review within the manage component of the *ASCA National Model* require that SCs collect achievement, attendance, and discipline data. These data are reviewed to identify trends, suggesting areas for improvement, and for achievement gaps, meaning, that there are considerable differences between subgroups of students, thus indicating areas for redress. For achievement indicators, SCs can collect disaggregated data on rates of graduation, promotion and retention, and dropouts. Standardized test data can include the proficiency levels for the state achievement tests by subject area (e.g., reading, math, science, etc.), number of students at or above grade level for achievement tests (e.g., Iowa Test of Basic Skills), and SAT/ACT and Advanced Placement (AP) exam scores. Other academic indicators could be grade point average and enrollment in advanced courses (e.g., AP, honors, International Baccalaureate, college preparation). Important data regarding attendance may include average daily attendance, students who have exceeded a threshold of absences, or identifying percentage of student subgroups with greater absences than other student groups. Relevant discipline data may include the total number of disciplinary referrals for a specific time period and subgroups of students who have higher referral rates or specific consequences (e.g., consequences).

Analysis of data may identity possible reasons for low academic or gaps in academic achievement. For example, a high number of discipline referrals may indicate poor teacher-student relations, or gaps between racial groups in terms of the number of discipline referrals may indicate a need for enhanced training of staff. Low attendance or gaps between groups in attendance could be due to various reasons, including difficulties in transportation, students' difficulty in seeing the importance of school to their future, etc. Collection of additional data can help further explore the likelihood of hypotheses. SCs can collect and analyze data concerning the types of issues for which students were referred for discipline. SCs may conduct focus group with teachers, students, and additional stakeholders to obtain their perceptions and suggestions for enhancing the functioning of the school. Whereas in past decades, SCs would often conduct needs assessments, which involved surveying students, teachers, parents, and other stakeholders regarding the focus of the school counseling program and the services provided, today, the development of a school counseling program also includes academic and behavioral data. The school data summary is used to identify potential areas for intervention, and analysis of the data collected for the summary over time can be used to identify the impact of the school counseling program.

Types of Data Within the ASCA National Model (2019b)

The *ASCA National Model* requires SCs to collect three types of data, process, the ASCA Student Standards (2021) data, and outcome data, to evaluate the impact of the school counseling program. Process data involves a description of the types of activities provided to whom. Examples of process data include:

- All the sixth-grade students received four 45-minute classroom lessons on anger management.
- Twenty parents of 11th-grade students attended an hour-long presentation regarding financial aid options.
- Fifteen ninth-grade students who failed two or more academic subjects in the preceding marking period participated in a study skills group comprised of six 45-minute sessions.

Process data is generally considered a necessary but insufficient form of data because it does not indicate how such activities impacted the participants.

The ASCA Student Standards data concerns students' progress toward acquiring the attitudes, knowledge, and skills embedded within these standards. SCs often assess students' acquisition of these standards using students' self-reports prior to and following the implementation of school counseling activities, including classroom lessons, group counseling, and even individual counseling and advising. SCs appear to have flexibility within the *ASCA National Model* in determining the attitude, knowledge, or skill that relates to the respective ASCA Student Standard. For example, for the ASCA Student Standard of effective coping skills (B-SMS 7.), SCs may either ask students a Likert-scale question, such as, "I can identify at least two ways to calm down," or they may present an open-ended question to students, asking them to identify at least ways to calm down. Assessing changes in students' perceived competence may include comparing the average number of strategies student participants identified prior to the start of a small group or series of classroom lessons on such topics of study skills (B-LS 3.), conflict resolution (B-SS 2.), anger management (B-SMS 7.), and bullying (B-SS 2.) to the average number of strategies identified by participating students upon completion of the school counseling activity.

Other variables that may be assessed in this fashion include the average number of variables considered in exploring a college/university (B-LS 7.), opportunities for financial aid (B-LS 7.), the number of careers within a career cluster (B-LS 7.), etc. An example of how the SC could report such a finding would be, "Before the implementation of the classroom lessons concerning selecting a college, students on average identified 1.4 variables they were considering, whereas at posttest, the average number of variables identified by participating students was 3.4." Student competency may also be assessed in terms of self-efficacy, which refers to students' degree of confidence in completing a respective task/issue. Bandura (2006), who created the term "self-efficacy," identified a variety of self-efficacy beliefs related to adolescents' confidence in using social resources (e.g., "Get teachers to help me when I get stuck on schoolwork"), engaging in self-regulated learning (e.g., "Get myself to study when there are other interesting things to do"), relating to peers (e.g., "Work well in a group"), and self-assertion (e.g., "Stand up for myself when I feel I am being treated unfairly"). His assessment involves asking students to rate their confidence on a 100-point scale in engaging in such tasks. Bandura's self-efficacy scale could be used as both a screener to identify students in need of more intensive services and as an indicator of change/progress.

SCs can also measure students' actual competencies, as opposed to students' perceived competencies. For example, an SC might instruct 11th-grade students in job interviewing skills in small-group counseling sessions. The SC could have the participating students conduct a simulated role-play of a job interview, and the SC could assess the students' use of the job interview skills either by observing the simulation or even analyzing a video of the simulation. The results could be reported as, "80% of the 11th-grade students effectively used at least four of the job interview skills taught at least at a standard level of performance within the mock job interview." This example implies that the SC developed a rubric that provided an explicit description of performance at the standard and below the standard level (a rubric for a mock job interview is provided in the subsequent section on authentic/performance assessment). Other examples of what is referred to as performance-based assessments include assessing students' mastery of conflict resolution skills, using a college search tool such as college board, use of a particular study skills method, and so forth.

Gains in knowledge can either include a pre- and postassessment comparison or an assessment at the completion of a school counseling activity. An example of a change in knowledge using a pre- and postassessment is: "Prior to the beginning of the three classroom lessons on conflict resolution, 42% of the seventh-grade students were able to identify at least two strategies for effectively managing conflict, whereas at the completion of the lessons, 81% of the participating students were able to identify at least two strategies for effectively managing conflict." An example of just using a postassessment of knowledge is: "At the completion of the six-session study skills group, 75% of students were able to correctly identify the terms of the SQ3R reading method."

Outcome data may be considered a more valid form of assessment by stakeholders because it indicates how students' participation in school counseling–related activities (process data) and changes in attitudes, knowledge, and skills (ASCA Student Standards data) impact students' achievement, attendance, or discipline. Examples of outcome data provided within the *ASCA National Model* include promotion rates, reading levels, standardized tests, absences, discipline referrals, grade point average, progress toward graduation, dropout rate, etc. Changes in the graduation rate for an entire grade may be reported, or the graduation rate of students participating in a school counseling–related activity, such as a group, can be compared to the graduation rate for the rest of the grade. The impact of school counseling activities on standardized tests, such as respective state assessment tests or other standardized achievement tests, can be reported in terms of changes in the average score or the percentage of students who achieved a rating at the proficient or advanced levels. Some SCs will track the progress of students for whom they provided individual and group counseling and compare their scores on standardized achievement tests in comparison to students who did not receive school counseling–related services. For example, an SC could compare the changes in the percentile rank (the percentage of scores in its frequency distribution that are the same or lower) for students participating in a school counseling–led study skills group versus the rest of the students in the grade. Such a comparison could be reported in the following manner: "The average percentile rank for the reading scale of the Iowa Test of Basic Skills (ITBS) for the 16 students who participated in the eight-session study skills group increased from the 38th percentile rank to the 44th percentile rank between grades 7 and 8, whereas the rest of the grade decreased one percentile rank between grades 7 and 8." Rates of attendance and discipline referrals can also be evaluated in terms of the changes in their percentages for the entire grade or changes in students who participated in a school counseling–related program. Such changes can then be compared to the rest of the grade. While the collection of data may at first appear to be time-consuming, much of standardized data is available to SCs in the school's student information system.

In summary, while process and ASCA Student Standards data may prove to be useful to SCs in assessing the impact of school counseling–related activities, stakeholders are more likely to evaluate the school counseling program as a whole in terms of its ability to impact outcome data. SCs should use process and perception data to modify school counseling activities but should be mindful of the greater importance in implementing activities that are likely to impact the outcome data.

Accountability Identification and Reporting

The *ASCA National Model* has two types of results reports: classroom and group ASCA Student Standards and closing the gap. The *ASCA National Model* identifies guiding questions that assist SCs in analyzing the results of these three types of action plans. The next step in the accountability process is to share the results of the data analysis to stakeholders in a manner that enables them to understand the impact of the school counseling program. There are a number of different evaluation programs available to SCs for sharing results with stakeholders. MEASURE is one of the most common approaches used by SCs to analyze and disseminate the results of school counseling activities (Stone & Dahir, 2010). This six-step process stands for Mission, Elements, Analyze, Stakeholders Unite, Results, and Educate. One of the examples we will use to elucidate the MEASURE process is an intervention to improve students' scores on a state's academic achievement tests.

Step 1: Mission

The goals and activities of the school counseling program should readily relate to the academic mission of schools (Stone & Dahir, 2010). Academic outcome indicators may include the following:

- Scores on standardized tests, such as the state achievement tests, SAT, or ACT
- Grades for a marking period or number of subjects passed; enrollment patterns in Advanced Placement (AP), International Baccalaureate (IB), and/or honors classes

- Rates regarding graduation, retention, promotion/dropout; acceptance to postsecondary institutions; number of visits to postsecondary institutions
- The number of variables identified in exploring a career/college

School counseling activities/interventions that are not necessarily concerned with promoting an academic behavior, such as in the case of a social skills group or series of lessons on bullying prevention, should still use academic outcome indicators in addition to indicators that are more directly linked to the objectives of the activity. Outcome indicators that may be relevant for school counseling–related interventions that concern social/emotional development include:

- Discipline referrals
- Suspension rates
- Attendance patterns
- Participation rates in mediation
- Extracurricular activity participation
- Standardized measurements assessing a psychological construct, such as self-esteem, self-efficacy, emotional intelligence, attitudes toward the use of violence, depression, anxiety, happiness, etc.

Career-oriented activities could include such outcome indicators as:

- The number of variables students consider in selecting a career
- The ability to identify career clusters
- Patterns in the use of a school's career resource center, and standardized measures of career maturity

Step 2: Element

School improvement plan committees identify data elements that can be analyzed to indicate areas for improvement, and one way SCs can demonstrate leadership is through participation on the school's improvement plan (Stone & Dahir, 2010). Important data elements can often be found on the district's or school's report card, which are coordinated by state as part of the requirements of the ESSA (US Department of Education, n.d.). Furthermore, school systems also collect and house academic and demographic data, and often, SCs have ready access to such data as attendance/tardies, discipline referrals, etc. Analysis of the data must include disaggregation of a variety of categories that are required by ESSA, which include, among other variables, race, gender, economic disadvantage, special education, English-language learner (ELL) status, etc.

Step 3: Analyze

This step involves analyzing the data elements to identify which areas are in need of redress. A review of the disaggregated data may reveal gaps between respective groups, thus indicating which group may require targeting in order to increase the respective indicator. Table 4.1 provides the percentage of students at a fictitious school who scored either at the advanced or proficiency level of a state's achievement test in math and reading.

In Table 4.2, there are achievement gaps between White and Black students and between grade levels. Data only provide a picture of what is occurring but do not explain the why,

Table 4.1 Percentage of Students Scoring at the Proficient and Advanced Levels for Math and Reading on the State Achievement Test at Jane Doe Elementary School

Grade	Group	# of Students	% Advanced & Proficient in Math	% Advanced or Proficient in Reading
3	All students	70	71.4	68.6
3	Economically disadvantaged	58	70.0	67.1
3	Male	36	80.5	69.4
3	Female	34	61.8	67.7
3	White	22	86.4	86.4
3	Black	40	67.5	75.0
4	All students	72	75.0	58.3
4	Economically disadvantaged	57	71.9	54.4
4	Male	35	71.4	57.2
4	Female	37	78.3	59.4
4	White	19	84.2	68.4
4	Black	46	67.3	47.9
5	All students	71	63.4	71.8
5	Economically disadvantaged	53	60.3	66.0
5	Male	37	67.5	70.3
5	Female	34	58.8	73.5
5	White	28	67.8	71.4
5	Black	36	52.8	72.2

meaning, the variables that may contribute to the achievement gap. Often, contextual variables are important in helping to identify potential causes for such gaps. In other words, the SC can ask herself of himself what it is about the school environment that may contribute to the existence of such disparities. For example, helpful questions may include: Is there a lack of understanding of multiculturalism among the staff? Are there differences in how staff relate to White vs. Black students? Are there differences between the level of parental involvement between White and Black parents? The identification of gaps often reveals that additional information may need to be collected and analyzed. For example, the SC could attempt to determine if there are differential patterns in discipline referrals between White and Black students, involvement of White vs. Black parents, etc.

Step 4: Stakeholders Unite

Identify stakeholders with whom to collaborate in addressing the critical data elements, including both internal community members (e.g., administrators, teachers, school board members) and external community members (e.g., parents, faith-based groups). If possible, use an existing school committee, such as the school improvement team, data team, grade team, etc. In collaborating with the team of stakeholders, develop an action plan for improving the selected data elements. The plan should include strategies, a timeline, and responsibilities for achieving a selected target. A targeted goal of the data presented in

Table 4.2 Stakeholders Unite to Develop Strategies to Increase the State Achievement Test Scores of All Students and Reduce the Achievement Gap between Black and White Students

Beginning Date: September
Ending Date: June

Stakeholders	Strategies
School Counselors	—Implemented the Student Success Skills (SSC: Brigman & Webb, 2004) curriculum in group counseling sessions to all 4th- and 5th-grade students who did not achieve advanced or proficient in either math or reading the previous year —Arranged for presentations by community members, including Black members, regarding how education assists them in their postsecondary training and their current occupation —Coordinated college pride week in which teachers and community volunteers wore the T-shirts and baseball caps of their college in order to help students understand the relationship between academic achievement and college readiness —Provided training for teachers in using solution-focused strategies in consulting parents, including discussion of how to develop rapport with Black parents, during in-service day —Coordinated a mentoring/tutoring program with local colleges and universities, training the mentors in active listening and tutoring skills
Teachers	—Used standards-based instructional practices to improve skill attainment, including inquiry and problem-solving, collaborative learning, continual assessment embedded in instruction, and higher-order questioning —Used improvement-focused teacher evaluation systems, including measuring effective teaching (setting expectations, using multiple measures, and giving 33% to 50% of decision-making weight to student achievement measures), ensuring high-quality data (monitoring validity, ensuring reliability, and assuring accuracy), and investing in improvement (making meaningful decisions, prioritizing support and feedback, and using data for decisions at all levels
Administrators	—Provided funding for training for the mentoring/tutoring program —Reorganized several consultation rooms to provide space for the mentoring/tutoring activities
Clerical Staff	—Assisted in the scheduling of the mentoring/tutoring program
Business Partners	—Served as speakers regarding the importance of education for postsecondary training and occupations
Colleges and Universities	—Hosted "College for a Day" programs for 5th-grade students —Provided mentors for Black students

Table 4.2 could be increasing by four percentile points the number of Black students who achieve proficiency or advanced levels for the state's math and reading achievement tests.

Step 5: Results

This step involves refining the action plan and strategies developed to achieve the goal. The stakeholders must reunite to identify what aspects of the plan they believe were effective, based on analysis of the data, which interventions appear to be effective, which require modification, and which should be discarded.

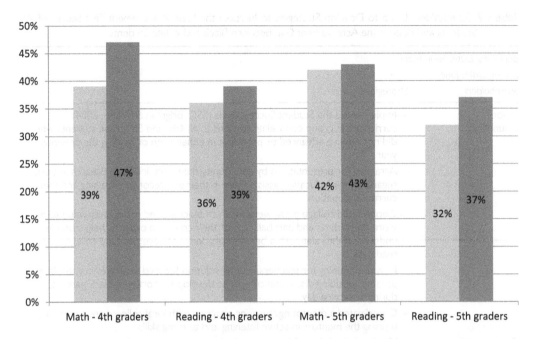

Figure 4.1 Change in the percentile rank on the math and reading state achievement tests for the 4th- and 5th-grade students who received the Student Success Skills (SSS) Curriculum (Brigman & Webb, 2004).

Step 6: Educate

It is crucial that schools educate both internal and external stakeholders about the results of school counseling–related activities in order to demonstrate that SCs and the school counseling program are vital contributors to the school's educational mission and to exhibit accountability. SCs should use visual depictions of data in the forms of graphs and charts to clearly indicate the impact of initiatives. For example, Figure 4.1 illustrates how the SC in the scenario depicted in Table 4.2 could use a bar graph to inform stakeholders of the results of one of the school counseling activities identified in the Stakeholders Unite Plan.

As the figure reveals, the hypothetical application of the Student Success Skills (SSS: Brigman & Webb, 2004) curriculum to the fourth- and fifth-grade students who did not achieve a passing score on either of the state's math or reading achievement test during the previous year appeared to have a positive impact on the students' scores. The SC in this hypothetical situation could have also elected to report the mean of the student scores or the total percentage of the grade who achieved a passing score. The results of such programs should be listed on the school counseling program's webpage and may also be disseminated at public forums, such as school board and parent-teacher association (PTA) meetings and newsletters.

Measuring the Impact of School Counseling Activities

As previously mentioned, the *ASCA National Model* recommends that SCs use three types of data to measure the impact of school counseling activities: process, ASCA Student Standards, and outcome. With the emphasis on accountability and data-driven decision-making within education, there are many forms of outcome data that are available in the schools, including standardized test scores, attendance and graduation rates, and behavioral data, such as office discipline referrals and suspensions. Outcome data is considered to be the most valid form of data and is thus the most likely to influence stakeholders. SCs should always attempt to use outcome data as indicators for school counseling–related activities.

Outcome data can be regarded as summative data in that it is an indicator of the overall impact of a school counseling–related activity. However, educators also may wish to have more immediate feedback to determine the effectiveness of a single lesson or a group counseling session. The ASCA Student Standards data concern what students learn through participation in school counseling activities (ASCA, 2019b) and can be seen as a type of formative data in that it provides SCs with information immediately following a school counseling activity. SCs can use the ASCA Student Standards as an indicator of the effectiveness of a school counseling activity and can also use the data to make midcourse adjustments. For example, if an SC is conducting three lessons on career development with ninth-grade students and after the first lesson determines that only 32% of the students can name more than one career cluster, the SC can cover the material in greater depth and use different and more effective instructional activities for the next lesson. If an SC is conducting a group on social skills, analysis of questions regarding the content knowledge students received is likely to be more helpful in modifying the intervention.

Establishing Objectives

The first step of assessment is determining the objectives. Dimmitt et al. (2007) outline a series of questions that guide the development of objectives. The first question is: What do we want students to know or be able to do following the school counseling activity? The learning outcomes should be connected to ASCA's Student Standards (2021a) and state curriculum standards for academic content areas. Students should be informed of the learning outcomes. The second question is determining how students' learning can be measured. What do students currently know? Is there data in the system that helps us determine what students know? What method(s) of assessment should be used to indicate learning?

Common Methods of Assessment Used by SCs

There are many methods that can be used to measure student achievement. This section explores some of the more common methods used by SCs.

Existing Assessment Tools

Increasingly, commercially available curricula include assessments, but they are not necessarily well-developed and may need to be revised to match the developmental level and/or language capabilities of the students (Dimmitt et al., 2007). Although historically SCs often did not use standardized measurements other than the academic and behavioral measurements that are used by schools, the increased emphasis on accountability suggests that, at some point, standard practice will involve the more frequent use of objective measurements for school counseling–specific activities. For example, SCs may regularly use a standardized measurement of career development, such as the Career Decision-Making System-Revised (O'Shea & Harrington, 2003). The Strengths and Difficulties Questionnaire (SDQ; Goodman, 1997), which yields subscores regarding emotional symptoms, conduct problems, hyperactivity/inattention, relationship problems, and prosocial behavior, has been used by SCs both as behavioral screener and as a pre- and postmeasure for individual and group counseling (Alvarez & Logan-McKibben, 2019).

Scales

Likert-type scales, which assess agreement (5 = "strongly agree") or disagreement (1 = "strongly disagree") on a four- or five-point scale, are commonly used.

Box 4.5

Did You Know?

The Likert scale is named after its inventor, Rensis Likert, who developed it during his doctoral research. Likert demonstrated, with empirical comparisons, that his "much simpler method (asking the respondent to place himself on a scale of favor/disfavor with a neutral midpoint) gave results very similar to those of the much more cumbersome (though more theoretically elegant) Thurstone procedure (based on the psychophysical method of equal-appearing intervals)" (Kish, 1982, p. 124).

Bandura (2006) recommends the use of measuring self-efficacy, which refers to people's perceptions of their ability to perform a task, as self-efficacy has been found to be a fairly reliable indicator of performance. Bandura (2006) has developed self-efficacy questions for a variety of domains, and Likert-scale questions can be used to assess these self-efficacy domains. One domain is self-efficacy for self-regulated learning, which has such assessments as, "I feel confident that I can finish my homework assignment by deadlines," and, "I feel confident that I can arrange a place to study without distractions." Example questions for the domain of social self-efficacy include, "I feel confident that I can work well in a group," and, "I feel confident that I can make and keep friends of the opposite sex."

A different type of scale is response choice, in which the scale items include all the possible range of answers. Dimmitt et al. (2007) provide the following example of a response choice question, "How much time, on average, do you spend on homework every day?" (p. 122). The choices for this question include: "1: More than 2 hours," "2: Between 1 and 2 hours," "3: Between 30 minutes and 1 hour," "4: Less than 30 minutes, more than none," and "5: None" (p. 122).

Some important guidelines should be used when developing surveys that employ scales. In order to maintain students' attention and increase the likelihood that they will complete the survey and future surveys, surveys should use the least number of questions to obtain the information that is sought. The questions must be age-appropriate. Surveys for kindergarten through second-grade students should use a two- or three-point scale involving visuals for the response choices: a frowning face for *no*, a smiling face for *yes*, a confused face for *not sure*. Surveys should use parallel language and response choices as much as possible. Other common problems in survey construction involve questions that include more than two issues, which are referred to as "double-barreled questions." The following is an example of a double-barreled question: Identify if you agree or disagree with the following statement: "My friends and I have an equal amount of control in our relationships. I sometimes talk about other people when I'm angry with them, but that doesn't happen often." This question should be separated to make two questions. Survey designers should have colleagues and students of the age group who will receive the survey review the survey to assess the reading level and clarity of the questions.

Authentic/Performance Assessment

Authentic or performance-based assessments involve having students apply acquired knowledge, often referred to as skill development (Dimmitt et al., 2007). It can be argued that having students apply knowledge is a more valid form of assessment than assessments that merely ask students to identify a correct answer or assess students' ability in using newly acquired knowledge. Dimmitt et al. (2007) provide the following examples of skill-based assessment that may be relevant for school counseling activities: completing a job application, financial aid form, or a four-year plan of study; calculating grade point average, portfolios, PowerPoint, or audiovisual presentations of information students have learned in their career exploration; and using their assignment/agenda planner. Other authentic assessments include various types of role-playing (e.g., job interview, using communication skills for negotiating conflict) and uses of technology (e.g., using at least three variables in using a search engine to learn about colleges, etc.). The difficulty with authentic assessments is that student performance must be rated, typically through the use of a rubric, and the rating process and the development of the rubric require a significant time investment. Table 4.3 provides an example of a rubric for a performance assessment of responding to job interview questions.

Table 4.3 Rubric for Job Interview Performance

Question/Indicator	Below the Standard	Approaching the Standard	Meets the Standard	Exceeds the Standard
Talks about strengths and interests	Does not mention any strengths/interests	Mentions several strengths/interests, but they are not directly related to the job/duty	Mentions at least 2 strengths/interests, and they are related to the job/duty	Mentions at least 2 strengths/interests that are related to the job/duty and provides examples of strengths/interests
Explains how one would deal with customers	Fails to answer the question	Identifies a strategy/approach, but they are not appropriate to the job/duty	Identifies at least 2 strategies/approaches that are appropriate to the job/duty	Identifies at least 2 relevant strategies/approaches and provides an example of how it would be applied
Give an example of a time you worked well with others/"team player"	Fails to answer the question	Example provided is not highly related to job/duty	Provides at least 2 relevant examples	Provides at least 2 relevant examples and relates the examples to strengths/interests
Communication skills	Fails to use oral communication skills (e.g., clear speech) or effective body language (e.g., intermittent eye contact, faced interviewer, appropriate posture)	Uses effective communication skills (e.g., clear speech) or effective body language (e.g., intermittent eye contact, faced interviewer, appropriate posture)	Uses effective communication skills (e.g., clear speech) and effective body language (e.g., intermittent eye contact, faced interviewer, appropriate posture)	Uses effective communication skills (e.g., clear speech) or effective body language (e.g., intermittent eye contact, faced interviewer, appropriate posture) and also demonstrated active listening skills (e.g., paraphrased interview, asked open-ended questions)

Multiple-Choice Questions

The advantages of using multiple-choice questions are that they are easy to score and they allow for ready pre- and posttest comparisons. However, one of the challenges with constructing multiple-choice questions that are to be used for measuring change between the pre- and posttest is to achieve an appropriate level of difficulty. The questions should not be so obvious as to enable most students to answer the question correctly prior to the lesson. The questions must also be directly connected to the instruction. Multiple-choice questions can be designed to assess factual knowledge or the ability to apply knowledge. An example of a factual-based multiple-choice question would be asking students to identify how many credits they need to graduate from high school, the different types of financial aid available for postsecondary education, or the definition of what constitutes a college preparatory course (Dimmitt et al., 2007). While performance-authentic based assessment may be a more valid way to measure students' mastery of a skill, multiple-choice questions can also attempt to assess students' ability to recognize the accurate application of concepts, skills, etc. Examples of application-based multiple-choice questions include identifying an example of the use of a particular study skill or anger management technique. Application-based multiple-choice questions do not ensure that the student will use the skill or method, but at least they assess students' ability to identify accurate examples of the application of the skill or method. In Table 4.4, sample learning goals, the related Behavior Standards from ASCA's Student Standards, and corresponding pre- and posttest questions are provided.

Online Software to Support School Counselor Accountability

Sink et al. (2019) concluded that many of the available free online software programs can be used effectively for data analysis and management by school counselors who have only limited technology skills but that practice is necessary if school counselors want to maximize each program's capabilities.

Survey Development and Data Collection

SurveyGizmo (www.surveygizmo.com) is an advanced questionnaire development tool that enables users to create professional-looking survey, polls, forms, and data summary reports. Surveys are distributed to participants through a link (Sink et al., 2019). The free version of SurveyMonkey (www.surveymonkey.com) is suitable for creating uncomplicated surveys which can be distributed to participants via the web, email, and data collection. Google Forms (www.google.com/forms/about/) is part of several data-related tools (e.g., Google Docs, Google Sheets) which are accessed by users through their Gmail accounts. Question formats include short answer, paragraph, multiple-choice, checkboxes, drop-down, linear scale, and multiple-choice grid. Data can be analyzed either within Google Forms or it can be imported into spreadsheet applications, such as Google Sheets and Microsoft Excel. The free version of Qualtrics (www.qualtrics.com) offers premade surveys and templates.

Data Management and Analysis

Microsoft Excel Online (https://www.office/com/launch/excel?ui=en-US&rs=US&auth=2) offers both simple tools for school counselors, such as tracking tasks and making schedules, and more sophisticated data management (Sink et al., 2019). EZAnalyze (www.

ezanalyze.com) is an add-in software application that provides a tab to the Excel menu which enables users to conduct statistical analyses and make graphs and tables. Google Sheets (https://docs.google.com/spreadsheets/) and Google Fusion Tables (https://support. google.com/fusiontables/answer/2571232?hl=en) enable users to collect, analyze, visualize, and share data. The *Time Elapsed Analysis & Reporting System (TEARS)* is a Microsoft Excel add-in that automatically calculates the total amount of time SCs devote to particular activities, and the *SC Use of Time Analysis (SCUTA)* is a smartphone app that provides the same purpose.

Reporting Data and Presentation

Microsoft PowerPoint Online (https://office.com/launch/powerpoint?ui=en-US&rs=US&auth-2) can be easily integrated with Microsoft Excel and Word. Users can insert tables, charts, photos, sounds, and clip art. Online assistance is readily available and easy to understand. Google Slides (https://docs.google.com/presentation) is an easy-to-use presentation tool that is accessed through one's Gmail account.

Table 4.4 Sample Learning Goals and Related Pre- and Postquestions

1. Learning Goal (6th Grade)	Students will understand the strategies of effective communication in working as a group member.
ASCA Behavior Standard	Uses effective oral and written communication skills and listening skills (B-SS 1).
Question	Which of the following is the correct definition of paraphrasing?
	a. Apologizing.
	b. Telling a person how to think/feel about something.
	c. Stating back to another person in your own words what you believe another person has said.*
2. Learning Goal (8th Grade)	Students will learn the SSCD method of learning new vocabulary while reading.
ASCA Behavior Standard	Use time-management, organization, and study skills (B-LS-3).
Question	When encountering a new word, Jennifer attempts to understand the meaning of the word by looking for clues in the surrounding passages. In the Sound, Structure, Context, and Dictionary (SSCD) method of learning new vocabulary while reading, this is an example of which of the following?
	a. Sound
	b. Structure
	c. Context*
	d. Dictionary
3. Learning Goal (6th Grade)	Students will learn to use the SMART goal format in setting goals.
ASCA Behavior Standard	Identify long- and short-term academic, career, and social/emotional goals (B-LS 7).
Question	Which of the following is an example of a goal that is specific, measurable, attainable, realistic, and timely (SMART)?
	a. I will increase my grade in language arts from a "C" to a "B" for the next marking period.*
	b. I will get better grades.
	c. All my grades will increase from "Ds" to "As" for the next marking period.

(Continued)

Table 4.4 (Continued)

4. Learning Goal (9th Grade)	Students will know how to think rationally to manage their anger.
ASCA Behavior Standard	Demonstrate self-discipline and self-control (B-SMS 2).
Question	Which of the following is an example of replacing self-talk with more rational self-talk?
	a. I cannot believe my sister; she always takes my clothes and never thinks of what I want.
	b. My mother needs to solve this problem for us.
	c. I am angry at my sister. I wish she did not borrow my shirt when I planned to wear it today. I wonder if she is mad about me borrowing her shirt last week.*
	d. My sister needs to never come in my room again.
5. Learning Goal (9th Grade)	Students will learn cognitive and behavioral self-motivation strategies.
ASCA Behavior Standard	Demonstrate ability to delay immediate gratification for long-term rewards (B-LS 7).
	Which of the following is an example of the use of a self-reinforcement strategy?
	a. Miguel helps Jennifer with her homework.
	b. Miguel always completes his homework at the library.
	c. Miguel starts his homework after watching television for several hours.
	d. After Miguel completes his math homework, he responds to texts for 15 minutes before starting his homework for foreign language.*

The SC's Role in Accountability within Multitiered Systems of Support (MTSS)

ASCA (2021b) describes SCs "as stakeholders in the development and implementation of multitiered system of supports (MTSS)." Response to intervention (RtI) is an MTSS used for academic instruction. While the role of SCs in addressing academic deficits in the RtI model is unclear, it is evident that SCs can play a vital role in the behavioral domain of RtI, which sometimes is referred to as behavioral RtI, or school-wide positive behavioral interventions and support (SWPBIS). This section examines some of the different approaches for SCs in collecting student behavioral data.

Universal Screens

In SWPBIS, data must be collected at the universal level in order to determine the effectiveness of the school's approach to ensuring that students meet behavioral expectations and to identify students who may be in need of additional services. Some commonly used assessment methods at the universal level include office discipline referrals (ODRs) and multiple-gate screening systems (Kalberg et al., 2010).

Office Discipline Referrals (ODRs)

An ODR is a checklist of behavioral concerns that school personnel use to refer a student for violation of a school's code of conduct. Many schools input ODR information into the student information system, which an SC can access to determine which students have been receiving a large number of infractions (Gruman & Hoelzen, 2011). The data can be useful for developing a list for the school behavioral team and identifying systems-wide trends. However, ODRs are not used to monitor individual student progress for several reasons. First, ODRs generally do not have a high degree of reliability, as teachers often have different expectations for student behavior, refer students inconsistently, and their referrals may be influenced by cultural bias (Shores, 2009). Second, while ODRs have been found to be a reliable indicator of externalizing problem behaviors (McIntosh et al., 2009), defined as disruptive, aggressive, and defiant behaviors, they are ineffective in identifying students who may be experiencing internalizing behaviors, which include extreme shyness, anxiety, withdrawal, and depressive symptoms. Another problem with ODRs is that they can be described as reactive rather than preventative, as staff must wait for students to demonstrate a negative pattern (Burke et al., 2014).

Multiple-Gate Universal Screening

Multiple-gate universal screening involves several steps of assessments. The first step in the assessment process is the use of a broad screener to identify at-risk students, whether it be for academic, behavioral, or emotional difficulties. Those students who are identified as being at risk then receive a more intensive, reliable assessment. Donohue et al. (2016) recommend that SCs are members of the school's team that coordinates the use of screens, and recommend that SCs can provide individual and group counseling to students who are identified through the screening process and develop classroom lessons to address school-wide trends. Screening instruments can also be used to measure intervention outcomes if the instrument is closely related to the objectives of the intervention program (Bardhoshi et al., 2019). There are a number of a commercially available multiple-gate universal screening programs for social and emotional concerns that are considered psychometrically sound and that are free (see Table 4.5).

Maloney's (2015) use of a multiple-gate screening procedure in the four elementary schools in the Hempfield Area School District (Pennsylvania) will be described as an example of the multiple-gate assessment process and the role of SCs in providing services to students who are identified through this process. In the first stage of the assessment process, teachers use the Systematic Screening for Behavior Disorders (SSBD; Walker & Severson, 1992) to rank all students for internalizing and externalizing behaviors. The behavior of the three students who receive the highest ratings for internalizing and externalizing behaviors are then measured using the Walker Assessment Scale/Walker Survey Instrument (WAS/WSI: Walker & McConnell, 1988). The third gate in the Hempfield Area School District involves a review of data in the following areas over a nine-week period: ODRs (two or more), nonemergency visits to the nurse (four or more), attendance (six or more absences), and behavior grades on the most recent report card (25% of scores indicate "needs improvement"). Students who receive the threshold score on the WAS/WSI and who meet at least one other of the criteria listed prior are then referred to tier two intervention.

If the parent provided consent, students in the tier two intervention participate in the Behavior Education Program (BEP), which is also known as check-in/check-out (CICO). In *CICO*, students receive daily monitoring and feedback through the use of a daily behavior report card (DBRC) to assess students' progress in meeting the school-wide expectations for tier one. Each morning, the student "checks in" with his or her assigned adult facilitator, then takes the DBRC to each class and receives feedback and reinforcement from the teacher using a point system. At the conclusion of the school day, the student

Table 4.5 Free-Access Assessment Instruments for Socioemotional Concerns

Instrument	Format	# of Items	Minutes to Complete	Construct	Free-Access Location
Generalized Anxiety Disorder (GAD-7)	Self-report	7	5	Anxiety	www.integration.samsha.gov/clinical-practice/GAD708.19.08Cartwright.pdf
Hamilton Rating Scale for Depression (HAM-D)	Counselor report	17	10	Depression	www.ouctometracker.org/library/HAM-D.pdf
National Institute for Children's Health Quality (NICHQ) Vanderbilt Assessment Scales				ODD, CD, anxiety, depression	www.nichq.org/resource/nichq-vanderbilt-assessment-scales
Posttraumatic Stress Disorder (PCL-5)	Self-report	20	10	PTSD	www.ptsd.va.gov/professional/assessment/documents/PCL-5_Standard.pdf
Swanson, Nolan, and Pelham IV Rating Scale (SNAP-IV)	Parent & teacher report	90	30	ADHD, ODD	www.aacap.org/App_Themes/AACAP/docs/member_resources/toolbox_for_clinical_practice_and_outcomes/symptoms/SNAP-IV_18_item.pdf
Strengths and Difficulties Questionnaire (SDQ)	Parent, teacher, & self-report	33	15	Emotions, conduct, ADHD, peer relationships	www.sdqinfo.com
Student Risk Screening Scale (SRSS)	Teacher report	21	10–15	Externalizing behaviors	https://education.missouri.edu/ebi/2015/10/28/student-risk-screening-scale-srss/

"checks out" with his or her adult facilitator and takes the form home to be reviewed by a parent/guardian (Crone et al., 2010). In the Hempfield Area School District elementary schools, the SC is the students' assigned CICO adult facilitator.

Maloney (2015) conducted a study comparing the effectiveness of *BEP/CICO* to small-group social skills training, which is another commonly used tier two intervention for students exhibiting behavioral deficits. Students who were identified through the multiple-gate screening procedure were randomly assigned to either the BEP/CICO program or a social skills training group that used the Strong Kids Curriculum (Merrell et al., 2007). The Strong Kids Curriculum is designed to promote students' social and emotional competence, and the topics of the curriculum include understanding feelings, managing anger and stress, understanding others' feelings, clear and positive thinking, problem-solving. The students assigned to the Strong Kids Curriculum met once a week with their SC for a 30-minute session for an eight-week period. In each session, previous skills were reviewed, after which the students role-played new skills.

Students in both the BEP/CICO group and the Strong Kids Curriculum social skills training group showed significant increases in behaviors upon completion of the program (Maloney, 2015). At a four-month follow-up, students who received the social skills training showed continued improvement from the posttest and outperformed the students who received the BEP/CICO whose behavioral gains were maintained but did not increase from the initial posttest. Students who were identified as those with externalizing behavior problems exhibited greater behavioral gains than those with internalizing behavior problems at the four-month follow-up point. The SCs reported that they perceived the BEP/CICO and Strong Kids Curriculum social skills training group to be programs that could be feasibly implemented within the school setting and were within the scope of their role as SCs. For the BEP/CICO, the four SCs achieved an average fidelity rating of 84.5%, with 80% being considered an acceptable rating (Horner et al., 2004). For the Strong Kids Curriculum, the SCs averaged a 95.4% satisfaction rating, again compared to an 80% target.

Observation Methods

Gruman and Hoelzen (2011) encourage SCs to use behavioral observations to determine the effectiveness of services provided within SWPBIS. Anecdotal and interval observations can be used to identify the severity of a child's problem; communicate with school personnel, parents, and any external professionals assisting the child; and assess changes following the implementation of an intervention.

Anecdotal Observations

In anecdotal observations of behavior, an observer records all the behaviors and interactions that occur during a specified period of time. A "time stamp" is used to note behavioral changes by the student or environment changes. Anecdotal observations are used in functional behavioral analysis (FBA) to identify the antecedent-behavior-consequence (ABC) links associated with a child's behavior, which may indicate environmental contributions of peers or a teacher to a child's problematic behavior. Limitations of anecdotal observations include difficulty in quantifying and sharing the data with others and time-intensiveness.

Box 4.6

8:45 Listening attentively to other students as they presented their book reports.

9:20 Talked out ("This sucks") while doing morning seatwork in which there was no clear purpose to the seatwork. John's friend Tom laughed. John was verbally redirected by the teacher and then received a warning that he would receive a time-out if he continued the behavior.

9:55 Shouted out to his classmate Mike while lining up for the next class, which got Mike's attention. He was verbally redirected by the teacher.

10:10 Fell out of his chair while doing seatwork. Mike looked over at him. He was verbally redirected by the teacher, and the teacher stood by him for five minutes, reading with him and going over the directions.

10:20 The class started a reading assignment, but he refused. His peers and the teacher ignored him.

10:30 He dumped his books on the floor and swore. Tom looked over at John. He received a time-out for five minutes.

10:45 Paying attention while teacher showed a video on dinosaurs.

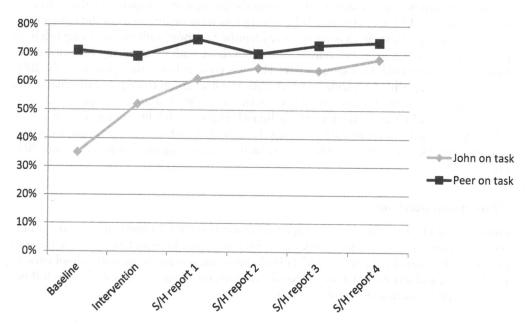

Figure 4.2 Interval observation data comparing John's on-task behavior to a composite of selected peers' on-task behavior measured at different points in the intervention process. Each data point represents 120 intervals collected in 20 minutes of classroom observations. Intervention = behavioral modification point card implemented; S/H report = school-home report intervention.

Interval Observations

Interval observations assess the frequency of specific student behaviors associated with academic achievement (e.g., inattention, disorganization, attention-seeking). Interval observations are objective and more readily understood by parents, teachers, etc. In order to conduct an interval observation, the observer chooses times when the class will be involved in individual or small group tasks. The observer tallies behavior for the target student and a same-gender peer on an established interval schedule. At each time point, the observer selects behaviors from an established list of behaviors (e.g., on-task, off-task, out-of-seat, talk-out). Usually, several observations are conducted, and data are analyzed to determine the behavioral "average." For example, if an observer uses a 20-second interval and records data for ten minutes for four different observations, the data set would yield 120 data points for both the target and comparison students. The data points are then graphed, and percentages can be shared with team members (see Figure 4.2).

Summary

The use of data-driven decision-making to demonstrate accountability has irrevocably modified education. Historically, SCs have avoided measuring the impact of their activities and programs, often due to a belief that the multifaceted and ambiguous role of the SC did not lend itself to program evaluation. However, as politicians and the public challenge educators to demonstrate the impact of their efforts, SCs no longer have the luxury of standing along the sidelines. SCs must understand and meet these new expectations head-on.

Recently, an SC explained to one of the authors his belief that the *ASCA National Model* (2019) was unrealistic. This SC stated that his job is to have an open-door policy, in which he is always available for any student's immediate need. This SC proudly recounted how he had helped a boy dig out his retainer, which he had accidentally discarded. This SC also appeared to be proud of the fact that he did not collect or analyze data. While the SC's retelling of helping the boy find his retainer may appear compelling, SCs must understand that such stories are not likely to have much impact if the school board is seeking to reduce the district budget by trimming school personnel who do not have a clear record of effectiveness.

References

Alvarez, J., & Logan-McKibben, S. (2019). *Free, valid, and reliable assessments to enhance SCs' data-driven practices.* Evidence-based School Counseling Conference.

American School Counselor Association. (2019a). *ASCA standards for school counselor preparation programs.* Author. www.schoolcounselor.org/getmedia/573d7c2c-1622-4d25-a5ac-ac74d2e614ca/ASCA-Standards-for-School-Counselor-Preparation-Programs.pdf

American School Counselor Association. (2019b). *The ASCA national model: A framework for school counseling programs* (4th ed.). Author.

American School Counselor Association. (2021a). *ASCA Student Standards: Mindsets & behaviors for student success.* Author.

American School Counselor Association. (2021b). *The school counselor and multitiered system of supports.* Author.

American School Counselor Association. (2022). *ASCA ethical standards for school counselors.* Author.

Bandura, A. (2006). *Self-efficacy beliefs for adolescents.* Information Age Publications.

Bardhoshi, B., Cobb, N., & Erford, B. T. (2019). Determining evidence-based outcomes in school-aged youth: Free access instruments for SC use. *Professional School Counseling*, 22(1b), 1–10. https://doi.org/10.1177/2156759X19834431

Beghetto, R. (2003). *Scientifically based research.* ERIC Clearinghouse on Educational Management.

Brigman, G., Villares, E., & Webb, L. (2018). *Evidence-based school counseling.* Routledge.

Brigman, G., & Webb, L. (2004). *Student success skills: Classroom manual.* Atlantic Education Consultants.

Burke, M. D., Davis, J. L., Hagain-Burke, S., Lee, Y., & Fogarty, M. S. (2014). Using SWPBS expectations as a screening tool to predict behavioral risk in middle school. *Journal of Positive Behavior Interventions*, 16(1), 5–17. https://doi.org/10.11771098300712461147

Carey, J. C., Dimmitt, C., Hatch, T. A., Lapan, R. T., & Whiston, S. C. (2008). Report of the national panel for evidence-based school counseling: Outcome research coding protocol and evaluation of student success skills and second step. *Professional School Counseling*, 11(3), 197–206. https://doi.org/10.1177/2156759X0801100306

Carey, J. C., Harrington, K., Martin, I., & Hoffman, D. (2012a). A statewide evaluation of the outcomes of implementation of the ASCA National Model school counseling programs in rural and suburban Nebraska high schools. *Professional School Counseling*, 16(2), 100–107. https://doi.org/10.1177/2156759X0001600203

Carey, J. C., Harrington, K., Martin, I., & Stevenson, D. (2012b). Implementation of ASCA National Model counseling programs in Utah high schools. *Professional School Counseling*, 16(2), 89–99. https://doi.org/10.1177/2156759X0001600203

Council for the Accreditation of Counseling and Related Educational Programs. (n.d.). *2016 CACREP standards.* www.cacrep.org/for-programs/2016-cacrep-standards/

Crone, D. A., Hawken, L. S., & Horner, R. H. (2010). *Responding to problem behavior in schools* (2nd ed.). Guilford Press.

Dimmitt, C. (2009). Why evaluation matters: Determining effective school counseling practices. *Professional School Counseling, 12*(6), 395–399. https://journals.sagepub.com/doi/pdf/10.1177 /2156759X0901200605?casa_token=4ZbGti-HwZkAAAAA:yO17p1DpMycYohgHgxcr-tXhk-2CrAI4OjumQ_KqWJSbUXg2AWR9JWWGmNLY_0EF8zNqq6JVYI8d2

Dimmitt, C., Carey, J. C., & Hatch, T. (2007). *Evidence-based school counseling*. Corwin.

Donohue, P., Goodman-Scott, E., & Betters-Bubon, J. (2016). Universal screening for early identification of students at risk: A case example from the field. *Professional School Counseling, 19*(1), 133–143. https://doi.org/10.5330/1096-2409-19.1.133

Erford, B. (2018). Accountability: Assessing needs, determining outcomes, and evaluating programs. In B. Erford's (Ed.), *Transforming the school counseling profession* (pp. 94–130). Pearson.

Goodman, R. (1997). The strengths and difficulties questionnaire: A research note. *Child Psychology & Psychiatry & Allied Disciplines, 38*(5), 581–586. https://doi.org/10.1111/j.1469-7610.1997. tb01545.x

Goodman-Scott, E., Taylor, J. V., Kalkbrenner, M. T., Darsie, J., Barbosa, R., Walsh, K., & Worth, A. (2020). A multivariate analysis of variance investigation of school-level RAMP status across two states. *Counseling Outcome Research and Evaluation, 11*(1), 31–44. https://doi.org/10.108 0/21501378.2019.1575696

Gruman, D. H., & Hoelzen, B. (2011). Determining responsiveness to school counseling interventions using behavioral observations. *Professional School Counseling, 14*(3), 183–190. https://doi. org/10.1177/2156759X1101400302

Horner, R. H., Todd, A. W., Lewis-Palmer, T., Irwin, L. K., Sugai, G., & Boland, J. B. (2004). The school-wide evaluation tool (SET): A research instrument for assessing school-wide positive behavior support. *Journal of Positive Behavior Interventions, 6*(1), 3–12. https://doi.org/10.117 7/10983007040060010201

Kalberg, J. R., Lane, K. L., & Menzies, H. M. (2010). Using systematic screening procedures to identify students who are nonresponsive to primary prevention efforts: Integrating academic and behavioral measures. *Education & Treatment of Children, 33*(4), 561–584. https://muse.jhu.edu/ article/398177

Kish, L. (1982). Rensis Likert (1903–1981). *The American Statistician, 36*(2), 124–125. https://doi. org/10.1080/00031305.1982.10482804

Lapan, R. T., Gysbers, N. C., & Petroski, G. F. (2001). Helping seventh graders be safe and successful: A statewide study of the impact of comprehensive guidance and counseling programs. *Journal of Counseling & Development, 79*(3), 320–330. https://doi.org/10.1002/j.1556-6676.2001. tb01977.x

Maloney, L. A. (2015). *A comparison of two interventions in a Response to Intervention (RtI) framework across student problem type* (Unpublished doctoral dissertation). Duquesne University.

McIntosh, K., Campbell, A., Carter, D., Russell, D., & Zumbo, B. (2009). Concurrent validity of office discipline referrals and cut points used in schoolwide positive behavior support. *Behavioral Disorders, 34*(2), 100–113. https://doi.org/10.1177/019874290903400204

Merrell, K. W., Carrizales, D., Feuerborn, L., Gueldner, B. A., & Tran, O. K. (2007). *Strong kids 3–5: A social & emotional curriculum*. Paul H. Brookes Publishing Co.

Milsom, A., & Morey, M. (2019). Does RAMP matter? Comparing elementary student grades and absences in one district. *Professional School Counseling, 22*(1), 1–8. https://doi.org/10.1177/215 6759X19847977

No Child Left Behind Act of 2001, Pub. L. No. 107–110 (2002).

O'Shea, A. J., & Harrington, T. F. (2003). Using the career decision-making system-revised to enhance students' career development. *Professional School Counseling, 6*(4), 280–286. www. jstor.org/stable/42732441

Paulsen, C. A., & Dailey, D. (2002). *A guide for education personnel: Evaluating a program or intervention*. Ph.D. Elementary and Middle Schools Technical Assistance Center (EMSTAC). American Institutes for Research.

Resch, A., Berk, J., & Akers, L. (2014). *Recognizing and conducting opportunistic experiments in education: A guide for policymakers and researchers* (REL 2014–037). US Department of

Education, Institute of Education Sciences, National Center for Education Evaluation and Regional Assistance, Analytic Technical Assistance and Development. http://ies.ed.gov/ncee/edlabs

Shores, C. (2009). *A comprehensive RTI model: Integrating behavioral and academic interventions.* Corwin.

Sink, C. A., Adkins, C., Cooney, M., & Garverick, T. (2019). An exploratory study of online software to support accountability practices. *Professional School Counseling, 22*(1b), 1–11. https://doi.org/10.1177/2156759X19834443

Sink, C. A., Akos, P., Turnbull, R. J., & Mvududu, N. (2008). An investigation of comprehensive school counseling programs and academic achievement in Washington state middle schools. *Professional School Counseling, 12*(1), 43–53. https://doi.org/10.1177/2156759X0801200105

Sink, C. A., & Stroh, H. R. (2003). Raising achievement test scores of early elementary school students through comprehensive school counseling programs. *Professional School Counseling, 6*(5), 350–364. www.jstor.org/stable/42732452

Stone, C. B., & Dahir, C. A. (2010). *School counselor accountability. A MEASURE for student success* (3rd ed.). Prentice Hall.

Super, D. E. (1992). Toward a comprehensive theory of career development. In D. Montross & C. Shinkman (Eds.), *Career development: Theory and practice* (pp. 35–64). Charles C. Thomas.

US Department of Education. (n.d.). *Every student succeeds act (ESSA).* Author. www.ed.gov/essa?src%3Drn

Walker, H. M., & McConnell, S. R. (1988). *The Walker-McConnell scale of social competence and adjustment.* PRO-ED.

Walker, H. M., & Severson, H. H. (1992). *Systemic Screening of Behavior Disorders (SSBD)* (2nd ed.). Sopris West.

Ward, C. A. (2009). *An examination of the impact of the ASCA National Model on student Achievement at Recognized ASCA Model Program (RAMP) elementary schools.* (Doctoral dissertation). Retrieved from Dissertation Abstracts International, Proquest. (UMI No. 3401416).

Whiston, S. C., & Quinby, R. F. (2009). Review of school counseling outcome research. *Psychology in the Schools, 46*(3), 267–272. https://doi.org/10.1002/pits.20372

Whiston, S. C., Tai, W. L., Rahardja, D., & Eder, K. (2011). School counseling outcome: A meta-analytic examination of interventions. *Journal of Counseling & Development, 89*(1), 37–55. https://doi.org/10.1002/j.1556-6678.2011.tb00059.x

Wilkerson, K., Perusse, R., & Hughes, A. (2013). Comprehensive school counseling programs and student achievement outcomes: A comparative analysis of RAMP vs. non-RAMP schools. *Professional School Counseling, 16*(3), 172–184. https://doi.org/10.1177/2156759X1701600302

Chapter 5

Instruction

Box 5.1 2016 Council for the Accreditation of Counseling and Related Educational Programs (CACREP, n.d.) School Counseling Specialty Area Standards

3.b Design and evaluation of school counseling programs
3.c Core curriculum design, lesson plan development, classroom management strategies, and differentiated instructional strategies
3.d Interventions to promote academic development
3.l Techniques to foster and collaboration within schools
3.n Use of accountability data to inform decision-making

Box 5.2 ASCA (2019a) Standards for School Counselor Preparation Programs (ASCA CAEP SPA)

2.1 Describe established and emerging counseling and educational methods, including, but not limited to, childhood and adolescent development, learning theories, behavior modification and classroom management, social justice, multiculturalism, group counseling, college/career readiness, and crisis response.
3.2 Identify research-based individual counseling, group counseling, and classroom instruction techniques to promote academic achievement, college/career readiness, and social/emotional development for every student.
4.1 Plan, organize, and implement a variety of instructional and counseling strategies as part of a comprehensive school counseling program (direct and indirect student services) to improve pre-K–12 student attitudes, knowledge, and skills.
6.1 Explain appropriate school of practice for school counselors, defined as the overall delivery of the comprehensive school counseling program, providing education, prevention, intervention, and referral services to students and their families.

The *ASCA National Model* (2019b) requires the development and implementation of a curriculum that is planned, comprehensive, preventive, and developmental. The school counseling curriculum must support the program's vision, mission, and annual student outcome goals, with the ASCA Student Standards (2021) serving as the frame for the instructional content. The school counseling curriculum is regarded as a universal tier one intervention in the response to intervention (RtI) model. Providing classroom instruction is considered one of the most effective delivery methods for SCs, as a large number of students can be reached simultaneously.

The notion that SCs are educators who are expected to deliver instruction in a classroom setting is often unsettling to SC students in training, who often enter the profession without a teaching background and rather envision their primary role as developing close relationships with students in need through individual counseling. Obtaining proficiency in conducting school counseling lessons is a difficult developmental process, as there are many layers of competence, from curriculum development to classroom management, which are necessary for providing effective instruction. The delicate balance between being a disciplinarian in the classroom or allowing an "anything goes" approach takes time for SCs to develop. Use of an authoritarian approach by SCs often leads students to distance themselves from the SC and gives the student an additional negative experience with an adult. On the other hand, the passive SC, who does not respond to negative behaviors, sends a message of powerlessness of the adult and undermines the students' respect, which can ultimately render the lesson ineffective (Goodnough et al., 2007). SCs in training are encouraged to seek to challenge their personal discomfort with learning to deliver instruction, and hopefully the realization that through classroom instruction they are more likely to positively impact students may serve as a personal motivation for providing classroom instruction. This chapter includes a review of Marzano's (2007) empirically supported instructional strategies, approaches for school counseling lesson planning, school counselors' approach to classroom management, differentiated instruction, and culturally responsive teaching.

Marzano's (2007) Research-Supported Teaching Strategies

A major initiative of the educational reform movement of the past several decades has been the identification and proliferation of evidence-based strategies in teaching. Although many SCs do not receive intensive training in providing instruction, given that they do not provide subject-based instruction, we urge SCs to be familiar with the research literature regarding evidence-based instructional strategies to be better prepared to collaborate with educators and provide effective instruction. Through meta-analytic procedures (an aggregation of multiple studies to identify an average effect size, quantifying the magnitude of impact), Marzano (2007) identified teaching strategies which have empirical support. Marzano (2017) cautions against the use of the term "high-yield instructional strategies," noting that typically instructors must utilize a variety of teaching strategies in concert in order to promote student learning. However, the strategies identified by Marzano may be regarded as a general framework for effective teaching. In the section that follows, Marzano's (2007) empirically supported instructional strategies are listed in order from the strongest to the weakest in terms of their impact on students' academic achievement. SCs are not likely to use all these instructional strategies in a single lesson but will likely find that effective incorporation of at least several of the strategies will enhance their instructional effectiveness.

Identifying Similarities and Differences

This strategy includes comparing, classifying, creating metaphors, and creating analogies. Providing students with the opportunity to divide a concept into its similar and dissimilar characteristics enables students to analyze and solve complex problems by approaching them in a simpler way. An example of the way in which an SC could incorporate this instructional strategy in delivering the school counseling curriculum is providing students with examples and nonexamples of the characteristics of effective goal-setting while having the students develop hypotheses about what principles are unique to the examples presented.

Summarizing and Note-Taking

This strategy involves teaching students how to engage in effective summarization/note-taking, which includes eliminating unnecessary information, replacing some information, rewriting, and analyzing information. Summarization and note-taking have been shown to increase student recall and are believed to contribute to students' deeper understanding of concepts. While SCs typically do not emphasize the use of note-taking, given that they do not provide subject instruction, they may utilize this strategy in asking students to consider what they learned from the school counseling curriculum lesson, or asking students to name one thing they are likely to use or do within the next week.

Reinforcing Effort and Providing Recognition

Reinforcing effort refers to enhancing students' awareness that learning is difficult and requires sustained and active effort on the part of the learner. Surprisingly, many younger students, who are more likely to have an external locus of control, do not attribute learning to their own efforts. Instead, they see the instructor as the person responsible for their learning. SCs can help students explore times that they have been successful and help them identify the various thoughts, feelings, and behaviors they had that associated with their success. Providing recognition for these successes involves giving students symbolic or tangible rewards for achievement. SCs may provide students with tangible rewards for completing activities associated with a lesson. For example, the SCs could provide students with a reward for those who completed a journal worksheet identifying various physiological and cognitive indicators of emotions they experienced during a specified period of time. Also, SCs can integrate both these instructional strategies by teaching students to recognize and praise themselves for their effort and achievements, which promotes students' intrinsic motivation.

Homework and Practice

Homework and practice provide students with the opportunity to apply their learning, which is associated with deeper understanding. An example of how an SC might utilize homework is provided in the discussion of the previous instructional strategy. SCs should always seek to provide opportunities for practice when conducting school counseling lessons. For example, for a lesson regarding time management, SCs should have students use a scheduling sheet to plan their schedule for the upcoming week. As indicated in the sample lesson plan concerning communication skills provided in Table 5.1, the SC could model the use of assertive talking and listening and then have students pair up and practice the specific assertiveness skills taught. One student could be asked to think of a time when he or she was really angry with someone and practice communicating his or her anger in a respectful and assertive manner. Correspondingly, the listener might play the person with

Table 5.1 Lesson Plan Template

Lesson Plan for Communication Skills

School Counselor: Jane Doe

Target Audience: Each eighth-grade Jane Doe Middle School student

Evidence-base: Action Research

ASCA's Student Standards (limit of 3):

- Self-Management #9: Personal safety skills
- Social Skills #1: Effective oral and written communication and listening skills
- Social Skills #2: Positive, respectful, and supportive relationships with students who are similar to and different from them

Lesson 1 of 3

Learning Objective(s)/Competency

Students Will:	At least 80% of the students will be able to identify three negotiation styles: (a) collaborative, (b) bullying, and (c) responsive, as indicated through multiple-choice questions.
Student Will:	At least 80% of the students will be able to identify and use paraphrasing and "I" messages as indicated with the use of a rubric developed by the instructor.

Materials:

Playing cards, PowerPoint document, "Meet or Fight" scoring key (Curhan, 1998)

Evidence Base:

__ Best Practice

_x Action Research

__ Research-Informed

__ Evidence-Based

Procedure: Describe how you will . . .

Introduce	Students will first be paired to play the card game "Meet or Fight" (Curhan, 1998), which provides students with insight regarding their style of negotiation. The activity concludes with a discussion of how trust is related to conflict resolution and negotiation.
Communicate Lesson Objective	Students will be informed through PowerPoint of the lesson's objectives following the "Meet or Fight" activity (Curhan, 1998).
Teach Content	Students will be taught effective communication skills, including the skills of "I" messages and paraphrasing, through visual depictions in a PowerPoint, YouTube video, and demonstration by the instructor.
Practice Content	Students will first practice ineffective forms of communication to help realize poor forms of communication. After demonstration of effective communication, students will practice "I" messages and paraphrasing in a paired role-play.
Summarize/Close	Students will be reminded of the benefits/advantages of effective communication.
	Students will be asked to identify one skill/thing they learned in the lesson that they are likely to use more frequently henceforth.

Data Collection Plan
Participation Data

Anticipated Number of Students	All 425 eighth-grade Liberty Middle school students will participate in the lesson.
Planned Length of Lesson(s)	The lesson will comprise one 90-minute block/period.

(Continued)

Table 5.1 (Continued)

ASCA Student Standards Data

Posttest administered after lesson:

Multiple-choice questions

1) Mike is angry at Jim for not coming over to his house after school when he said he was going to. At school the next day, Mike confronts Jim with the following statement: "I cannot believe you didn't come over." If Jim were really listening and understanding of Mike, he would say which of the following:

    a) So what? Bobby came over, and we wanted to do something else.
    b) You're angry that I didn't show up.
    c) You'd better not talk to me like that.

2) A bullying negotiation style is defined as:

    a) Taking turns to make sure that each person gets what they want at least every other time.
    b) Achieving a compromise to make sure that people get what they want.
    c) Only thinking of what you want and not the wants of another person.

3) Which of the following statements is an example of a good "I" message?

    a) "I was really annoyed when you didn't tell me what happened."
    b) "You better stop doing that or I'm leaving."
    c) "I cannot believe you did that again . . . there is really something wrong with you."

Outcome Data

Discipline: The number of office discipline referrals (ODRs) for verbal and physical aggression for eighth-grade students will decrease by 10% in comparison to the class's number of ODRs for verbal and physical aggression for seventh grade.

Reproduced with permission, American School Counselor Association, www.schoolcounselor.org.

whom the student is angry and focus on using paraphrasing to identify the student's anger in a nondefensive manner.

Nonlinguistic Presentations

This includes use of graphic presentations, mental pictures, drawings, pictography, and kinesthetic activities. The use of nonlinguistic presentations has been associated with increased brain activity. SCs can incorporate nonlinguistics activities in school counseling lessons by incorporating visuals in PowerPoint presentations, by having students create a picture or symbol of their understanding of the material, and through the use of applied activities in the form of role-playing, group problem-solving, etc.

Cooperative Learning

The school counseling profession acknowledges the importance of social interactions through the profession's emphasis on social/emotional development. SCs can include cooperative learning in a variety of ways. They can divide the class into small groups to work on scenario-based issues. For example, for a lesson in which the SC seeks emotional empathy, students can be assigned to small groups to identify the likely emotions and irrational thoughts of a depiction of a similar-aged student and develop possible responses for assisting the student experiencing emotional distress. Students could be assigned to role-play a job interview in which one student functions as the interviewer, one the interviewee, and another student to serve as an observer who evaluates the interviewees' ability to use specified interview skills. Importantly, extant research suggests that when creating groups, it is important to instruct students regarding the expected roles of group members and the expectations of the group work.

Setting Objectives and Providing Feedback

Student achievement is enhanced when students understand the objectives of the lesson, and SCs should also explain how the objectives are relevant for students' development. Feedback from SCs varies somewhat from teacher feedback in that SCs do not typically provide formal grades. Rather, SC feedback is more likely to be connected to a specific learning activity, and in such cases, the focus of feedback should be on the student's mastery of a task, such as communication skills, the use of the career search engine to locate relevant information, etc. One SC developed a comprehensive way in which to provide feedback through a Likert-scale rubric to assess students' videotaped role-play of a job interview. As is the case with all kinds of feedback, such information should be provided to students in a timely and constructive manner.

Generating and Testing Hypotheses

The generation and testing of hypotheses involves the use of inductive and deductive reasoning through problem-solving. An example of an SC's use of this instructional strategy is helping students identify a social problem, research the various causes of the social problem, and implement an applied project to address one of the causes of the social problem identified by the students. Given the long-term nature of this instructional strategy, it may not be as applicable for SCs, who are not likely to conduct a long series of lessons.

Cues, Questions, and Advanced Organizers

Cues are reminders to students about what they are about to experience, and highlighting the most essential information, questions can help students analyze what they already know, and advanced organizers can assist students in relating new information to what they already know. SCs can incorporate these strategies by asking students early in a lesson about their understanding and experiences with a topic. For example, when teaching a lesson on assertive communication, an SC may ask students about their experiences in receiving or eliciting poor communication skills and what strategies they have developed for maintaining good relationships with peers and family members.

School Counseling Lesson Planning

Lesson Objectives

Instruction in the *ASCA National Model* (2019b), categorized as a direct student service, is one of the primary ways in which SCs and collaborators implement the school counseling

Table 5.2 Bloom's Taxonomy

| | The Cognitive Process Dimension | | | | | |
The Knowledge Dimension	Remember	Understand	Apply	Analyze	Evaluate	Create
Factual Knowledge	List	Summarize	Classify	Order	Rank	Combine
Conceptual Knowledge	Describe	Interpret	Experiment	Explain	Assess	Plan
Procedural Knowledge	Tabulate	Predict	Calculate	Differentiate	Conclude	Compose
Meta-Cognitive Knowledge	Appropriate Use	Execute	Construct	Achieve	Action	Actualize

Reprinted with permission: http://oregonstate.edu/instruct/coursedev/models/id/taxonomy/#table Designer/Developer. Dianna Fisher.

program. Classroom lessons should be designed to reflect the mission and vision of the school counseling program and meet the program's annual student outcome goals. As discussed in Chapter 4, the school counseling program is developed by identifying student needs through an analysis of student data. SCs use the classroom and group ASCA Student Standards action plan template to identify the knowledge, attitudes, and skills, informed by the ASCA Student Standards, that will be taught to students. ASCA's (2019b) lesson plan template provides structure for the lesson (see Table 5.1 for an example of a lesson using ASCA's lesson plan template).

The importance of SCs using standards-based instruction is highlighted by the fact that the first component of the ASCA lesson plan template requires the practitioner to identify one to three ASCA Student Standards that are contained in the lesson. The second component of the ASCA lesson plan template requires that the objectives of the lesson plan are stated in clear, measurable terms, and ASCA (2019b) recommends the use of Bloom's taxonomy (Krathwohl, 2002) in writing measurable learning objectives. The revised Bloom's taxonomy is comprised of a two-dimensional table, with one dimension identifying the knowledge that will be learned, and the other dimension identifying the cognitive process used to learn (see Table 5.2; Krathwohl, 2002). The objectives should be designed in accordance with what the SC wants the students to know and be able to do and the behaviors that will be demonstrated following the implementation of the unit.

The following hypothetical example demonstrates SCs' use of creating measurable learning objectives using Bloom's taxonomy (Krathwohl, 2002). In analyzing discipline data and follow-up surveys with teachers and students, the members of the advisory council of Jane Doe Middle School concluded that the high rate of disciplinary referrals was related to students' lack of proactive conflict-resolution skills. The advisory council created the annual student outcome goal of reducing the percentage of discipline referrals for verbal aggression by 25%. The SCs elected to conduct a three-lesson unit for fifth-grade students on conflict resolution which included material from the *Second Step* curriculum (Committee for Children, 2011). For the lesson concerning assertiveness, one of the objectives of the Second Step curriculum is that "students will be able to identify passive, aggressive, and assertiveness responses" (p. 32). This objective is fairly measurable, but its measurability can be enhanced by more specifically including the assessment within the language of the objective, such as, "At least 80% of the students will be able to correctly identify whether forms of communication exhibited in three multiple-choice questions presenting realistic social scenarios represent passive, aggressive, or assertiveness responses."

Evidence Base for School Counseling Lessons

The ASCA lesson plan template includes an evidence base section consisting of a continuum between best practice and evidence-based (Sparks, personal communication) with action research and research-informed existing within the continuum. SCs are encouraged to employ evidence-based activities, but given that an evidence base often does not exist, SCs can use other aspects of research to inform their work. Best practice may lack empirical support, but it is selected by the SC in lesson planning because it is an accepted practice within the profession. *Program evaluation* can be considered an equivalent term for *action research*, as the intent of the practitioner is to determine the impact of the activity upon the students with whom they are working, and the practitioner is not seeking to generalize the findings to other students or settings. ASCA's recommendation that SCs examine pre- and posttest data to identify the impact of school counseling lessons can be considered a form of action research. Such action research is particularly relevant when an SC creates the curriculum, which remains commonplace given that there is a dearth of empirical studies on topics for which SCs conduct lessons and because schools will not provide funding for SCs to purchase empirically supported curriculums. *Research-informed* generally refers to procedures or techniques for which there is research evidence. For example, for this section of the ASCA lesson plan template, SCs could list instructional strategies that Marzano (2007) identified as having empirical support. Finally, the term *evidence-based* means that the intervention in its entirety has empirical support, meaning, that studies have demonstrated that they have a positive impact upon various groups of students and settings and have been successfully implemented by different persons. SCs may find it comforting to know that SCs' use of classroom instruction, regardless of which specific curriculum is in use, has been revealed to yield a statistically significant and small to moderate impact on students, with some evidence suggesting that school counseling lessons produced a larger effect than did individual and group counseling and crisis response (Whiston et al., 2011).

Meta-analytic studies generally have found that SEL programs promote small to moderate positive outcomes (Moy et al., 2018). However, the increased emphasis on accountability within the education profession has created an environment in which the expectation is that educators are expected, if possible, to provide evidence that the specific curriculum which they are using has empirical support. If the data indicate a need for a prevention or intervention strategy that would best be delivered through the school counseling curriculum, the SC should first review the research literature to determine if there exists an evidence-based program for the topic.

SCs may use a variety of sources for identifying evidence-based school counseling lessons. Dimmitt et al. (2019) identify tier one interventions that are considered evidence-based (see Table 5.3). The websites of the Center for School Counseling Outcome Research (CSCORE), What Works Clearinghouse (WWC), and the Substance Abuse and Mental Health Services Administration (SAMSHA) list school-based programs that they have identified as having empirical support. ASCA (n.d.) maintains the School Counseling Analysis, Leadership and Evaluation (SCALE), in which members of ASCA can access for free curriculum, small-group, and closing-the-gap results reports. These reports can be considered best practice, in that they have been implemented by SCs and include evaluation

Table 5.3 Dimmitt et al.'s (2019) Tier One Evidence-Based Interventions

Program Name/Grade Level	Topic	Website for More Information
4Rs (K–6)	Social/Emotional Integrated with Language Arts	www.morningsidecenter.org
Bully Busters	Bullying Prevention	www.researchpress.com/books/455/bully-busters
Career Academies	Career Development	www.ncacinc.com
Caring for School Community (K–6)	Social/Emotional	www.devstu.org
Grad Nation (HS)	Dropout Prevention	http://ies.ed.gov/ncee/wwc/Practice Guide.aspx?sid=11
I Can Problem-Solve (Pre-K–5)	Problem-Solving	www.researchpress.com/product/item/4628
Life Skills Training (3–10)	Substance Use Prevention	www.lifeskillstraining.com
Lion Quest (K–12)	Substance Use and Violence Prevention	www.lions-quest.org/
Michigan Model for Health Education (K–12)	Social Responsibility and Substance Use Prevention	www.michiganmodelforhealth.org/
Navigation 101 (6–12)	Career Development	www.k12.wa.us/Secondary Education/careerCollegeReadiness/Default.aspx
Olweus Bullying Prevention Program (K–9)	Bullying Prevention	www.violencepreventionworks.org/public/index.page
Peacebuilders (K–12)	Conflict Resolution/Bullying and Violence Prevention	www.peacebuilders.com
Positive Action (K–12)	Social/Emotional	www.positiveaction.net/
Promoting Alternative Thinking Strategies (Pre-K–6)	Social/Emotional	www.channing-bete.com/paths
Resolving Conflicts Creatively (Pre-K–8)	Conflict Resolution	https://casel.org/guideprogramsresolving-conflict-creatively-program-rccp/
Responsive Classroom (K–6)	Social Responsibility	www.responsiveclassroom.org
School-Wide Positive Behavioral Interventions and Supports (K–12)	Positive Student Behavior	www.pbis.org
Second Step (Prek-K–8)	Violence Prevention	www.secondstep.org
Social Decision-Making/Problem-Solving Program (K–5)	Social Responsibility	http://ubhc.rutgers.edu/sdm/index.html
Steps to Respect (K–6)	Bullying Prevention	https://youth.gov/content/steps-respect%C2%AE
Student Success Skills (4–9)	Academic, Social, and Self-Management Skills	studentsuccessskills.com
Too Good for Drugs (K–12)	Prevention Education through Social/Emotional Learning	www.toogoodprograms.org/
Too Good for Violence (K–12)	Prevention Education through Social/Emotional Learning	www.toogoodprograms.org/

data, but would not be considered evidence-based, given that generally they have not been evaluated using rigorous research methods, such as use of random assignment and inferential statistics.

Data Collection Plan

The ASCA lesson plan template requires that SCs collect participation data, ASCA Student Standards data, and outcome data. *Participation data* simply refers to the number of participants who received the service, and with the case of a lesson, this means the number of students who received the lesson. The ASCA lesson plan template encourages SCs to collect pre- and posttest data to measure the lessons' impact upon the selected ASCA Student Standards (2021). While many of the published curriculums include methods for assessing the lesson, or unit, these assessment questions would not directly correspond to *the* ASCA Student Standards (2021), and thus, SCs would likely need to develop additional assessment methods to determine the impact of the intervention on the selected ASCA Student Standards. For students grades K–3, a visual format of assessment is recommended in which the item responses include a smiley face, a neutral face, and a frowning face (LaFountain & Garner, 1998). Multiple-choice and open-ended questions can be used with older children (Perusse et al., 2018). One of the objectives for Second Step curriculum for fifth grade (Committee for Children, 2011) is that "[s]tudents will be able to identify social situations" (p. 32), which corresponds to the ASCA Student Standard "effective collaboration and cooperation skills" (B-SS 6.). For a lesson in which a school counselor taught students how the components of Covey's (2014) habit of seeking to understand, a relative multiple-choice question would be, "Which of the following is NOT one of the important parts in seeking to understand another's perspective? (a) Making eye contact with the person, (b) repeating back in your own words what you hear the person saying, (c) seeking to identify the emotion which underlies the person's message, (d) ensuring that they first understand how you see the situation." Or an open question to assess students' understanding would be, "What are the three parts of Covey's seeking to understand?" Web-based platforms such as Google Classroom have greatly expedited the process of data collection. In addition to electronically delivered pre- and postassessments, SCs can assess the impact of a lesson or unit using the following methods: a round, asking each student to respond to a particular question or asking each student to say something new he or she learned; a brief written response to a question as an exit ticket from the classroom; a board blitz, in which students come to the board and write the answers to the questions; a gallery tour, where all the work done by the students is presented around the room; role-plays demonstrating the skills learned; journaling; and classroom student presentations (Williams et al., 2008).

The ASCA lesson plan template also requires that SCs identify a form of outcome data that measures the impact of the lesson upon students' achievement, attendance, or discipline. Outcome data is considered the most valid form of data, and the form of data that is most likely to impress stakeholders, as it is based on measurable behaviors and includes an external criterion. In returning to the previous example of the school counseling curriculum for Jane Doe Middle School which included a three-lesson unit for fifth-grade students on conflict resolution, the data collection plan for outcome data could be the following: "The rate of fifth-grade students' suspensions for verbal and physical aggression will decrease by 25% in comparison to rates for last year's fifth-grade students."

Box 5.3 Suggested Proposal Planning Format

1) Identify the local and national data that indicate the need for intervention.
2) Review and document the research literature that identifies effective interventions.
3) Crosswalk and align the ASCA Student Standards (2021) with the educational course in which this intervention might be presented.
4) Develop overarching unit goals and objectives.
5) Identify the baseline data that will be used in the lesson's/unit's effectiveness.
6) Present the proposal to the necessary stakeholders, advisory council, administrators, and teachers for approval.

The activities for the lesson should be thoroughly developed since students will often sense an ill-prepared endeavor. Thorough development of the activities also assists more novice SCs to manage their understandable anxiety about presenting to a class. SCs may develop a script to organize their thinking and approach to the lesson, but they should avoid reading from a script, as this may suggest to students that the school counselor is anxious and may result in off-task behaviors. When developing step-by-step delivery of the lesson, consider the small details. Planning of the simple details can make or break a lesson; even how the SC assigns students to groups should be considered beforehand. SCs who have not decided upon how they will group students may find that the most disruptive students wind up in the same group. Be creative and unpredictable in the pairing or grouping, introductions, and assessments. An example of pairing up students might be lining up students according to their birthday in one straight line and taking the first six students into one group. Another aspect of the lesson delivery is the arrangement of the room. SCs must consider the type of arrangement that would work best for the respective activity, the time necessary to arrange the room in the preferred manner, and should also obtain the approval of the classroom teacher to make such arrangements.

Differentiation

Differentiation is the intentional planning for effective SC lessons that incorporate students' cognitive strengths and challenges (Tomlinson & Imbeau, 2012). Cultural diversity, English proficiency, economic backgrounds, and individual students' learning challenges must all be factored into an effective classroom instruction, thus the need for differentiated instruction (Akos et al., 2007; Tomlinson & Imbeau, 2012). By the way, learning style, or what is also referred to as modality preference, is generally no longer considered an important construct in education as there is considerable research to suggest that teaching to different learning styles has no impact on student achievement (e.g., Lodge et al., 2016). Differentiation is a pedagogical philosophy that promotes a focus on the educational needs of the individual student (Tomlinson & Imbeau, 2012).

> Differentiation is an instructional approach and does not dictate curricula. . . . The primary goal of differentiation . . . is to help teachers develop and use multiple pathways for students to learn whatever they teach, including content standards.
>
> (Tomlinson & Imbeau, 2012, p. 2)

Akos et al. (2007) suggest that the basic tenets of differentiation are to focus on addressing the learning needs of all students using a variety of learning strategies. These tenets of differentiation are remarkably similar to the core beliefs of the school counseling profession. Differentiated school counseling lessons operate within the belief that the variety of interests, learning profiles, and readiness levels of the learners must be addressed for a more equitable and effective delivery of the information. When developing school counseling curriculum lessons, one strategy for the SC to employ is classroom observation prior to the lesson, in order to assess the learning readiness and needs of the students. The differentiated strategies for school counseling lessons are factored into the lesson planning.

Intervention practices that are associated with positive effects upon learning include direct instruction, learning strategy instruction, and the use of a sequential, simultaneous, structured multisensory approach (Learning Disabilities Association of America, n.d.). In using such interventions, some strategies that SCs may find to be useful in developing classroom lessons include repetition of information; chunking information into smaller amounts; frequent probes to assess learning; timely, meaningful feedback; the use of pictorial representations of information (e.g., graphics and diagrams); well-designed, intensive independent practice; modeling and prompting; and the use of process questions, such as, "Is this strategy helpful? Where else might you be able to use it?" (Learning Disabilities Association of America, n.d.).

An overall approach that seems to be effective with diverse learners is the use of scaffolding. The SC can begin a lesson using explicit instruction, in which he or she is extensively directing the course and pace of instruction and gradually encouraging students to acquire the skill, increasingly approaching the goal of student-mediated instruction (Learning Disabilities Association of America, n.d.). As students become more comfortable with the learning concepts, the SC can urge students to become more independent and self-directed in their learning. An example of this may be in teaching students to use study skills to improve their performance on assessments of their learning. The SC can begin by explicitly teaching mnemonic strategies in memorizing. After the students have understood the principle being used, they can be encouraged to develop mnemonics for other hard-to-remember facts, such as the capital of each of the 50 states or the periodic table of elements.

Culturally Responsive Teaching and Standards Blending

The ASCA Standards for School Counselor Preparation Programs (ASCA, 2019a) require that SCs be prepared to use culturally responsive teaching (CRT) practices.

Gay (2018) identified five components of CRT: (1) developing a culturally diverse knowledge base, (2) incorporating culturally relevant content within classroom lessons, (3) cultural caring and establishing a learning community, (4) facilitating effective cross-cultural communications, and (5) infusing congruity in classroom instruction. While CRT has received much attention, the impact of CRT on student achievement is only beginning to emerge. Similarly, currently there is not much literature regarding how SCs incorporate CRT in their classroom instruction. One way that SCs may incorporate CRT in classroom instruction is through the use of standards blending.

Standards blending involves the integration of specific core academic standards with the ASCA Student Standards (2021) in a culturally competent manner (Schellenberg, 2008). Standards blending uses a student-centered approach in that it draws upon students' previous knowledge and encourages them to personalize the material. Students are provided opportunities to socially interact with their peers and teachers in small learning communities, where the respective material is examined and resolved. Schellenberg recommends that language arts and mathematics standards be the focus in standards blending, versus other core academic standards, because these academic areas serve as the foundation for other core academic areas. Examples of standards blending are provided in the following paragraphs.

Schellenberg (2008) provides an example of the use of standards blending in eighth-grade school counseling classroom lessons to address career development standards from the school counseling program's curriculum, the language arts curriculum's standard of interviewing techniques to acquire information, and the math standards of estimating, data analysis, and conjectures, and determining means. The school counseling curriculum standard regarded learning how to research different careers by gaining and interpreting information. Students also learned how to conduct informational interviews and explored how this form of information-gathering compared to techniques they had used in the past to obtain information. In order to demonstrate their knowledge, students conducted an informational interview (language arts competency) to engage in career exploration (school counseling competency). Each student constructed ten questions for their interview (language arts competency), and at least five of the questions had to include proportions, such as scaling questions (math competency). Students role-played the interview with the school counselor and other students, recording the responses (language arts competency). Students had to use a table or graph to present the results of the scaled responses and identify patterns and similarities within their results and compare their results to their classmates' (math competency). The entire class discussed the inferences of their findings (math competency) and the effectiveness of the interviews (language arts competency) for career exploration (school counseling competency) and the usefulness of interviews for their personal, academic, and professional lives.

Schellenberg and Grothaus (2011) used standards blending while conducting a large-group intervention with four classes of diverse public high school students. Analysis of the school's outcome data revealed that a disproportionate number of students of color and students receiving special education services were not achieving success in language arts and were also not meeting positive behavioral expectations in career and technical education (CTE) classes. The CTE faculty and school counselor decided to implement a tier two response. The lead author conducted four one-hour, large-group lessons that sought to promote the students' employability skills and as well as selected language arts and school counseling curriculum standards. Use of paired sample t-tests revealed that the posttest scores were significantly higher than the scores for both the language and school counseling content areas. Black and Latin@ students made statistically significant gains in both content areas, while the students receiving special education services exhibited statistically significant gains for the school counseling curriculum items. Schellenberg and Grothaus (2009) applied standards blending to a school-based counseling group for six low-achieving third-grade Black males in an urban public elementary school. The "Me I Wanna Be" group sought to promote participants' self-esteem and identification of cultural strengths to empower the participants and thus facilitate their academic achievement. The group was comprised of four 30-minute sessions. Session 1 involved assigning students into pairs who interviewed each other and then presented a brief biography of their partner following a discussion of the characteristics of biographies and autobiographies (language arts competency). There was also discussion regarding the importance of friendship and positive relations. The objective of session 2 was to promote participants' sense of individualism while in connection with others. Participants spent 5–10 minutes talking to each other to acquire information regarding how each student is different and alike. Following the information gathering, students reflected upon the information obtained, comparing and contrasting themselves in relation to the other student, and reported their findings to the group. The goal of session 3 was to increase students' problem-solving skills. They were instructed to select one of three goals listed on the board to accomplish during the session. The goals were to (1) say something positive to a group member, (2) say something positive to the school counselor, and (3) ask someone for help during the session. Students were asked to select from a deck of cards, each of which had a goal on one side and the corresponding steps on the other side. They then took turns in sharing the goal and asking group members to identify possible steps to achieve the goal. The cards were preselected by the group leader to illustrate the mathematical concept of inverse operations (math competency). The goals of the final session were to teach students how to modify their internal dialogue to enhance their self-efficacy. This internal dialogue, or self-talk, was defined and modeled. The impact of positive vs. negative self-talk was discussed, and examples were indicated on 20 individual strips of paper. The strips of paper were described as consisting of a whole and then being divided in order to illustrate fractions (math competency). The results indicated that all six students exhibited knowledge development related to both the academic curriculum and the school counseling content, and the self-reported self-esteem of the participants increased by 72% from the beginning to the completion of the group.

Schellenberg (2008) argues that standards blending enables SCs to develop and implement programming which leads them to be viewed by educational personnel as valuable partners in closing the achievement gap and promoting academic achievement while simultaneously maintaining their unique role of an educational specialist who is also committed to promoting students' personal/social and career development. Schellenberg and Grothaus (2009) suggest that SCs can train teachers to use standards blending by incorporating students' cultural knowledge and strengths.

Classroom Management

It is not uncommon for SCs who enter the profession to report that they perceive older SCs to be resistant to implementing comprehensive, developmental programming. It is possible that SCs' reluctance to pursue the implementation of comprehensive, developmental programming is related to concern about using more preventive oriented delivery models, including classroom instruction. In other words, standing before a large group of students who may or may not be interested in what one has to say can be very anxiety-provoking. As mentioned previously, many SCs enter the profession with the expectation that their primary role will be to provide individual counseling to students, and many SCs seem a bit taken aback when it is suggested that providing instruction is a necessary part of delivering a comprehensive school counseling program. Research regarding preservice teachers consistently reveals that one of their biggest fears is classroom management (e.g., Matoti & Lekhu, 2016). It is likely that SCs have similar fears to preservice teachers about managing student behavior. Indeed, Goodman-Scott (2019) found that some SCs believe that SCs who lack previous teaching experience face a steep learning curve in managing student behavior.

Although there is extensive research regarding evidence-based classroom management strategies for teachers (e.g., Mitchell et al., 2017), some (e.g., Goodman-Scott, 2019) have argued that SCs' roles are distinct from teachers, and thus SCs may benefit from using a unique approach to classroom management. For example, SCs tend to refrain from applying punitive discipline, given that it may harm relationships with teachers (Buchanan et al., 2017). Some have recommended that SCs request that teachers assist in their delivery of classroom lessons so that teachers may discipline students if the need arises (Buchanan et al., 2017). Teachers' structuring of the physical space of the classroom is considered an important component of effective classroom management, which is not a luxury typically available to SCs, given that they conduct their lessons in their host teachers' rooms (Runyan et al., 2019). Likewise, SCs are not likely to be able to avail themselves of such instructional supports as guided notes, peer tutoring, and computer assistance, given that they are not consistently instructing the same set of students when conducting classroom lessons.

Goodman-Scott's (2019) study of practicing SCs revealed that they perceived the following to be effective classroom management strategies: (1) acting proactively, (2) engaging students, (3) implementing positive reinforcement, (4) using varied modalities, and (5) utilizing discipline. SCs act proactively by clearly explaining their behavioral expectations to students at the beginning of a lesson. According to SCs in the Goodman-Scott's (2019) study, student engagement is best achieved by making lessons interactive, using technology, and providing extra attention or tasks to students who tend to be disruptive. SCs often reported making use of positive reinforcement, praising students when they are on task, and some of the SCs used the school's formal behavioral modification framework. Using a variety of modalities to both communicate and engage students is perceived by SCs to be effective. Some of the SCs reported using both verbal behaviors, changing their vocal tone or pausing, and nonverbal behaviors, such as body language and eye contact, to indicate their expectations to students. Some SCs reported using physical proximity to prevent disruptive behavior and using activities that involved students in physical movement to enhance students' interest. In regards to discipline, SCs in Goodman-Scott's (2019) study appear to be divided. Some of the SCs recommend assigning consequences to students who disrupt the learning of other students, including removing students from the classroom, while others relied upon the classroom teacher to punish misbehaving students as they perceived punishment to be incompatible with the SC's role.

Goodman-Scott's (2019) study also identified several factors that influence SCs' classroom management. SCs reported that it is important for SCs to manage their personal characteristics when providing instruction, as SCs should seek to display calm, confidence, consistency, and genuineness. Knowing students was perceived by SCs to be an important aspect of classroom management. SCs recommended developing rapport with students by talking to students, often outside the classroom, about their interests, and by using humor and respect. For students exhibiting disruptive behavior, some SCs reported seeking to identify the potential motivations of the student, asking themselves if the student is being triggered or is confused. Many SCs find it helpful to follow the teacher's classroom management style and procedures and to model their approach to classroom management on those of teachers they perceived as effective.

Interestingly, the primary difference between successful and unsuccessful behavior managers is not the manner in which they handle discipline problems but instead in the number of discipline problems they encounter, with the successful managers creating a structured environment and managing behavioral antecedents to diminish the likelihood of behavior problems ever occurring (Elliott et al., 2002). In an effort to avoid potential behavior problems, one of the first considerations is developing procedures, which is essentially a way to accomplish an action. Each time you want to accomplish something, there should be a procedure or set of procedures to achieve it (Wong et al., 2018). For elementary SCs, this could be something like:

Box 5.4   Getting Ready for Our Counseling Corner

1)   Put away our books.
2)   Get out our counseling folders.
3)   Come to the carpet quietly.

Middle and high school counselors may also use procedures, but they should be tailored to the developmental levels of the students. An example might be a PowerPoint slide that precedes a counseling session:

Box 5.5   Procedures for Counseling Exercises

1)   If you are finished with your work, submit it to your teacher.
2)   On your laptop, go to the district's school counseling webpage.
3)   Log in and answer the warm-up question.

Wong and colleagues (2018) suggest that it is necessary for students to understand that classroom procedures are used to make their days flow more efficiently and peacefully. Procedures function as a way to eliminate confusion, establish a routine, and enable the students' focus to be on the work of the lesson. Students should practice these procedures until they demonstrate mastery.

In order to diminish the opportunity for talking and misbehavior that a transition point may imply, having students complete planned work, such as a warm-up activity, is often beneficial. The SC can post a question to ascertain students' prior knowledge or ask them to respond to a quotation about the topic that will be presented. For elementary school students, having them draw a picture that shows a particular behavior, for example, may maintain their interest and bridge the time between the previous instructional activity and the counseling session scheduled for the day. Similarly, ending the session with a routine wrap-up activity, such as, "This week, I am going to use _____ that I learned today," may reduce a tendency to become inattentive or disruptive as the class returns to their instructional activities (Wong et al., 2018).

Expectations for students should be communicated proactively, with active strategies used to help maintain student behaviors. These active strategies may include both nonverbal and verbal interventions. Nonverbal interventions include such techniques as planned ignoring, proximity control, and signal interference, while verbal intervention may include verbal redirection, contingent praise, and tension reduction. While these techniques are helpful in managing unwanted behavior, the most effective method of encouraging desired behavior is reinforcement. Reinforcement increases the probability that a behavior will be demonstrated, either through positive reinforcement, in which the behavior is followed by a preferred stimulus, or negative reinforcement, in which an adverse stimulus is removed after the desired behavior has occurred (Shepherd & Linn, 2015).

There are many suggestions that are offered in handling difficult behaviors (e.g., Dollarhide & Saginak, 2016; Guillaume, 2015; Williams et al., 2008). Through the use of various tools and strategies, the basic rules that may help the SC develop a respectful and productive classroom environment include:

1. Develop a respectful atmosphere with effective boundaries.

   Strategies: Include the class in developing the guidelines for the class behaviors; establish boundaries that are not so rigid students cannot have fun; respond effectively and immediately when derogatory names are used; set a precedent that you will discuss inappropriate behaviors away from the rest of the class so student's will not be embarrassed.

2. Provide engaging curriculum.

   Strategies: Utilize a variety of media that will appeal to the students, like songs, videos, YouTube clips; allow students to be active and participate through role-plays or acting out scenes; utilize a variety of teaching styles, not just "sit and get"; empower students to develop their own effective strategies; allow students to teach the topic.

3. Be creative with your lessons and your classroom management.

   Strategies: Not every behavior, unless it is disrespectful, requires a response; allow the class members to determine if they are ready to proceed with the activity; sometimes students can manage their peers more effectively than the teacher, especially if they really want to participate in the activity; front-load an activity to prepare students for the expected behaviors, i.e., "The topic we are discussing today requires a very mature audience. I will know you can handle this topic if I see these types of behaviors . . . ."

   (Guillaume, 2015; Williams et al., 2008)

Classroom Lesson Structure/Sequence

Beginning a Lesson

Walking into the classroom to tell students why they need to know this information will not promote enthusiasm or engagement from the students. An attention-grabbing introduction to the lesson or unit will be a valuable part of the first session. Students need to understand why this information is being presented and how it will be applicable to them. A creative introduction will help students engage in the lesson and minimize negative behaviors. Suggestions include using music the students listen to, a story that catches their attention, or a role-play that will be a model for students learning. An introduction to the sexual harassment unit might be: Why should students and faculty care about what sexual harassment is? After several answers, all of which may be correct, the SC can indicate that the main reason is that sexual harassment is illegal! Statistics and percentages of girls and boys that are sexually harassed daily will surprise the learners and encourage them to gain interest in the topic. This introduction can include a guessing game comparing the percentage of girls vs. boys of the respective age group who report having been sexually harassed. The real answers are often surprising and alarming to the students and promotes their interest in the topic.

After conducting an activity that captures students' attention, the objectives and agenda should be shared with the students. Listing the objectives of the lesson on the board or reciting them to the students reinforces the intent of the lesson and how it will be measured. Reviewing the agenda for the lesson helps students know what to prepare for and often reduces student anxiety. As Dollarhide and Saginak (2016) suggest, a description of what the lesson will entail also demonstrates respect for the learner. This informs the students so they can determine the amount of investment they commit to the lesson. Furthermore, obtaining student agreement prior to the lesson will likely enhance student attention and decrease disruptive behavior.

Lesson Activities

No matter the age of the students or audience, most learners do not appreciate long "sit and get" methods of teaching, and this type of instruction is not associated with student retention of information (Williams & Riedo, 2008). While lecture-style instruction may be time-efficient and easier for the presenter, it also encourages passive learning. A more interactive and inductive method of teaching engages the learner and allows for more self-discovery. People typically learn best by doing (Kovalik & Olsen, 2005) rather than being directly told the information. Experiential learning has a longer effect on information retention. The developmental skills of the learners are important to consider in lesson planning. Consider: Are the students developmentally capable of doing what is asked of them? Are the students capable of success with the selected activity? Time is another consideration. Is there enough time for the planned activities and for effective processing of the activities?

Debrief the Activity

The point of an activity is not in the doing of the activity but in the processing of what happened in the activity, the purpose of the activity, and the application to real life (Williams & Riedo, 2008). Such processing increases the likelihood that students will engage in transfer of learning, meaning, that they will develop the skills, attitudes, and/or behaviors that they can apply to real-world contexts. Be sure to carefully plan the debriefing questions in advance. This will help alleviate the spontaneous and distracting, on-the-fly questions that may not promote the objective of the activity.

Furthermore, readers are encouraged to follow the debriefing process outlined in the chapter on group counseling. There are three main types of debriefing questions. The WHAT questions ask about the immediate experience: What just happened? Additionally, the SO WHAT questions ask about the purpose of the activity: Why do you think we did this activity? Finally, the NOW WHAT questions are about application and tying the activity to the students' own lives: How does the learning you just had in this activity apply to your daily life? (Williams et al., 2008). Each question may elicit a number of responses.

Summary

The school counseling curriculum can have a powerful impact on students within the school system. Research indicates that not only is this type of school counseling programming an efficient delivery method, but when delivered effectively, it can also impact all three domains of the school counseling program: academic, career, and social/emotional. Collaborating with the teacher in whose class the school counseling curriculum lesson will be presented regarding the goals and objectives aids in the educational alliance. A thorough proposal for school counseling curriculum can help teachers understand the importance of the lessons and the scope and sequence of unit being developed. Aside from the curriculum used, one of the keys to effective school counseling lessons is how well it is delivered. It is important for school counselors to develop effective teaching strategies and to be able to deal with classroom management issues that may arise. With proper and intentional planning of the lessons and the pedagogy, school counseling lessons can be fun and informational for both the students and the school counselor while impacting the school climate in a positive way.

References

Akos, P., Cockman, C. R., & Strickland, C. A. (2007). Differentiating classroom guidance. *Professional School Counseling, 10*(5), 455–463. https://doi.org/10.1177/2156759X0701000502

American School Counselor Association. (2019a). *ASCA school counselor professional standards & competencies.* www.schoolcounselor.org/asca/media/asca/home/SCCompetencies.pdf

American School Counselor Association. (2019b). *The ASCA national model: A framework for for school counseling programs* (4th ed.). Author.

American School Counselor Association. (2021). *ASCA student standards: Mindsets & behaviors for student success.* Author.

American School Counselor Association. (n.d.). *What is SCALE?* https://scale-research.org/?category=Crisis%2FTrauma&year=&s=

Buchanan, D. K., Mynatt, B. S., & Woodside, M. (2017). Novice school counselors' experience in classroom management. *Journal of Counselor Preparation and Supervision, 9,* 33–62. https://doi.org/10.7729/91.1146

Committee for Children. (2011). *Second step: Skills for social and academic success: Grade 5.* Author.

Council for the Accreditation of Counseling and Related Educational Programs. (n.d.). *2016 CACREP standards.* www.cacrep.org/for-programs/2016-cacrep-standards/

Covey, S. (2014). *The 7 habits of highly effective teens.* Simon & Schuster.

Curhan, J. (1998). *Young negotiators student activity book.* Houghton Mifflin.

Dimmitt, C., Zyromski, B., & Griffith, C. (2019, March). *Identifying evidence-based school counseling interventions.* Evidence-Based School Counseling Conference.

Dollarhide, C. T., & Saginak, K. A. (2016). *Comprehensive school counseling programs: K-12 delivery systems in action* (3rd ed.). Pearson Education, Inc.

Elliott, S. N., Witt, J. C., Kratochwill, T. R., & Stoiber, K. C. (2002). Selecting and evaluating classroom interventions. In M. A. Shinn, H. M. Walker, & G. Stoner (Eds.), *Interventions for academic and behavior problems II: Preventive and remedial approaches* (pp. 243–294). National Association of School Psychologists.

Gay, G. (2018). *Culturally responsive teaching: Theory, research, and practice* (3rd ed.). Teachers College Press.

Goodman-Scott, E. (2019). Enhancing student learning by "building a caring climate": School counselors' experiences with classroom management. *Professional School Counseling, 22*(1), 1–12. https://doi.org/10.1177/2156759X19852618

Goodnough, G. E., Perusse, R., & Erford, B. T. (2007). Developmental classroom guidance. In B. T. (Ed.), *Transforming the school counseling profession* (2nd ed., pp. 142–165). Pearson Education.

Guillaume, A. M. (2015). *K-12 classroom teaching: A primer for new professionals* (5th ed.). Pearson Education Inc.

Kovalik, S. J., & Olsen, K. D. (2005). *Exceeding expectations: A user's guide to implementing brain research in the classroom* (3rd ed.). Author.

Krathwohl, D. R. (2002). A revision of Bloom's taxonomy: An overview. *Theory Into Practice, 41*(4), 212–218. https://doi.org/10.1207/s15430421tip4104_2

LaFountain, R. M., & Garner, N. E. (1998). *A school with solutions: Implementing a solution-focused/Adlerian-based comprehensive school counseling program.* American School Counselor Association.

Learning Disabilities Association of America. (n.d.). *Adult literacy, pre-k thru high school for educators.* Author. http://ldaamerica.org/successful-strategies-for-teaching-students-with-learning-disabilities/

Lodge, J. M., Hansen, L., & Cottrell, D. (2016). Modality preference and learning style theories: Rethinking the role of sensory modality in learning. *Learning: Research and Practice*, 2(1), 4–17. https://doi.org/10.1080/23735082.2015.1083115

Marzano, R. J. (2007). *The art and science of teaching: A comprehensive framework for effective instruction*. Association for Curriculum and Supervision Development.

Marzano, R. J. (2017). *The new art and science of teaching: More than fifty new strategies for academic success*. Association for Curriculum and Supervision Development.

Matoti, S. N., & Lekhu, M. A. (2016). Sources of anxiety among pre-service teachers on field field placement experience. *Journal of Psychology in Africa*, 26(3), 3–4–307. https://doi.org/10.1080/14330237.2016.1185921

Mitchell, B. S., Hirn, R. G., & Lewis, T. J. (2017). Enhancing effective classroom management in schools: Structures for changing teacher behavior. *Teacher Education and Special Education*, 40(2), 140–153. https://doi.org/10.1177/0888406417700961

Moy, G., Polanin, J. R., McPherson, C., & Phan, T. (2018). International adoption of the *Second Step program*: Moderating variables in treatment effects. *School Psychology International*, 39(4), 333–359. https://doi.org/10.1177/0143034318783339

Perusse, R., Parzych, J., & Erford, B. T. (2018). Implementing the developmental school counseling core curriculum in the classroom. In B. T. Erford's (Ed.), *Transforming the school counseling profession*. Pearson.

Runyan, H., Grothaus, T., & Michel, R. E. (2019). Classroom management competencies for school counselors: A Delphi study. *Professional School Counseling*, 22(1), 1–12. https://doi.org/10.1177/2156759X19834293

Schellenberg, R. (2008). *The new school counselor: Strategies for universal academic achievement*. Rowman & Littlefield Education.

Schellenberg, R., & Grothaus, T. (2009). Promoting cultural responsiveness and closing the academic achievement gap with standards blending. *Professional School Counseling*, 12(6), 440–449. https://doi.org/10.1177/2156759X0901200613

Schellenberg, R., & Grothaus, T. (2011). Using culturally competent responsive services to improve student achievement and behavior. *Professional School Counseling*, 14(3), 222–230. https://doi.org/10.1177/2156759X1101400306

Shepherd, T. L., & Linn, D. (2015). *Behavior and classroom management in the multicultural classroom: Proactive, active, and reactive strategies*. Sage.

Tomlinson, C. A., & Imbeau, M. B. (2012). Common sticking points about differentiation. *School Administrator*, 69(5), 18–22.

Whiston, S. C., Tai, W. L., Rahardja, D., & Eder, K. (2011). School counseling outcome: A meta-analytic examination of interventions. *Journal of Counseling & Development*, 89(1), 37–55. https://doi.org/10.1002/j.1556-6678.2011.tb00059.x

Williams, R. L., Lantz, A., & Noorulamin, S. (2008). *Making smart choices: Social and emotional skills for adolescent girls*. American School Counselor Association.

Williams, R. L., & Riedo, S. (2008). *A handbook for leading positive youth development programs*. Smart-Girl.

Wong, H. K., Wong, R. T., Jondahl, S. F., & Ferguson, O. F. (2018). *The classroom management book* (2nd ed.). Harry K. Wong Publications, Inc.

Chapter 6

Individual Counseling

Box 6.1 2016 Council for Accreditation of Counseling and Related Educational Programs (CACREP, n.d.) School Counseling Specialty Area Standards

3.d Interventions to promote academic development
3.f Techniques of personal/social counseling in school settings

---

Box 6.2 ASCA (2019a) Standards for School Counselor Preparation Programs (ASCA CAEP SPA)

2.2 Demonstrate strengths-based counseling and relationship-building skills to support student growth and promote equity and inclusion.
2.3 Describe established and emerging counseling theories and evidence-based techniques that are effective in a school setting, including but not limited to rational emotive behavior therapy, reality therapy, cognitive behavioral therapy, Adlerian, solution-focused brief counseling, person-centered counseling, and family systems.
3.2 Identify research-based individual counseling, group counseling, and classroom instruction techniques to promote academic achievement, college/career readiness, and social/emotional development for every student.
4.1 Plan, organize, and implement a variety of instructional and counseling strategies as part of a comprehensive school counseling program (direct and indirect student services) to improve pre-K–12 student attitudes, knowledge, and skills.
4.4 Demonstrate pedagogical skills, including culturally responsive classroom management strategies, lesson planning, and personalized instruction.

In the *ASCA National Model* (2019b), counseling an individual student, along with instruction, appraisal, advisement, and counseling students in groups, is categorized as a direct service. These services are steeped in the history of schools, where interventions were directed toward individual children who required support after showing distress. However, as the school counseling profession has moved away from the student services model, which focused more upon meeting the needs of at-risk students, and toward models that

DOI: 10.4324/9781003167730-6

emphasize impacting the entire student population through comprehensive programming, SCs have been encouraged to spend less time providing counseling to individual students.

This philosophical shift in the *ASCA National Model* has brought into focus a long-standing controversy within counselor education programs in which SCs often comprise a plurality of the student body, and yet the majority of the backgrounds of most of the faculty are clinical in nature. Such faculty may fail to demonstrate an understanding of the educational context in which services are delivered. As such, these faculty members tend to train SCs to function as mental health therapists who apply their skills in the school setting. However, the *ASCA National Model* states that counseling provided to individual students is short-term, and that when students require long-term counseling, SCs collaborate work with families and other professionals in making appropriate referrals.

Accordingly, this chapter will identify and describe theories, techniques, and frameworks that are relevant to SCs in providing individual, brief counseling within an educational context. It is essential to remember the primary mission of the school is promoting academic success—interventions that remove children from the classroom potentially interfere with this mission. SCs should attempt to minimize students' removal from the classroom by scheduling individual counseling sessions during less instructionally intensive times, such as during homeroom, study halls, elective classes, lunch periods, etc. Individual counseling conducted within school settings must be time limited. Individual sessions typically run from 10 to 30 minutes, and the amount of time is often dictated by the school's schedule. For example, when a student seeks to talk with the SC, the SC often seeks to attempt to assist the student with his or her issue, helping the student construct an approach to the issue, by the end of the period or before the next important school activity, such as an exam or the start of a lesson. Thus, the SC may only have 10 minutes to assist the student with the issue. As the SC listens to the student and gathers information about the issue, he or she must assess the time and number of sessions it may take to assist the student with his or her issue, or whether the student should be referred outside of the school. The SC seeks to instill a sense of empowerment in the student, providing the message that the student possesses the resources to address whatever issue he or she is presenting, and avoids implying that meeting with the school counselor again is essential for addressing the issue. However, if the student and SC agree to meet again, the SC should ask the student to identify times for future meetings which are less likely to interfere with the student's academics.

Another reason SCs must use brief approaches in individual counseling may not be an efficient use of time in comparison to the time spent in group counseling and classroom guidance. SCs who primarily use individual counseling are not likely to impact the entire student population and thus may not be regarded as valuable members of the school staff. The *National Model* states that students who require long-term therapy should be referred to relevant community resources.

Although SCs are encouraged by the *ASCA National Model* to provide individual counseling in a brief format, this does not diminish the importance of this service. Studies comparing brief counseling to long-term therapy have revealed no difference in effectiveness (e.g., Brown & Minami, 2010). Furthermore, while the *ASCA National Model* recommends that SCs refer students to community resources who require long-term therapy, only a small number of families follow through on an SC's referral for mental health services outside the school system. Thus, the brief counseling provided is often the only therapy the child will receive. In recognition of this, it is imperative that SCs seek to maximize their effectiveness in providing brief counseling.

Effectiveness of Individual Counseling with Children

Research literature regarding positive responses to counseling services shows that counseling is effective and results in fairly large benefits for both adults (e.g., Wampold, 2010) and children (Kelley et al., 2010). The research also seems to indicate that a variety of counseling theories/approaches are equally effective, and there are factors that are common to all counseling approaches which are responsible for facilitating positive outcomes; this is referred to as the common factors model. Lambert's (1992) analysis of the research literature indicated that client factors account for 40% of the change shown in response to the counseling provided. Client factors associated with change include their strengths, severity of the disturbance, capacity to relate to others, psychological mindedness, ability to identity particular goals, and motivation. An additional 30% of client outcome is predicted by client-counselor relationship factors, such as the ability to build and maintain rapport and effective communications; 15% of the client's outcome is accounted for by the client's hopefulness, meaning, their expectation that counseling will benefit him or her. Finally, 15% of client change is attributed to the specific counseling model or technique. In summary, research seems to indicate that SCs should primarily seek to develop a caring and genuine relationship with students as it is the factor under the control of the SC which has the strongest relationship to positive outcomes for students.

It is understood that in most programs students will complete a course on counseling theories and techniques. The intent of this chapter is to provide a review of several the counseling theories which are identified in the ASCA (2019a) standards for school counseling program as being particularly helpful in conducting counseling in a school setting, including person-centered therapy, reality therapy, solution-focused therapy, and cognitive behavioral therapy. Other counseling theories that are explicitly identified in ASCA

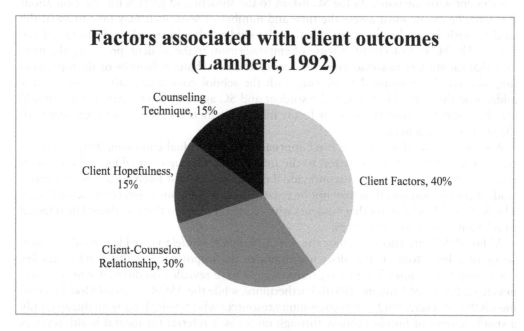

Figure 6.1 Factors associated with client outcomes. Adapted from Lambert, M. J. (1992). Implications of outcome research for psychotherapy integration.

Source: In J. C. Norcross & M. R. Goldfried (Eds.), *Handbook of psychotherapy integration* (pp. 94–129). Basic Books.

standards that are not covered in this chapter due to space limitations are rational emotive behavior therapy and Adlerian therapy.

Person-Centered Therapy

Nearly all counseling theories emphasize the need for counselors to establish a positive relationship with students. However, it can be argued that Rogers's person-centered therapy (Raskin et al., 2018) is the only major therapy that claims that the relationship is in itself necessary *and* sufficient for producing client growth and thus speaks most directly about the nature of the client-counselor relationship. Rogers believed that people are inherently oriented toward growth but become maladjusted when they deny or distort aspects of their experience. People often deny experiences in order to maintain an ideal image of themselves. For example, men and boys are often fearful of appearing weak and thus may deny or distort negative feelings as sadness, hurt, rejection, etc. that they believe imply vulnerability and weakness to others. The incongruence enables the male to maintain the ideal image, but at the cost of failing to symbolize or integrate aspects of his experience, eventually leading to more significant maladjustment.

Box 6.3

Did You Know?

Carl Rogers committed the latter part of his life to applying his theories to national social conflict and political oppression, working in Northern Ireland, South Africa, Brazil, and the Soviet Union (Raskin et al., 2018).

The person-centered counselor facilitates a caring, democratic, nonjudgmental, nondirective environment that enables the student to become more fully aware of various aspects of his or her experience, thus activating the student's innate tendency toward growth. Within this theoretical framework, the role of the counselor can be likened to that of a facilitator who provides the conditions for change rather than being responsible for directing the client's change. The conditions that the counselor provides are congruence, unconditional positive regard, and empathic understanding of the client's internal frame of reference. The counselor himself or herself must be congruent, meaning, that he or she can assimilate and integrate various aspects of his or her own experience. In other words, the counselor should be psychologically mature, self-aware, and open and accepting of himself or herself and others.

Box 6.4

Person-centered therapy—popularized by Carl Rogers and theorizes that the client-counselor relationship is both necessary *and* sufficient for producing client growth (Raskin et al., 2018).

Also, the counselor must demonstrate an unconditional positive regard for the student, accepting without judging the student's thoughts, feelings, motivations, etc. Accepting the student without judgment is meant to enable the student to identify and integrate aspects of his or her experience that he or she has been denying or distorting. Students often enter counseling through the urging of parents, teachers, and administrators who want the student to change in some fashion, and in the beginning of the relationship with the counselor, students often repeatedly defend their views and positions. However, the nonjudgmental position of the counselor often enables students to eventually examine aspects of themselves heretofore they have been unwilling to consider. Some SCs may struggle to accept aspects of students, parents, or teachers which they consider abhorrent and problematic. A perspective that is often helpful when viewing persons counselors are seeking to assist is recognizing that in the vast majority of situations, people have good intentions and are doing what they know how to do. Problematic behaviors often do make sense from their point of view.

Box 6.5

Necessary Aspects of Person-Centered Therapy (Raskin et al., 2018)

- Counselor must be *congruent* and assimilate various aspects of their own experience.
- Counselor must demonstrate *unconditional positive regard* toward the student.
- Counselor must demonstrate *empathetic understanding* of the client's internal frame of reference.

The last condition the SC is responsible for providing is empathic understanding of the client's frame of reference. The counselor seeks to enter and understand the worldview of the student at a deep level, paraphrasing the student's implied thoughts, feelings, goals, and values, which is referred to as advanced empathy. By paraphrasing the student's implicit communications, the student gains self-awareness, as he or she is presented with his or her thoughts and feelings with which he or she is struggling to better understand and assimilate. The establishment of these conditions helps students and clients develop an expanded view of themselves, clarify their goals and values, and enhance confidence in their decision-making.

Research literature clearly demonstrates the importance of the client-counselor relationship, and SCs may wish to consider using Rogers's person-centered therapy as the foundation for their work with students. Indeed, strengthening positive adult-child relationships is the hallmark of good work in the school context. However, there are some myths about why an SC may object to using person-centered therapy; each of these is considered below.

Some assert that SCs provide counseling rather than therapy, and as a result, the SCs' use of a theoretical orientation may be regarded as "therapy." This argument can be rejected on several grounds. First, the distinction between "counseling" and "therapy" is not clear. For some, the distinction between the two appears to be in terms of the length, but as discussed earlier, the length of the relationship does not necessarily appear to be a predictor of effectiveness. Although counseling theories do not appear to be substantially different in terms of their effectiveness, it can be argued that the failure to base one's work in a counseling therapy increases the likelihood that the SC will impose his or her values and thus increase the probability of causing harm. SCs are particularly vulnerable to imposing values on others because rules governing a child's behavior are implied within the school context; unchecked advice-giving about behavior expectations can devolve into dogmatic judgments. SCs often find a balance by avoiding the use of terms and language with parents and administrators that imply they are providing "therapy." Instead, SCs describe their counseling work as an "approach" or "framework" in order to capture the benefits of counseling but also remain less intrusive.

Another common criticism of person-centered therapy is its lack of effectiveness with less abstract and expressive students, but later in this chapter, we discuss how school counselors should select counseling theories that are consistent with the student's developmental level. As such, this criticism is not unique to a person-centered approach. A related criticism of person-centered therapy suggests the nondirective stance is not well-suited for the brief time available within schools. Although the person-centered school counselor assumes a nondirective stance with students, since he or she believes in the capability of the student to generate his or her own solutions, this does not mean that the SC cannot be structured in his or her approach. In the following section, we describe how the person-centered approach, and other counseling theories for that matter, can be integrated with Ivey et al.'s (2017) five stages of the well-formed interview to produce an approach that fosters students' own problem-solving while, at the same time, providing a framework that assists the students in progressing through a structured problem-solving sequence.

Basic Listening Sequence

Ivey et al.'s (2017) stages of the well-formed interview, or the basic listening sequence (BSL), provides SCs with a logical, sequential framework where they can use active listening skills to guide students through the process of problem-solving. It is particularly relevant for early concrete operational and formal operational students who have, or are at the beginning of acquiring, the capacity for their own sequential reasoning. SCs using the well-formed interview stages assist students in exploring their thoughts and feelings but do so in a focused, purposeful manner so that the exploration is related to a particular goal or outcome. This structured focus is particularly relevant to the brief nature of individual counseling conducted with a school context.

Box 6.6

Basic listening sequence—a logical, sequential framework that counselors can use to guide students through the process of problem-solving.

The basic listening skills can be integrated with any counseling therapy.

Relationship Stage

In the first stage of the BSL, the primary functions are to establish a positive relationship and explain the process of counseling (Ivey et al., 2017). Children vary considerably in the amount of time needed for counselors to establish trust, which is necessary for students to share thoughts and feelings. Younger children and children who are not self-referred are often reluctant to self-disclose. SCs can increase students' comfort by explaining the counseling process. Children often are not familiar with counseling and may require explanation, in language that is at their level, about the purpose of counseling and what is expected of the school and the student. The following summary from the counselor may be helpful:

> Students often talk with me when they are having big feelings, such as when they are angry, upset, or confused, or if they have a goal in mind, like getting better grades or making more friends. I help students better understand their thoughts and feelings, their goals, and together we can help you develop a plan to achieve your goals.

For children who are not self-referred, a somewhat common mistake for beginning SCs is to fail to discuss why the SC is meeting with the child. That is, SCs sometimes assume the child is aware of the adults' concerns about the child's behavior or academic progress. In situations when a child is meeting with the SC at the urging of an adult, it is best for the SC to obtain the permission of the adult to share, in general terms, why the adult encouraged the child to meet with the SC. Honest and direct communications are likely to decrease the child's suspicions and defensiveness, thus helping to develop the child's trust. In such a situation, the SC might say, "Your dad called because he was concerned about your grades and he thought I might be able to help."

The SC can also increase the child's comfort by first engaging in safe activities or discussing issues that are not emotionally charged. For example, after explaining the process of counseling, the SC might say, "I know we only met at the beginning of the school year, and I was hoping to get to know you a little better. What do you like to do when you are not here in school?" Other safe activities include games like Jenga and Connect Four, playing with stress balls, shooting baskets, coloring, etc. Activities that facilitate child-counselor interactions are especially helpful. That is, watching the child color is less engaging than coloring together. Counselors can use the child's preferences as the basis for selecting safe activities.

Story and Strengths Stage

In this stage, the primary functions are to gather data, by exploring the student's perspective, thoughts, feelings, and strengths/resources. During this stage, the SC is particularly nondirective and should mainly use open-ended questions, paraphrases, or reflection of feelings as the student shares his or her perspective on the issue that led him or her to seek counseling or led an adult to encourage the student to seek counseling. The SC seeks to understand both the student's explicit statements and also the student's implied thoughts, feelings, meanings, motivations, and solutions, which when reflected back to the student may help him or her develop a deeper understanding of his or her perspective of the situation. Person-centered therapy believes in the student's ability to generate his or her own solutions, and often during this stage, the student will imply solutions for his or her situation, depending upon how he or she discusses an issue. For example, a student who is unhappy with a recent grade in a class may talk about how he or she does not like the teacher, which some may regard as the student disowning responsibility. Although that may be the case, it may also imply that he or she views their relationship with the teacher as part of the problem, and thus possibly as part of the solution.

Goals Stage

In this stage, the SC formally clarifies the student's goal. After collecting data in the story and strengths stage, the SC should summarize the student's perspective and then ask the student, "We've been talking for a while. Let me ask you, what do you want in this situation?" It is a mistake for the SC to assume that he or she knows the student's goal, as often the exploration that occurred in the story and strengths stage has helped to clarify and thus slightly change the student's goal. The SC can follow up this initial question with an exploration of the student's vision of the goal, meaning, what the student thinks he or she may gain by accomplishing the described goal. The SC can encourage the student to define the goal in specific terms, asking, "So what specifically are the types of grades you want to have by the end of the marking period?"

Restory Stage

The primary function of this stage may be seen as developing solutions or perspective that may assist with achievement of his or her goal. The SC can maintain a nondirective stance by exploring the student's ideas for achieving his or her goals. For example, the SC might say, "You mentioned that you have thought about talking with your friend about your belief that she spread a rumor about you, but you also said that you are not sure if you want to do this."

This example reflects another function of this interview stage, which is to explore the student's incongruities or dilemma. In this example, the student's dilemma is that on one hand, she wants to talk with her friend, but on the other hand, she is reluctant to do so. Often, students have generated options, but they are concerned about carrying out an option, and the active listening provided by the SC enables the student to examine his or her concerns about the various options, which often helps them with decision-making. For situations that involve the potential of communicating with someone else, whether it be a peer, teacher, or parent, the SC can help the student examine what he or she believes is the other person's perspective. This process may help the student develop insight regarding his or her contribution to the situation and how to explore how the other person might respond if the student was to approach him or her.

During this stage, the SC can also highlight strengths or resources that the student mentioned or implied in a previous stage which may be relevant to the student's achievement of his or her goal. Solution-focused therapy, which will later be discussed in greater detail, uses the techniques of exception-seeking to explore times when the goal in question has been realized or when the problem does not exist. For example, the student might be asked to explore when he or she has been successful at earning good grades, motivating himself or herself to do something that he or she did not want to do, or managing conflict with a peer or adult, managing his or her emotions, etc., with which the SC follows up by exploring how the skills or techniques that enabled him or her to achieve past success can be modified or used in the current situation.

Action Stage

In the last stage, the SC helps the student transfer the information discussed, gained, or clarified in the previous stages by exploring what the student plans to do with the information. The emphasis is on helping the student develop a concrete plan of action to implement. Given that SCs are typically limited to only several meetings with a student, the SC wants the student to leave even a first session with a specific plan of action. In order to increase the likelihood the student will engage in transfer of learning, the SC should examine with the student the what, who, when, where, and how of their plan. For example, for a student who has decided that he wants to increase the amount of time he studies for a subject, the SC can help him consider how much time he will spend studying, what he will focus upon, where he studies best, and who might assist him in realizing his plan. For situations in which the student is leaning toward communicating with another person, the SC might suggest that they role-play the potential interaction. The SC can end the individual meeting by summarizing the student's intended plan, asking the child if he or she would like to meet again and if the student would like the SC to ask the student when they next encounter each other how the plan worked out.

Box 6.7

Stages of the Basic Listening Sequence (Ivey et al., 2017)

- *Relationship stage.* Building trust and explaining expectations.
- *Story and strengths stage.* Exploring the student's thoughts, feelings, and strengths/resources.
- *Goal stage.* Clarification of student goals.
- *Restory stage.* Development of solutions or perspectives that may help the student achieve their goal.
- *Action stage.* Helping the student transfer previously discussed information or strategies into concrete action steps.

Developmental Approach to Individual Counseling

One of the most challenging aspects of providing counseling to children is that they vary widely in terms of their socioemotional and cognitive development. A number of counseling developmental theorists, such as D'Andrea (1988), assert that counseling theories vary in their applicability to the developmental stages and that the task of the counselor is to identify the child's developmental level and apply the counseling therapy that is relevant to the student's level of cognitive complexity. These counseling developmental theories are based on Jean Piaget's cognitive developmental theory, which asserts that there are specific cognitive tools or "operations" associated with each stage of cognitive development. According to D'Andrea (1988), counseling theories vary in the degree to which they match the cognitive complexity of the various stages of development of the child.

Cognitive Developmental Stages

At the preoperational level, in which children are typically in between infancy and 7 years of age, children are learning to use symbols such as words and images to understand how the world operates, and they tend to express themselves in terms of physiological sensations and actions and often talk in a random and disorganized fashion (Ivey et al., 2017). At this developmental level, the child lacks control of his or her thoughts, feelings, and impulses because he or she lacks the ability to reflect upon the source of the psychological phenomena.

Children usually function within the concrete operational stage between the ages of 7 and 11. The advantage of concrete operations is that the child can reason logically—in contrast to the preoperational child, who tends to base their logic on appearance (e.g., concrete, observable events) and thus fails to consider cause and effect or sequential transformations. Children within this developmental stage tend to focus upon linear, sequential details regarding social interactions and events, and they struggle to understand the perspective of others and how their actions may have contributed to events. In other words, the child is learning to think in a sequential, logical manner but is not yet able to do so.

Children may acquire the capacity for formal operational thinking around the age of 11. Formal operational thinkers are capable of deductive reasoning, enabling them to examine various solutions and options, understand abstract concepts such as justice, democracy, love, etc., and identify behavioral patterns and reflect upon their meaning. They are able to "think about their thinking."

Individual Counseling With Preoperational Children

Because of preoperational children's limited capacity for self-awareness, SCs can use behavior therapy to teach the child specific behavioral skills, through the use of modeling, practice/role-playing, and either tangible or verbal reinforcement. There are a limitless number of behavioral skills that SCs may teach children, and the child's specific needs can be determined through the use of observation and consultation with the children's teachers and parents. Commonly taught behavioral skills include anger management, conflict resolution, anxiety management, social skills, attending, organization, etc. Such behavioral skills can also be taught within the context of structured play approaches, in which the SC acts out through puppets, stuffed animals, etc. the various components of a behavioral skill. SCs help children use games they play during recess for the skills they need in the classroom. For example, games like red light/green light and Simon Says are particularly useful in teaching children listening skills, physiological control, and how these skill sets are coordinated. Both games teach children what to listen for (i.e., green light) and how to act when you do hear the cue compared to when you do not. Classrooms that use visual prompts (green, yellow, and red lights) to prompt behavioral expectations and control can capitalize on the similarities of these games. Teachers that reinforce attentive listening through games (e.g., staying in your seat, lining up when asked) are especially effective. Researchers have shown that teaching children behavioral self-regulation also improves academic readiness skills (Tominey & McClelland, 2011).

Counseling children at this developmental level should also include a psychoeducational component such that the SC can help the child begin to develop the language to identify and express his or her thoughts, feelings, and physiological sensations. With this knowledge comes the understanding that such development will, in the future, increase the child's capacity to reflect upon and manage these psychological phenomena. It is useful, for example, to help children begin to differentiate between thoughts, feelings, and behavior. An SC could ask the child, "Tell me three happy thoughts." Here, counselors are helping children find positive associations. Once this is mastered, an SC may ask, "Tell me three things you did that worked out well," which helps promote a focus upon cause and effect. In developmental order, the SC wants to help children distinguish between thoughts and feelings and then move to how the child can effect outcomes through actions. SCs may point out, "Because you studied, you got a good grade," "Because you showed good effort, your teacher was happy with your project," "Because you listened to your classmate, she said you were a good friend."

However, many children at this age may not understand the extent to which behavioral outcomes are under their control. Accordingly, the next task is to ask the same questions about others: "Tell me something that worked out well for someone else," and then, "Tell me what they did to make it work out well." With these basic questions, the SC can help children understand cause and effect and whose actions led to the outcome. This is a critical skill, because young children often confuse the cause and effect of their problems (e.g., "My parents are divorcing

---

Box 6.8

Development-Related Goals of Counseling with *Preoperational* Children (D'Andrea, 1988)

- Improve language skills related to thoughts, feelings, and physiological sensations.
- Differentiate between thoughts, feelings, and behavior.
- Help foster cause-and-effect thinking and understanding of child's own thoughts and feelings.
- Help foster cause-and-effect thinking and understanding of others' thoughts and feelings.

---

because I didn't clean my room"). Furthermore, we want students to appropriately connect their efforts with their outcomes; otherwise, it is difficult for them to detect how they might be able to influence the outcomes they desire.

Individual Counseling With Concrete Operational Children

Students in the concrete operational stage are beginning to understand logical sequences but are not yet ready for hypothetical thinking or inferences. They do understand an object can be round and green and small, but will miss more complex logic; if the bird is bigger than the cat and the cat is bigger than the dog, then the dog, by definition, is also smaller than the bird. Concrete operational children are most likely to benefit from counseling that assist such children in expanding their thinking in a logical, sequential manner, which includes reality therapy, solution-focused therapy, certain techniques of behavioral therapy, and structured cognitive therapy approaches, such as those developed by Kendall (2011).

Reality Therapy

Choice theory, a major tenet of reality therapy, asserts that the brain functions like a thermostat, in that it regulates behavior in order to change the environment to meet our five basic needs, which are belonging, power, freedom, fun, and survival (Wubbolding, 2010). Reality therapy includes a psychoeducational aspect, in that students can be taught about these basic needs and be helped in determining which of their needs are

---

Box 6.9

Reality therapy—counseling technique that teaches students how to recognize which of their basic needs are currently met and which should to be pursued (Wubbolding, 2010).

currently satisfied and which of their needs they wish to pursue. Students are taught the WDEP system, in which *W* stands for "wants," *D* is concerned with "direction and doing," *E* regards "evaluation," and *P* is for "planning." The WDEP system is essentially a method of problem-solving, and students can be taught these steps using WDEP as a mnemonic device.

Box 6.10

Did You Know?

William Glasser, the founder of reality therapy and choice theory, was a psychiatrist. However, many psychiatrists considered Dr. Glasser's theories to be controversial, as Dr. Glasser was very critical of modern psychiatry and what he considered to be an excessive emphasis on diagnosis and use of psychotropic medications, particularly for children (Wubbolding, 2010).

First, the SC helps a student identify their wants by accessing their "quality world," which consists of the student's ideals. An SC helps the student generate or describe his or her quality world through guided imagery, exploring an ideal day, or a situation in which the student would feel a sense of pride. Helpful questions include, "If you could wave a magic wand and get whatever you want, what it would be?" or "When have you gotten part of what you wanted?" Upon identifying the student's desires or wants, the school counselor can help the student identify what he or she believes would be the advantages of achieving his or her goal, which often leads to further exploration of their priorities. The SC can use a scaling question to have the student rate his or her level of commitment to achieving the goal, posing the following type of question: "On a scale of 1–10, with 10 being the thing you want the most and 1 being not that important, how important is it for you to increase your grades to at least all Cs?"

Assessing the student's level of commitment enhances the student's self-awareness and helps the SC understand the degree to which a topic should be focused upon in the counseling session. Next, the SC has the student identify his or her "doings," meaning, the various thoughts and behaviors related to the issue. The SC can use an element of brainstorming during this phase, in which he or she can have the student write down his or her thoughts and behaviors about his or her goals/wants or have the student generate a list of his or her daily activities that will ultimately be compared to how he or she relates to a desired goal.

In the next phase, the SC has the student *evaluate* the degree to which he or she thinks the various behaviors and thoughts he or she identified are either "helping" or "hindering" the process of achieving his or her goal, which enables the student to identify which behaviors and thoughts he or she wants to increase or decrease or eliminate altogether. The SC should refrain from providing advice, regardless of the immaturity of the student's ideas, but should perceive his or her role as facilitating the student's problem-solving.

For example, it is not uncommon for male students to first identify violence as an option for achieving their goal, and the SC should refrain from immediately rejecting this option but should instead assist them in exploring the potential consequences of using aggression. In this manner, the SC hopes to help the student learn to "think through the consequences of his or her actions." It is tempting to tell the child what to do; however, people are more likely to engage in options which they have generated, and the objective of this process is to help the child learn the process of problem-solving rather than solving a particular problem/issue in a manner preferred by the adult. Usually, students have thought about various aspects of the problem/goal, and if the SC is patient, often the student will share the variety of options he or she has generated and his or her preferences for various perspectives about the problem/goal. The task of the SC then becomes helping the student sort through the potential positive and negative consequences of his or her various ideas.

During the *planning* phase, the SC assists the student in organizing his or her goals and ideas identified through brainstorming to develop a plan for achieving the goal. The SC can teach the student about the characteristics of effective planning through the SAMIC[3] acronym: (s)imple, (a)ttainable, (m)easurable, (i)mmediate, (c)ontrolled, (c)omitted, and (c)onsistent. Subsequent meetings with the student involve reviewing the student's implementation of his or her plan, or lack thereof. Lack of progress may be due to lack of commitment on the student's part, to which the SC can respond by exploring the student's ambivalence, identifying other goals that the student would be more interested in pursuing, or exploring the potential consequence of not making progress.

For example, if the student is receiving pressure from teachers or parents to improve his or her performance, the SC may help the student guess how his or her parents or teachers might respond to his or her lack of progress, and then the student can consider his or her willingness to accept the consequences. Lack of progress may also indicate that the student's goal is unrealistic. For example, some students, without explicitly saying so, want to be popular, but that student's level of status may be very resistant to change; the school counselor may lead the student to redefine the goal of popularity as developing a friend or making the effort to connect with others while focusing less on whether others actually respond. Finally, a common reason for lack of progress is related to an inadequate or underdeveloped plan; in this case, the SC should use the same WDEP phases to help the child revise his or her plan.

Box 6.11

Phases of Reality Therapy (Wubbolding, 2010)

(W)ants
(D)irection and Doing
(E)valuation
(P)lanning

Reality Therapy Case Study. Reality therapy was used with Brandy, an African American, seventh-grade student who sought out the SC after receiving detention from her math teacher, Mr. Johnson, for what Mr. Johnson identified as her "poor attitude." Brandy was angry with Mr. Johnson, explaining that she did not think he was an effective teacher as it was her perception that he used a lot of worksheets, did not respond adequately to students' questions, and seemed to favor certain students in the class. Previously, the SC had developed a good relationship with Brandy as he had helped her resolve a conflict through mediation with one of her cousins who was also in seventh grade. The SC's perspective was that Brandy had a number of strong leadership characteristics in that she could be very assertive and compassionate, but some of the seventh-grade teachers, including Mr. Johnson, appeared to regard Brandy as verbally aggressive.

After using active listening skills to identify Brandy's thoughts and feelings, the school counselor asked Brandy what she was hoping to get out of the situation. Brandy indicated that she wanted to be removed from Mr. Johnson's class, but the SC explained that the administration did not permit such schedule changes two months into the school year. Brandy expressed anger that she could not change her math teacher, but eventually Brandy identified her goal of improving her math grade, as she knew her mother would be unhappy if she received another "C" in math for the next marking period.

Next, the SC assisted Brandy in identifying her various thoughts and behaviors related to her performance in her math class and evaluating whether they were helping or hindering her in achieving her goal. Through this exploration, Brandy indicated that she was engaging in a number of behaviors that were not helping her, including choosing to sit in the back of the math class with a friend with whom she often talked while she was supposed to be working on worksheets, and not asking Mr. Johnson for help because she did not like him. The SC and Brandy also identified her strengths/assets for achieving her goal, which included her independence and outspokenness. The SC provided two reframes, stating that maybe Brandy's challenge was to learn to use her strength of outspokenness in a way that Mr. Johnson could hear, and to learn to work with someone she did not like, which unfortunately is part of getting older, and these reframes appeared to resonate with Brandy.

With Brandy's consent, the SC and Brandy proceeded to role-play how to approach Mr. Johnson for help, with Brandy playing herself and the SC playing Mr. Johnson. Following the role-play, the SC asked Brandy to evaluate her performance, and the SC provided his feedback as well, commending her on the polite way she approached the pretend Mr. Johnson. Several weeks later, when questioned in the hallway by the SC, Brandy indicated that she had developed a better relationship with Mr. Johnson and that her scores on recent quizzes had improved.

Solution-Focused Therapy

Solution-focused therapy can be effectively applied with both concrete and formal operational children. Solution-focused therapy is widely used by SCs for both counseling and consultation, as it is designed to be brief and it emphasizes students' strengths. Solution-focused therapy is similar to person-centered therapy in that it assumes that people are growth-oriented and proactive self-healers (Murphy, 2015). A basic tenet of solution-focused therapy is, people have their own resources to achieve their goals, and these resources lie within their personal histories. Solution-focused therapy is influenced by the theory of social constructivism, which asserts that people actively construct their reality, as opposed to an objective reality, through the use of language. The primary task of the SC is to expand a student's perception of a problem or issue, which the SC accomplishes by encouraging the student to change the way he or she talks about the problem or himself or herself.

> **Box 6.12**
> **Solution-focused theory**—a commonly used tactic for counseling and consultation that focuses on students' strengths and resources that can be used to achieve goals, and on refocusing students toward solutions rather than problems (Murphy, 2015).

Box 6.13

Did You Know?

Insoo Kim Berg and Steve de Shazer, two of the leading pioneers of solution-focused therapy, were married and died within two years of each other. Berg was from Korea and was originally a pharmacist, while de Shazer originally trained as a classical musician (Taylor, 2005).

Students often enter counseling with what solution-focused therapists refer to as a "problem-saturated perspective." According to Taylor (2005), people often begin a counseling relationship with a focus on what they do not want, when things go wrong, aspects of the situation they cannot change, when they have not been successful in addressing the issue, and when they are pessimistic about the future. The task of the counselor is to shift the conversation and the student's language to discuss what the student wants, explore times when he or she has been successful, or at least partially successful, and aspects of the situation that the student can change.

Similar to person-centered therapy, the SC initially seeks to understand the student's worldview, listening intently to the student, looking to emphasize or reinforce the student's communications that imply positive possibilities. The SC eventually uses a number of questions or techniques that are designed to help shift the student's perspective (Murphy, 2015). Exception-seeking questions involve asking the student to identify times when he or she has been successful in dealing with the respective issue. For example, the SC may ask the student to describe a time when he or she believed he or she had effectively managed anger, resolved a conflict with a peer or adult, was assertive, completed homework, performed well on a test, etc. Exception-seeking questions are followed up with "not-knowing questions," in which the SC helps the student minutely analyze the things he or she did to be successful, exploring the specific thoughts, behaviors, steps, motivations, etc. he or she used.

Scaling questions involve having the student rate his or her success regarding an issue. For example, the SC might ask, "On a scale of 1–10, with 10 being managing your anger extremely well and 1 being not handling your anger well at all, what number would you currently give yourself in managing your anger?" Students typically respond with a rating of anywhere from 3 to 7, and regardless of the number the student identifies, the SC explores with the student what he or she did positively to get to a 3, once again, minutely analyzing the various thoughts and behaviors that helped him or her achieve that positive number. This is followed by asking the student what he or she would be doing when he or she is at the next number or half-numbered step. This question helps the student see the small things he or she needs to do in order to make progress, rather than overly focusing on the large, often-unrealistic goal of fully achieving the goal. Scaling questions can also be used to explore times when the student believes he or she had a higher rate of success.

In the miracle question, the SC instructs the student to imagine that the problem has been resolved overnight, then has the student explore as concretely as possible how things would be different, asking the student to identify how he or she would feel, think, behave, what he or she would do during that day, what he or she would do next, and what friends, parents, and teachers would notice about him or her. The miracle question helps the student move beyond a problem-saturated perspective, which may help the student see himself or herself and the situation in a different light and may generate new thoughts, feelings, and ideas that are helpful for making progress.

Box 6.14

Types of Questions Used During Solution-Focused Theory Sessions (Murphy, 2015)

- *Exception seeking*. Student identifies a time when problem was handled effectively.
- *Scaling*. Student labels his or her level of skill or distress on a 1–10 scale, which can lead to discussions of how to move higher along the scale.
- *Miracle*. Student describes how his or her life would be different if the problem were to vanish overnight.

Cognitive Behavioral Therapy

The structured cognitive-behavioral approach used by Kendall (2011) highlights the connections between the body's responses to anxiety-provoking situations and how the student's thinking about those feelings can increase or decrease their ability to cope.

Box 6.15

Cognitive-behavioral theory (Beck & Weishaar, 2018)—focuses on connections between the body's responses and the student's thinking while using skill training and practice sessions to help improve student coping.

Kendall's approach has two primary segments; the first is a focus on skills training, and the second focuses on skills practice. During skills training, a counselor reviews the body's anxiety reactions (e.g., heart racing, quick breathing, sweating, skin turning red and feeling hot, feeling sick to your stomach, tightness around your rib cage, fearfulness, etc.), including those experienced by most people, those the student reports, and those the SC has had. The message here is that it is normal for the body to respond to anxiety-provoking situations and it is important to notice your own patterns. The SC should highlight that physical feelings are cues from the body to let us know that we need to help our body relax. Catching on to the cues early can help us mange our feelings before they escalate.

In the skill practice section, SCs begin by helping students identify their own fears and expectations about a specific situation. Identifying the student's self-talk (e.g., what he or she says to himself or herself) about the situation and his or her own reactions allows the student to modify his or her expectations. Next, the SC helps the student problem-solve about which attitudes or actions would be more effective. Finally, the student should evaluate if his or her efforts have been effective in helping them cope and feel better. If so, he or she should reward his or her own success.

The FEAR plan is used to counsel students exhibiting anxiety. *F* stands for "Feeling frightened?" and is to remind students to be aware of their physical feelings of anxiety. *E* stands for "Expecting bad things to happen?" and asks students to recognize their own self-talk. *A* stands for "Attitudes and actions?" reminding students to use previously identified behaviors and self-talk that will manage or decrease feeling of anxiety. *R* stands for "Results and rewards?" reminding students to consider the usefulness of their response to anxious feelings and to reward themselves for success.

Kendall and his colleagues are credited with establishing the effectiveness of manualized treatment—a treatment plan used in a predetermined order—for children and adolescents reporting feelings of anxiety. His work, the Coping Cat Program, is widely used and routinely updated (Kendall, 2011). Students reporting relatively minor disruptions, as well as those identified with clinical disturbances, have shown improvement after participating in the Coping Cat Program. SCs are on safe ground identifying this program as an evidence-based practice when required to do so in their school districts.

Individual Counseling With Formal Operational Children

During formal operational thought, students can make decisions based on prior experiences and think logically about abstract concepts. Not only can students recognize patterns in their own behaviors, but they also can identify causality between their emotions and behaviors. As reviewed in the preceding passages, there can be some crossover in working with concrete operational and formal operational students. However, once formal operations are well established, person-centered and structured cognitive behavioral approaches that are frequently used with adults are useful. Primarily, the difference between those approaches, when used with students who are now in the formal operational stage, is the degree of emphasis on individual choice and insight. That is, as students age, free choice and responsibility are highlighted, whereas psychoeducational information-sharing is emphasized for students in the concrete operational stages. As students age, it is expected that the sources of their distress (e.g., insight) become more apparent to them and thus are available for student-driven efforts.

Person-Centered Therapy

Person-centered therapy can be considered to be the preferred approach in working with formal operational adolescents, as such youths have the capacity for problem-solving and developing complex understandings of their self-concept, values, and patterns regarding how they relate to others. The role of the SC using this approach is that of a facilitator, who helps the student enhance their meaning-making by providing them with a safe environment in which to explore their various thoughts and feelings and to enhance the clarity of their perspective.

Person-Centered Therapy Case Study. Jodi, a 15-year-old, ninth-grade student, sought assistance from the SC, reporting that she was experiencing difficulty "controlling [her] emotions." Jodi explained that she often would "tear up" in class, meaning, that she would begin to cry for no apparent reason.

Jodi moved back to the school district in the middle of her eighth-grade year. She had attended elementary school in the district but moved in fifth grade to another state when her parents separated and her mother married a man Jodi believes her mother had been having an affair with for several years. Jodi reported that her mother's new husband sexually abused her on several occasions. Jodi reported that when she informed her mother of the abuse, her mother became "depressed" and felt betrayed. Jodi's mother initiated steps to separate from Jodi's stepfather, but her mother ultimately decided that it would be best for Jodi to return to live with her father. Jodi reported that she had not seen her mother or her older sister for over a year and that her mother did not seem very interested when they talked sporadically on the phone. Jodi's mother sought counseling for Jodi, but Jodi stopped attending when she resisted the SC's suggestion that she attempt to re-experience the sexual abuse in order to reduce her emotional intensity connected to the event.

Jodi reported being fearful and angry with her father. Her dad allegedly had been quite physically punitive with her when she was younger, and he had been investigated by Child Protective Services. She did not want to return to live with her dad and tried to keep her distance from him. Jodi also had "crying spells" at home, to which her dad would become agitated, telling her that she needed to get over it. She also saw her dad as dictatorial and controlling and that much of their interactions involved him telling her that she needed to assume more responsibility for cleaning the home, doing dishes, etc.

Jodi had frequent altercations with other girls, often leading her to being referred to the SCs for mediation or to the principal's office. During such a mediation, the SC observed that Jodi would be quite verbally aggressive, telling other girls that they had better shut up or she would make them.

Jodi began dating a boy named Mike, who was a junior at the school she attended, shortly after she returned to live with her dad. She described their relationship as chaotic in that they frequently verbally argued and she worried that either he or she would eventually escalate the argument to physical aggression. She saw Mike as controlling in that he did not want her to spend time with her group of friends. She considered breaking up with Mike and did for a short time when he confirmed that he had slept with another girl, as she feared losing her independence.

Jodi was unsure about her goals for the future. In eighth grade, she received an overall score of 110 on a group intelligence test. She received mostly Bs and Cs in her academic subjects and was not taking any advanced academic classes. She had not given much thought to a career or post–high school plans.

The SC used a nondirective approach in counseling Jodi, meeting with her once a week for six weeks. By reflecting Jodi's implicit thoughts and feelings, the SC helped Jodi identify important themes in her worldview and patterns in her life. The SC affirmed Jodi's ambivalent feelings about her mother and stepfather, as well as her anger regarding her mother's apparent decision to select Jodi's stepfather by sending Jodi to live with her father. The SC helped Jodi recognize how her relationships with her parents influenced her current relationships. For example, Jodi offered that her tendency to become angry quickly with both female and male peers was related to a high level of anger for the past years of her life, and the SC and Jodi explored what she regarded as positive mechanisms for managing her feelings. Jodi gradually expressed ambivalence about her relationship with her boyfriend and men in general in that she longed for closeness and yet was terrified by it as well.

The SC helped Jodi recognize that her current conflicted feelings were normal and were also related to her past. Eventually, the SC helped Jodi explore her anxiety about relating to her father in a more mature way, and Jodi reported some success in developing a closer relationship with her father. The SC assumed a slightly more directive approach by asking Jodi about her goals for the future. The SC helped Jodi identify her personal strengths and how they could apply to the world of work. Jodi appeared to engage in more serious explorations of who she was and what she wanted for herself.

Cognitive Behavioral Therapy

As cognition becomes well-developed in the formal operational stage, cognitive behavioral therapy (CBT) emphasizes the freedom of the individual to accept or revise their views about themselves, other people, and the world (Beck & Weishaar, 2018). The assumption is that problematic thinking precedes and results in problematic emotions or behaviors; by changing one's thinking—or one's perceptions of the problematic thinking—a person will change his or her feelings and/or behaviors. Counselors help people examine the validity of their conclusions, helping persons devise experiments to determine the accuracy of their beliefs. For example, for a student who is experiencing anxiety, counselors using exposure and response prevention (ERP) (Abramowitz et al., 2019), which is a form of CBT, might instruct a student to engage in behaviors they have been avoiding, such as speaking in class. Meta-analytic studies have revealed that exposure-based CBT is the most empirically supported counseling approach for anxiety (Carpenter et al., 2018) and that it is effective with youth (Hoffman et al., 2012). The student would be taught that, in the case of anxiety, avoidance and common safety behaviors (e.g., deep breathing, reassurance seeking) are negatively reinforced as they provide temporary relief, confirming the person's conclusion that the respective situation is unsafe and can only be managed either through avoidance and safety behaviors (Abramowitz et al., 2019). However, the avoidance and safety-seeking behaviors do not allow the person to examine whether the respective situation results in their feared outcomes and whether their anxiety is intolerable. Counselors encourage clients to expose themselves to the situations that invoke anxiety, while refraining from the use safety behaviors, to determine whether their feared outcomes occur and the degree of discomfort that they experience. In vivo or live exposures are preferable, but imaginal exposures may be used for situations where it would be difficult or impossible to expose oneself to. For example, for an adolescent who believes that their parent will die if the adolescent leaves the house, through imaginal exposure, the adolescent would practice imagining the worst-case scenario, their parents' death, in vivid detail, for ten minutes a day, helping the adolescent learn that such unwanted intrusive images, while uncomfortable, are tolerable and are more likely to dissipate when the adolescent no longer seeks to eradicate the image or engages in safety behaviors to neutralize the image. Counselors teach persons that such unwanted intrusive images are very common but tolerable and that seeking to avoid or eliminate such unwanted intrusive images are often counterproductive, as it typically results in endless rumination. In summary, persons learn through ERP that they can function and even enjoy themselves when having uncomfortable thoughts, images, and feelings.

Box. 6.16

Did You Know?

Aaron Beck (Beck & Weishaar, 2018), the founder of cognitive therapy, was originally trained as a Freudian psychoanalyst.

Effectiveness of Counseling Therapies

There is strong support for the efficacy of CBT, including for children with anxiety disorders (Hoffman et al., 2012). While there has not been nearly as much research regarding person-centered therapy as there has been for CBT, there is considerable evidence that many of the principles of person-centered therapy, including therapeutic alliance (e.g., Wampold & Imel, 2015) and empathy (e.g., Laska et al., 2014), contribute to positive counseling outcomes. Gingerich and Peterson (2013) concluded from a review of 43 controlled studies that there is empirical support for using solution-focused therapy for children experiencing academic and behavioral problems, depression, couples and families, and with criminal behavior of adolescents. The limited number of controlled studies of reality therapy has mostly involved school settings, indicating that reality therapy yields a moderate and practical benefit (Radtke et al., 1997).

Summary

SCs are not likely to provide long-term individual counseling to students. Students and families requiring long-term clinical care are likely to receive those services through other professionals in the building (e.g., social workers or school psychologists), or they will be referred to community-based facilities. However, SCs do need to have clinical skills. SCs are called upon to help school teams understand and promote behavioral change so that students may benefit from their educational environment and advance in their academic skills. Short-term counseling is routinely required for students in crisis, in acute distress (e.g., peer rejection), and to promote stalled or uneven social-emotional development. Understanding the usefulness of specific therapies and being able to apply those therapies with appropriate age groups to facilitate academic and social-emotional development is a critical skill for SCs.

References

Abramowitz, J. S., Deacon, B. J., & Whiteside, S. P. H. (2019). *Exposure therapy for anxiety: Principles and practice* (2nd ed.). Guilford Press.

American School Counselor Association. (2019a). *ASCA standards for school counselor preparation programs.* Author. www.schoolcounselor.org/getmedia/573d7c2c-1622-4d25-a5ac-ac74d2e614ca/ASCA-Standards-for-School-Counselor-Preparation-Programs.pdf

American School Counselor Association. (2019b). *The ASCA national model: A framework for school counseling programs* (4th ed.). Author.

Beck, A. T., & Weishaar, M. E. (2018). Cognitive therapy. In D. Wedding & R. J. Corsini (Eds.), *Current psychotherapies* (11th ed., pp. 237–272). Cengage.

Brown, G. S., & Minami, T. (2010). Outcomes management, reimbursement, and the future of psychotherapy. In B. L. Duncan, S. D. Miller, B. E. Wampold, & M. A. Hubble (Eds.), *The heart and soul of change: Delivering what works in therapy* (2nd ed., pp. 267–297). American Psychological Association.

Carpenter, J. K., Andrews, L. A., Witcraft, S. M., Powers, M. B., Smits, J. A., & Hoffman, S. G. (2018). Cognitive-behavioral therapy for anxiety and related disorders: A meta-analysis of randomized placebo-controlled trials. *Depression and Anxiety, 35*(6), 502–514. https://doi.org/10.1002/da.22728

Council for the Accreditation of Counseling and Related Educational Programs. (n.d.). *2016 CACREP standards.* www.cacrep.org/for-programs/2016-cacrep-standards/

D'Andrea, M. (1988). The counselor as pacer: A model for the revitalization of the counseling profession. In R. Hayes & R. Aubrey (Eds.), *New directions for counseling and development* (pp. 22–44). Love Publishing.

Gingerich, W. J., & Peterson, L. T. (2013). Effectiveness of solution-focused brief therapy: A systematic qualitative review of controlled outcome studies. *Research on Social Work Practice, 23*(3), 266–283. https://doi.org/10.1177/1049731512470859

Hoffman, S. G., Asnaani, A., Vonk, I. J. J., Sawyer, A. T., & Fang, M. A. (2012). The efficacy of cognitive behavior therapy: A review of meta-analyses. *Cognitive Therapy and Research, 36*(5), 427–440. https://doi.org/10.1007/s10608-012-9476-1

Ivey, A. E., Ivey, M. B., & Zalaquett, C. P. (2017). *Intentional interviewing and counseling: Facilitating client development in a multicultural society* (9th ed.). Cengage Learning.

Kelley, S. D., Bickman, L., & Norwood, E. (2010). Evidence-based treatments and common factors in youth psychotherapy. In B. L. Duncan, S. D. Miller, B. E. Wampold, & M. A. Hubble (Eds.), *The heart and soul of change: Delivering what works in therapy* (2nd ed., pp. 325–355). American Psychological Association.

Kendall, P. C. (Ed.). (2011). *Child and adolescent therapy: Cognitive-behavioral procedures* (4th ed.). Guilford Press.

Lambert, M. J. (1992). Implications of outcome research for psychotherapy integration. In J. C. Norcross & M. R. Goldfried (Eds.), *Handbook of psychotherapy integration* (pp. 94–129). Basic Books.

Laska, K. M., Gurman, A. S., & Wampold, B. E. (2014). Expanding the lens of evidence-based practice in psychotherapy: A common factors perspective. *Psychotherapy, 51*, 467–381.

Murphy, J. J. (2015). *Solution-focused counseling in schools* (3rd ed.). American Counseling Association.

Radtke, L., Sapp, M., & Farrell, W. C. (1997). Reality therapy: A meta-analysis. *Journal of Reality Therapy, 17*(1), 4–9.

Raskin, N. J., Rogers, C. R., & Witty, M. C. (2018). Client-centered therapy. In D. Wedding & R. J. Corsini (Eds.), *Current psychotherapies* (11th ed., pp. 101–156). Cengage.

Taylor, L. (2005). A thumbnail map for solution-focused brief therapy. *Journal of Family Psychotherapy, 16*(1–2), 27–33. https://doi.org/10.1300/J085v16n01_07

Tominey, S. L., & McClelland, M. M. (2011). Red light, purple light: Findings from a randomized trial using circle time games to improve behavioral self-regulation in preschool. *Early Education & Development, 22*(3), 489–519. https://doi.org/10.1080/10409289.2011.574258

Wampold, B. E. (2010). The research evidence for the common factors models: A historically situated perspective. In B. L. Duncan, S. D. Miller, B. E. Wampold, & M. A. Hubble (Eds.), *The heart and soul of change: Delivering what works in therapy* (2nd ed., pp. 49–70). American Psychological Association.

Wampold, B. E., & Imel, Z. E. (2015). *The great psychotherapy debate: The evidence for what makes psychotherapy work* (2nd ed.). Routledge.

Wubbolding, R. E. (2010). *Reality therapy: Theories of psychotherapy.* American Psychological Association.

Group Counseling

Box 7.1 2016 CACREP (n.d.) School Counseling Specialty Area Standards

3.c Core curriculum design, lesson plan development, classroom management strategies, and differentiated instructional strategies.

3.d Interventions to promote academic development.

3.f Techniques of personal/social counseling in school settings.

3.l Techniques to foster collaboration and teamwork within schools.

3.m Strategies for implementing and coordinating peer intervention programs.

Box 7.2 ASCA (2019a) Standards for School Counselor Preparation Programs (ASCA CAEP SPA)

2.1 Describe established and emerging counseling and educational methods, including but not limited to child and adolescent development, learning theories, behavior modification and classroom management, social justice, multiculturalism, group counseling, college/career readiness, and crisis response.

2.2 Demonstrate strengths-based counseling and relationship-building skills to support student growth and promote equity and inclusion.

3.2 Identify research-based individual counseling, group counseling, and classroom instruction techniques to promote academic achievement, college/career readiness, and social/emotional development for every student.

3.3 Identify research-based individual counseling, group counseling, and classroom instruction techniques to promote academic achievement, college/career readiness, and social/emotional development for every student.

4.1 Plan, organize, and implement a variety of instructional and counseling strategies as part of a comprehensive school counseling program (direct and indirect student services) to improve pre-K–12 student attitudes, knowledge, and skills.

4.4 Demonstrate pedagogical skills, including culturally responsive classroom management strategies, lesson planning, and personalized instruction.

DOI: 10.4324/9781003167730-7

Meeting the needs of students drives SCs' work and vision. SCs use group counseling interventions to promote students' academic, career, and social/emotional development through the application of developmentally based approaches. This chapter will explore the SC's role of group facilitator and discuss some of the relevant issues for conducting group counseling in the school setting. The availability of groups for students in schools is crucial to their overall development and has been an integral part of the *ASCA School Counselor Professional Standards and Competencies* (2019b). Providing students with the opportunity to come together and learn about themselves and others allows space to address the ASCA Student Standards (2021) as well.

Small-group instruction, which typically involves a group of up to ten students, is classified as a direct student service within the *ASCA National Model* (2019c). Groups address the three broad developmental domains of the *ASCA National Model*: academic, career, and social/emotional. Examples include:

- *Academic Development Groups.* Issues addressed include, but are not limited to, time management, study skills, test-taking strategies, and institutional transition issues (middle to high school, high school to college).
- *Career Development Groups.* Issues addressed include goal-setting and decision-making, transitioning into postsecondary life, exploration of options, financial literacy, and college planning.
- *Social/Emotional Groups.* Issues addressed include, but are not limited to, grief and loss, fears and anxiety, building healthy friendships, self-esteem, dealing with relational aggression, dating relationships, sexual identity, personal empowerment, accepting a newborn sibling, or dealing with divorce or separation from parents (incarceration, hospitalization, etc.).

Figure 7.1 Group counseling session.

Source: Copyright www.istockphoto.com/.

Group counseling is regarded as an effective form of service delivery for SCs for a variety of reasons (Bruce et al., 2009). Group works is time-efficient as it enables SCs to provide services to more than one student at a time. From a developmental and pedagogical perspective, students often learn best from each other (due to shared feelings and experiences). Groups provide an excellent forum for students to experience this student-to-student learning process (mentoring, supporting, understanding, empathizing). Groups are a microcosm of society and, as such, provide real-life settings in which students can work out issues and problems.

Box 7.3   Important Questions in Creating School-Based Counseling Groups

Answering these questions might prove helpful in establishing an effective group program:

- Why is this group relevant to students?
- Who is this group meant to serve (ages, grade level, issues addressed, and number of students)?
- Will this be a homogeneous or heterogeneous group, based on what criteria?
- How will you recruit members?
- How will you screen for appropriate fit of members for the group?
- How often will the group meet, and for what period of time (6 weeks, 12 weeks, etc.)?
- What will be the location of the group meeting?
- What will be the structure of the group meetings?
- How will you evaluate the groups' effectiveness?

Ethical Considerations Regarding Groups

There are several ethical concerns to be considered when establishing small-group counseling into the program. These ethical concerns encompass group participant screening, informed consent for students and parents, confidentiality, school counselor group facilitation competency, and cultural awareness in the group setting. All these topics are explicitly addressed in the *ASCA Ethical Standards for School Counselors* (2022). Section A.7 of the 2022 *Ethical Standards for School Counselors* directly discusses group work in the school setting, which is markedly different from group work conducted in a clinical setting. SCS are required to "take precautions to protect members from harm as a result of interactions with the group" (A.7.i). This necessary precaution considers students in conflict or students with severe behavioral problems. While these issues may interfere with the progression of the group, the biggest ethical concern is that they may also cause damage to individual group members. Questions to consider in the screening process might include: Does this student work well in groups? Are they capable of understanding the material covered? Do the direction, intention, and goals of this group work for this student? Not all students necessarily benefit from the small-group process, as their social skills may not be up for the challenges of group dynamics. This screening is also an opportunity to evaluate whether the individual student's needs may be effectively addressed through the group process. The success and effectiveness of the group can be sabotaged by lack of screening.

At the time of the screening process, the informed consent can be presented for the potential participants. Section A.2 of the ASCA *Ethical Standards* explains that SCs must "[i]nform students of the purposes, goals, techniques, and rules of procedure under which they may receive counseling." This informed consent should be provided in a developmentally appropriate and meaningful manner inclusive of a check for understanding. Additional information that should be presented to students in a developmentally appropriate manner include how they were selected for the group, what they will get out of the group, techniques and theoretical approaches, and what they can expect regarding confidentiality.

Box 7.4

Did You Know?

Bruce et al. (2009) suggest that a group counseling format may be culturally responsive for Black students as it is consistent with the Black community's shared value on connectedness. A group setting may also provide Black students with an opportunity to bond and discuss personal issues while also working toward a shared goal.

Confidentiality is the cornerstone of the counseling profession; however, in working with minors and groups, there are some intrinsic limits to confidentiality. SCs are required to inform group participants that confidentiality is a group norm but also explain that confidentiality cannot be guaranteed (A.7.e). Clarity about the limitations of confidentiality includes any harm to self, harm to others, or being harmed, any of which could be disclosed in the group situation. Best ethical practice seeks parent's/guardian's permission for their child's participation in group sessions utilizing a parental permission form. Appendices A and B are parental consent letters, one in English, one in Spanish.

Stages of Groups

Throughout the group process, members become fluid in their development, and the group takes on characteristics that resemble unique stages that are achieved as the members collectively process information and demonstrate characteristics that Corey (2015) described as formation, orientation, transition, working, and consolidation. Within each stage of group development, members maintain growth from the previous stage and build on the knowledge and coping skills from the stage achieved. Corey's (2015) description of the counseling stages is reviewed in the following section.

Forming Stage

Forming identifies the initial process members go through at the onset of the group and is characterized by group members' anxiety, curiosity, and feeling of hope as they learn about the purpose and objectives of the group process. The facilitator takes care of the logistical aspect of the group formation, by setting up the meeting times and location, inviting and screening potential members, obtaining consent for participation if working with students, and planning each session (as needed, depending on the type of group) so members are aware of any curriculum plan for the group meetings.

Orientation Stage

Orientation involves the members moving into a deeper level of understanding regarding the group process as feelings of distrust, anxiety, and skepticism surface. The facilitator is responsible for creating a safe and welcoming environment in which the members will work. An effective facilitator will allow for members to introduce themselves in a way that connects one to another and make the group goals known to the group (either through collaborative development or sharing of predetermined goals). This is also a time for members and facilitators to voice concerns and expectations for group participation. The facilitator will also address specific needs and concerns of the group members, in order to cultivate trust and support open communication.

Transition Stage

Transition is the phase where members become less willing to share emotional burdens with the group, for fear of overdisclosing or retribution by the facilitator or other members. The group begins to experience conflict among members that prompts members to resort to a "fight or flight" stance on issues they deem uncomfortable to discuss openly. The facilitator's role in this stage is to validate and provide support for members' feelings of anxiety. Normalizing feelings, while acknowledging strong emotional responses, will help build trust among the group members. It is important for the facilitator to remain objective and not personalize the potentially strong reactions members may have to conflict in the group. By acknowledging the conflict among members as part of the group process, and as something to be expected, not feared, members may begin to let go of anxiety and irritation toward one another and begin to practice the coping skills that the facilitator has demonstrated for them during this phase.

Working Stage

Working can be recognized by the group facilitator when members appear to be connected and freely interact with one another without being prompted. They demonstrate a shared commitment to the group and each other. This stage is marked by members challenging each other to work on individual goals while recognizing each member's contribution to the group as a whole. The facilitator continues to model appropriate coping skills as members begin to practice these skills within and outside the group. Collaboration and openness to feedback are also seen at this stage in the process, whereas some members will spend an entire group session working on a personal issue with the support of the others. Many groups stay in this stage for long periods of time without disruption; others will begin working and suffer a setback in which they regress back to the transition stage. This is common and not something that should be feared. All groups have a personality of their own, and if the facilitator can remain objective and allow the group room to grow, the outcome will be much richer than if the facilitator attempts to control the movement of the group in and out of the stages.

Consolidation Stage

Consolidation is characterized by the ending of the group process and termination of group meetings. Many members will reflect on their accomplishments and satisfaction of their goals, while others will shy away from ending the group because of the feelings of loss that might accompany it. Some members might feel ambivalent toward the group terminating, and these feelings should be normalized. Each member will react to the consolidation process differently. While some will want to celebrate accomplishments, others will feel sad and lonely at the thought of something ending in their life. The facilitator supports this closure by providing each member the opportunity to talk about what the group meant to them, what they gained, what they might be looking forward to doing with their newfound skills, and what they will do to prevent relapse. The facilitator also offers information about upcoming groups or other resources within the community that might be of benefit to the members.

Homogeneous and Heterogeneous Groups

When looking at the makeup of a group, it is prudent to decide the characteristics you would like to include. There are two types of groups, those that contain members with similar challenges and those experiencing different challenges but who are able to learn coping skills to tackle a wide range of student concerns. The facilitator is tasked with deciding which type of group to create and how members will be selected. Once that decision is made, members may be recruited based on needs and appropriateness for each group.

A homogeneous group is comprised of students who are struggling with similar issues. By grouping students together that have a common interest in a particular subject (i.e., grief, loss, substance abuse, social issues, divorce, dating violence), the counselor brings students that might not connect into the same room. Students are able to identify with one another, whereas someone without knowledge of the issue may not understand. Students may feel less alone or isolated in this type of group, where members may offer support for one another. According to Yalom (2020), this idea of "universality" is what makes groups successful. Participants learn that they are not alone and engage with others on a level of common understanding.

Heterogeneous groups form around a common means for solving a problem, with specific psychoeducational information provided (i.e., solution-focused problem-solving, or choice theory) as a means of working with all members. Within heterogeneous groups, individual student concerns may vary. Some students may have challenges in certain areas of their lives but still serve as a model for others within the group, providing examples of healthy responses to stressful situations. With these student-models as guides, other members are encouraged to test out new, healthy behaviors within and outside the group. This process works best if not all students lack the coping skills the facilitator hopes they each develop. The facilitator may also model certain behaviors as a means of reinforcing psychoeducational material presented.

Effective Group Facilitation

Group Leadership Skills

When implementing group work in a school setting, many people think about the activities and curriculum first and often miss other essential aspects of creating effective groups. Actually, the most important component that makes groups work is the quality and skills of the facilitator (Brown, 2008). As a facilitator, the SC brings not only their skills and techniques but also their personality, including playfulness and supportiveness (Corey, 2015). The authenticity and uniqueness of the group facilitator can make or break a group. Brown (2008) avows "effectiveness is tied to the groups' perceptions of what you demonstrate rather than what you say. Who you are ends up being more influential on group members than your actions or your words" (p. 4). The group's progress can be based on the authenticity of the facilitator. Depending on only techniques and curriculum forces the facilitator to become mechanical (Brown, 2008). While many experienced group leaders caution that there is no "right" way to facilitate, Corey (2015) warns that the primary goal of good facilitation is being fully present with the group members and understanding their experiences.

The leader's skills and personality are balanced with the complexities of multitasking skills of facilitation. Group facilitation requires a focus on the whole of the group, which is a change from the individual counseling perspective. Additional suggested perception shifts (Brown, 2008) for effective group leading include:

- Observing and understanding interactions among and between members, which are often projections, transference, and a reflection of their daily interactions.
- Being honest with the group members regarding observations and feedback in a way that can be understood by group members without provoking defensiveness.
- Identifying similarities among members, offering an understanding of universality, which impacts feelings of separation.
- Using group dynamics effectively, which is a major source of information about group members' responses offering insight into potential intervention strategies.
- Making group process commentary, revealing negative and positive group interactions is a primary responsibility of the group facilitator.
- Demonstrating acceptance of all participants in the group and not labeling or judging individuals.
- Recognizing the impact of the various cultural and diversity factors which are presented in the group even when all members appear to be from the same culture or diversity is not apparent.
- Detecting the facilitators' own countertransference reactions, misusing leadership power, and attempting to meet the group leaders own needs at the expense of the members.

Box 7.5 Cooley's (2009) Recommendations for How Group Facilitators Demonstrate Effective Leadership Skills

- Express concern regarding the member's behavior without calling names or labeling.
- Resist the urge to address a sarcastic remark with sarcasm.
- Be open about how the group process works and answer questions as they arise.
- Address members' feelings of resistance in the moment.
- Describe disruptive behavior without labeling, criticizing, or condemning the member involved. Model the effective use of "I" statements.
- When expressing hunches or observations, avoid generalizations and provide specific examples that lead to your discovery.

Group Planning

Group counseling is inherently more challenging than individual counseling because there are many moving parts. It offers more professional growth for the facilitator and arguably more personal growth for the participants. Group counseling gives a view of the individual's microcosm while exposing macrocosmic aspects of the group interaction. Allowing this flow to occur requires the three Ps of group development. Planning, performing, and processing are best practice framework for group facilitation, as determined by the Association for Specialists in Group Work (Thomas & Pender, 2008).

Planning

The planning stage refers to all the preparatory aspects of setting up a group. This may include a needs assessment for what types of groups to offer, group curriculum and design, logistics with time and site, identification of group members, parent permission (Conyne et al., 2008). This portion of the group planning process has often been a neglected area. Frequently, the success or failure of a group is attributed to unmotivated participants, inadequate curriculum, or parent interference, when, instead, it may ultimately lie at the door of poor or negligent planning (Malekoff, 2015). In order to effectively determine a plan for your group, keeping in mind ecological impact factors, the areas in Box 7.6 should be addressed.

Box 7.6   Important Aspects of Group Planning

Needs: the concerns and issues specific to the group and individual participants.
Purpose: the focus and intentions of the group function.
Composition: the members participating in the group and the group facilitator.
Structure: inclusive of not only the logistics of time and place for the group but also considers the physical and emotional safety of the group.
Content and curriculum: the means to achieve the purpose.
Screening process: the preliminary evaluation and invitation of potential participants.
Context: the culture and climate within the group.

Intentional Techniques

Another aspect of effective group facilitation is intentional planning of techniques and activities. Conyne et al. (2008) define *techniques* as "the interventions ('tools of the trade') that are used by group leaders- and sometimes by group members-to focus group processes, try out behavior, accentuate thoughts and feelings, and provide opportunities for learning" (p. 8). Some facilitators chose to use a "canned" curriculum of techniques, while others develop their own. It may be easiest to follow an established curriculum, but if it does not meet the conceptual framework of the group (Conyne et al., 2008) or the group goals, nor does it address the dynamics of the members, then the curriculum will fail.

Talk groups used with adults do not fit well with the developmental needs of the younger group participants (Conyne et al., 2008; Malekoff, 2015). Adolescent and children learn best by doing; thus, experiential activities actually teach lifelong learning skills. In planning for this type of experiential learning and choosing activities, the facilitator must first assess which techniques will best serve the interactions of each particular group.

Box 7.7   Conyne et al. (2008) Suggest Using the Purposeful Group Techniques Model (PGTM) That Includes Five Steps

1. *Identify* the group type and purpose, the relevant best practice area, and the developmental stage that it may be in at the present time.
2. *Analyze* the presenting group situation by applying ecological concepts of context, interconnection, collaboration, social system, meaning-making, and sustainability.
3. *Review* possible group techniques, considering focus and level.
4. *Select* a best-fit technique for that situation that holds promise for success.
5. *Implement and evaluate* how well the technique worked.

After the decision on activities has been made, an effective group leader must carefully consider three main components of every activity: concept introduction, the activity, and debrief (Williams et al., 2008).

Concept introduction. How will the group leader get the group members to buy in to the activity? Just as a paper is written with an introduction, a body of information, and a conclusion, the facilitator must follow the same pattern with an experiential activity. To encourage engagement and enthusiasm, the facilitator develops a creative method of introducing the concept in the activity. In addition, it is important to keep in mind the objective for the activity.

Conduct the activity. Experiencing the experience is when the actual learning occurs for the participants, if facilitation is done well. Conducting the activity includes attaining the necessary materials needed and prioritizing physical and emotional safety of all the group members. After the directions of the activity are given and questions are answered, the role of the facilitator shifts to that of an observer. Facilitators do not solve the problem for the participants but allows for exploration within the group, encouraging effective communication, team building, and problem-solving without rescuing the participants.

Debrief the activity. The third, and most valuable, component of facilitation is processing the experience. No activity should be done unless there is time to debrief the experience, which is where the intention of an activity comes to fruition (Williams et al., 2008). Done immediately following an activity, the facilitator structures the debrief so individuals are encouraged to reflect on how the group planned and how the members interacted, analyze the communication, and transfer meaning to the group learning that just occurred. There are many suggested processing structures; however, the one that seems most concise and meaningful is the reflective model presented by Rolfe et al. (2001). This technique consists of asking three basic questions, "What?" "So what?" and "What now?"

What Questions. This line of questioning is about the immediate response of the group members regarding the activity. Examples: So what just happened? What was that activity like for you? It encourages the group to reflect on the immediate feelings that occurred during the activity. These questions can refer to actions, attitudes, and behaviors of the group or individuals.

So What Questions. These questions ask about the purpose of the activity. Examples: Why do you think we did this? What was the point of this activity? These questions are intended to draw conclusions about the actions of the group and success of the strategies employed by the group. This portion of the debrief process allows for group members to consider actions that worked well and consider changing actions that were not successful.

Now What Questions. The final level of debrief questions is about the real-life application or meaning of the experience for each person. Example: What did you learn about yourself in this activity? What are the behaviors you brought to this activity that helped with the groups' success? These application questions are the intent of doing activities so the members learn from the experience and apply this to their own lives.

Encouragement to utilize activities and techniques comes with the caution of balance. Be intentional in your planning and purpose. Activities are more than tools or exercises (Malekoff, 2015). Ideally, activities are used to promote new personal awareness and more effective behaviors. It is the essence of experiential learning. But this does not occur by happenstance. Simply doing an activity does not give meaning and application to the participants. It is through the processing of the activity that meaning is attached and learning occurs (Williams et al., 2008).

Assessing Group Functioning

- Causes members to be reliant on others.
- Outcomes of experience cannot be totally predictable.
- Possibility to learn from natural consequences, mistakes, and/or success.
- Provides opportunities for learning and experiencing in a unique and physical setting—kinesthetic learning.
- Holistic, involving all senses, using variety of learning styles.
- Immediate feedback on performance.
- Activities are novel and multidimensional.
- Educators recognize spontaneous opportunities for learning.
- Learnings are personal and basis for future learning.
- Relationships are developed.
- An activity that is structured to encourage individuals to plan, reflect, describe, analyze, and communicate about experiences.
- Can be used to:

  - Help individuals focus awareness on issues.
  - Facilitate awareness to promote change.
  - Reflect, analyze, describe, or discuss.
  - Reinforce perceptions of change and promote integration.

When group members engage in the assessment process, reflection and understanding become part of their awareness. Without this necessary function, members may not fully understand the depths to which they have connected with others in the group or with the group facilitator. While this process relies mostly on the work of the members, the facilitator has an obligation to provide the structure necessary for members to engage in meaningful ways. The skills needed by the facilitator vary, depending on the overall development of the members, but having adequate training is a must for those who hope to engage in group work with students.

Group Dynamics

Leading a counseling group within a school is considered by Perusse et al. (2009) to be a highly specialized skill, requiring specific training in how to facilitate groups. Group facilitators also need to be grounded in counseling theory and practice in order to be effective. When students apply what they learn in the group setting to their own lives, they come back to the group to share their experiences. This sharing may open students up to emotional risk. Encouraging students to keep confidentiality supports the notion that the group is a safe place to experience emotional growth, promote trust among members, and develop a sense of inclusion. Group facilitators help students understand that they are not alone by connecting students to each other in meaningful ways. This is used to promote healing by allowing students to share their personal experiences in a supportive environment.

Structure of a Group

Solution-Focused Groups in Schools

Solution-focused theory is one of seven counseling theories identified in the ASCA Standards for School Counselor Preparation Programs (ASCA, 2019a) that are relevant approaches for providing counseling in a school setting. Solution-focused theory involves strengths-based inquiry and does not look to explore past issues but only the present and future orientation of the students (Murphy, 2015). While looking at students as agents for change in their own lives, SCs cultivate power within students' perspective and become advocates for individual change within the system. The more control they believe they have to solve their own problems, the more likely they will be to do so. However, the SC must provide the appropriate level of information and guidance in order for students to fully integrate this approach into their daily lives.

Traditional group counseling models are based on students sharing their feelings, finding common ground with others who suffer a similar plight, and gaining strength to overcome their issues. Through this process, students learn to communicate their feelings in a more effective way and relate to others on a deeper level. Solution-focused group work emphasizes looking internally to discover strengths and resiliency toward solving problems in the past that may lead to healthy beliefs of future-oriented problem-solving ability. Building on past successes and relating those behaviors to current situations help the students gain power over their behavior and ultimately compile a mental list of coping skills they may draw from in the future.

Cooley (2009) identified eight assumptions of solution-focused brief counseling. These assumptions guide the process of working from this perspective and help to form a template for change with groups. These include:

1) All students have resources and strengths, even if they are not yet obvious to us or to the student.
2) If what you are doing is working, do more of it, and if what you are doing is not working, at least try something different.
3) Problems are not constant. There are times when the problem either does not exist or is less frequent.
4) Big problems do not necessarily require complex solutions.
5) Changes in one area will affect other areas.
6) Even if temporarily confused or uncertain, the student is the expert on the problem.

7) The solution may not necessarily be directly related to the problem. The solution can be found at the intersection of the future focus, the student's strengths and resourcefulness, and the counselor's respectful curiosity.
8) Change is inevitable. (p. 21)

Determining Necessity

The first step in creating a group is to determine if the group is really necessary and how many students suffer from similar issues. SCs can determine necessity of a group by evaluating their school's achievement and discipline data and the results of universal screens of such issues as students' risk for internalizing and externalizing behaviors. In addition, SCs can administer a needs assessment to students, teachers, parents, and administrators. Oftentimes, parents and teachers believe a problem such as "bullying" is of high concern, only to find out that the real issue is low self-esteem among the students. By obtaining data related to students' needs, the SC will save precious time and energy determining what students believe is important to them and tailoring their group interventions to those specific needs. By making an effort to gain information from students, it will empower them not only to have a voice but to also feel they have an outlet to vent their concerns. The SC will already have begun to form relationships with students by merely asking them to share their feelings. Obtaining information from a formal needs assessment might also help the parents and teachers develop a better understanding of the students' needs and how to support them. Additionally, surveying administrators, teachers, and parents regarding their perceptions of students' needs increases the likelihood that they will support the SC in conducting groups. Final approval of the group topics should be sought from the administrator(s).

Laying the Groundwork

The next step is to educate students, parents, teachers, and administrators on what the group counseling process is, the purpose, details about time and space, and what they might expect if they participate. By making the process known to the stakeholders in the school, the SC will likely gain support and participation for this movement. Once the needs of students have been determined and members of the school community have been briefed on why groups are effective within the school setting, the SC may begin to accept referrals for groups that have been created based on need. Referrals may come from sources within the school community or from outside sources (i.e., family therapist, juvenile justice, social services). It is the SC's responsibility to determine a student's readiness for group participation, not the referring party. In order for groups to be successful, the SC facilitating the group needs to be knowledgeable of the needs of each member and have enough information to manage the interaction between members during group sessions.

Timing Is Everything

To increase the likelihood of obtaining the cooperation of teachers and administrators, groups must be scheduled in a manner that is least disruptive to the academic mission and the school's schedule. SCs often use a staggered schedule in which the group meets at different times in order to distribute students' missed time evenly among their classes (Greenberg, 2020). For example, at the middle/junior high and high school levels, the number of group sessions coincides with the number of school periods, and groups meet once for each period. In elementary schools, which do not have specified class periods, a tiered schedule involves meeting one week at 9:30, the next week at 1:30, the third week at 10:30, and so on. The SC should first consult with teachers before scheduling groups to obtain their ideas regarding creating the least disruptive schedule. The SC can obtain the future testing/exam schedule of teachers to avoid scheduling groups during such times.

Another concern with scheduling of groups is the number of group sessions. In middle/junior high and high schools, the number of group sessions often coincides with the number of periods in the school. For example, if a school has eight periods, the group will be comprised of eight sessions; thus, students only miss a class or a portion of a class once. The problem with staggering the schedule of groups is that the members may forget the group meeting times. SCs can remind students of the meeting times by sending notes to both the teachers and the group members the day before the group meets and asking group members to remind each other of the meeting times.

Missed Work

The most disruptive aspect of groups in a school setting is the work worked missed by students. The SC should often remind students of their responsibility for making up missed work and to inform teachers of this group requirement (Greenberg, 2020). On days when the group meets, group members can obtain any homework assignments by meeting with their teacher, such as before school begins, during lunchtime, at free period, or even after school. The SC should often ask teachers whether group members are keeping up with their work, and failure to do so could result in having the student leave the group.

Location, Location, Location

Choosing a room that is appropriate for a confidential group session can be tricky in schools. There may not be a room that is available at the time you desire, and with limited access to conference rooms that offer privacy, facilitators may need to be creative in finding places to hold groups. One way to ensure group space is to work with a teacher or other professional within the building that may have space available during her/his planning period. Often, classrooms are free when students have recess or lunch. Utilizing a first-grade classroom for a fourth-grade group while the class is at recess just might be the ticket to successful time and space management. Other creative options include meeting in the band room while the band director has a planning period and other students (your group members) eat lunch. As long as the band director is fine with students eating lunch in the band room and you adhere to the set time frame agreed upon, this option may also be feasible.

The Screening Process

As stated earlier in the chapter, when a referral is made, the SC must interview each member to find out (a) if they are committed to the process, (b) what issues they anticipate surfacing if they participate, (c) any other potential resistance issues the member has toward fully engaging in the group process, and (d) what the student hopes to gain from participating in the group. Finding out if the challenges they are facing match the referral, and determining if additional challenges to their success are present, may help the facilitator rule out certain members for a particular group but also allow for group reassignment prior to the onset of any groups. For example, if Juan (a reserved fourth grader) approaches you to become part of a "Healthy Friendship" group but tells you he refuses to be in a group with any of the boys in Mr. Thomas's class, you ask Juan to tell you about his interaction with the other boys, and he reveals that they have been bullying him about his family's financial situation since first grade. You express concern and let him know you will support him, no matter what group he finds himself in, and that by being placed with those particular boys, he may discover common ground and actually build some new friendships. Juan refuses to hear anything about being with the other boys and asks to be removed from any possible group that semester. Do you accommodate Juan's request and place him in another group, away from the other boys, or let him sit this one out and hope he comes around next semester? In this case, it might be best to allow Juan to be in another group until he gains the confidence to work through his issues with the other boys. If he is convinced that this experience will be awful and he refuses to show up, the facilitator may be sabotaging the group's success before it even starts. Upon completion of the initial group process, it would then be appropriate to communicate with Juan your desire for him to join a group with the boys with whom he has issues (real or perceived), with the intention of successfully navigating that relationship.

As discussed earlier in the chapter, once the student expresses a commitment to the group counseling process, SCs should obtain parental consent in order to include a student in the group (see Appendices A and B). An exception to this would include students who are over the age of consent (check your state's laws on minor's age of consent), where parental permission is not required for participation. It is also prudent to check your school district policy on consent for counseling participation. Many districts have a blank consent policy that parents sign in the beginning of the school year in order to cover school-related events and participation in activities. There may also be an opt-out form that parents or guardians sign when they choose not to allow their children to participate in counseling or other mental health–related services. If a parent signed the opt-out form but you believe the student may benefit from group participation, you may choose to contact the parent in an attempt to inform them of your program and what you offer to your students. In many cases, the parents will consent to group interventions offered to many students versus individual counseling, requested just for their child.

At this point in the process, students, parents, and teachers might notice something called "pretreatment change" happening with students. This phenomenon occurs when a student demonstrates some type of change as a result of being introduced to the group concept but prior to the initial group meeting. The idea of change can be cultivated in individuals long before the actual changes in behavior occur. SCs may nurture the pretreatment change process by discussing how students' behavior may have changed as a result of being included in the group formation. Student interaction may look different, but by recognizing this phenomenon within the first group meeting, participants may feel drawn to participate due to an already-evident impact the process is having on their thoughts, feelings, or behavior.

At the onset of the first group meeting, the facilitator gains the support and buy-in of the members by creating a comfortable, inviting, and inclusive environment for the students. This may be accomplished by encouraging members to get to know one another through the use of an activity. Members who find something in common with others in the group will have a greater chance of returning, especially if they deem the group as an effective use of their time. Membership in the group must be seen as something worthwhile and productive; whether or not the student has worked on any of their own issues or just helped support others, a sense of community must develop in order for the group experience to be deemed a success.

Once the members have become acquainted with one another and the facilitator, the next step is to develop a "group agreement" that will guide the behavior of group members and help foster feelings of trust within the group. To reiterate, a conversation about confidentiality and how a breach might impact the group process is one way to instill the value of privacy and respecting self and others. Remember, this may be a relatively new concept for some students, and a very important factor for the potential participation of others. By talking openly about how the group might deal with confidential issues and offer suggestions when faced with tough situations (i.e., a friend asks you what was said in the group), members will have a better idea of how to respond to potential threats to confidentiality. The group will also be responsible for addressing breaches of confidentiality, and as part of the agreement, they agree to abide by the rules and support the goals of the group. The agreement should be unanimously supported by all members. If there is dissention regarding a particular group guideline, the members must work it out until a consensus is reached and all members are in agreement.

The facilitator is in charge of all group materials and the overall management and organization of the group process. Students must believe that the facilitator will be on time and show up prepared. For some students who have experienced abuse in their past, the facilitator's lack of preparedness, timeliness, and accountability may lead to feelings of fear, anger, or uncertainty. It is imperative that the facilitator notify the students as soon as they are able regarding any changes to the group schedule (i.e., room, time, day, topic) so they may mentally prepare for the change. By not doing this, the facilitator runs the risk of losing the member's trust, and potentially the group's support for the process.

Goal setting is an important part of group work. Each student develops their own goals, which are fluid in nature and can evolve and change over the course of the group process. By setting goals, students take an increased role in ownership and emotional investment in the development of the group and their own growth. By demonstrating how to set a goal, students learn a lifelong lesson in how to work toward something positive in their lives and gain emotional muscle in the process. With each goal accomplished, students become more confident that they can achieve success. The more often they set goals, the more likely they will be to achieve what they want.

According to the ASCA (2019c), goals should be specific, measurable, attainable, results-oriented, and time-bound. These guidelines are meant to deter group members from setting goals that are too broad in scope, cannot be measured, have negative consequences (i.e., setting a goal to get expelled from school in order to have more time to play video games), or seeks the absence of something and not the addition of something that will help alleviate the problem symptoms. For instance, when a student states they are depressed and sets a goal to not be depressed anymore, that student is not giving an indication as to what "not being depressed anymore" looks like. By encouraging the student to set a goal that outlines what they will be doing instead of being depressed (whatever that looks like for the individual), then there is a clearer picture of what to aim for. The group members may be able to assist the student in creating a picture of what a nondepressed day might look like, or activities the student might engage in when not depressed. This helps foster a sense of community among group members, with each invested in the others' well-being. When students feel connected to the group and responsible for the goals they set, it increases the likelihood that they will continue to work hard to achieve them.

Using the Miracle Question

In order to assist students with goal formation, it may be helpful to ask them to consider what life would be like if the problem no longer existed (Cooley, 2009). For students that struggle to come up with a specific goal, the facilitator might ask:

> *Let's suppose that when you went to sleep tonight, a miracle happened in your life and the problem that you've been talking about no longer existed. When you woke up, how would you know that the problem was gone? What would be different? How would your parents or teachers know that the problem didn't exist anymore? Who else might notice, and what would they say was different?*

This type of questioning often allows the student to "free think" about how their life might be without the existence of the problem (Cooley, 2009). For some, this task allows them to ponder who might be impacted as a result of the problem not being an issue. For others, this might prove to be a way to name specific factors that have been eliminated and thus help them to outline goals rather quickly. The facilitator and group members may take note as the person is speaking and restate the information back to them in the form of possible goals to work toward. Some members may be grieving the loss of a person, pet, or relationship. In many cases, the member would state something like, "Ya, I'd have my mom back," in response to the miracle question. When that happens, the facilitator needs to support the member as she/he grieves the loss and revisit the goal-setting once the person has had a chance to get to a point where goal-setting is appropriate. Pushing goals that suggest their grieving is being ignored is inappropriate and will most likely lead to the member discontinuing the group. Encouraging short-term goals (i.e., going to school each day, interacting with friends, completing homework), the school counselor is helping the student stay connected to the school community while demonstrating compassion for the heartache and loss they are experiencing.

Once the group members have established their goals for the group, they may be ready to look for exceptions to their problems or consider times when the problem was not a problem. For example, Channin came to group with complaints about her father always yelling at her in the morning, and as a result, she was always upset and had a terrible time paying attention in her first-period math class. When asked about a time when her father did not yell at her, Channin thought about it and quickly retold the story from last week when she had a great morning. She said that when she woke up on Tuesday morning, she quickly got dressed, brushed her hair and teeth, fed the dog without being asked, and ate the breakfast her father had prepared for her. When she left for school, she remembered him telling her that he was proud of her and gave her the $3.00 she had asked for so she could get ice cream after school with her friends that day. When she recalled that moment, a big smile came across her face. She also recalled that she did well on a quiz in her math class that morning as well. Drawing from that particular experience, Channin was able to set a goal for getting up and ready in the morning without being asked. The absence of arguing with her father in the morning (the exception) set the tone for more great mornings and lowered the likelihood of being distracted and angry during her first-period math class. By eliminating the cause of her distress in the morning, she may continue to excel.

In Channin's case, the facilitator did not have to search for the strengths that she possessed or the exceptions to her problem. In some cases, however, students are challenged by their situations and have little to offer when asked to recall times when the problem did not exist. The facilitator's role is to help members see their strengths and promote a healthy self-image. When a member struggles to find an exception to a difficult situation, the facilitator may recall a time when they used good judgment when a conflict arose between group members, or when they returned a lost book to a classmate and showed compassion for someone else. There may be days when the facilitator is hard-pressed to find exceptions to a student's behavior, but by focusing on what the student has done well rather than their failures, the strengths-based approach will result in positive outcomes (Cooley, 2009). Being purposeful and persistent in helping find exceptions will result in a student's continued commitment to individual growth and the group process.

Group facilitation skills are developed over time. When using specific techniques, counselors must be aware of how the questions they ask may impact the flow or mood of the group. If a student begins to tell a story that has a negative outcome and the student engages in self-blame or doubt, the facilitator may use a technique from solution-focused therapy called "reframing" to help the student see another side to the story. This technique, in which the counselor repeats the same information back to the student, but from a positive, empowering place instead of a negative, harmful one, can be very effective in helping students begin to see hope in their situation. The new meaning of the story may serve as a catalyst for future "glass half-full" thinking instead of looking at the negative side to a situation. By demonstrating concern and compassion for finding strengths, this process may also help solidify the facilitator's role as a caring adult with whom students can rely.

Another technique used in solution-focused therapy groups is to ask the members to rate their feelings on a scale from 0 to 10, with 0 being the very worst they could ever imagine and 10 being the best they could ever imagine. This exercise, known as using "scaling questions," helps students truly determine how their current situation has impacted their life. In many cases, the worst possible situation is the death of a loved one, and the best is the achievement of a long-term goal, such as graduation from college or winning the lottery. When students put their current problem into perspective, it helps diffuse irrational self-blame, doubt, or loathing. Oftentimes, students recognize when a problem has been given too much energy or how hard they've worked to remain stuck in a situation. By discussing the true highs and lows in a student's life, current problems become more manageable. Other useful ways to use the scaling question is to ask students to rate their current mood at the beginning and again at the end of group each session. Practicing this technique within the context of the group will allow each member the opportunity to express feelings and find common ground with others who might be experiencing similar situations. Gaining the knowledge that she/he is not alone can sometimes normalize a situation for the group member, and in turn, the member may decide to discontinue asserting personal energy toward the problem.

Asking follow-up questions may help the members discover the results of the work they've done toward identifying their strengths and "doing more of what works" throughout the week. For example, when Kenyon, a sixth grader who joined a group for kids struggling with issues in blended families, was asked to identify how she was feeling at the onset of the weekly group, she stated she was "6" this week. The facilitator then asked a follow-up question: "Last week you said you were at 4 at the end of group, up from a 3. What happened this week to lead you to the 6 you're at today?" Another question might be, "Kenyon, how has your situation changed in order for you to be up to a 6 today?" By asking appropriate follow-up questions, the group members have the opportunity to express deeper feelings and share their accomplishments since the group met last. The facilitator may encourage other members to also ask follow-up questions as a means of helping members relate to one another. This encouraging process helps bring the group closer through common understanding and empathic support for one another. Appropriate modeling of the process must take place over several meetings in order for the facilitator to reasonably expect members to engage in this type of questioning. While the members may feel comfortable with one another, they may look to the facilitator for guidance before asking another member to go deeper in their response.

Activities in Groups

Oftentimes, the school counselor will begin to plan a group with specific activities or curriculum in mind. This process leads to the question, "How will I use this curriculum or activity to promote growth in my students?" Finding the right fit for your needs and the needs of your students can be challenging. With such an incredible amount of information available through professional organizations, recommendations from colleagues, and websites like *Pinterest*, where school counselors "pin" their favorite guidance and group activities, knowing where to begin can be stressful. While looking for curriculum to address a specific problem or issue, make sure to follow these simple steps, making sure the intervention you choose is age-appropriate, time-sensitive (can be completed within one group session), and engaging for students. Students will tune out after the first few minutes of the group if they believe the activity is boring, consumes too much energy to complete, or is irrelevant to their life (Cooley, 2009).

Cliques in Groups

One of the most challenging aspects of group counseling is addressing cliques that form between and among members in a group. As a group facilitator, it might be instinctual to avoid confronting members who show signs of resistance or choose to form their own alliances within the group (Cooley, 2009). This type of intrusion may pose a threat to the effectiveness of the group process. With that in mind, it is important for the facilitator to check her/his own biases toward the members of the group that appear to be aligning away from the other members. At times, counselors have difficulty dealing with members whose character traits mimic problematic behaviors within themselves or others in their lives. By checking biases at the door and looking at the potential causes of the clique, the facilitator may then be able to understand how it occurred and how best to deal with those members' actions within the context of the group.

Recognizing the conflict among members and openly addressing the impact the clique has had on the group will allow the facilitator to demonstrate leadership skills and model how to effectively defuse disruption within the group process. Each member of the group should have a chance to discuss the specific ways in which the clique has impacted them, while allowing all participants a chance to respond. When a member uses sarcasm to avoid dealing with the situation, responding with humor is appropriate. However, responding in kind with a sarcastic quip only attempts to equally degrade their character without solving the problem. Stick with a calm demeanor and focus on getting the issue out in the open. The intention of this process is to dissolve the clique and realigning all the members with the original purpose of the group. Once all members have successfully recommitted to the group process, the facilitator may encourage continued processing of feelings related to other topics as they arise.

Group Behavior Management

When group facilitators are asked about the hardest part of leading a group, managing behaviors is the typical response (Williams et al., 2008). There is no "one size fits all" response to group behavior management; however, the effective facilitator develops a "tool kit" of responses so the group can stay on target and be productive. Again, as a facilitator, you are a guide facilitating, and rarely are you the sheriff lecturing or the teacher lecturing. As a facilitator, the role is about managing the interactions, not giving the answers or directing the group. This is not a hierarchy in which the facilitator has all the power and control, as opposed to the classroom, where the teacher is the authority. An effective group facilitator gives the power back to the group and allows the group to practice the lifelong skills of problem-solving and risk-taking.

Power-Sharing Techniques

There are several ways in which an effective group facilitator can use power-sharing instead of overpowering (Williams et al., 2007). Power-sharing attributes the bulk of power and decision-making to the participants in the group.

Circle Format

The simplest application of power-sharing is utilization of the circle format (Williams et al., 2007). The circle has no head or tail, and all participants—and this includes the facilitator—are part of the circle. A hierarchy does not exist in the circle. This inclusive format keeps the focus on the group as a whole. It also allows for the facilitator to monitor the body language of all the participants. If a group member demonstrates inappropriate behaviors, the circle format makes the monitoring and intervention easier for the facilitator or cofacilitator. In a circle, eye rolls and discounting body language can be immediately noticed and addressed by the facilitator.

Behavior-Management Techniques

Another group facilitation tip utilizes the guidelines that were developed by the group members. To allow natural responses and interactions to occur, the facilitator must assist the group members to establish group norms, guidelines, or boundaries within which the members will operate. These norms create a safe space and help the group members hold each other accountable. If the group leader has facilitated the creation of the group norms or guidelines in an effective manner, the participants will "own" the guidelines as their own. Using these member-developed guidelines allows the facilitator to draw attention to the guidelines if inappropriate behavior is escalating. A simple reminder, asking all group members if they are following the group guidelines or if the group guidelines need to be changed, can refocus groups or individual members into more appropriate behavior.

It is important, as a facilitator, to not direct negative behaviors toward a specific participant but to indirectly address behaviors (Williams et al., 2007). The group guidelines can be the initial behavior management technique; however, helping the group members learn to manage their own behaviors is a life skill. When something happens in the group, instead of directing attention toward the culprit, the facilitator can redirect the attention toward the group as a whole. Such questions as "How is the group working right now?" or "What helps this group be most successful?" may help the group work more effectively. Because the facilitator wants to focus on the behavior and not blame the person, it is important to avoid directing unnecessary attention to the individual. Discussing behaviors that work in the group and behaviors that will not work in a group also mitigates negative behaviors. However, there are always those participants that act out negative or distracting behaviors to the group. Sometimes those behaviors need specific interventions.

Naysayer

There will occasionally be participants who are negative. This behavior can be annoying to facilitators and participants alike. It can also be contagious if the person has power in the group. The impact of a toxic person can be debilitating to a group; however, to avoid directly responding to the individual as a negative person, one suggestion is for the leader to give the naysayer some type of leadership role to promote positive energy (Williams et al., 2007). Another suggestion would be to ask all participants what they liked about an activity and what they would change so that the naysayer does not have all the power. The group can also create a guideline that says if a participant is going to say something negative, they have to provide an idea about how to change it. As a last resort, a facilitator can remind group members that attendance is voluntary. The facilitator can remind members that if they are unhappy, they can ask permission to leave after they explain why they are making that choice to the rest of the group.

Overtalker

The overtalker can quickly drain the energy from everyone in the group. As a facilitator, you cannot roll your eyes when the individual talks or avoid calling on the overtalker every time they want to talk (Williams et al., 2007). Ignoring the behavior may only make it more blatant. One suggested technique is the use of pipe cleaners. Each participant gets three pipe cleaners (or any other collection of objects). When one person wishes to talk, she/he has to put one pipe cleaner into the middle of the circle. When that person runs out of pipe cleaners, they cannot share any more information. This strategy may also encourage the participant who does not talk very often. (It is important to not allow the participants to negotiate pipe cleaners or trade them.)

Quiet/Shy Person

The pipe cleaner strategy is as helpful with the quiet participant as with the overtalker. Directly asking each participant to share one thing about the activity gives the quiet person a chance to practice having a voice (Williams et al., 2007). The facilitator can gently encourage anyone who has not had the chance to speak to share first, or to give the quiet person a task where they can contribute to the group in some way.

Cliques

Factions of students can quickly overpower the rest of the group members and disempower group effectiveness. It is vital that the group facilitator continually divide group members in creative ways (Williams et al., 2007). As a facilitator, being unpredictable in how you divide up the groups for different activities will minimize clique manipulations. The facilitator may have to speak directly about how it feels to be left out of group activities.

Additional Group Management Techniques

A Handbook for Leading Positive Youth Development Programs (Williams et al., 2007) offers a variety of additional group management techniques that may help participants have a more positive experience:

Rounds. Ask one question and go around the group so everyone contributes an answer. Although it might take longer, depending on the size of the group, it equalizes the energy and power in the group and gives all members a voice.

Passing. If there is a group member who does not want to talk at that moment, giving the person a pass for the time being is helpful. However, it is important to let the person know that the facilitator will come back to them after everyone else has spoken. This gives the person time to think about their answer while making them accountable for an answer. Accountability is important so that the "pass" does not become the norm for the group.

Talking Stick. This strategy is a tried-and-true method for effective group management. The only person who can talk is the person holding the talking stick. An addition to this strategy is to have the next speaker receiving the talking stick repeat what they just heard the previous speaker say. This reinforces active listening for the members of the group.

Freeze Frame. This is a minimally used strategy when the facilitator feels the physical or emotional safety of the group or a member is in jeopardy. Overuse of this strategy can cause members to dismiss it. However, used sparingly, it is an effective message that there is an important reason that the facilitator needs to take control of the group.

While there will always be disruptive behaviors in group counseling, effective facilitation can mitigate the negative impact on the group process. The facilitator focuses on the behavior and not on blaming the person. One of the most powerful reasons to implement small-group programs is to help group members learn to manage their own behaviors through feedback and modeling in the group process. Changing one participant's behavior can influence others' behaviors. Learning through group process!

Assessment

SCs should, as much as feasible, collect participation, ASCA Student Standards, and outcome data for SC-led interventions. SCs can design for the group participants both questions regarding students' self-efficacy and multiple-choice questions that relate to both the focus of the group and ASCA Student Standards (2021). For example, a relevant ASCA student standard for a grief counseling group would be "effective coping skills" (B-SMS 7). A relevant pre- and posttest assessment of students' self-efficacy could be, "I am confident that I can use at least two coping skills when I identify that I am having strong feelings regarding the loss I have experienced." For a study skills group, a relevant perception-based question would be, "I am confident that I can use two study skills in preparing for tests" (B-LS 2). Multiple-choice questions can be used to assess students' mastery of the content of a group curriculum. For example, of an academic group which had the objective of teaching students to create self-directed SMART goals, a relevant multiple-choice question would be the following: "Which of the following is an example of a specific, measurable, attainable, results-oriented, and time-bound (SMART) goal? (a) I will seek to improve my grades, (b) I will try my hardest in school, (c) I will seek to attain at least all B grades in my academic subjects for this marking period." An example of a multiple-choice question concerning the social skill of empathy (B-SS 9) is the following: "Juanita tells Olivia that she cannot believe that she did not respond to her texts last night as something was really bothering Juanita. Which of the following would be the most relevant response to demonstrate that Olivia understands Juanita's concern? (a) Why did you not text me again? (b) You are disappointed as you really wanted to talk. (c) Why do you always get upset with me?"

The perceptions of students often provide valuable information to SCs regarding what activities to modify. However, such feedback is not likely to impress administrators and teachers who are increasingly being held accountable for demonstrating measurable gains in student achievement. Likewise, SCs must seek to impact student achievement in a more objective, measurable manner. Depending upon the objectives of the group, behavioral data might be used to measure the rates of attendance or homework completion (ASCA, 2019c) and on-task behavior. Forms of academic data that might be relevant to assess include standardized test data, grade point average, and number of classes passed.

Summary

There are considerable challenges to conducting group counseling in a school setting. Data must be collected to determine the necessity of group topics. SCs must work hard to obtain the support of administrators, teachers, parents, and students. There is a considerable amount of coordination and paperwork as parents' written consent should be obtained, teachers and students must be consistently reminded of the group schedule, students must complete missed work, and evaluations must be conducted. Given the challenges in conducting group counseling, some SCs elect not to conduct groups. However, we encourage SCs to accept these challenges as the rewards may be worth the effort. Some studies have found that small-group interventions can yield up to a moderate effect size on student achievement (Whiston et al., 2011).

References

American School Counselor Association. (2019a). *ASCA standards for school counselor preparation programs*. Author.

American School Counselor Association. (2019b). *ASCA school counselor professional standards & competencies*. www.schoolcounselor.org/asca/media/asca/home/SCCompetencies.pdf

American School Counselor Association. (2019c). *The ASCA national model: A framework for school counseling programs* (4th ed.). Author.

American School Counselor Association (2021). *ASCA Student Standards: Mindsets & behaviors for student success*. Author. https://www.schoolcounselor.org/Standards-Positions/Standards/ASCA-Mindsets-Behaviors-for-Student-Success

Brown, N. W. (2008). *Becoming a group leader*. Allyn & Bacon.

Bruce, A. M., Getch, Y. Q., & Ziomek-Daigle, J. (2009). Closing the gap: A group counseling approach to improve test performance of African-American students. *Professional School Counseling, 12*(6), 450–457. https://doi.org/10.1177/2156759X0901200603

Conyne, R. K., Cromwell, J. L., & Newmyer, M. D. (2008). *Group techniques*. Pearson Education.

Cooley, L. (2009). *The power of groups: Solution-focused group counseling in schools*. Corwin/Sage.

Corey, G. (2015). *Theory and practice of group counseling* (Revised ed.). Author.

Council for the Accreditation of Counseling and Related Educational Programs. (n.d.). *2016 CACREP standards*. www.cacrep.org/for-programs/2016-cacrep-standards/

Greenberg, K. R. (2020). *Group counseling in K-12 schools: A handbook for school counselors.* Pearson.

Malekoff, A. (2015). *Group work with adolescents: Principles and practice* (3rd ed.). The Guilford Press.

Murphy, J. J. (2015). *Solution-focused counseling in schools* (3rd ed.). American Counseling Association.

Perusse, R., Goodnough, G. E., & Lee, V. V. (2009). Group counseling in the schools. *Psychology in the Schools, 46*(3), 225–231. https://doi.org/10.1002/pits.20369

Rolfe, G., Freshwater, D., & Jasper, M. (2001). *Critical reflection in nursing and the helping professions: A user's guide.* Palgrave Macmillan.

Thomas, R. V., & Pender, D. A. (2008). Association for specialists in group work: Best practices guide 2007 revisions. *The Journal for Specialist in Group Work, 33*(2), 111–117. https://doi.org/10.1080/01933920801971184

Whiston, S. C., Tai, W. L., Rahardja, D., & Eder, K. (2011). School counseling outcome: A meta-analytic examination of interventions. *Journal of Counseling & Development, 89*(1), 37–55. https://doi.org/10.1002/j.1556-6678.2011.tb00059.x

Williams, R. L., Lantz, A., & Noorulamin, S. (2008). *Making smart choices: Social emotional intelligence for adolescent girls.* American School Counselor Association.

Williams, R. L., Riedo, S., & DeBard, S. (2007). *A handbook for leading positive youth development programs.* Smart-Girl.

Yalom, I. D. (2020). *The theory and practice of group psychotherapy* (6th ed.). Station Hill Press.

Chapter 8

Consultation and Collaboration

Collaboration and consultation are vital components of a school counseling program. SCs must partner with various stakeholders in order to support the school's academic mission, implement and maintain a comprehensive school counseling program, and effect systemic change. In the *ASCA National Model* (2019b), consultation and collaboration are defined as indirect services within the delivery component of the framework.

DOI: 10.4324/9781003167730-8

Within the literature, there are various definitions of consultation and collaboration. Among the various definitions of these terms, an element that is common to both collaboration and consultation is involvement with another to impact a third party. SCs consult and collaborate with parents, teachers, administrators, and other important stakeholders in order to benefit students. Collaboration and consultation may be regarded as the primary behaviors through which schools contribute to systemic change. In this chapter, readers will learn about the models and theories of collaboration and consultation that are relevant for SCs, including strategies and models of collaboration and consultation that can be regarded as particularly relevant for working with low-income and minority parents.

Collaboration

As the school counseling profession has moved away from primarily emphasizing providing direct service to at-risk students, it has instead focused on the implementation of a program and serving as an integral team player to advance the academic mission of the school, and thus the importance of collaboration has correspondingly increased. The SC's training in communication skills, in group dynamics, and in working with systems puts him or her in a unique position to collaborate with others. SCs seek to promote systemic change by providing leadership and advocacy, and collaboration is an essential part of all three of these model themes.

SCs collaborate with colleagues in order to be a vital contributor to the school's academic mission. Traditional definitions of both collaboration and consultation emphasize the role of experts sharing their area of expertise. Historically, training for SCs have emphasized understanding students' career development and labor trends, the college admissions process, children's social/emotional development, and mental health services available in the community. SCs are often members of various school committees addressing school improvement, such as teacher teams and/or data teams, and also participate on committees focusing on academically or behaviorally at-risk students, such as the Instructional Support Team (IST)/child study team, Individualized Education Planning (IEP) team, Student Assistance Program (SAP), etc. SCs also typically work as the school's liaison with community agencies, providing parents and students with referrals and coordinating the communication between the community agencies while providing services to at-risk children and their families. Finally, SCs are frequently involved in planning and presenting teacher-in-service sessions.

While SCs are primarily responsible for creating and implementing the school counseling curriculum, there are various collaborative components emphasized in the ASCA National Model. Several aspects of the ASCA National Model reflect the importance of designing a program that meets the unique needs of the community. The vision and mission statements and the goals of the school counseling program are expected to support the school's and district's mission, and SCs are tasked with identifying and removing barriers to educational access for traditionally disadvantaged groups that are specific to the setting. In order to meet the unique needs of the school and community, SCs conduct needs assessments and gather already-existing data to understand the perspectives of the various stakeholders.

Ideally, school counseling programs have an advisory council, consisting of 8–20 members who reflect the diversity of the community, and which includes students, parents, SC(s), administrators, school board members, and business and community members. The advisory council is a key element of the democratic process essential for changing prevailing values and norms and developing support for implementation of the programs of the school counseling program. The advisory council assists with needs assessments, analyzing the collected data, disseminating the results to various stakeholders, creating the foundation of the program, and managing and delivering the program.

SCs are also expected to meet annually with an administrator in identifying the school counseling program's priorities. In this conference, SCs can educate administrators regarding the benefits of a comprehensive school counseling program. Lastly, SCs collaborate with colleagues through their coordination of the various programs that may be closely associated with the school counseling program, which may include the school-wide positive behavioral interventions and supports (SWPBIS), bullying and violence prevention programs, mentoring and tutoring programs, etc.

Family-School Collaboration

Both the No Child Left Behind (NCLB, 2002) Act and the Every Student Succeeds Act (ESSA; US Department of Education, n.d.) emphasize family-school collaboration. State departments of education and school districts must provide professional development opportunities that enhance educators' and parents' understanding of the importance of collaboration and the skills to achieve goal-oriented partnership programs. Schools must share with parents and the community information and decisions about students' placements and the performance of the school, including the aggregated and disaggregated results of state achievement tests, attendance and graduation rates, and information about teachers' qualifications. Finally, schools are expected to increase equity in education by making more of an effort to include families, even those who are not currently involved, and by ensuring that communications with parents are clear, useful, and executed in languages that all parents understand.

Box 8.3

One group of students that is at risk for inequitable educational outcomes are those from families that are low-income. SCs can work to develop family-school partnerships by:

- Challenging bias
- Training school personnel to work with all families
- Initiating outreach activities with families
- Conducting research to establish effective practices
- Highlighting the benefits of collaborative problem-solving
- Accessing student and family strengths (Grothaus & Cole, 2010)

Epstein and her colleagues (2018) have developed the most comprehensive model for family-school collaboration and have conducted a rigorous program of evaluation that has demonstrated the effectiveness of the model in promoting family-school collaboration and enhancing students' academic achievement. In their model, the home, school, and community are referred to as "overlapping spheres," which influence both children and the conditions and relationships in the three contexts. The external model is comprised of the external contexts in which students live (e.g., home, school, and community), and the theory assumes that student achievement is enhanced when these external contexts collaborate. The internal model refers to the interactions and patterns of influence that occur between individuals at home, at school, and in the community.

Interactions between the three contexts occur both at the institutional level (e.g., the school creating a system by which parents can verify homework assignments) and at the individual level (e.g., parent-teacher conference). Epstein and her colleagues identified six main types of involvement interactions which are used to organize the school's activities in promoting parental and community involvement. She adapted a model indicating how school counselors can use the six types of family involvement in a prevention mode and in a treatment mode (Epstein & Van Voorhis, 2010).

Meta-analyses have consistently identified positive benefits of family involvement on specific academic outcomes (e.g., Jeynes, 2012). Use of Epstein's et al. (2018) parent-involvement model has resulted in increased family-school collaboration and is associated with increases in school climate, improved student behavior and school discipline, and increased reading achievement scores. Epstein and Sheldon's (2002) longitudinal study found that specific family-school collaboration activities were associated with increased attendance among elementary students, including providing workshops for parents regarding attendance matters, communicating with all families, and providing a school contact person for parents to call. Although the effectiveness of Epstein's adaptation of the parent-involvement model for SCs has not been evaluated, the widespread use of the parent-involvement model among many state departments of education establishes its relevance for the role of SCs in fostering family school collaboration.

Griffin and Steen (2010) used Epstein's six types of school-family-community involvement interactions in understanding SCs' experience with partnering with parents and community organizations. The findings revealed that although many SCs perceive school-family-community partnerships to be useful and report confidence in developing such partnerships, most SCs indicate that they do not participate in such partnerships. The activities of SCs who did report partnering with parents fit into the categories of parenting and collaborating with the community within Epstein's model, with low involvement reported in decision-making, volunteering, learning-at-home activities, and communicating with parents. The study also revealed that SCs reported engaging in collaborative activities that did not fit into any of the categories in Epstein's model. Griffin and Steen (2010) categorized these advanced collaborative activities as forms of leadership and advocacy, including establishing a leadership council, presenting to school boards, etc.

Griffin and Steen (2010) concluded that SCs could increase their use of communication, volunteering, decision-making, and leadership and advocacy practices, and the authors provided recommendations based on a review of the literature. SCs can communicate with parents regarding how they can support their child in establishing educational goals while also advertising their role as SCs. Moreover, SCs can establish a family resource center containing educational resources, such as audiovisuals, brochures, and announcements concerning academic, career, and social/emotional issues. SCs have enhanced training in interpersonal communication skills and may be in the best position to initially establish a working alliance between family members and school personnel, using constructive communication skills and emphasizing student's and families' strengths, establishing the trust essential for addressing more challenging and potentially conflictual issues.

SCs may not only model such constructive communication and teaming skills during parent-teacher conferences but may also collaborate with respected teachers in providing in-service trainings for the staff regarding effective strategies for relating to parents and collaborative decision-making, as many teachers do not feel prepared to interact with parents. SCs can use parent volunteers to support the school counseling program, including designing and implementing workshops for other parents (Sheldon, 2003), identifying community resources, and tutoring (Griffin & Steen, 2010). The authors of this text have found that parents are often eager to hear the experiences of parents of children who have recently undergone important transitions, such as entering middle or high school, applying to college, etc., and that such parents can be included on such panel topics.

SCs can collaborate with teachers in providing workshops for parents to increase their understanding of the academic curriculum, with SCs contributing their expertise regarding how to structure such workshops to be informative for parents who have less formal education (Griffin & Steen, 2010). SCs can involve parents in decision-making by surveying parents regarding their perceptions of needed services and by including parents as part of the school counseling program's advisory council.

Involving Low-Income Parents and Parents of Color

While parent involvement seems to be clearly associated with academic achievement for White students, the relationship between parent involvement and achievement for minority and low-income students is more mixed. School-family-community partnerships have been associated with improvements in academic achievement tests, grade point averages, and attendance rates for Black male students (Henry, 2014). However, Bower and Griffin (2011) found that while parents of elementary students with a high rate of poverty and minority student enrollment were involved with their children, implementation of Epstein's parent-involvement model did not increase parent involvement or student achievement. They recommend that schools develop a broader definition of parental involvement, which may decrease the frustration that many teachers expressed regarding the low rate of parent participation in the parent teacher organization meetings and informal open houses. To increase parental involvement, they recommend that schools seek a long-term approach to acquire the trust of parents and that schools must conduct continued outreach efforts, even when initial attempts at connecting with parents appear to be unsuccessful. SCs can coordinate cultural awareness workshops.

Literature has indicated a number of factors that explain lower rates of involvement of minority parents and parents of color (Holcomb-McCoy, 2010). These factors include language barriers, the fact that schools do not provide a welcoming environment, a cultural disconnection between schools and communities, and the lack of opportunities for parent involvement. Unfortunately, there is some evidence to suggest that SCs in the past have contributed to the barriers to the involvement of low-income and minority families in discouraging such students from pursuing postsecondary education (e.g., Hart & Jacobi, 1992).

It has been suggested that parent involvement, which has been traditionally defined as volunteering, attending school conferences and events, and communicating with teachers, has been defined in ways that discount how other cultures promote achievement in their youth (Bower & Griffin, 2011). A broader definition of parent involvement can include providing nurturance and limit-setting, providing assistance with homework, establishing high expectations, and discussing with children their aspirations (e.g., Abdul-Adil & Farmer, 2006). Latino families tend to defer to school personnel and are less likely to contact regarding potential problems, which may be interpreted by school personnel as a lack of involvement (Gaetano, 2007). Low-income families are more likely to have informal conversations and do unscheduled visits, which are often viewed as inappropriate by teachers (Fields-Smith, 2007).

Schools must work hard at welcoming minority and low-income parents who are likely to be reluctant to participate with schools given past negative experiences and beliefs that their views will not be welcomed. School personnel should seek to understand the perspectives of minority and low-income parents and thank parents for sharing their ideas and perspectives and should avoid becoming defensive if parents' perspectives are seemingly critical. Schools need to be creative and flexible in how and when they provide opportunities for parental involvement. Schools should schedule some events in the evening and may increase parent participation by providing food and day care. Schools can provide opportunities within the community, providing informational sessions at churches, community agencies, etc. Schools should avoid excessive use of the technical language of education, including such acronyms as Individualized Education Plans (IEP), 504, percentile rank, etc., and should provide clear explanations of such language.

Teachers in the elementary school in the Bower and Griffin (2011) study that implemented Epstein's model of parental involvement developed home learning activities in which parents could participate. For example, in teaching measurement and capacity, teachers encouraged parents to ask their children to look in the refrigerator and kitchen to identify the capacity of objects (e.g., liters of milks, identifying the measurements used for ingredients, etc.).

Consultation

Consultation in schools is a service delivery model in which a clinician, serving as a consultant, uses problem-solving strategies (in order to alter an existing set of circumstances to become a desired set of circumstances) to address the needs of a consultee and a client (Kratochwill, 1990). Both a time- and cost-efficient way to provide service to a large number of clients (e.g., children, families), consultants work with consultees, such as teachers and other educators, who then work with clients (children and their families) guided by consultative treatment plans. Consultants and consultees work collaboratively to share their knowledge bases to help solve academic, behavioral, and social/emotional problems in children. Thus, consultation is an indirect vehicle through which school-based educational and mental health professionals can combine their expertise to positively impact upon children's development and functioning. Although there are various models of school-based consultation, this chapter will focus upon solution-focused, systems, and behavioral consultation, as these consultation models may be considered to be the most frequently used by SCs.

Solution-Focused Consultation (SFC)

The principles of solution-focused theory are compatible with the collaborative model of consultation. Notably, most of the models of consultation for schools use the collaborative, problem-solving model (Kahn, 2000), in contrast to the triadic-dependent consultation model. In the triadic-dependent approach to consultation, the consultant is regarded as an expert who is generally active and directive in prescribing an intervention for the consultee. Collaborative consultation de-emphasizes the power differential between the consultant and consultee, rather, seeing each member of the consultation team as possessing potentially important insights and resources. The task of the consultant is to facilitate a constructive process that enables the consultee to develop more effective approaches in working with the student(s) in question. In the triadic-dependent model, the consultant offers his or her expertise, whether it be instructional strategies, behavior modification, and so forth, to the consultee, whereas in the collaborative consultation model, the consultant's primary source of expertise is his or her ability to facilitate a constructive process.

A primary assumption of solution-focused theory is that individuals, whether they are students, teachers, or parents, have the resources to obtain their goals. However, such people may currently be experiencing difficulty because of their perspective of the problem. This is often referred to within solution-focused theory as having a problem-saturated perspective. The task of the solution-focused consultant is to help the consultee develop new perspectives of the students, himself or herself, and the situation through the consultant's artful use of language. This implies another founding principle of solution-focused theory, which is that reality is partially a social construct and maintained through the use of language.

Consultants' view of the student or the student's problem is influenced by their language. For example, a student's learning disability or behavioral disorder may become problematic for the teacher or parent because it is viewed in the most negative and pessimistic manner and may be assumed by the parent or teacher to be objective reality. The solution-focused consultant attempts to access the consultee's "frame" of the situation and help the consultee develop slightly modified or new frames which are more constructive. In illustration of this, a teacher may see a child's obsessive behaviors of checking to make sure his or her pencil is on his or her desk as interfering with the child's completion of academic tasks. A modified frame of this problem might be that the child's perseveration in making sure the pencil is on the desk is to help manage his or her anxiety and to allow him or her to focus on the academic work.

SFC emphasizes a positive frame by assisting consultees to identify and use their strengths, resources, and past successes to establish goals (Kahn, 2000). Rather than extensively focus on the problem, the consultant encourages the consultee to focus upon past successes and exceptions to the problem, meaning, when the problem did not exist or was less of a problem. The consultant does not provide direct suggestions but rather engages the consultee in a constructive conversation that helps the consultee develop a new perspective of the situation, resulting in the consultee devising his or her own solutions. Solutions that are generated by the consultee are considered preferable because the consultee is likely to use those solutions, since they stem from the consultee's resources and perspective. Another difference of SFC in comparison to traditional models of consultation is that there is less focus on the student or the object of the consultation and more focus on those aspects of the situation that the consultee controls, such as his or her viewpoint of or interactions with the child.

SFC does not strictly adhere to distinct stages in comparison to traditional models of consultation, as the focus is primarily to help the consultee develop more constructive frames, but there is a general process that is followed. Kahn (2000) adapted the steps of Juhnke's (1996) solution-focused supervision model to the consultation process, which are as follows: (a) presession and initial structuring, (b) identifying consultation goals, (c), exploring exceptions, (d) helping the consultee decide upon a solution, and (e) summarizing and complimenting.

Presession and Initial Structuring

In the presession and initial structuring steps, the goals are to help the consultee identify strengths and objectives. Kahn (2000) adapted Juhnke's (1996) presession supervision questionnaire to the consultation process. The questionnaire instructs teachers to identify the strengths and resources they can contribute to the consultation process, such as their teaching skills or interpersonal strengths. The questionnaire may also include goals for the student and consultee, including, "How would you like the student to be? How would you like to be with your student? With your class? And how will you know such consultation is successful?" (p. 249). Such questions may create a shift in the consultee's thinking, as the consultee may be focused upon the negative aspects of the situation, such as the student's lack of progress or the consultee's inability to facilitate the student's progress, leading the consultee to think more about future possibilities to increase the consultee's hopefulness.

Establishing Consultation Goals

In examining the consultee's goals, there is little emphasis on discussing the problem, which is not considered productive, since the focus should be upon solutions. However, these authors recommend spending at least five to ten minutes listening attentively to the consultee's perspective, even it is quite negative, and reflecting the consultee's perspective back to the consultee using active listening skills. One reason it may be helpful to first explore the consultee's perspective is that it helps the consultant understand the consultee's "frame of the problem," possibly indicating how the consultee's frame may be contributing to the problem. Also, it has been the authors' experience that some consultees are not ready to engage in problem-solving until they believe that their perspective of the problem has been understood and acknowledged. SFC shares similarities with behavioral consultation in that effective goals are considered to be concrete, behavioral, defined in measurable terms, and identified in the affirmative expectation (rather than identifying the absence of a behavior).

Exploring Exceptions

A primary solution-focused technique used during this phase is exception seeking. This technique involves asking the consultee to identify times in which the problem did not occur, or occurred to a lesser degree, and then exploring with the consultee how or she contributed to the success of that respective situation. In SFC, the consultant seeks to help the consultee identify the very specific thoughts and behaviors that may have contributed to the exception and which consultees often overlook. For example, the consultee may be asked to provide specific details about how he or she asked the student to participate in a class discussion, what the consultee was thinking which contributed to his or her decision to invite the student's participation, how the student responded in terms of his or her behavior, and what these behaviors might indicate about the student's thoughts and feelings, etc. Scaling questions may be used during any of the consultation phases and have particularly relevance for exploring exceptions as well.

Scaling Questions

The consultee can be asked to assess on a 10-point scale the degree to which a student is demonstrating the respective goal. Typically, consultees and clients provide a rating in the range of 3–8. The consultant then asks the consultee to identify how he or she thinks the student achieved whatever rating the consultee identified, and how the consultee contributed to the child's success. The consultant may use what is referred to as a "not knowing questions." Examples include the following: "What was it that you did that helped your son complete his homework on Thursday night?" "How did you help the child develop more interest in the reading assignment?" After exploring the things that have helped the child and consultee achieve at least a limited degree of success, the consultant asks the consultee what one additional point of success would look like on the scale—in other words, what is the next step the consultant could take. This question serves to counter the tendency of consultees to think in all-or-nothing terms and instead think in terms of small incremental steps toward change, which solution-focused theory would suggest is more consistent with the nature of lasting change.

Helping Consultees Decide on a Solution

This phase is often brief, as the previous consultation phases should have helped the consultee develop new perspectives and solutions. The primary task of the consultant in this phase is to summarize and emphasize the new perspectives, solutions, and resources that the consultee has implied will likely contribute to progress, and asking the consultee to identify the concrete steps he or she plans to pursue.

Case Consultation: An Illustration of Solution-Focused Consultation (SFC)

Mrs. Dwyer is the mother of James, a seventh-grade student in a suburban middle school. Mrs. Dwyer has sought out the SC to discuss her concerns about James's inconsistency in completing homework.

Counselor: It is good see you, Mrs. Dwyer. I always appreciate it when parents contact me about their concerns, and I admire your interest in your son's education. Please tell me about your concerns.

Parent: Well, I'm just so frustrated with James. His teachers informed me that he hasn't been submitting his homework on a regular basis, and for this last marking period, his grades dropped from Bs to Cs in most of his academic subjects. His father and I accepted Bs, hoping James would pull them up to As, and now he seems to be going in the opposite direction.

Counselor: Let me see that I'm hearing you correctly. You and your husband were satisfied with the Bs that James received for the previous marking period, but you are obviously unhappy with the Cs he received this marking period, and his teachers have identified his inconsistency in completing homework as one reason for the decline in his grades in academic subjects.

Parent: Yes! I mean, I am just not sure what to do when it comes to his homework. I think my husband and I thought that we could back off a bit, since he seemed to be doing well, and friends of ours who have children in high school had told us how at some point we have to allow James to be more responsible in doing his work. Now we're wondering if we should go back to staying on top of him more.

Counselor: You're wondering about how to help James with his homework. You want James to assume more responsibility for doing his work but are thinking about going back to what you did last marking period when it came to his homework.

Parent: Yeah, I know I feel sort of caught, and I think my husband feels similarly.

Counselor: So if I understand it, your goal right now is to help James increase his homework completion. Is that accurate?

Parent: Yes, from what I understand from the teachers, they believe this is what brought James's grades down, as his scores in tests and quizzes were generally in the B range.

Counselor: Okay, on a 10-point scale, with 10 being James is handling his homework well, where you would like him to be, and 1 being James is not assuming any responsibility for his homework completion, what number would you currently give James?

Parent: I'd say he is at about a 3, since he is completing his homework sometimes.

Counselor: How about last marking period? What number would you give James when it came to completing his homework on that 10-point scale?

Parent: More like an 8. My husband and I believe he was completing and turning in his homework every time, but rather than a 10, I would give James an 8, because we often had to ask numerous times if he had homework before we would even look to see if he did, and we sometimes had to sit with him when he did it to make sure that he wouldn't go and do something else.

Counselor: And I heard that part of your goal is that you want him to complete his homework, but with less prodding from you and your husband. Could you tell me a time where you saw this happening, that James did his homework with less prodding from you and your husband?

Parent: Well, it hasn't happened a lot, but I can think of a time about a month ago. James did all of his homework right when he got from school without me even saying anything to him when he got off the bus.

Counselor: Wow, interesting. So what is your sense of how you helped James do that?

Parent: Well, the night before, both my husband and I sat down with James and explained to him that we want him to get his work done right after school, as we thought he is more focused then. We also shared that once he gets his work done, that gives us more time to do something fun with him, like play a video game.

Counselor: So you think sharing your perspective with James, that he is more focused right after school, and then explaining how this gives him more time to do fun things with you and your husband helped to motivate him?

Parent: Yeah, it seemed to work that night.

Counselor: Wow, it sounds like you have seen the success you are looking for.

Parent: I guess you're right. I guess we keep need to keep it going. It is hard because I don't think James did his homework the following night, and then we fell into what we do sometimes, which is to nag him, which just leads to an argument.

Counselor: So we know what an 8 looks like. What would a 9 look like—meaning, what would be James be doing if he were at a 9?

Parent: Well, obviously he would be doing his homework right away when he gets from school, and he would be more organized. Sometimes it takes me and James a while to figure out what homework he has to do, as he doesn't write down in his agenda like he is supposed to.

Counselor: Okay, so a 9 would be James is getting his work after school, and he knows what he needs to do. What is your sense of how you can help him to be a 9?

Parent: We've told him about the importance of using his agenda. I've been wondering if he doesn't have too much stuff in his backpack. I mean, he has to pull out tons of stuff just to get to his agenda.

Counselor: Ah, so you think you want to teach him to pare down to essential things?

Parent: Yes, and you know, I think it is something that my husband and I need to learn to better model for James. I mean, we tend to be a bit disorganized around the house, and I've been thinking I need to better show James how to organize things.

Counselor: It sounds to me like you have a number of ideas about what helps James to complete his work. You sense that reminding him the night before of your expectations seems to work and helps you to avoid nagging him and provide a reinforcer, something he can look forward to for completing his work. You see the next step as helping him to be organized in keeping track of what are his homework assignments, and you have several ideas regarding how you can help him to do that.

Case Discussion and Conclusions

Several aspects of solution-focused theory are displayed in this case example. First, the SC focuses on positives throughout the session. The counselor initiates the session by praising the mother for being involved in her son's education, which helps to both establish the tone for the session and to develop rapport with the mother. Rather than focusing on what has not been working, the SC focuses on the exceptions, meaning, when things have gone well, and explores the details of what James did during the exception and the mother's perceptions regarding her and her husband's contributions to James's exceptions.

The SC uses a scaling question to identify what successes the mother perceives to already have happened. Furthermore, the counselor helps the mother identify what will be the small steps that will yield future progress. Scaling questions help to combat people's tendency to think dualistically. When frustrated, people tend to minimize their strengths/resources and exaggerate the degree of change needed to achieve a goal. Asking people to identify the progress they have already made and what a point above success they have already experienced will look like helps people identify the small changes and details that will lead toward their goals. In other words, it encourages people to focus on the process of change rather than concentrate on whether they have or have not achieved the respective goal, which often is not particularly helpful in making progress toward that goal.

The SC assisted the mother in generating her own ideas and solutions in assisting her son, which reflects another core principle of solution-focused theory—that people have the resources to resolve their own problems. The SC could have readily offered direct suggestions but refrained from doing so because of the fact that people tend not to follow the suggestions of others. Rather, the SC helped the mother identify solutions that had already worked in her family and were generated by her, two conditions that are likely to increase the likelihood that the mother will use the ideas she generated. The authors' experience is that most people have done considerable thinking about their problem and have identified potential solutions for that problem, and rather than offering solutions that would work from the consultant's worldview, it is more effective to facilitate the consultee's exploration of the solutions he or she is considering.

The process and techniques used in SFC are extremely similar to the process of solution-focused counseling. The primary difference is that the consultant asks the consultee to identify his or her contributions to changes in the person of concern.

Empirical Support for Solution-Focused Consultation (SFC)

There is not much research regarding the effectiveness of SFC. Two efficacy studies involving SFC with parents yielded support for the approach. One study positively impacted parent stress and competence along with high levels of satisfaction among parent participants (Sommers-Flanagan et al., 2015). The other investigation yielded improvement on a number of child and parent measures three and six months following the intervention, whereas the treatment-as-usual comparison group showed improvement three months following the consultation but failed to demonstrate continued improvement at six months postconsultation (McGarry et al., 2008).

There is also some empirical support that school psychologists and teachers regard SFC as a viable model. A qualitative study revealed that solution-focused thinking was one of only three theories used by ten educational psychologists from the United Kingdom (Kennedy et al., 2008). In an examination of a consultation model employed by educational psychologists that integrated appreciative inquiry and solution-focused thinking in assisting teachers to promote students' emotional and social skill development, investigators found that teachers believed that the model increased their professional development, and teachers perceived the miracle question, which is a predominant technique in SFC, to be the most powerful question of the consultation (Doveston & Keenaghan, 2010).

Conjoint Behavioral Consultation (CBC)

CBC (Sheridan & Kratochwill, 2010) is a family-school partner model which seeks to address children's needs across both home and school environments and to enhance relationships between parents and teachers. It probably has the most empirical support of any school-consultation model, more of which will be discussed later. CBC incorporates a traditional model of behavioral consultation along with the ecological model which seeks to understand and address children's behavior by intervening within the various systems in which children exist. The mechanism of children's behavior change is through modification of the mesosystems and microsystems in which the child is embedded. The microsystem is enhanced by providing parents and teachers with behavioral techniques and strategies. The mesosystem is addressed through efforts to improve parent-teacher relationships by (a) emphasizing shared ownership and responsibility for problem identification and solutions, (b) acknowledging the unique expertise of both the teacher and parent, (c) targeting needs across rather than within settings, and (d) enhancing parent-teacher communication. Research has demonstrated that within in the context of CBC, children's improvements in learning, attention, adaptive behaviors, and social skills are mediated by improvements in the parent-teacher relationship (Sheridan et al., 2017). Similar to other behavioral consultation models, the four stages in the CBC process include conjoint needs (problem) identification, conjoint needs (problem) analysis, plan implementation, and conjoint plan evaluation (Sheridan & Kratochwill, 2010). Prior to the initial conjoint needs (problem) identification stage, relationship building, which is emphasized throughout the consultative process, is pursued through establishing shared expectations, clarifying roles, and strengthening partnerships.

Conjoint Needs (Problem) Identification Stage

The goals of the initial problem identification stage involve prioritizing needs, clarifying and defining target concerns, and establishing procedures for collecting baseline data

(Sheridan & Kratochwill, 2010). The team collaborates in prioritizing the student's needs, considering a behavior's severity, relationship to other behaviors, and existence in both the school and home environments. Behavioral targets of concern are identified and operationalized in objective, measurable terms. For example, the target behavior that is described as a classroom disruption may be redefined as "the number of times the student speaks without raising their hand during class or without being called upon by the teacher." There is an emphasis on identifying behaviors that a child needs to develop in order to enhance their functioning, as opposed to focusing on the elimination of undesirable behaviors, unless the child is exhibiting behaviors that are harmful to oneself or others. The consultant considers the likelihood of behavioral constellation, meaning, that behaviors are rarely singular but typically reflect a larger constellation (e.g., depression, anxiety). The consultant also keeps in mind the principle of response covariation, meaning, that the consultant reflects upon the correlation between various behavioral responses, none of which alone may be problematic or symptomatic but, taken together, may provide insight regarding a student's underlying concerns.

Once there is agreement among the team regarding the priorities, the behaviors of concern are defined in measurable, objective terms. Data collection is conducted to establish a baseline and enable data-driven decision-making. Data is collected from a variety of persons, including teachers, parents, peers, and even the child themselves, when it is important to know the child's subjective experiences, such as cognitions and feelings. A variety of data collection methods may include rating scales, interviews, and observations. Data is also collected within a variety of home and school settings (e.g., classroom, lunchroom, playground, community settings, and others). Whereas other behavioral consultation models tend to focus on only child-related variables, conjoint behavioral consultants emphasizes environmental assessments with deep consideration being given to the settings in which the behaviors occur and the events preceding and succeeding the behaviors of concern.

Conjoint Needs (Problem) Analysis

Parents and teachers evaluate the baseline data, select behaviors for the child, and explore various factors that may influence the child's behavior. Hypotheses are generated regarding the conditions that may support the occurrence of the behaviors of concern, and an intervention plan is developed that can be used across the school and home. The team seeks to determine the potential function of a child's behavior, as all behavior is seen as purposeful, or whether the child has the ability to demonstrate the behavior expected. In order to identify the potential function of a child's behavior, the team considers the antecedents to the behavior, which might include such things as the instructions given by a teacher, interactions with certain peers, or school bus rides, and the consequences, meaning, the events that follow the behavior, which may include attention from a parent, removal of expectations, and avoidance of tasks. Patterns across home and school settings are examined to identify whether events that occur in one setting contribute to behaviors in another setting. For example, the team may consider how the child's sleep and nutrition or morning routine may impact school performance, or whether school events, such as bullying victimization or poor performance on a test, may contribute to expressions of anger at home. The function of the child's behavior may be to obtain something, such as attention or approval, or avoid something, such as an exam or interacting with a particular peer. In order to determine whether the child's behavior is due to lacking the required skill set, the consultant must identify the skills required to complete a task, divide the skills down into component steps, assess the child's capacity to demonstrate each step, identify the highest level at which the child can conduct the skill, and develop an intervention starting at that point. For example, a child with poor social skills who has difficulty initiating conversations with peers may need to first learn common ways to introduce topics of conversation. The consultant should ask both teachers and parents what they perceive as the function of the child's, emphasizing the consequences for the child's behavior rather than internal explanations (e.g., "He is lazy").

The development of a specific plan includes several considerations. One, the plan must address whether the child appears to be either motivated by attention or escape. Second, the plan should include evidence-based strategies that the consultant can share with the team. Evidence-based strategies can be researched through such resources as the US Department of Education's "What Works Clearinghouse" website (https://ies.ed.gov/ncee/wwc). Finally, to ensure that both teachers and parents implement the plan within their respective environments, it is crucial that the consultant obtain the parents' and teacher's acceptance of the plan. The plan must be consistent with the teachers' and parents' beliefs, require reasonable effort, and be within the consultees' skill set.

Plan Implementation

During the implementation stage, the consultant maintains close contact with the consultees in order to provide support, ensure understanding of the plan, reinforce consultees' intervention efforts, and identify whether there is a need for modifications to the plan. The consultant seeks to reinforce consultees' implementation of the plan by creating a written description of the plan (e.g., manual) or using previously used interventions, providing scripts or checklists, providing training or feedback to the teachers and parents, and asking consultees to self-monitor their implementation of the plan. The consultant might also consider conducting an assessment of the immediate intervention effects.

Conjoint Plan Evaluation

The consultant, teachers, and parents examine the collected behavioral data to determine the impact of the intervention. There are several strategies for determining whether the intervention is responsible for any observed behavioral changes. Data collection must be conducted early in the case. Objective data, such as frequency counts, must be used rather than subjective data. Data are collected and graphed continuously throughout a case. Standardized assessments, such as structured interviews, are to be used. Goal attainment scaling (GAS) is often used to assess consultees' perceptions regarding whether the consultation goals have been achieved. In GAS, involved individuals rate the child's behavior on a scale of –2 (least favorable) to +2 (most favorable). For example, for homework completion, which is a common focus in CBC, a rating of +2 might be the child completing 80% of their homework assignments, a rating of 0 would indicate the baseline, and a rating of –2 could be completing none of their homework.

Effectiveness of Conjoint Behavioral Consultation

Studies have revealed that CBC is effective in improving social skills (Sheridan et al., 2017) and decreasing off-task, noncompliant behavior for youth at risk of developing behavioral disorders (Garbacz et al., 2020; Sheridan et al., 2017). CBC has been found to be more effective in reducing hyperactivity for children diagnosed with attention-deficit/

hyperactivity disorder (ADHD) than a treatment of the usual condition, but that differences at a one-year follow-up were not maintained.

Participatory Culture-Specific Intervention Model (PCSIM)

In an effort to develop a model of consultation that incorporates clients' cultural experiences, Nastasi and colleagues developed a model, the PCSIM, that integrates an ethnographic (qualitative) research method and action research process with a collaborative approach to consultation (Nastasi et al., 2000). In this approach, consultation operates as applied research, in which the consultant works as a reflective practitioner or action researcher who "engages in a continual process of explicating and evaluating his/her application of theory and research to service delivery" (Nastasi et al., p. 168). This model involves the integration of behavioral, ecobehavioral, and conjoint behavioral consultation and incorporates models of program development and evaluation, including those for capacity building, empowerment evaluation, program planning and evaluation, and organizational development.

In using PCSIM, consultants employ naturalistic inquiry to construct a comprehensive understanding of culture which is then used to develop interventions that are culture-specific (Nastasi et al., 2000). Naturalistic inquiry is conducted in real-life settings based upon the assumption that phenomena are highly influenced by context and culture. Culture-specific theory and intervention are based upon the identification and description of phenomena from the perspective of the target population. Other methods of inquiry include key informant and intensive interviews, participant observation, artifacts, and activity logs. A sense of trust by clients is engendered through the investigator's work in engaging long-term and intensively with the population and setting, using various sources, methods, and perspectives, seeking confirmation from stakeholders on the validity of the data and interpretations, and presenting the research in sufficient detail to enable replication.

The foundational assumption of PCSIM is, like ecological theory, consultation incorporates culture in understanding behavior (Nastasi et al., 2000). In PCSIM, culture includes the shared language, beliefs, values, and behavioral norms and the interpretations of these cultural experiences of the members of the culture. Through the use of this model, PCSIM consultants facilitate sustainable and systemic cultural change.

PCSIM to Promote Psychological Well-Being (PWB)

In one investigation, Bell and colleagues (2015) used the PCSIM model to promote psychological well-being (PWB) in a K–2 charter school in New Orleans in which the student population was predominately low-income African American students. In order to connect students to the mental health services in the community, promote PWB, and prevent population-level disturbances, the objective of the consultation was to develop multitiered systems of student support. In the goal identification phase, the consultants conducted semistructured focus groups with teachers, parents, and students, through which they examined valued competencies and expectations, stressors, reactions to stress, support, and reactions to support (Nastasi et al., 2000). The university team also collected ecomaps from students, in which they drew and labeled (e.g., stressful, supportive, or ambivalent) important people in their life, which were followed by individual interviews regarding particularly stressful and supportive relationships (Nastasi et al., 2011).

During the four-year partnership, multiple significant challenges emerged, which prompted a two-year problem identification and analysis phase (Bell et al., 2015). Challenges at the macrosystem level included a reluctance on the part of school personnel to reduce academic time and instruction, given the academic needs of the low-income students, a lack of mental health providers in the community, and a lack of financial resources to hire a staff member to provide PWB services.

Through the consultant-consultee partnership, challenges were addressed by disseminating formative research data to administrators and teachers, and in particular, universal screening reports and qualitative data regarding local risks and supports, to eventually obtain school personnel's support to increase the focus on PWB services. Bell and colleagues (2015) enumerated several successes of the consultative partnership, including the implementation of a universal screening procedure, which helped school staff understand the PWB needs of students, and school staff members' increased understanding of the need to balance students' academic and socioemotional needs.

Culture-Specific Participatory Action Research to Promote Psychological Well-Being

In another study, Bell et al. (2017) describe the use of a culture-specific participatory action research approach, which incorporated the PCSIM approach (Nastasi et al., 2000) among several others, for the process of implementing a social-emotional learning (SEL) program. Explicit instruction and ongoing student practice in the competencies of self-awareness, self-regulation, social awareness, relationship skills, and responsible decision-making are typically delivered by teachers using an evidence-based curriculum in the SEL program (Collaborative for Academic, Social, and Emotional Learning; CASEL, 2013a).

In particular, promotion of the school climate by addressing school policy- and practice-related factors, such as safety, caring relationships, and parent involvement, is included in SEL programming. The efficacy of SEL program has been stablished by numerous studies that have documented effects, including enhanced academic achievement and decreases in externalizing and internalizing problems (e.g., Durlak et al., 2011). Nevertheless, varying cultural values, priorities, resources and strengths, and phenomenologies of behavior that occur within the family, school, and community can represent a consistent barrier to effective school-based programming, such as SEL programs (Burke, 2008). Indeed, the cultural factors of skills, norms, behaviors, and values are essential to the success of evidence-based programs through the compatibility of the program with the people delivering and receiving it (Forman et al., 2013). With this in mind, the culture of the school must be a paramount consideration for consultants implementing programs in engaging in systems reform (Nastasi & Hitchcock, 2016).

In another investigation, Bell and colleagues (2017) studied the application of a culture-specific participatory action research approach to address SEL and school climate in an urban public school which was an open-enrollment charter school comprised of 96% African American students and 4% Latin@ students, who were mostly from low-income families. Eighteen of the 23 classroom teachers (78%) were European American. The authors developed and implemented a SEL-specific consultation model consisting of four existing models: Nastasi et al.'s (2000) PCSIM, Hess et al.'s (2012) public health problem-solving model for schools, the National School Climate Council's (2007) school climate reform model, and Devaney et al.'s (2013) social and emotional learning implementation cycle.

The first three stages of the SEL cycle concern system entry activities, stages 4–8 included traditional problem-solving steps, and stage 9 was the integration of the model, which included:

- Stage 1: Gaining commitment to the SEL cycle from the principal
- Stage 2: Creating a school action research team (stage 2)
- Stage 3: Developing relationships with the staff before designing formative research
- Stage 4: Problem identification
- Stage 5: Problem analysis
- Stage 6: Program design
- Stage 7: Implementation
- Stage 8: Process or program evaluation
- Stage 9: Institutionalization of the action research process

Five principles are infused in each stage, with multiple stakeholders (e.g., students, parents, and teachers) being included in the process. Cultural specificity is addressed through ensuring the acceptability of methods, process, and programs among the stakeholders. Participants engage in local data-based decisions for each of the research, planning, and implementation phases. Problem analysis and program design incorporate evidence base and practice. Lastly, the principal is supported in providing facilitative leadership for the SEL-focused initiatives.

STAGE 1: PRINCIPAL COMMITMENT

In order to help the principal make an informed commitment to the SEL cycle, several strategies were employed (Bell et al., 2017). Following the principal's review of literature on SEL that included a summary of the research, definition, and effectiveness indicators (CASEL, 2003), the principal and primary consultant met to discuss the resources required for the program. The meeting resulted in an agreement to offer a professional development presentation for the instructional staff on the principles of SEL. The principal agreed to inform the staff and school board that SEL was a priority for him and that the upcoming school year would involve formative research and planning that would address the specific needs of the school, and the subsequent school year would be used to implement pilot programs.

STAGE 2: ACTION RESEARCH TEAM CREATION

The school action research team (SART) and the principal agreed that the team must include representatives from various stakeholders (e.g., teachers, parents, and students). In addition, the principal added the criteria that SART nominees had to have been employed at the school for at least one year and had committed to being there for the next year, the teacher nominees must represent different grade levels, and because the principal could not allot time to the endeavor during the school day, the teacher nominees would be willing to attend after-school meetings, and students and parents could provide their own transportation. The nominees were informed of the purpose, procedures, and time commitment. The SART ultimately consisted of ten stakeholders: one seventh-grade student, one parent, one administrator, seven teachers, and the consultant.

STAGE 3: FORMING PARTNERSHIPS AMONG THE SART

As group cohesion was important to the success of the endeavor, several strategies were used to promote unity within the SART. The first SART meeting involved a team-building exercise that included sharing personal stories and values while emphasizing active listening and trust. Group norms were developed and were then reviewed at the beginning of all meetings. Furthermore, the consultant developed rapport with the SART members through informal, non-work-related weekly check-ins, including sitting with SART members during planning periods or during lunch.

STAGE 4: BROAD-LEVEL FORMATIVE RESEARCH TO IDENTIFY PROBLEM OR GOAL

The SART team administered the CASEL (2013b) Survey of Social-Emotional Skills and Climate, which is a comprehensive SEL and school climate questionnaire comprised of 63 Likert-scaled items containing 22 distinct factors. The instructional staff received the complete data set along with a polarized ranking of the top five most unfavorably endorsed items during a 1.5-hour faculty meeting (Bell et al., 2017). During this meeting, eight SART members each led a small-group discussion in which teachers reviewed a list of data analysis questions designed to elicit the group's top three suggested problems for investigation and programming for change. The three most common suggested priorities were bullying and safety issues on the bus, problems with anger-regulation skills, and excessive teasing. At the SART meeting the following week, the team prioritized the issue of anger regulation to be analyzed and addressed because it was perceived to be a core issue that was related to other concerns, including bus behavior.

STAGE 5: UNDERSTANDING THE PROBLEM IN CONTEXT (PROBLEM ANALYSIS)

In the next stage, the SART team co-constructed a problem analysis methodology in order to develop a comprehensive understanding of the problem of inappropriate anger regulation. In pursuit of the goal of stage 5, the team developed a local model that defined culturally problematic anger regulation behaviors, along with the ecological risk and protective factors that are contributory or protective against problematic anger regulation. Subsequently, within two meetings, the SART and consultant developed a research methodology to develop the research questions, select appropriate methods to answer the research questions, and obtain the necessary resources for data collection efforts. SART members read Hess et al.'s (2012; pp. 69–78) chapter on problem analysis and reviewed a visual model of factors involved in problem analysis created by the consultant (Bell et al., 2017). Then, consensus was achieved among the SART that the following four broad research questions would guide the problem analysis: (a) What triggers students at the school to become angry at each ecological level? (b) What does appropriate and inappropriate anger look like? (c) What are the reasons a student will exhibit inappropriate anger control? and (d) What are the reasons a student will exhibit valued or appropriate anger control?

The SART agreed that qualitative focus groups would be used, as they would allow for detailed responses from a large sample while avoiding the difficult task of coding multiple handwritten responses. Then, student focus groups were conducted with 36 teacher-nominated students with representation from each of the grade levels and anger-regulation abilities. Eight teachers from varying grade levels participated in three teacher focus groups, and six parents with at least several children attending the school participated in two evening focus groups. The principal committed funds for dinner for the adult focus groups and snacks for student groups.

Following Meyers and colleagues' (2010) eight steps for qualitative analysis, the consultant, two interested SART members, and three university-based research assistants received consultant training and then engaged in whole-group coding of several focus group transcripts. Following the practice exercises, each coder independently analyzed transcripts they had been assigned and then discussed her or his coding decisions during a series of weekly group meetings. The team subsequently analyzed codes to determine if they were identified by all the stakeholder groups (parents, students, and teachers). Then, a visual model of the codes was created and presented to all focus groups for checking.

The SART team then independently reviewed all 150 codes, identifying what they believed to be the key themes. A theme was categorized as higher-order insight when it was reflected in data across or within the deductive domains (i.e., triggers, protective factors, risk factors, and undesired behaviors). Twelve meta-themes were identified through this process. For example, three conclusions for the domain of triggers were reached among SART members. The team identified an inherent tension between the purpose of public schooling and the trigger of academic frustration. Second, the school emphasized college readiness and academic rigor, and there was consensus among all the stakeholder groups that students' frustration with academic material was a frequent source of anger. The third issue was the failure of the prevention of the frequent triggers for anger, including those at home, with students not being provided with the methods to manage anger. The final theme concerning triggers involves the tension between classroom management and the enforcement of discipline. There was a vicious cycle in which students would react angrily upon receiving discipline, at which time they would receive another consequence for the inappropriate response.

STAGE 6: DESIGNING A CULTURE-SPECIFIC PROGRAM

The process of designing a program to address anger regulation involved five steps (Bell et al., 2017). First, the SART members created a list of five to ten potential prevention or intervention activities in response to the themes from the visual model of the data and also treat multiple ecological variables. Second, at a SART meeting, participants discussed and identified commonalities in members' suggestions. Third, the SART members agreed upon three interventions: a social emotional curriculum delivered by all teachers, a SEL-focused teacher-to-teacher mentorship program, and the implementation of a peer mediation program. Fourth, SART was divided into three committees and met weekly for a month to select an evidence-based program, coordinate the program implementation, identify and acquire the needed resources, and identify the intervention objectives and short- and long-term data needed to evaluate fulfillment of the objectives. After completing the committee planning for each intervention, the consultant engaged in a series of four meetings with the school administrators to identify and obtain the human, fiscal, and material resources required to implement each program.

CONCLUSION

Through this example, Bell et al. (2017) provided an extensive case study studying the way in which consultants can engage in a culture-specific, co-constructed model for a mental health program design that contrasts with the typical top-down managerial approaches. The sequence of consultation within each stage typically involved a consultant-led introduction to theory and practice and logic modeling, followed by SART's assumption of responsibility for developing processes and programs that were compatible with the unique culture of the school. The results of surveys and focus group members with SART members suggest that the process was acceptable and socially valid, suggesting the ability for the program perhaps to be generalized to other schools within the district.

Summary

It is likely that school SCs will be increasingly called upon to engage in collaboration and consultation for a variety of reasons. The NCLB Act (2002) and ESSA (US Department of Education, n.d.) require that school personnel make concerted efforts to increase parent involvement, including hard-to-access parents, given that research demonstrates the positive relationship between parent involvement and academic achievement. Enhanced use of consultation and collaboration by SCs is also consistent with the trend in the school counseling profession to maximize the impact of the school counselor through the utilization of comprehensive interventions that are more likely to impact the larger school environment in comparison to direct services, such as individual counseling.

It is possible that SCs who positively influence teachers, administrators, and parents by imparting their training and expertise achieve a more significant impact than SCs who rely upon solely providing direct service to students. As a colleague of one of the authors stated, "If I help a teacher more effectively manage her class, teach a subject, or relate to students, it will likely help thousands of students over time." By using consultation and collaboration, SCs thus adopt an expanded view regarding the way in which they can help students both at school and at home. School counselors are likely in a key position to promote the increased emphasis on facilitating school-family-community partnerships given their training and expertise in group dynamics, communication skills, and child and adolescent development. Moreover, enthusiastic adoption of this role may contribute to the further development of the identity of the school counseling profession.

References

Abdul-Adil, J. K., & Farmer, Jr., A. D. (2006). Inner-city African American parental involvement in elementary schools: Getting beyond urban legends of apathy. *School Psychology Quarterly*, *21*(1), 1–12. https://doi.org/10.1521/scpq.2006.21.1.1

American School Counselor Association. (2019a). *ASCA standards for school counselor preparation programs*. Author. www.schoolcounselor.org/getmedia/573d7c2c-1622-4d25-a5ac-ac74d2e614ca/ASCA-Standards-for-School-Counselor-Preparation-Programs.pdf

American School Counselor Association. (2019b). *The ASCA national model: A framework for school counseling programs* (4th ed.). Author.

Bell, P. B., Larrazolo, H. L., & Nastasi, B. K. (2017). Promoting universal psychological well-being in an urban U.S. public school using a culture-specific, participatory action research approach to consultation. *International Journal of School & Educational Psychology*, *5*(3), 178–191. https://doi.org/10.1080/21683603.2016.1276815

Bell, P. B., Summerville, M. A., Nastasi, B. K., Patterson, J., & Earnshaw, E. (2015). Promoting psychological well-being in an urban school using the participatory culture-specific intervention model. *Journal of Educational and Psychological Consultation*, *25*(2–3), 72–89. https://doi.org/10.1080/10474412.2014.929955

Bower, H. A., & Griffin, D. (2011). Can the Epstein Model of parental involvement work in a high minority, high-poverty school? A case study. *Professional School Counseling*, *15*(2), 77–87. https://doi.org/10.1177/2156759X1101500201

Burke, R. W. (2008). *Political and systemic issues of public schools as settings for mental health programs and services.* Center for School Mental Health. http://csmh.umaryland.edu/Resources/Briefs/SMHTeacherBrief.pdf

Collaborative for Academic, Social, and Emotional Learning. (2003). *Safe and sound: An educational leader's guide to evidence-based social and emotional learning (SEL) programs.* Mid-Atlantic Regional Educational Laboratory, the Laboratory for Student Success (LSS). www.communityschools.org/assets/1/AssetManager/1A_Safe_Sound.pdu

Collaborative for Academic, Social, and Emotional Learning. (2013a). *Effective social and emotional learning programs.* Author. www.casel.org/library/2013-casel-guide

Collaborative for Academic, Social, and Emotional Learning. (2013b). Student, staff, and parent survey of social-emotional skills and climate for needs and outcome assessment. In E. Devaney, M. U. O'Brien, H. Resnik, S. Keister, & R. P. Weissberg (Eds.), *Sustainable schoolwide social and emotional learning (SEL): Implementation guide and toolkit* (pp. 161–197). Author.

Council for the Accreditation of Counseling and Related Educational Programs. (n.d.). *2016 CACREP standards.* www.cacrep.org/for-programs/2016-cacrep-standards/

Devaney, E., O'Brien, M. U., Resnik, H., Keister, S., & Weissberg, R. P. (2013). *Sustainable schoolwide social and emotional learning (SEL): Implementation guide.* Collaborative for Academic, Social, and Emotional Learning.

Doveston, M., & Keenaghan, M. (2010). Teachers and educational psychologists working together: What can we learn? *Support for Learning, 25*(3), 131–137. https://doi.org/10.1111/j.1467-9604.2010.01451.x

Durlak, J. A., Weissberg, R. P., Dymnicki, A. B., Taylor, R. D., & Schellinger, K. B. (2011). The impact of enhancing students' social and emotional learning: A meta-analysis of school-based universal interventions. *Child Development, 81*(1), 405–432. https://doi.org/10.1111/j.1467-8624.2010.01564.x

Epstein, J. L., Sanders, M. G., Sheldon, S., Simon, B. S., Salinas, K. C., Jansorn, N. R., Van Voorhis, F. L., Martin, C. S., Thomas, B. G., Greenfield, M. D., Hutchins, D. J., & Williams, K. J. (2018). *School, family, and community partnerships: Your handbook for action* (4th ed.). Corwin Press.

Epstein, J. L., & Sheldon, S. B. (2002). Present and accounted for: Improving student attendance through family and community involvement. *The Journal of Educational Research, 95*(5), 308–318. https://doi.org/10.1080/00220670209596604

Epstein, J. L., & Van Voorhis, F. L. (2010). School counselors' roles in developing partnerships with families and communities for student success. *Professional School Counseling, 14*(1), 1–14. https://doi.org/10.1177/2156759X1001400102

Fields-Smith, C. (2007). Social class-and African-American parental involvement. In J. A. VanGalen & G. W. Noblit (Eds.), *Late to class: Social class and schooling in the new economy* (pp. 167–202). State University of New York Press.

Forman, S. G., Shapiro, E. S., Codding, R. S., Gonzalez, J. E., Reddy, L. A., Rosenfield, S. A., Sanetti, L. M. H., & Stoiber, K. C. (2013). Implementation science and school psychology. *School Psychology Quarterly, 28*(2), 77–100. https://doi.org/10.1037/spq0000019

Gaetano, Y. D. (2007). The role of culture in engaging Latino parents' involvement in school. *Urban Education, 42*(2), 145–162. https://doi.org/10.1177/0042085906296536

Garbacz, S. A., Beattie, T., Novotnak, T., Kurtz-Nelson, E., Zahn, M., Yim-Dockery, H., Cohenhour, J., & Jordan, P. (2020). Examining the efficacy of conjoint behavioral consultation for middle school students with externalizing behavior problems. *Behavioral Disorders, 46*(1), 3–17. https://doi.org/10.1177/0198742919888844

Griffin, D., & Steen, S. (2010). School-family-community partnerships: Applying Epstein's theory of the six types of involvement to school counselor practice. *Professional School Counseling, 13*(4), 218–226. https://doi.org/10.1177/2156759X1001300402

Grothaus, T., & Cole, R. (2010). Meeting the challenges together: School counselors collaborating with students and families with low income. *Journal of School Counseling, 8.* www.jsc.montana.edu/articles/v8n27.pdf

Hart, P., & Jacobi, M. (1992). *From gatekeeper to advocate: Transforming the role of the school counselor.* College Entrance Examination Board.

Henry, L. M. (2014). *Just love: A collaborative evaluation of a faith-based school-family-community partnership through the voices of the children* (Unpublished doctoral dissertation). University of Florida.

Hess, R. S., Short, R. J., & Hazel, C. E. (2012). *Comprehensive children's mental health services in schools and communities.* Routledge.

Holcomb-McCoy, C. (2010). Involving low-income parents and parents of color in college readiness activities: An exploratory study. *Professional School Counseling, 14*(1), 115–124. https://doi.org /10.1177/2156759X1001400111

Jeynes, W. H. (2012). A meta-analysis of the efficacy of different types of parent involvement programs for urban students. *Urban Education, 47*(4), 706–742. https://doi. org/10.1177/0042085912445643

Juhnke, G. A. (1996). Solution-focused supervision: Promoting supervisee skills and confidence through successful solutions. *Counselor Education and Supervision, 36*(1), 48–57. https://doi. org/10.1002/j.1556-6978.1996.tb00235.x

Kahn, B. B. (2000). A model of solution-focused consultation for school counselors. *Professional School Counseling, 3*(4), 248–254.

Kennedy, E. K., Frederickson, N., & Monsen, J. (2008). Do educational psychologists "walk the talk" when consulting? *Educational Psychology in Practice, 24*(3), 169–187. https://doi. org/10.1080/02667360802256733

Kratochwill, T. R. (1990). *Behavioral consultation and therapy.* Plenum.

McGarry, J., McNicholas, F., Buckley, H., Kelly, B. D., Atkin, B. D., Atkin, L., & Ross, N. (2008). The clinical effectiveness of a brief consultation and advisory approach compared to treatment as usual in child and adolescent mental health services. *Clinical Child Psychology and Psychiatry, 13*(3), 365–376. https://doi.org/10.1177/1359104508090600

Meyers, J., Truscott, S. D., Meyers, A. B., Varjas, K., & Smith Collins, A. (2010). Qualitative and mixed methods designs in consultation research. In W. P. Erchul & S. M. Sheridan (Eds.), *Handbook of research in school consultation* (pp. 89–114). Routledge.

Nastasi, B. K., & Hitchcock, J. (2016). *Mixed methods research and culture-specific interventions: Program design and evaluation.* The New Mixed Methods Research Series.

Nastasi, B. K., Jayasena, A., Summerville, M., & Borja, A. (2011). Facilitating long-term recovery from natural disasters: Psychosocial programming in tsunami-affected schools of Sri Lanka. *School Psychology International, 32*(5), 512–532. https://doi. org/10.1177/0143034311402923

Nastasi, B. K., Varjas, K., Bernstein, R., & Jayasena, A. (2000). Conducting participatory culture-specific consultation: A global perspective on multicultural consultation. *School Psychology Review, 29*(3), 401–413. https://doi.org/10.1080/02796015.2000.12086024

National School Climate Council. (2007). *The school climate challenge: Narrowing the gap between school climate research and school climate policy, practice guidelines and teacher education policy.* Author. http://schoolclimate.org/climate/policy.php/

No Child Left Behind Act of 2001, Pub. L. No. 107–110 (2002).

Sheldon, S. B. (2003). Linking school-family-partnerships in urban elementary schools to student achievement on state tests. *The Urban Review, 35,* 149–165. https://doi.org/10.1023/A: 1023713829693

Sheridan, S. M., & Kratochwill, R. T. (2010). *Conjoint behavioral consultation: Promoting family-school connections and interventions* (2nd ed.). Springer.

Sheridan, S. M., Witte, A. L., Holmes, S. R., Coutts, M. J., Dent, A. L., Kunz, G. M., & Wu, C. R. (2017). A randomized trial examining the effects of conjoint behavioral consultation in rural schools: Student outcomes and the mediating role of the teacher-parent relationship. *Journal of School Psychology, 61,* 33–53. https://doi.org/10.1016/j.jsp.2016.12.002

Sommers-Flanagan, J., Polanchek, S., Zeleke, W. A., Hood, M. H. E., & Shaw, S. L. (2015). Effectiveness of solution-focused consultations on parent stress and competence. *The Family Journal, 23*(1), 49–55. https://doi.org/10.1177/1066480714555696

US Department of Education. (n.d.). *Every student succeeds act (ESSA).* Author. www.ed.gov/ essa?src%3Drn

Chapter 9

Academic Development

Box 9.1 2016 Council for the Accreditation of Counseling and Related Educational Programs (CACREP, n.d.) School Counseling Specialty Area Standards

2.a School counselor roles as leaders, advocates, and systems change agents in P-12 schools

2.b School counselor roles in consultation with families, P-12 and postsecondary school personnel, and community agencies

2.d School counselor roles in school leadership and multidisciplinary teams

3.d Interventions that promote academic development

3.i Approaches to increase promotion and graduation rates

Box 9.2 ASCA (2019a) Standards for School Counselor Preparation Programs (ASCA CAEP SPA)

2.1 Describe established and emerging counseling and educational methods, including but not limited to childhood and adolescent development, learning theories, behavior modification and classroom management, social justice, multiculturalism, group counseling, college/career readiness, and crisis response.

4.1 Plan, organize, and implement a variety of instructional and counseling strategies as part of a comprehensive school counseling program (direct and indirect student services) to improve pre-K–12 student attitudes, knowledge, and skills.

A historic criticism of the role of SCs is that by primarily focusing on the mental health needs of a comparatively small number of students rather than on the academic development of all students, SCs have functionally reduced their potential positive impact. The aspects of school counseling services that have typically benefited all students, such as class scheduling and tracking students in academic/career paths, are increasingly viewed as administrative responsibilities instead of the developmental interventions that SCs are trained to provide (Galassi & Akos, 2012). Although SCs, among their other

DOI: 10.4324/9781003167730-9

responsibilities, can be critical educational team members in promoting students' academic development, they may lack confidence in their ability to effect change in children's academic performance. As an example of this, in one study, SCs expressed doubt that they could impact student achievement on standardized tests with the interventions they typically use (Brigman & Campbell, 2003). SCs' lack of confidence in impacting students' academic achievement may also be compounded by the fact that SCs often do not have a background in providing instruction. As of 2021, only Kansas, Kentucky, Louisiana, Nebraska, North Dakota, Oregon, and Texas still required teaching experience as requirement to become a school counselor (ASCA, n.d.). One potential reason that many states eliminated the teaching requirement for SCs is that studies have consistently demonstrated that having prior teaching experience is not an indicator of perceived effectiveness for school counselors (e.g., Moyer & Yu, 2012).

The profession's expectation that SCs focus on academic development is clearly reflected in the first two SC mindsets of the *ASCA National Model* (2019b), which are that "[e]very student can learn, and every student can succeed" (M 1.: p. 6), and the mindset that "[e]very student should have access to and opportunity for a high quality-education" (M 2.: p. 6). The apparent challenge to the school counseling profession is the question of how SCs make a meaningful contribution to academic development when most lack a background in instruction. The profession of school counseling is evolving in its definitions of the role of the SC in promoting students' academic achievement. It is implied within the *ASCA National Model* (2019b) that SCs facilitate students' academic development by influencing those student behaviors that are indirect indicators of academic achievement, namely, attendance, behavior, and discipline, rather than providing direct instruction of an academic discipline (e.g., mathematics, reading, etc.). This chapter will focus on how SCs can facilitate student achievement through teaching students study skills, a growth mindset, focusing on improving students' attendance and remaining in school, and how school counselors can promote parent involvement. Finally, we also explain how SCs can utilize the theoretical frameworks of motivational interviewing and the transtheoretical model of change for promoting academic achievement.

Empirical Support for School Counselors' Impact on Students' Academic Achievement

As discussed in previous chapters, the impact of comprehensive school counseling programs upon students' academic achievement is mixed. There are a number of statewide studies that have found that students from schools which have comprehensive school counseling programs, comapared to those who do not have one, tend to have higher grades and better attendance (e.g., Carey et al., 2012). Research comparing schools with RAMPs versus those that do not have it yielded more mixed results, with some studies finding that schools with RAMP status appeared to promote greater academic achievement than schools without RAMP (e.g., Ward, 2009), while other studies found no differences in the academic achievement of RAMP vs. non-RAMP schools (e.g., Goodman-Scott et al., 2020). Given that SCs are often closely associated with social emotional learning (SEL) programs, a related line of research is the impact of SEL programs on students' academic achievement. A meta-analytic study revealed that SEL programs promote students' academic achievement (Durlak et al., 2011). It has been theorized that SEL programs promote students' learning outcomes because they (1) enhance students' core problem-solving skills, (2) improve relationships between students and teachers, and (3) improve teachers' classroom management (Schonfeld et al., 2015). One study revealed that SCs' time usage was positively associated with positive student outcomes (Shi & Brown, 2020). When SCs expended more time on scheduling and other counseling duties, students were more likely to be retained in ninth grade. The more time SCs spent on college readiness/application was positively associated with students' enrollment in Advanced Placement (AP) courses and four-year universities.

School Counselors' Use of Direct Services to Promote Academic Development

SCs can promote academic development in their application of direct student services, which includes the school counseling curriculum, appraisal and advising, and responsive services. Much of the research literature in the past two decades concerning SCs' use of direct services to promote students' academic development involves teaching students study skills through small-group counseling and school counseling lessons.

Student Success Skills (SSS)

Student Success Skills (SSS) is a classroom lesson and group counseling curriculum developed by school counselor educators to be implemented specifically by SCs to promote students' academic achievement (Webb et al., 2019). This curriculum was developed in response to studies that found a set of skills to be fundamental to students' school success: cognitive and metacognitive skills, including goal setting, progress monitoring, and memory skills; social skills, including interpersonal skills, problem-solving, listening and teamwork skills; and self-management skills, including the ability to manage attention, motivation, and anger. The SSS curriculum uses Wang et al.'s (1994) Ask, Tell, Show, Do, Feedback instructional method.

A meta-analytic study of the first five SSS studies found that that the curriculum promoted statistically significant increases in mathematics and reading scores on achievement tests, and these gains were considered to be large effects (Villares et al., 2012). However, a more recent study found that while SSS improved students' behavioral engagement, disruption, assertion, cooperation, and test anxiety, it did not result in increases in reading and mathematics test scores (Webb et al., 2019).

Format for Group Sessions Within SSS

This group counseling intervention entails eight weekly sessions of 45 minutes each, after which four booster sessions occur. Brigman and Campbell (2003) explain that the group format is comprised of three sections: the beginning, middle, and end. The beginning phase of the session had four tasks, including a temperature check on feelings/energy, a review of the past session, a focus upon goals and progress associated with academic achievement and school success behavior, and a preview of the day's meeting and a rationale or benefits statement that related to engagement in the activity (Brigman & Campbell, 2003).

The middle phase of each session included the introduction of the main activity, in which the leader used the "Ask, Tell, Show, Do" method of skill and knowledge building (Brigman & Campbell, 2003). Before the presentation of a new topic, counselors "ask" students to define and relate their existing knowledge and how they currently use this skill or concept. Second, the students "tell" or offer new information related to skill/information being discussed and, third, "show" the use of this skill or information. Finally, the "do," or guided practice, provides the students with the chance to apply the new ideas/skills; this typically involves role-play and feedback but may also include art, music, games, or story-telling or reading with different endings suggested by the student.

The ending of the group session also includes four tasks (Brigman & Campbell, 2003). The first is a review of the content that was covered in the session, while the second is to process or discuss the thoughts and feelings of participants during their participation in the activities of the session. The third task is for students to set a goal, consider what was most meaningful in the session, and choose how they will use a particular technique the next week to reach their goal. The final task of the session is a preview of the next session conducted by the leader.

Format for School Counseling Lessons Within SSS

The format for the school counseling lessons involves three main topics: (1) cognitive skills, including memory strategies, setting of goals, and progress monitoring; (2) social skills, including conflict resolution, social problem-solving, and teamwork skills; and (3) self-management skills, including anger management, motivation, and career awareness (Brigman & Campbell, 2003). The school counseling lessons are taught in a four-part format in accordance with the small-group sessions. Activity 1 includes the use of an introduction, something that stimulates the children's attention, and a rationale that encourages children to value the topic being taught. Children share what they already know, provide a definition of the topic being discussed, and may think about ways to handle a proposed problem through the use of quotations, puppets, visual aids, and so forth. SCs may also use pair sharing and group discussion skills to respond to student comments and inter-weave students' ideas with one another. Once the activity is completed, small groups present their information to the entire class, after which students summarize the content of the lesson and engage in setting a goal. Students consider the activity, what they learned, and how they can use the information learned. Children are encouraged to think of something they had learned from the lesson that they could use and to share this with their partners, while volunteers report on how they would apply the lesson with the entire class.

Teaching Students to Use Study Skills

One way that SCs often seek to promote students' academic achievement is by providing students with study skills. Information included in the following section comes from an excellent chapter regarding best practices in school psychologists' practice in teaching study skills, by Smith Harvey and Chickie-Wolfe (2007). Interested readers are encouraged to consult this resource for more information on this topic.

Students who are able to effectively organize their time and have good test-taking skills are able to achieve better grades as well as perform more proficiently on standardized tests.

Box 9.3

Did You Know?

Some studies have found that test-taking skills training benefits students from low socioeconomic backgrounds more than twice as much as students who are not from low socioeconomic backgrounds (Scruggs, 1986).

Study skills involve self-regulation, in which students learn to use a variety of techniques to incorporate fundamental principles of effective learning into their studying and learning. Smith Harvey and Chickie-Wolfe (2007) explain that best practice in teaching study skills should include the techniques being embedded in the curriculum, since study skills taught in isolation are less likely to be maintained or used in multiple settings. A team of collaborative members that include SCs, teachers, parents, and students should be developed in order to teach the study skills, which first includes an ecological assessment of four steps (Smith Harvey & Chickie-Wolfe, 2007).

Ecological Assessment: Step 1

First, team members analyze the problem together and define it using measurable and specific terms. This may include a classroom observation in which the students' academic skills and behaviors are identified and compared with peers, followed by a student interview, in which students' motivation, emotions, and behaviors regarding study skills, environmental supports toward the use of study skills, and students' cognitive skills, reading skills, writing and reporting skills, math, science, and technology skills, test preparation and test-taking skills, and use of metacognitive strategies are measured. A work session observation, in which the school counselor observes a student completing academic tasks, is conducted. During this first step, the student should describe his or her work methods, approaches to studying, textbooks, notebooks, assignment books, and completed work, along with the observer's analysis of classroom-completed work and homework samples from the student. A parent-and-teacher interview should occur, followed by the assembly of information to identify strengths and needs (Smith Harvey & Chickie-Wolfe, 2007).

Box 9.4

Did You Know?

There are numerous study skills checklists and assessments available on the internet.

Ecological Assessment: Step 2

Following the assessment, the second step involves team members meeting to review gathered information, coming to an agreement about the desired or acceptable level of performance by the student(s), and identifying resources, including materials and supportive people. The potential interventions should be enumerated along with their positive and negative attributes. After interventions are selected, a time frame to teach the study skills and implementation strategies is identified. The responsibilities for each team members are named, written, and reinforced through the writing of a signed contract (Smith Harvey & Chickie-Wolfe, 2007).

Ecological Assessment: Step 3

In the third step, interventions are actualized, through interventions being implemented with guided instruction and modeling, with a transition to fading instruction as self-sufficiency is evidenced. Results should be tracked until the behavior reaches the acceptable levels of performance identified prior to the implementation of the intervention. Ideally, the student will monitor his or her own behavior, as self-monitoring is related to more independent and sustained learning (Smith Harvey & Chickie-Wolfe, 2007).

Ecological Assessment: Step 4

After successful strategies have been ascertained, in the fourth step, the team should plan and initiate strategies in order for the student to generalize and maintain the study skills learned. In this level, goals should be set for successful generalization. Progress monitoring can be used to track progress in using the study skills effectively and consistently across settings. Smith Harvey and Chickie-Wolfe (2007) explain that goal setting and progress monitoring will likely need to be used in at least three settings to promote successful generalization of skills.

Consideration of Students' Motivation, Emotions, and Behavior

After an ecological analysis of the problem, team members should consider the students' motivation, emotions, and behavior. Developing short- and long-term goals for each subject and including them into the student's weekly planners can be a helpful intervention. School counselors should determine to what the student attributes academic success and difficulty, as pupils with an external locus of control need to experience the connection between the use of study skills and the result of academic success. Students also need to identify the purpose of the learning material, such as why the teacher gave the assignment or how the assignment will be useful in life (Smith Harvey & Chickie-Wolfe, 2007).

Another consideration for SCs is to determine what kind of homework the student enjoys and dislikes, since many students assume that they generally dislike homework when in fact they do enjoy some homework assignments. Less-preferred homework assignments may be completed first, sandwiched between preferred assignments, or completed after easier work has been accomplished. Finally, SCs should determine whether the student suffers from disabling academic anxiety. There is a curvilinear relationship between anxiety and performance; some anxiety is helpful in encouraging an optimal level of functioning, while too much anxiety can be crippling. Test anxiety affects between a third and a half of intermediate-level students and can be identified by students during individual interviews or self-report measures. Direct interventions to diminish anxiety may range from relaxation techniques to medication, while indirect interventions include study skill training, including test-taking strategies (Smith Harvey & Chickie-Wolfe, 2007).

Consideration of Environmental Supports

After considering students' motivation, emotions, and behaviors, attention should next be paid to the student's environmental supports. First, to what extent are the students' parents checking assignments and monitoring homework completion? Children typically require help from their parents in time management and organization of materials, and while students generally need less supervision as they age, those with learning difficulties will likely require more support for a longer period of time than typically developing adolescents. SCs should check to see whether there is a regular, quiet time set aside for homework completion and if there is enough support at home for the establishment of solid study strategies. This may require the identification of an alternative location to complete homework, such as an after-school program. Another consideration is what the student does when he or she gets stuck with homework completion at home. Is there a person from whom the student may seek help? Additionally, is there adequate communication between home and school to foster the student's homework completion? (Please see discussion on parent-school involvement later in the chapter.) Teachers need to be able to talk with parents about problems with homework; likewise, parents need to be able to consult with teachers for assistance with children's homework and their organization (Smith Harvey & Chickie-Wolfe, 2007).

Consideration of Students' Cognitive Skills

Next, the SC should analyze the students' cognitive skills that may promote or inhibit his or her learning. For example, does the student plan for learning, such as bringing home all necessary supplies for homework? Students should document short-term assignments in a homework book and keep track of long-term assignments, such as projects or papers, in a calendar. SCs will also want to establish whether the student uses estimation skills to gauge the amount of time necessary for assignments and schedules such assignments accordingly. When the student submits assignments, does he or she include his or her name, the title of the assignment, and a date? SCs should also determine whether or not the student corrects his or her papers before submission. Other necessary cognitive skills include the abilities to organize papers, keep work areas clean and organized, follow directions and information given, and take notes in class. Finally, the student should be able to pre-read reading materials before listening to a lecture, as such a practice tends to increase his or her understanding of the material presented (Smith Harvey & Chickie-Wolfe, 2007).

Test Preparation and Taking

Perhaps one of the most important set of skills that students may possess is to be able to effectively prepare for assessments of their learning (see Box 9.6). This includes spacing learning across several study sessions, conducting weekly reviews, and using effective memory-enhancing strategies, such as rehearsing, making organizational charts, using associative strategies (e.g., peg words), and using graphic organizers. School counselors should also determine whether the student uses study guides while studying. It is typically helpful to assemble information into meaningful groupings, although teacher-provided study guides that require students to add their own elaborative information can also be valuable. SCs should also ask whether or not the student is able to predict test questions and use corrected assignments and tests as a learning tool. Finally, it is important to recognize if the student knows and can use good test-taking strategies. For example, he or she should come to an exam with all necessary materials, skim through a test to determine its layout prior to allocating time to each section, record memorized material as soon as possible, try to answer every question, immediately eliminate incorrect multiple-choice responses, and so forth (Smith Harvey & Chickie-Wolfe, 2007).

Encouraging School Attendance and Preventing Student Dropout

Of course, in order for students to be academically successful, they need to stay in school.
One in seven students in the United States is chronically absent (Swaak, 2018). Chronic absenteeism is associated with lower math and letter recognition scores in elementary students (Erlich et al., 2013), is an early predictor of dropping out of school (MacIver,

2010), and is a predictor of poverty, negative physical health, and increased involvement in the criminal justice system (US Department of Education, 2019). While the percentage of students who drop out of high school declined from 8.3% in 2010 to 5.1% in 2019 (National Center for Education Statistics, n.d.), it is still a cause for concern for educators. The high school dropout rate varies by ethnicity: 1.8% for Asians, 4.1% for Whites, 5.1% for two more races, 5.6% for Blacks, 7.7% for Latin@, 8.0% for Pacific Islanders, and 9.6% for American Indian/Alaska Native. Thirty-six states include attendance rates as part of their school performance profile (Swaak, 2018).

A national review of attendance data identified three types of students who are chronically absent from schools, which include those who cannot attend, those who will not attend, and those who do not attend (Balfanz & Byrnes, 2012). For students who cannot attend school, the primary reasons for missing school involve physical illness, poverty issues, such as housing instability or the need for employment, and involvement in the juvenile justice system. For students who will not attend school, reasons for school absenteeism include school refusal or school phobia. These students report bullying and feelings of harassment as reasons for their absenteeism. For students who do not attend school, many of them do not see school as being related to their future and report that their culture does not value education. Obviously, SCs are encouraged to attempt to tailor interventions to address the reasons students are chronically absent (Eklund et al., 2022). Eklund et al. (2022) notes that there are not many studies using designs which compared one intervention to another. A meta-analytic study revealed that each of the four types of attendance promotion programs, which include behavioral (e.g., peer and adult mentoring, token reinforcement systems, school-based truancy court, and social-emotional learning instruction), academic, family-school partnerships (e.g., home-school communication), and policy-oriented interventions, yielded a positive and statistically significant but small impact upon attendance.

A meta-analytic study of dropout prevention programs found that programs that involved family engagement, behavioral intervention, career development/job training, and literacy development strategies were the most effective in preventing students from leaving school (Chappell et al., 2015). Other types of dropout prevention programs which have empirical support include those that focused on enhanced academic support, after-school, health and wellness, life skills development, mentoring, and school/classroom environment. Weinstein et al. (2021) conducted one of the few empirical studies of an SC-led dropout prevention program, finding that students who participated in the Student Success Skills (SSS) group curriculum, discussed previously in this chapter, demonstrated greater gains than a treatment group in school attendance, core grade point average, and the mathematics and reading state assessment tests.

White and Kelly (2010) summarize the best practices for school counselors in preventing school dropout, including strategies addressing protective factors, such as social support (e.g., instituting a peer mentoring system or buddy system), monitoring and mentoring (e.g., assigning adult mentors or advocates to identified at-risk students to track progress and collaborate with parents), personal and social skill development (e.g., providing explicit social skills instruction), and parent involvement (e.g., offering parent training), and addressing risk factors such as academic instruction (e.g., assisting teachers in providing more academic instruction and less time on behavior management), and academic support (e.g., offering after-school study skills and time management classes). Galassi and Akos (2012) recommend that SCs access dropout data in one's own district (to identify particular subgroups of students that are at risk for dropping out), identify initiatives to discourage dropout in one's own district, and develop, propose, and advocate for individual and systems-level interventions to combat the problem of student dropout in one's own school system. Furthermore, given that students report a variety of reasons for absenteeism (Balfanz & Byrnes, 2012), SCs should interview students to identify their reasons for being chronically absent.

Promoting a Growth Mindset

There has been a fair amount of attention in the education literature given fostering students' growth mindset. Individuals with a growth mindset believe that personal characteristics (e.g., intelligence, athletic ability) can be modified through persistence and effective strategies (Yeager & Dweck, 2012). Growth mindset is contrasted with a fixed mindset, in which people believe that personal characteristics are fixed and therefore cannot be modified. A growth mindset among students is associated with self-regulatory learning, specifically setting learning goals, help-seeking, persistence, remaining confident when encountering obstacles (Burnette et al., 2013). Students with a fixed mindset are more likely than students with a growth mindset to focus on bettering their peers, proving their ability, and avoiding mistakes. Studies have also shown that adults can impact students' mindsets. When students are provided with praise for their effort, they are more likely to assume more challenging tasks and have a mastery focus (Skipper & Douglas, 2012). In contrast, when students are praised for their intelligence, they tend to be more concerned with their grades and appearing intelligent rather than actually learning. Dweck (2007) recommends that adults provide students with praise regarding the process for how they learned material, making such comments as, "It was neat to see that you tried a variety of strategies before you found one that worked for you." Or for students who continue to struggle with comprehending a new concept, "I see the hard work you have been putting into learning, and I would like to work together with you to help you understand what you have learned and what you are still seeking to figure out." A meta-analytic study revealed that the relationship between mindset and academic achievement is not strong, and interventions to enhance growth mindsets generally do not have a strong impact on academic achievement (Sisk et al., 2018). However, the results of the meta-analytic study did find some support for the contention that improving mindsets may be more impactful for academically at-risk students and students with low socioeconomic status.

Brougham and Kashubeck-West (2018) conducted the lone study that could be identified in the literature to date of a school counselor–led intervention to specifically enhance students' growth mindset. The investigators argue that growth mindset is relevant to the school counseling profession as developing a growth mindset is consistent with each of the mindsets of the ASCA Student Standards (2021) and a number of behavior standards, including applying self-motivation to learning and the self-management skills of assuming responsibility, employment self-control and discipline, working independently, delaying gratification for long-term gains, persevering, overcoming learning barriers, and using coping skills. Sixty-nine students from two urban high schools received either the treatment or control sessions. The treatment condition consisted of three group sessions in which students learned about how the brain learns, read a testimonial about a student who struggled and improved with effort, and wrote a letter of encouragement to a future freshmen regarding what they learned about learning. While the students in the treatment condition had enhanced growth mindset in comparison to students from the control group, the treatment group participants did not outperform the control group participants in terms of either grade point average or attendance. The investigators concluded that the positive impacts of a growth mindset intervention may only be revealed over a longer period of time, citing the results of Blackwell et al. (2007), who found that a growth mindset orientation predicted academic achievement over a two-year time frame.

Parent Involvement

A quantitative synthesis of nearly half a million families found that parents' naturally occurring involvement in children's schooling had a positive but small association with children's academic, social, and emotional adjustment and is negatively related to children's delinquency (Barger et al., 2019). Parents' attendance at school events and discussion of school with children were positively related to children's adjustment, but parents' assistance with homework was negatively associated with children's achievement, but not motivation or engagement. The finding that parental involvement in children's homework was negatively associated with academic achievement is consistent with previous research. For example, one study found that parental involvement with children's homework has a negative impact upon student's achievement over time (e.g., Silinskas et al., 2015). Barger et al. (2019) suggest that likely reasons for the finding that parental involvement in homework is negatively associated with achievement may be because parental involvement interferes with student's skill development, or that homework involvement may be dependent upon the quality of a parent's involvement.

There is much research regarding the advantages of families in children's educational lives. The quality of family-school interactions has been found to be not only positively related but also partly responsible for students' positive functioning (Sheridan et al., 2017). In the school counseling literature, parent involvement is often conceptualized as school-family-community partnerships (SFC), which are collaborative relationships between school personnel, families, and community members in which all are considered to be equal in the planning, coordinating, and implementing of programs and activities at home, at school, and in the community to help increase the social, academic, and emotional success of students (Smith et al., 2020). Many approaches present a limited conception of family involvement, where parents and teachers work in parallel rather than collaboratively. For example, Storytelling for the Home Enrichment of Language and Literacy Skills (SHELLS; Boyce et al., 2010) teaches parents to support their children's literacy by employing three kinds of elicitation strategies: "support" (e.g., following the child's lead while encouraging the child's active participation), "ask" (asking children about what they are reading), and "expand" (e.g., building on the child's responses, connecting the child's responses to their previous experiences). Smith et al. (2020) conducted a meta-analysis of parent-involvement programs that also included relational elements, meaning, that they either strengthened or increased meaningful relationships between parents and teachers, through such mechanisms as home-school notes and collaborative conferences involving mutual decision-making. Smith et al. (2020) found that SFC interventions significantly and positively impacted students' academic achievement, behaviors, social-behavioral competence, and mental health. Specific components of SFCs that were particularly impactful were home-based involvement, school-to-home communication, and bidirectional communication. The benefits of SFCs applied equally to students of various racial backgrounds. It would seem that SCs would have an essential role in promoting SFC partnerships, given their training in communications and child development.

Griffin et al. (2021) present a seven-stage model for SFC parternships designed specifically for the purposes of promoting Black male students' education success and equity. Griffin et al. (2021) explains that an equity-focused approach is essential for meeting the needs of Black male students, given their history of oppression and barriers to educational access. Equity-focused partnerships are based on four principles: democratic collaboration, empowerment, social justice, and strengths. Democratic collaboration means that all stakeholders are involved, including Black males and their family and community members, in decision-making, planning, and evaluation processes. Empowerment is reflected in the view that Black youth, parents, and community members are experts in their own lives who must be equally involved in decisions that affect them. Equity-focused partnership also seek to empower Black males, helping them understand the education and community problems impacting them, acquire a positive racial/culture identify, and develop advocacy skills. Equity-focused partnerships also have the goal of promoting social justice so that Black males obtain access to information, opportunities, and resources and they can identify and challenge systemic racism and inequity. Equity-focused partnerships view Black males from a strength-based perspective, as opposed to the commonly used deficit perspective.

The first stage of Griffin et al.'s (2021) model for equity-focused partnerships involves *preparing to partner*. The SC must seek to educate themselves about the experiences of Black students, collect data on disparities that exist within the school, and learn about antiracist strategies. Preparing to partner also involves beginning to build a coalition of stakeholders (e.g., other SCs, administrators, teachers, community members, organizations) who are committed to promoting equity. In stage 2, SCs *assess the needs and strengths* of Black male students by conducting needs and strengths assessments through interviews, surveys, and focus groups with the various stakeholder groups and identifying current and potential resources and allies. Stage 3 involves *coming together* through the formation of a partnership leadership team which is informed of the results of the assessments from stage 2. In stage 4, *creating a shared vision and plan*, the leadership team moves toward consensus regarding the program goals, timeline, and evaluation plan, which includes identifying the relevant instruments and/or surveys for measuring the program goals. Stage 5, *taking action*, involves recruiting volunteers (e.g., mentors, tutors) from the Black community, delegating responsibilities, and building alliances among teachers, family, and community members to support the program. In stage 6, *evaluating and celebrating progress*, Black family and community members are included in the evaluation process and celebrated for their contributions to the program. The final stage, *maintaining momentum*, involves continuing to build support for the program by developing additional alliances and seeking to strengthen the program based upon the evaluation results.

Motivational Interviewing and the Transtheoretical Model (TTM) of Change

MI and the TTM of Change are two psychological frameworks, which are often used in conjunction, that currently are not widely used among school counselors but may have considerable relevance in promoting students' academic development. Simply defined by Miller and Rollnick (2012), "[m]otivational interviewing is a collaborative conversation style for strengthening a person's own motivation and commitment to change" (p. 29). The helpee is encouraged to be an active member in achieving lifestyle change as the helper assumes a collaborative approach, working "with" and "for" the helpee that enables him or her to activate their own motivation and resources for change.

MI embodies elements of person-centered counseling theory (Miller & Rollnick, 2012). Person-centered therapy focuses on the ideas that a person is trustworthy and can solve their own problems and that people truly want to self-actualize and be the best version of themselves. Carl Rogers (1954) theorized that a counseling relationship that is rooted in acceptance but not approval of actions and empathy for a person's experience promotes self-change. Much like person-centered theory, MI allows this process to happen because the purpose is to see the world through another person's eyes and allow the person to set an agenda for change (Miller & Rollnick, 2012). MI allows a person to see their options to reaching a goal through the use of conversation to elicit a person's personal thoughts and attitudes toward change. MI assumes that a person has the strengths and reasons for acting a certain way, and they must overcome their ambivalence about changing. Another person cannot force someone else to change; they must want it for themselves (Miller & Rollnick, 2012). MI provides an environment of support and understanding that a person needs in order to make a commitment to change.

In MI, counselors create an environment that promotes the person's autonomy and decision-making skills. Counselors must realize that a person may desire to change a behavior, or they may be seeking counseling to accept a behavior or condition (Miller & Rollnick, 2012). MI is often used in conjunction with Prochaska et al.'s (1994) theory of change. The TTM of change is effective in eliciting change of behaviors and acknowledges that change can happen on a continuum. This theory hypothesizes that people who make significant behavioral changes, such as quitting smoking or modifying their diet, undergo a series of changes or stages in which they display changes in thoughts, feelings, and behaviors that can be characterized as increasingly adaptive. Prochaska et al. (1994) found that there are six stages of change people pass through while trying to adjust their habits. The six stages of change include precontemplation, contemplation, preparation, action, maintenance, termination (Prochaska et al., 1994). Within TTM, the counselor meets the person at his or her stage of change. A person must be cognizant of his/her stage of change in order to make progress. TTM allows a person to overcome their ambivalence about change, see their reasons for certain behaviors, and acknowledge feelings associated with the desire to change. It is essential to recognize and understand these stages of changes since a person can rotate and cycle through these stages numerous times before the termination of the behavior occurs. Table 9.1 provides a brief summary of the six stages of change proposed by Prochaska et al. (1994) and describes how these stages can be seen in an academic setting.

Several studies have found empirical support for the use of TTM for understanding students' academic development. In comparison to students in the lower stages of TTM, students in the more advanced stages of TTM show greater academic achievement (Moreira et al., 2018), higher self-efficacy for learning (Grant & Franklin, 2007), engagement, well-being, more advanced learning approaches, and demonstrated less emotional/behavioral problems (Moreira et al., 2020). Moreira et al. (2020) concluded that the TTM framework is a useful framework of identifying students who are academically at risk, informing differentiated academic interventions, and monitoring the effectiveness of academic interventions in students over time through an assessment of a student's stage of development.

Many educators assume that students should be fully motivated to learn and experience frustration with academically at-risk students. MI and TTM imply that educators must first understand the student's desire to change and not ignore the fact that students may be ambivalent about academic underachievement and may not regard it is as a significant problem. MI provides teachers with a framework to help students overcome their ambivalence and find motivation to change without demoralizing or forcing a change to happen.

Strait et al. (2012) found that middle school students who participated in an MI process were more likely to exhibit increase class participation and positive academic behavior over

Table 9.1 Transtheoretical (Stages of Change) Model for Academic Behaviors

Stage of Change	Characteristic	Student Statement	Appropriate Intervention	Sample Dialogue
Pre-contemplation	No intention of changing and avoids discussion of the issue. Either sees situation as hopeless or denies existence of issue.	"I will be okay. I'm fine." "Grades do not count until I get to high school." "Why do people keep annoying me about this?" "I just have to be here so they stop bugging me."	In a respectful manner discuss the possible consequences of continued academic underachievement.	"What do you think will likely happen if your grades stay the same as they are now?"
Con-templation	Aware of problem and considers making changes but lacks commitment. May remain in this stage for considerable time.	"I want better grades, but it is hard to do my homework every night." "I can't study every night for an hour, and my teacher is too busy to help. I will try something else next time."	Discuss advantages and disadvantages of making changes.	"Would you like to explore what you see as the advantages and disadvantages of getting better grades?"
Preparation	Recognizes advantages of making changes and thinking about how to change. May have made small behavioral changes.	"I really want to get better grades, and I have ideas on how to do so." "Last week in math, when I was frustrated, I was able to take a break and come back to the problem in a little while." "I know I could improve my math grade if I organized my binder, studied every night for an hour, asked my teacher to explain what I don't understand, or asked a friend to help me."	Explore the student's perspectives regarding his or her small steps, asking what the student thinks has been effective and what are additional steps the student plans to take. Ask the student if he or she is interested in learning about evidence-based strategies, such as strategies for note-taking, test-taking, etc.	"It sounds like you feel proud about the changes you have started to take."
Action	Actively engaging in steps to change.	"I'm working hard to get better grades." "For the last week, I've been completing my homework each night as soon as I get home from school for one week."	Explore the student's self-generated strategies for improvement, including what he or she has found to be effective, why the student thinks it is effective, what the student plans to increase. Explore the student's thoughts and feeling regarding the progress he or she is making in an attempt to instill in the student a sense of pride.	"What have you learned about what works?" "What do you plan to do more or less of?"

Maintenance	Achieved goals. Student adjusts his or her behaviors to maintain commitment to changes/goals. The student may be aware of obstacles to maintaining progress, such as tendency to not follow through on plans when around peers.	"I do not want anything to get in the way of the changes I've made, as I really want to get into that college." "It is really hard to keep things up when I am around some of my friends." "My friends don't have to do their homework right after school, but I know if I don't, I will not complete it. I will try to finish it right after school or in a study hall if I know I want to do something with friends after school."	Help student identify potential obstacles to maintaining changes and solutions to address identified obstacles.	"You are really committed to this. It is really important to you."
Termination	Behavioral changes have been achieved and are thoroughly integrated into the student's daily functioning. There is little chance of relapse.	"I'm really into what I'm doing. It is hard to believe that I used to struggle with school." "I've organized all my binders and folders so that I can easily find my work and classroom materials. I know that this takes me only a few minutes after class and has enabled me to complete my work on time and not become frustrated."	Help student reflect upon the various changes that he or she has made. Explore how the behavioral changes the student has made have resulted in changes regarding the student's self-efficacy/confidence.	"You have worked really hard. What does this say to you about your ability to achieve your goals?"

Modified from: Prochaska, J. O., Norcross, J. C., and DiClemente, C. C. (1994). *Changing for good: The revolutionary program that explains the six stages of change and teaches you how to free yourself from bad habits.* William Morrow.

time than students who did not participate in the MI process. The study required students to engage in an MI session with a school or clinical psychology graduate student in which they completed a self-assessment, received support and feedback, and developed a plan for change. The researchers believed that the intervention appeared to be successful because it helped students realize that they possessed the resources for progressing toward their goals. A systematic review of the literature found that MI improved student outcomes in such areas as academic achievement, attendance, engagement, and confidence with schoolwork among secondary school students in seven out of eight studies (Snape & Atkinson, 2016). Ratanavivan and Ricard (2018) found that the use of MI with elementary students in a disciplinary alternative education program yielded a moderate summative effect upon their classroom behaviors. A qualitative investigation of SCs who use MI revealed that they perceive MI to be effective for individual counseling with students, that SCs see evoking change talk as a particularly effective technique for helping students identify their reasons for failing and making changes for eventual improvement, and that discussing students' discrepancies often led to collaborative discussions between an SC and student in developing a student-led action plan.

Use of MI and TTM in Advising and Individual Counseling

SCs can infuse MI and TTM in individual counseling to promote academic development. When conducting advising or individual counseling, SCs must first identify where students are in the stages of change in order to see where to initiate the MI conversation. Since SCs often have limited time to work with students, MI can be applied in one to three quick individual sessions. The collaborative and conversational nature behind MI can be used to strengthen and develop a student's commitment to change (Miller & Rollnick, 2012). Students will be more likely to invest in this process because they are leading the conversation and their ideas are being used to solve their own problems, which is likely to increase students' academic efficacy.

SCs should follow the four processes of motivational interview, engaging, focusing, evoking, and planning with each student (Miller & Rollnick, 2012). Engagement establishes the connection between the student and the counselor and enables the student to begin to connect with someone who supports their ideas about changing. During the focusing piece of MI, a school counselor focuses on what the student wants to discuss as a problem. Areas of concern for counselors and students may or may not be the same, so a counselor must maintain a specific direction that will lead to a positive and necessary change for the student to become successful. Once the counselor and student have identified a problem, the MI process continues with evoking, and the student actively finds ideas and reasons for wanting to change their behaviors. Here the counselor is able to assist the student in finding realistic ways to solve a problem and narrow down their options while helping them to realize they can change and can do it independently. Finally, a student can develop a plan about how and when to change. Developing a commitment to change and creating a specific plan of action to change can be done with the school counselor's assistance. The student's plan can be changed and revisited as new challenges arise in order to maintain continuous commitment to the plan.

MI suggests that students will be more likely to be academically engaged because they have selected the goals and are a more active participant in the process of change. An example of using MI in schools would be for school counselors to enable students to create their own self-designed behavior contracts. These contracts could be for behaviors that occur (or do not occur) at school or home to increase appropriate behavior and academic success. To develop the contract, counselors can start with identifying the behavior that needs changed and use Miller and Rollnick's (2012) five beginning questions listed below to foster the student's ideas for change (see Box 9.5). From here a counselor and the student would begin to develop a contract and plan the student could follow. The counselor would be able to use MI in a few brief sessions to review the student's plan and progress.

Box 9.5   Miller and Rollnick's (2012) 5 Beginning Questions in Motivational Interviewing (p. 11)

1. "Why would you want to make this change?"
2. "How might you go about it in order to succeed?"
3. "What are the three best reasons for you to do it?"
4. "How important is it for you to make this change, and why?"
5. "So what do you think you will do?"

Source: Miller, W. R., and Rollnick, S. (2012). *Motivational interviewing: Helping people change* (3rd ed.). Guilford Press.

Use of MI and TTM in Consultation With Parents and Teachers

It is important to realize that MI in an academic setting requires the support of teachers and parents. SCs are in the unique position to advocate for the student's ability for self-directed change and assist parents and teachers in understanding how they can support students' continued commitment for academic improvement. SCs can encourage parents and teachers to be on the lookout for a student's strengths, good steps, and intentions. They should be "accentuating the positives," meaning, that even small progress should be acknowledged (Miller & Rollnick, 2012). Parents and teachers need to be aware of the fact that students may be resistant to change, and constantly focusing on the problem "behavior" or the negative "attributes" the student is ready to change will only be detrimental to the process of change. Change takes time, and the process can be frustrating for parents and teachers, and school counselors can help parents and teachers explore how they manage their frustration when relating to a student regarding academic difficulties.

SCs can explain the benefits and process of MI with parents and teachers. SCs can share with parents and teachers that students may feel angry, defensive, uncomfortable, and powerless when they are being "told" to change or have realized there is something they would like to change about themselves (Miller & Rollnick, 2012). They can be allowed to experience the natural consequences of what happens if they choose to continue a behavior that is self-defeating and need to see the benefits of self-directed change. This is especially true for students in the precontemplative stage, as they may not see their behaviors as a problem and will rarely take responsibility for their actions even if there is a negative consequence (Prochaska et al., 1994).

SCs can educate teachers and parents about the stages of change and how to respond to students at the various stages. SCs can assist parents with ways to stay engaged with the student, empower him/her to change, be open to their ideas, and make sure the student feels understood (Miller & Rollnick, 2012). Again, this can be a challenging process because many students feel as though they have tried everything possible or are in denial that the problem exists (Prochaska et al., 1994). For example, if a student is earning failing grades in math for two straight grading quarters and says he does not study or try, the school counselor may suggest that parents and teachers use MI techniques to help the student acknowledge his problem and develop a plan to be more successful. School counselors can remind parents and teachers to avoid demanding change, telling the student what he "should" do, or demeaning the students' efforts to change by saying they can do "better." It is important to remember that during the change cycle, a person is doing the best they know how in order to maintain a behavior or try to change it (Prochaska et al., 1994). SCs can train parents and teachers to ask the student what his process would be to earn higher grades in math, identify what would be "good grades" from the student's perspective, and explore with the student how improved grades might benefit the student.

Summary

Although SCs have not always been perceived as school personnel who can help promote students' academic development, their roles in contributing to students' academic success at the systems level, such as engaging in school reform activities, and at the student level, such as teaching study skills and success skills and promoting attendance and staying in school, are both intuitive to their professional responsibilities and supported by research. Furthermore, SCs can utilize their training and strengths in communication and socioemotional skills to foster collaboration between the family and school environments.

References

American School Counselor Association. (2019a). *ASCA standards for school counselor preparation programs.* www.schoolcounselor.org/getmedia/573d7c2c-1622-4d25-a5ac-ac74d2e614ca/ASCA-Standards-for-School-Counselor-Preparation-Programs.pdf

American School Counselor Association. (2019b). *The ASCA national model: A framework for school counseling programs* (4th ed.). Author.

American School Counselor Association. (2021). *ASCA student standards: Mindsets & behaviors for student success.* Author. www.schoolcounselor.org/Standards-Positions/Standards/ASCA-Mindsets-Behaviors-for-Student-Success

American School Counselor Association. (n.d.). *State certification requirements.* Author. www.schoolcounselor.org/school-counselors-members/careers-roles/state-certification-requirements

Balfanz, R., & Byrnes, V. (2012). *Chronic absenteeism: Summarizing what we know from nationally available data.* Johns Hopkins University. https://ies.ed.gov/ncee/edlabs/regions/west/relwestFiles/pdf/508_ChronicAbsenteeism_NatlSummary_Balfanz_Byrnes_2012.pdf#:~:text=Chronic%20absenteeism%20means%20missing%2010%20percent%20of%20a,days%2C%20different%20students%20make%20up%20that%2090%20percent

Barger, M. M., Kim, E. M., Kuncel, N. R., & Pomerantz, E. M. (2019). The relation between parents' involvement in children's schooling and children's adjustment: A meta-analysis. *Psychological Bulletin, 145*(9), 855–890. https://doi.org/10.1037/bul0000201

Blackwell, L., Trzesniewski, K. H., & Dweck, C. S. (2007). Implicit theories of intelligence predict achievement across an adolescent transition: A longitudinal study and an intervention. *Child Development, 78*(1), 246–263. https://doi.org/10.1111/j.1467-8624.2007.00995.x

Boyce, L. K., Innoccenti, M. S., Roggman, L. A., Norman, V. K. J., & Ortiz, E. (2010). Telling stories and making books: Evidence for an intervention to help parents in migrant head start families support their children's language and literacy. *Early Education and Development, 219*(3), 343–371. https://doi.org/10.1080/10409281003631142

Brigman, G., & Campbell, C. (2003). Helping students improve academic achievement and school success behavior. *Professional School Counseling, 7*(2), 91–98. www.jstor.org/stable/42732548

Brougham, L., & Kahubeck-West, S. (2018). Impact of a growth mindset intervention on academic performance of students at two urban high schools. *Professional School Counseling, 21*(1), 1–9. https://doi.org/10.1177/2156759X18764934

Burnette, J. L., O'Boyle, E. H., VanEpps, E. M., Pollack, J. M., & Finkel, E. J. (2013). Mind-sets matter: A meta-analytic review of implicit theories and self-regulation. *Psychological Bulletin, 139*(3), 655–701. https://doi.org/10.1037/a0029531

Carey, J., Harrington, K., Martin, I., & Hoffman, D. (2012). A statewide evaluation of the outcomes of implementation of the ASCA National Model school counseling programs in rural and suburban Nebraska high schools. *Professional School Counseling, 16*(2), 100–107. https://doi.org/10.1177/2156759X0001600203

Chappell, S. L., O'Connor, P., Withington, C., & Stegelin, D. A. (2015). *A meta-analysis of dropout prevention outcomes and strategies* (A technical report in collaboration with the Center for Educational Partnerships at Old Dominion University). National Dropout Prevention Center/ Network at Clemson University. http://dropoutprevention.org/meta-analysis-dropout-prevention-outcome-strategies/

Council for the Accreditation of Counseling and Related Educational Programs. (n.d.). *2016 CACREP standards.* www.cacrep.org/for-programs/2016-cacrep-standards/

Durlak, J. A., Weissberg, R. P., Dymnicki, A. B., Taylor, R. D., & Schellinger, K. B. (2011). The impact of enhancing students' social and emotional learning: A meta-analysis of school-based universal interventions. *Child Development, 82*(1), 405–432. https://doi.org/10.1111/j.1467-8624.2010.01564.x

Dweck, C. S. (2007). The perils and promise of praise. *Educational Leadership, 65*(2), 34–39.

Eklund, K., Burns, M. K., Oyen, K., DeMarchena, S., & McCollom, E. M. (2022). Addressing chronic absenteeism in schools: A meta-analysis of evidence-based interventions. *School Psychology Review, 51*(1), 95–11. https://doi.org/10.1080/2372966X.2020.1789436

Erlich, S. B., Gwynne, J. A., Pareja, A. S., & Allensworth, E. M. (2013). *Preschool attendance in Chicago public schools: Relationships with learning outcomes and reasons for absences.* https://files.eric.ed.gov/fulltext/ED553158.pdf

Galassi, J. P., & Akos, P. (2012). Preparing school counselors to promote academic development. *Counselor Education & Supervision, 51*(1), 50–63. https://doi.org/10.1002/j.1556-6978.2012.00004.x

Goodman-Scott, E., Taylor, J. V., Kalkbrenner, M. T., Darsie, J., Barbosa, R., Walsh, K., & Worth, A. (2020). A multivariate analysis of variance investigation of school-level RAMP status across two states. *Counseling Outcome Research and Evaluation, 11*(1), 31–44. https://doi.org/10.1080/21501378.2019.1575696

Grant, A. M., & Franklin, J. (2007). The transtheoretical model and study skills. *Behavior Change, 24*(2), 99–113. https://doi.org/10.1375/bech.24.2.99

Griffin, D., Williams, J. M., & Bryan, J. (2021). School-family-community partnerships for educational success and equity for Black male students. *Professional School Counseling, 21*(1c), 1–14.

MacIver, M. A. (2010). *Gradual disengagement: A portrait of the 2008–09 dropouts in Baltimore City Schools. Research Report.* Baltimore Education Research Consortium. https://files.eric.ed.gov/fulltext/ED553164.pdf

Miller, W. R., & Rollnick, S. (2012). *Motivational interviewing: Helping people change* (3rd ed.). Guilford Press.

Moreira, P. A. S., Faria, V., Cunha, D., Inman, R. A., & Rocha, M. (2020). Applying the transtheoretical model to adolescent academic performance using a person-centered approach: A latent cluster analysis. *Learning and Individual Differences, 78.* https://doi.org/10.1016/j.lindif.2019.101818

Moreira, P. A. S., Moreira, F., Cunha, D., & Inman, R. A. (2018). The Academic Performance Stages of Change Inventory (APSCI): An application of the transtheoretical model to academic performance. *International Journal of School Educational Psychology, 8*(3). https://doi.org/10.1080/21683603.2018.1530158

Moyer, M. S., & Yu, K. (2012). Factors influencing school counselors' perceived effectiveness. *Journal of School Counseling, 10*(6). www.jsc.montana.edu/articles/v10n6.pdf

National Center for Education Statistics. (n.d.). *Dropout rates*. https://nces.ed.gov/fastfacts/display.asp?id=16

Prochaska, J. O., Norcross, J. C., & DiClemente, C. C. (1994). *Changing for good: The revolutionary program that explains the six stages of change and teaches you how to free yourself from bad habits*. William Morrow.

Ratanavivan, W., & Ricard, R. J. (2018). Effects of a motivational interviewing-based counseling program on classroom behavior of children in a disciplinary alternative education program. *Journal of Counseling & Development*, 96(4), 410–422. https://doi.org/10.1002/jcad.12223

Rogers, C. (1954). *Psychotherapy and personality change*. University of Chicago Press.

Schonfeld, D. J., Adams, R. E., Fredstrom, B. K., Weissberg, R. P., Gilman, R., Voyce, C., Tomlin, R., & Speese-Linehan, D. (2015). Cluster-randomized trial demonstrating impact on academic achievement of elementary social-emotional learning. *School Psychology Quarterly*, 30(3), 406–420. https://doi.org/10.1037/spq0000099

Scruggs, T. E. (1986). Teaching test-taking skills to elementary-grade students: A meta-analysis. *Elementary School Journal*, 7(1), 69–82.

Sheridan, S. M., Witte, A. L., Holmes, S. R., Wu, C., Bhatia, S. A., & Angell, S. R. (2017). The efficacy of conjoint behavioral consultation in the home setting: Outcomes and mechanisms in rural communities. *Journal of School Psychology*, 62, 81–101. https://doi.org/10.1016/j.jsp.2017.03.005

Shi, Q., & Brown, M. H. (2020). School counselors' impact on school-level academic outcomes: Caseload and use of time. *Professional School Counseling*, 23(1), 1–8. https://doi.org/10.1177/2156759X20904489

Silinskas, G., Kiuru, N., Aunola, K., Lerkkanen, M. K., & Nurmi, J. E. (2015). The developmental dynamics of children's academic performance and mothers' homework-related affect and practices. *Developmental Psychology*, 51(4), 419–433. https://doi.org/10.1037/a0038908

Sisk, V. F., Burgoyne, A. P., Sun, J., Butler, J. L., & MacNamara, B. N. (2018). To what extent and under which circumstances are growth mind-sets important to academic achievement? Two meta-analyses. *Psychological Science*, 29(4), 549–571. https://doi.org/10.1177/0956797617739704

Skipper, Y., & Douglas, K. (2012). Is no praise good praise? Effects of positive feedback on children's and university students' responses to subsequent failures. *British Journal of Educational Psychology*, 82(2), 327–339. https://doi.org/10.1111/j.2044-8279.2011.02028.x

Smith, T. E., Sheridan, S. M., Kim, E. M., Park, S., & Beretvas, S. N. (2020). The effects of family school partnership interventions on academic and social-emotional functioning: A meta-analysis exploring what works for whom. *Educational Psychology Review*, 32, 511–544. https://doi.org/10.1007/s10648-019-09509-w

Smith Harvey, V., & Chickie-Wolfe, L. A. (2007). Best practices in teaching study skills. In A. Thomas & J. Grimes (Eds.), *Best practices in school psychology* (5th ed., pp. 1121–1136). National Association of School Psychologists.

Snape, L., & Atkinson, C. (2016). The evidence for student-focused motivational interviewing in educational settings: A review of the literature. *Advances in School Mental Health Promotion*, 9(2), 119–139. https://doi.org/10.1080/1754730X.2016.1157027

Strait, G. G., Smith, B. H., McQuillin, S., Terry, J., Swan, S., & Malone, P. S. (2012). A randomized trial of Motivational Interviewing to improve middle school students' academic performance. *Journal of Community Psychology*, 40(8), 1032–1039. https://doi.org/10.1002/jcop.21511

Swaak, T. (2018, July 31). Nearly 8 million students chronically absent from school each year, 36 states set out to tackle the problem in new federal education plans. *The 74 Million*. www.the74million.org/article/chronic-absenteeism-36-states-essa-plans/

US Department of Education. (2019). *Chronic absenteeism in the nation's schools*. www2.ed.gov/datastory/chronicabsenteeism.html

Villares, E., Frain, M., Brigman, G., Webb, L., & Peluso, P. (2012). The impact of student success skills on standardized test scores: A meta-analysis. *Counseling Outcome Research and Evaluation*, 3(1), 3–16. https://doi.org/10.1177/2150137811434041

Wang, M. C., Haertel, G. D., & Walberg, H. J. (1994). Educational resilience in inner cities. In M. C. Wang & E. W. Gordon (Eds.), *Educational resilience in inner-city America: Challenges and prospects* (pp. 45–72). Lawrence Erlbaum.

Ward, C. A. (2009). An examination of the impact of the ASCA National Model on student Achievement at Recognized ASCA Model Program (RAMP) elementary schools. *Dissertation Abstracts International*, Proquest, LLC. UMI #3401416. Texas A&M University.

Webb, L., Brigman, G., Carey, J., Villares, E., Wells, C., Sayer, A., Harrington, K., & Chance, E. (2019). Results of a randomized controlled trial of the Student Success Skills program on grade 5 students' academic and behavioral outcomes. *Journal of Counseling & Development*, 97(4), 398–408. https://doi.org/10.1002/jcad.12288

Weinstein, J., Villares, E., & Brigman, G. (2021). The effect of the Student Success Skills small group intervention on factors associated with dropout potential. *Journal for Specialists in Group Work*, 46(3), 256–271. https://doi.org/10.1080/01933922.2021.1945175

White, S. W., & Kelly, F. D. (2010). The school counselor's role in school dropout prevention. *Journal of Counseling & Development*, 88(2), 227–235. https://doi.org/10.1002/j.1556-6678.2010.tb00014.x

Yeager, D. S., & Dweck, C. S. (2012). Mindsets that promote resilience: When students believe that personal characteristics can be developed. *Educational Psychologist*, 47(4), 302–314. https://doi.org/10.1080/00461520.2012.722805

Chapter 10

College and Career Readiness

Box 10.1 2016 Council for the Accreditation of Counseling and Related Educational Programs (CACREP, n.d.) School Counseling Specialty Area Standards

1.c Models of P-12 comprehensive career development
2.c School counselors' roles in relation to college and career readiness
3.e Use of developmentally appropriate career counseling interventions and assessments
3.j Interventions to promote college and career readiness
3.k Strategies to promote equity in student achievement and college access

---

Box 10.2 ASCA (2019a) Standards for School Counselor Preparation Programs (ASCA CAEP SPA)

2.1 Describe established and emerging counseling and educational methods, including but not limited to childhood and adolescent development, learning theories, behavior modification and classroom management, social justice, multiculturalism, group counseling, college/career readiness, and crisis response.
3.2 Identify research-based individual counseling, group counseling, and classroom instruction techniques to promote academic achievement, college/career readiness, and social/emotional development for every student.

The *ASCA National Model* (2019b) provides SCs with a framework intended to guide comprehensive, inclusive, equitable school counseling programs that address the needs of all students. A robust career and college readiness program is an integral part of an SC program and can help engage students in academic courses if they are aware of the connection the coursework has to their future careers. Students must be provided with the tools and knowledge to make informed decisions regarding their current academic plans and future options. In this chapter, we review factors concerning students' college and career readiness (CCR), research regarding SCs' effectiveness in promoting college

DOI: 10.4324/9781003167730-10

readiness, and typical career development activities used by SCs. Relevant national organizations that support SCs' efforts to promote a career and college-ready workforce will also be discussed. We provide practical strategies for advisement, using Marcia's (2007) identity status theory, and supporting students in applying to college and financial aid. Finally, we will discuss specific considerations in promoting the CCR of students with disabilities.

While the ASCA asserts that SCs pursue a holistic focus in promoting students' academic, social/emotional, and career development (ASCA, 2019b), the origins of the school counseling profession concerned facilitating students' development. SCs generally have more expertise in career development than any other school-based professional, and it can be argued that career development provides an important niche for SCs. The *ASCA School Counselor Professional Standards & Competencies* require SCs to have the mindset that all students should graduate from secondary education prepared for postsecondary opportunities (ASCA, 2019b). The ASCA *Ethical Standards for School Counselors* (2022) indicates that ethical practice for SC includes collaborating with stakeholders to develop a culture of postsecondary readiness, conduct activities that facilitate college and career awareness, exploration, planning, and decision, and support students' acquisition of mindsets and behaviors for long-term career success.

Federal Legislation and College and Career Readiness

The focus on career development may also become more relevant given recent federal legislation. A criticism of No Child Left Behind (2002) is, while it mandated academic standards, it did not require that academic standards relate to students' CCR (Malin et al., 2017). The 2015 Every Student Succeeds Act (ESSA: US Department of Education, n.d.) increased the emphasis on CCR in a number of ways. Federal funds from ESSA can be used to encourage students' participation in dual enrollment programs and career and technical education (CTE), to encourage cross-sector partnerships with higher education institutions, and to prepare educators to integrate academic and CTE strategies, including funds to train SCs regarding the use of labor market information and financial literacy. Furthermore, ESSA granted states the right to use students' postsecondary readiness and completion of advanced coursework as indicators of school performance.

Components of College and Career Readiness

A widely used definition of college readiness is being academically prepared for postsecondary education, as indicated through standardized test scores, course completion, and grade point average (An & Taylor, 2015). Career readiness has been defined as having the skills necessary for success in the workforce. Increasingly, policy makers have advocated for a combined definition of CCR, meaning, that students should be prepared to graduate from high school being ready to pursue college or enter the workforce (Mattern et al., 2014). The National Office of School Counselor Advocacy (NOSCA) created the Eight Components of College and Career Readiness to provide SCs with a framework for providing CCR (College Board, 2010). The eight components are (a) college aspirations, (b) academic planning for CCR, (c) enrichment and extracurricular engagement, (d) college and career exploration and selection processes, (e) college and career assessments, (f) college affordability planning, (g) college and career admission processes, and (h) transition from high school graduation to college enrollment.

Students' College and Career Readiness

The number of jobs requiring average to above-average training increased to 68% between 1980 and 2015 (Pew Research Center, 2016). Many high school graduates are unprepared to enter college, as only 26% of students taking the ACT satisfied the benchmarks in all four subject areas (e.g., math, reading, writing, and science) (American College Testing, 2013). Early high school students generally possess limited information about postsecondary options (Gibbons & Woodside, 2014). Four-fifth of high school students overestimate the cost of four-year public tuition, and nearly two-thirds overestimate the costs of four-year private tuition (Nienhusser & Oshio, 2017). Large percentages of high school students and their parents lack awareness of financial aid sources (Montalto et al., 2019) or underestimate the amount of aid available (George-Jackson & Gast, 2015). Students with lower levels of information about college are less likely to intend to attend college (Dynarski & Scott-Clayton, 2013), apply to college (Roderick et al., 2011), or enroll in college (Bryan et al., 2011).

Students of color and low-income and first-generation college students appear to have particular challenges in accessing college. Although students attending urban schools exhibit strong aspirations for postsecondary education (Shamsuddin, 2016), they are less likely to enter college (Perna & Finney, 2014). In comparison to their more advantaged peers, students of color and low income have less information about the college entrance process (Hoxby & Turner, 2013) and have difficulty identifying the various types of colleges (Roderick et al., 2011). In regards to understanding the financial aspects of college, students from urban schools and low-income families have less information about the cost of tuition and sources of financial aid (George-Jackson & Gast, 2015). Although students in urban high schools are provided by SCs with considerable information about the college entrance process and requirements, students are often not informed regarding how to determine whether their current performance would make them competitive college applicants (Shamsuddin, 2016). Students of color and low income receive less information about attending college from family members who are less likely than nondisadvantaged parents to have attended college themselves (Welton & Martinez, 2014).

There also appears to be disparities in the college achievement of students with disabilities. While students with disabilities are nearly as likely as students without disabilities to attend postsecondary education, they are significantly less likely than their nondisabled peers to complete postsecondary training (Newman et al., 2011).

Jones et al. (2011) assert that a college-going culture has the following characteristics:

- Rigorous academic curriculum and programs
- Clear college-going mission and expectations
- Comprehensive college information and expectations
- Coordinated and systemic college support

Factors which predict whether students apply to and enroll in college include students' race/ethnicity, socioeconomic status (SES), parent involvement, AP course-taking, academic achievement scores, and students' educational aspirations (Cabrera & La Nasa, 2001).

School Counselors' Promotion of College Readiness

There is research that supports SCs' efficacy in promoting CCR. A national study revealed that student-counselor contact for college-career counseling in the early grades of high school is associated with students seeking out SCs for college admission and financial aid counseling in 12th grade and the number of college applications student submitted (Bryan et al., 2020). High school seniors are more likely to seek financial aid counseling and enroll in college when SCs spend more time in assisting students with financial aid college information FAFSA meetings. Students of parents who have contact with SCs apply to more college and were more likely to enroll in college. SCs' contact with lower-social-economic families is crucial, given that they are more likely to overestimate the cost of attending college, underestimate the availability of financial aid, and exhibit poor knowledge of the academic prerequisites for college admission (Deil-Amen & Tevis, 2010). While lower-income students are more likely to rely upon SCs for financial aid information, higher-income students are more likely to receive counselor for college admissions, apply to more college, and enroll in a bachelor's degree (Bryan et al., 2020). Poynton and Lapan (2017) also found that schools in which SCs spend considerable time conducting CCR activities have higher college-going rates, and this was particularly true for low-income students. Increased time spent with SCs for assistance with applying to college is associated with higher levels of academic motivation and school connection. College-related interactions with their SCs, teachers, and coaches have a moderate impact on students' rate of college enrollment (Bryan et al., 2017). Research also supports SCs in promoting college readiness at younger ages, providing instruction in financial aid as early as ninth grade (Bryan et al., 2020), and encouraging middle school students to enroll in rigorous coursework (College Board, 2010). Martinez et al. (2017) found that the CCR curriculum Preparing for Post–High School Education: Motivated, Informed, and Ready was more effective in enhancing students' knowledge and self-efficacy concerning postsecondary education than individualized learning. SCs delivered the program's eight units, which consisted of (1) introductions, (2) knowing students' setting and style, (3) knowing students' specific, measurable goals, (4) reading between the lines, (5) exploring careers that lead to majors, (6) holistic reviews, (7) pathways to college, and (8) financial planning. (See Box 10.3 for the College Board's suggestions regarding how the school counseling office can create a college-going culture.)

Box 10.3 Adapted from College Board's (2006) Suggestions for the School Counseling Office to Create a College-Going Culture

- Conduct advising sessions with each student, especially during the junior year, to monitor future plans.
- Invite local college graduates to present to current students.
- Hold a career day and college fair.
- Invite local admissions officers to speak to students.
- Host college information sessions with admissions offices during break periods.
- Create a "College of the Week" profile that includes photos.
- Attend college conferences and campus visits.
- Create a college center where students and parents can access information on scholarships, financial aid, applications, and specific colleges.
- Request for donations of college brochures and college guidebooks.
- Offer instruction in college issues, including writing essays, obtaining recommendations, preparing for entrance examinations, applying for financial aid, transitioning to college life.
- Repeat these sessions as parent nights, using translators if applicable.
- Celebrate students' acceptances publicly.
- Provide training to teachers regarding how to provide college advisement and write essays.
- Change the name of the department to "Counseling and Postgraduate Planning."

Table 10.1 Career Development Activities Prevalent in K–12 Settings

Experiential Activities (Work-Based Interventions)	Individual Activities (Individual Assessment and/or Advising)	Classroom Activities (Classroom Lessons or Group Activities)	Curriculum Activities (Curriculum-Based Interventions)
Service-Learning/ Volunteer Programs	Academic and/or 4-Year Planning	Career Day/Career Fair	Career Courses
Job Shadow	Career Assessments (RIASEC, SDS, Career Maturity, Career Clusters, etc.)	Career or College Field Trips	Career Academy/ Career Magnet School
Internship	College Admissions Testing	Community Member Presentations in Classroom	Career Information or Exploration Infused into Core Academic Curriculum
Work Study	Portfolio/Education Career Action Plan	Career Classroom Lessons	Dual Enrollment
Career and Technical Education (CTE) Programs		Technology/Computer- Assisted Guidance	Informational Interviewing
Mentoring Programs			Résumé Writing

Note: Falco, L. D., and Steen, S. (2018). Using-school-based career development activities to support college and career readiness: An integrative review. *Journal of School-Based Counseling Policy and Evaluation*, *1*(1), 51–67. https://doi. org/10.25774/v1t4-c816. Reprinted with kind permission from Dr. L. D. Falco.

School-Based Career Development

SCs provide a variety of career development activities. Examples include providing classroom lessons aligned with the College Board's (2010) eight components of CCR, inviting guest speakers representing various careers, job shadowing, providing service-learning opportunities, coordinating career fairs, administering career assessments, and coordinating CTE coursework (Falco & Steen, 2018). Table 10.1 provides a summary of Hughes and Karp's (2004) taxonomy of common school-based career development activities.

SCs typically use classroom lessons and small-group activities to present developmentally relevant career information. SCs promote students' awareness of their abilities through career interest inventories, such as Self-Directed Search (SDS: Holland & Messer, 2013), and career aptitude tests, such as the Armed Services Vocational Aptitude Battery (ASVAB: Military.com, 2020). Lessons and group activities are used to administer the instruments or demonstrate to students how to complete such instruments that are typically incorporated in the school's online career exploration programs. Popular online career exploration programs include Bridges (https://access.bridges.com/auth/login.do), Career Cruising (http://public.careercruising.com/en/), Discover http://career.iresearchnet. com/career-assessment/discover/), and Naviance (www.naviance.com/). For school districts that do not purchase online career exploration programs, free online career exploration programs are available through the College Board (www.collegeboard.org/), and some state departments of education offer such programs. Lessons and group activities are used to help students interpret the results of these assessments. SCs also use classroom lessons for a variety of career-related information, including promotion standards, elective options, graduation, college, and workforce requirements, workforce trends, career pathways, financial aid options for postsecondary education and training, etc.

Tier One: Empirically Supported Career Interventions

Dimmitt et al. (2019) identified two-tier career curriculums as having considerable empirical support: career academies and Navigation 101. A career academy is a small learning community which is often located within a larger school, although there are some stand-alone career academy schools. These small learning communities provide rigorous academics within the framework of a career-related theme, such as technology, business, or health sciences, and include work-based learning experiences (Stern et al., 2010). Decades of research indicate that career academies are associated with reduced dropout rates, improved attendance, increased interpersonal and academic skills, and employment outcomes (Stern et al., 2010). Navigation 101 is a postsecondary program that involves an advisory class in which students create a postsecondary plan and in which they also receive instruction in goal-setting, academic improvement, community involvement, and financial literacy (Baker et al., 2015). Students are assigned an educator-advisor. Students present their portfolio at student-led conferences. Students are encouraged to take advanced, dual-credit, or CTE courses.

There is not nearly as much research regarding the efficacy of career-based interventions at the elementary level as there is at the secondary level. Cerrito et al. (2017) found that among fourth and fifth graders, both a traditional career group curriculum, Journeys to Jobs (JTJ; Wosnik & Zwartjes, 2010), and a web-based career group curriculum, the Kuder Galaxy Program (KGP; Kuder, 2012), resulted in improvements in career information. However, the traditional career guidance group yielded greater gain scores than the web-based career guidance for career curiosity/exploration and locus of control.

Career and Technical Education (CTE)

What is now referred to as career and technical education (CTE) was once called "vocational education," which had a negative social stigma, being viewed as a step backward for students, pushing low-performing students toward poor-paying jobs (Malkus, 2019).

There has been an increase in popularity in the past decade as advocates note that less than 50% of college enrollees graduate (Long, 2018) and that CTE is associated with greater career awareness, a stronger career identity, and more specific career goals (Perry et al., 2010). CTE uses a career pathways approach with coursework involving work-based learning experiences and the provision of formal support for undergoing the career planning process, such as mentors and real-world classroom projects (McCharen & High, 2010). CTE introduces students to the world of work, providing general and occupation-specific workplace skills, and provides a real-world context to enhance academic skills (Stone, 2005). A study of South Carolina high school students revealed that CTE reported higher levels of involvement in career planning and career-related activities than non-CTE students (Mobley et al., 2017).

The ASCA's (2018) position statement regarding career and technical education indicates that SCs use their leadership skills to promote awareness of CTE programming options and collaborate with CTE stakeholders to advocate for these programs. Schenck et al. (2012) assert that socially just comprehensive school counseling programs must address the needs of all students and thus necessitate educating students about CTE. Career guidance is comprehensive in nature and enhances the opportunities for students and parents to gain an understanding of what academic and career options are available, but a one-size-fits-all approach is something of the past, not the future of postsecondary readiness. Alternative models of career exploration and coursework are necessary to truly provide access and equal opportunity to a wide range of diverse students.

SCs must be knowledgeable about the various two-year, four-year, and technical college curriculum and state/national organizations that support CTE. Through the Association for Career and Technical Education www.acteonline.org/ (ACTE) and the various state divisions, SCs can access a plethora of information to better assist their students in pursuing CTE courses and student organizations as part of their career- and college-readiness programs. There are currently 11 Career and Technical Student Organizations (CTSOs) recognized by the US Department of Education, with state divisions that support various career pathways in order to provide students with the opportunity to engage in their desired profession while still in high school (see Table 10.2).

Table 10.2 Career and Technical Student Organizations

Business Professionals of America	BPA is the leading CTSO (Career and Technical Student Organization) for students pursuing careers in business management, office administration, information technology, and other related career fields. BPA has 43,000 members in over 2,300 chapters in 23 states. BPA is a cocurricular organization that supports business and information technology educators by offering cocurricular exercises based on national standards.	www.ctsos.org/ctsos/business-professionals-of-america/
Distributive Education Clubs of America (DECA)	DECA prepares emerging leaders and entrepreneurs in marketing, finance, hospitality, and management in high schools and colleges around the globe. With over a 60-year history, DECA has impacted the lives of more than ten million students, educators, school administrators, and business professionals since it was founded in 1946. Their strong connection with our organization has resonated into a brand that people identify as a remarkable experience in the preparation of emerging leaders and entrepreneurs.	www.ctsos.org/ctsos/deca/
Future Business Leaders of America–Phi Beta Lambda	Future Business Leaders of America–Phi Beta Lambda is a nonprofit 501(c)(3) education association with a quarter million students preparing for careers in business and business-related fields. The association has four divisions: Future Business Leaders of America (FBLA) for high school students; FBLA–Middle Level for junior high, middle, and intermediate school students; Phi Beta Lambda (PBL) for postsecondary students; and Professional Division for businesspeople, FBLA-PBL alumni, educators, and parents who support the goals of the association.	www.bpa.org/
Family, Career and Community Leaders of America (FCCLA)	FCCLA is the only national career and technical student organization with the family as its central focus. Since 1945, FCCLA members have been making a difference in their families, careers, and communities by addressing important personal, work, and societal issues through family and consumer sciences education and through the opportunity to expand their leadership potential and develop skills for life.	www.fcclainc.org/
Future Educators Association	FEA is an international student organization dedicated to supporting young people interested in education-related careers. By staying true to its mission while incorporating the latest in technology and education research, FEA continues to help: • Attract exemplary future educators and begin averting teacher shortages at a local level, particularly within the areas of math, science, and special education. • Encourage students from diverse cultural and ethnic backgrounds to enter the education profession. • Elevate the image of teaching and promote it as a challenging and rewarding career.	www.futureeducators.org/

The National Career Cluster Framework

The National Career Cluster Framework, which consists of 16 separate clusters that are grouped by industry, is used as a conceptual framework for organizing CTE programs and education around the "world of work" (Blosveren, 2015). The 16 clusters include:

1. Agriculture, Food, and Natural Resources
2. Architecture and Construction
3. Arts, A/V Technology, and Communications
4. Business, Management, and Administration
5. Education and Training
6. Finance
7. Government and Public Administration
8. Health Science
9. Hospitality and Tourism
10. Human Services
11. Information Technology
12. Law, Public Safety, and Security
13. Manufacturing
14. Marketing, Sales, and Service
15. Science, Technology, Engineering, and Mathematics
16. Transportation, Distribution, and Logistics

Each career cluster represents a grouping of occupations and broad industries that share commonalities (Blosveren, 2015). Expectations at the cluster level indicate the skill and knowledge, both academic and technical, that students within the cluster should achieve regardless of their employment goals. By breaking down the individual courses a student may take within the school community into cluster areas, SCs are able to engage students in relevant conversations regarding the workforce jobs or college majors that may lead to employment within each industry (ACTE, n.d.). While this model is not new, many SCs are not familiar regarding the way in which they may use the clusters to foster student engagement and ultimately impact the sequence of courses students complete that lead to focused college or career preparedness. SCs provide guidance and information regarding what opportunities are available to students, but in many ways, the economic impacts of industry on the state in which they live dictate the needs and salary ranges for given occupations. Looking at global options that may be available in a particular career field may provide students increased power in career decision-making after high school.

Box 10.4

Did You Know?

Although SCs receive more training in career development than teachers, a survey of high school graduates revealed that students viewed teachers as offering more help in exploring college and career options than SCs (Johnson & Rochkind, 2010). This finding is likely due to a number of factors, including the large caseloads of school counselors. One implication of this finding is that SCs can train teachers in promoting students' career development.

Box 10.5 Web-Based Resources to Support Career and College Readiness

College and Career Readiness Success Center: www.ccrscenter.org/about-us
Career Development for Career Guidance Professionals: http://knowitall.scetv.org/careeraisle/guidance/index.cfm

National Career Development Association—Internet Sites for Career Planning: www.ncda.org/aws/NCDA/pt/sp/resources#list_resources_all-R102-NCDA

National Career Development Association—FREE Resources for School Counselors: www.ncda.org/aws/NCDA/pt/sd/news_article/6237/_self/layout_details/true

US Department of Education, National Initiatives in Career and Technical Education: http://cte.ed.gov/nationalinitiatives/gandctools.cfm?&pass_dis=1
Career Isle: **http://knowitall.scetv.org/careeraisle/students/index.cfm**

SPARC National has report cards that include Career Development Outcomes: http://sparc.schoolcounselorcentral.com/

Box 10.6 Video Resources

JobsMadeReal: www.jobsmadereal.com
Success in the New Economy: http://vimeo.com/67277269
Gigniks: Invent Yourself: www.youtube.com/user/GigniksCareerVideos
EEOC Youth@Work: Harassment and Discrimination: www.youtube.com/watch?v=LkhvV3g1zA8&feature=youtu.be
Is Your Daughter Safe at Work?: www.pbs.org/now/shows/508/
FAFSA Hooray: www.youtube.com/watch?v=e2d7IfFgxTs
Next Vista for Learning Careers Videos: www.nextvista.org/collection/light-bulbs/careers/
ESL Students Work Voices: http://blogs.kqed.org/education/category/post-secondary-esl/work-voices/page/2/
RoadTrip Nation: www.roadtripnation.com
Skills to Pay the Bills: www.dol.gov/dol/media/webcast/20121015-softskills/
Your Life, Your Money: www.youtube.com/embed/lpLBvrATSl4
The Dewey Bozella Story: www.youtube.com/watch?v=9AsxLuvHepk&feature=youtu.be

---

Advisement

One of the primary activities SCs use to promote career development is the use of advisement, which is categorized as a direct student service within the *ASCA National Model*. In the *ASCA National Model*, *advisement* is defined as the process through which SCs make recommendations based on appraisal of tests, inventories, and other data to help students make decisions for their future (p. 88). Most states now require that every student have an academic career plan by middle school (Knowledgeworks, 2018).

Many schools, particularly at the middle/junior high and high school levels, require that SCs meet individually with each student on their caseload every year to complete the student's individual student plan. Typically, classroom lessons and group activities are conducted in the first half of the year to provide career and educational information to students, and in the second half of the school year, the SC and student meet individually, processing the results of the student's career exploration activities, in order to select classes that support the students' career and postsecondary goals. In such individual meetings, the SC has the best opportunity to assess the student's career maturity, which may be defined as the degree to which the student's selected career path is based upon a thoughtful reflection of the student's career interests and abilities and life goals. There are a number of career development theories that may be used to assess career maturity. We recommend Marcia's (2007) identity phases to assess career maturity because it more broadly incorporates the entire student, assessing the student's psychosocial maturity, and thus has more clear implications for both career and personal/social development.

Use of Marcia's Identity Statuses in Advisement

Erikson (1968), in his psychosocial development theory, describes personality as developing in a series of stages. Adolescents, who are typically functioning within the "identity versus role confusion" stage in the ages from 13 to 18, are working toward acquiring a coherent identity in which they define both their place and purpose in society. Within this stage, individuals work toward making critical life and career decisions, which aids them in overcoming novel and unfamiliar challenges in career and life pursuits (Yeager & Bundick, 2009). In an expansion of Erikson's theory, Marcia (2007) posited that within the "identity versus role confusion" stage, individuals can be generally characterized as exploring any identity or committing to one.

Through exploration, an individual engages in active self-questioning, in which they are questioning and evaluating their values, worldview, abilities, and interests and pursuit for and testing of identity alternatives before deciding which goals, values, and interests to prioritize (Crocetti, 2017). Conversely, commitment is the selection of an identity and engagement in lifestyle choices that are coherent with their vision of the future. Based upon the extent to which an individual has explored and/or made specific commitments, an identity can be represented in one of four statuses: diffused status (low/no commitment, low/no exploration), foreclosure status (high commitment, low/no exploration), moratorium status (low/no commitment, high exploration), and achievement status (commitment following exploration; Marcia, 2007).

It may be helpful also to recognize that the term *identity development* has different meanings within the research literature (Verhoeven et al., 2019). The preponderance of the literature on adolescent identity development in educational settings utilizes a social framework that refers to adolescents' racial, cultural, ethnic, and gender identity. However, Erikson's (1968) and Marcia's (2007) theory of identity development focuses upon the more general and abstract aspects of adolescents' personal identity.

Researchers suggest that most individuals reach their identity achievement status around the age of 20 (Meeus, 2018). In early adolescence, most demonstrate identity diffusion or identity foreclosure. In the identity diffusion status, the individual is neither exploring nor committed to a worldview. Students exhibiting diffusion cannot typically identify a career or educational pathway beyond high school and are likely to demonstrate anxiety or avoidance when questioned about the future and career choices. In contrast, those in the identity foreclosure stage is committed to a particular worldview/set of values, which the student has typically acquired from their parents or other influential individuals without a period of reflection/exploration.

Those in identity foreclosure often can readily identity a career he or she wishes to pursue, and typically, the career that the student identifies is of high status (e.g., doctor, lawyer, engineer). However, when pressed, the student may have difficulty explaining what they find appealing about a profession. Those in identity moratorium are in the crisis phase of exploring their worldview and have not committed to an identity. Indeed, students in the identity moratorium status may have a variety of career interests and have difficulty differentiating among these interests. In contrast, the identity-achieved student has undergone an exploration of self and has a mostly consistent worldview/set of values. Students who have an achieved identity have moved beyond career exploration and have entered the phase of career decision-making, in which they are pursuing a career path compatible with their worldview.

Empirical support for Marcia's theory is provided in a meta-analysis of 73 longitudinal and cross-sectional studies that found that among adolescents and young adults, identity diffusion and foreclosure decrease over time, while identity achievement increases (Kroger et al., 2010). Some of the advantages associated with identity commitment are aspects of resiliency, such as extraversion and emotional stability (Morsunbul et al., 2014), self-concept and self-esteem (Sugimura et al., 2015), and nurturing family relationships (Crocetti et al., 2017). Additionally, a number of indicators of mental health and adjustment, positive well-being (Karas et al., 2015), life satisfaction (Sugimura et al., 2015), and academic achievement (Pop et al., 2016) are associated with identity commitment.

However, when identity commitment becomes reconsidered, in which a search occurs for alternative commitments because one's current commitments are not satisfactory, such status is negatively associated with self-concept and self-esteem (Sugimura et al., 2015) and desirable personality traits, such as agreeableness and extraversion (Hatano et al., 2016), and is predictive of low academic achievement (Pop et al., 2016). Additionally, reconsideration of commitment is strongly correlated with internal (e.g., symptoms of depression and anxiety) and external (e.g., involvement in delinquent behavior) psychosocial problems (Crocetti et al., 2008).

Identity Diffusion

The adolescent who is in identity diffusion lacks a commitment to personal values and a career path and is not yet engaging in such exploration (Marcia, 2002). In adolescence, the process of self-exploration assists in an eventual achievement of a clearer sense of identity, in which one has a general commitment to one's values, a career path, and a path for pursuing life meaning (Erikson, 1968; Marcia, 2002). The exploration of one's personal goals (Crocetti et al., 2016) and career options (Pisarik et al., 2017) have been found to be associated with anxiety, and those with greater anxiety are more likely to withdraw from career exploration (Hardin et al., 2006) to avoid the threatening situation of career decision-making. One way in which SCs may assist adolescents not yet in the exploration of their identity is to manage the anxiety associated with the journey.

For students with identity diffusion, the SCs' objective is to support the student's initiation of career- and self-exploration, either by engagement in exploration of multiple alternatives (i.e., exploration in breadth) or by focusing on deep investigation of one alternative (i.e., exploration in depth; Marcia, 2007). SCs can promote self-awareness during advisement by processing the results of career interest inventories, asking the student to describe their ideal picture of themselves within ten years, inquiring regarding what strengths the

Table 10.3 Marcia's (2007) Identity Statuses and Helper Questions

Identity Status	Characteristics	Helper Questions
Diffusion	Either avoided exploration of values or is no longer exploring.	What do you think your friends think that you particularly excel in?
		Do you agree? If so, what are some potential careers you are aware of that might align with your strengths?
		What careers have you ever thought looked interesting or what you would like to learn more about?
Foreclosure	Has not experienced identity crisis but expresses commitment to parents'/caregivers' choices and values.	What do you think of your dad's encouragement to become a carpenter? Does that fit with how you see yourself?
		What do you think about that career?
		What do you know about the activities of that career?
		What do you see as the potential things you would not like about that career?
Moratorium	Actively experiencing an identity crisis, exploring commitments, and developing a set of values and beliefs independent of parents/caregivers.	What is it like to be thinking about the future while also enjoying being in high school?
		How do you balance the stress of thinking about your future while also enjoying yourself?
Achievement	Has experienced an identity crisis and, after consideration of alternatives, is committed to an occupation and political and religious beliefs.	How can I be more help to you?
		What would you like to know more about?
		How is the information you seek related to your future goals?

student thinks others see in them, investigating what school subjects or elective school activities tend to interest the student, and exploring the student's ideas for how to obtain additional experiences and information (Kolbert et al., 2021). For example, SCs may ask such questions as, "What do you think your friends think that you particularly excel in?" followed by, "Do you agree, and if so, what are some potential careers that you are aware of that might align with your strengths?" "What careers have you ever thought looked interesting or what you would like to learn more about?" (See Table 10.3).

Online resources may be used, such as the Bureau of Labor Statistics, to help students understand the myriad of career opportunities, including the associated financial outcomes, typical job responsibilities, required training or education, etc. SCs may also encourage students to engage in job shadowing and visits to local colleges and career technical centers in order to gain a better sense of potential postsecondary interests. Because postsecondary success is largely dependent upon the rigor of academic course selection, particularly for underprivileged youth (Ohrt et al., 2009), SCs should strive to identify student strengths and encourage their enrollment in advanced courses. Such techniques and planning can help prepare students to be prepared to make highly important decisions about their future (ASCA, 2019b).

Identity Foreclosure

Students with identity foreclosure are committed to a career path, but they have not undergone sufficient exploration (Marcia, 2002). While such students may be able to easily name their career interest, they often have difficulty in explaining what they would enjoy about the career or do not have an in-depth amount of knowledge of the occupation and its educational or training requirements. SCs may have difficulty in advising students in identity foreclosure, as the student may appear confident in their career path and not recognize that they have simply adopted the perspectives of their caregiver(s) or peers. Similarly, such students may not have undergone an extensive review of their strengths and weaknesses because of the anxiety associated with career exploration. Questions that SCs may pose to such students, to encourage more critical analysis of their career choices, may include, "What do you think of your dad's encouragement to become a carpenter? Does that fit with how you see yourself?" "What do you think you would like about that career?" "What do you know about the activities of carpenters?" "What do you see as the potential things you would not like about that career?"

Identity Moratorium

Probably the most ideal situation for middle/junior high and high school students is to be in identity moratorium, exploring various career options as they learn more about themselves. Students of this age should be in the process of developing a worldview that is differentiated from their parents and peers, while being able also to maintain that connection with parents and peers. SCs can support students' self- and career exploration by helping them make sense of contrasting thoughts and values. The exploration process involves uncertainty and anxiety, which may result in students avoiding assuming responsibility for such large life choices by seeking others who will make decisions for them.

However, SCs should avoid pushing students to make large life decisions without a considerable process of reflection (Marcia, 2002). Therefore, it is important for SCs to normalize students' anxiety by exploring with the student how to effectively balance self-exploration and managing the anxiety associated with such self-exploration. Self- and career exploration indeed involves a focus on the future. However, the student can also be encouraged to think about how to alternate between thinking about the future and maintaining a present focus through leisure activities, exercise, relaxation exercises, mindfulness, etc. For example, SCs can ask students such questions as, "What is it like to be thinking about the future while also enjoying being in high school?" "How do you balance the stress of thinking about your future while also enjoying yourself?"

Identity Achievement

Students exhibiting characteristics of identity achievement have undergone a process of self- and career exploration and are committed to a set of personal values and at least a general career path. Such students, then, are most in need of gathering information (Marcia, 2002). SCs may provide specific information regarding academic course selection, extracurricular opportunities (e.g., internships), and career and postsecondary options (e.g., prestigious and competitive programs). Identity-achieved students typically have already identified important questions about their future, which SCs can leverage by providing information about finances (e.g., FAFSA, tuition) and deadlines of postsecondary options (e.g., college, career technical schools).

Those students who have reached identity achievement who have engaged in in-depth exploration about themselves and their futures may also be searching for deliberate opportunities to make them more competitive and prepared for their postsecondary plans. In response to such requests, SCs may encourage these students to seek out school and community-based opportunities that would complement their aspirations and current experiences. For example, SCs may develop a cooperative workspace for students to write their personal essays, ask questions about their portfolios, and acquire feedback from peers. Additionally, students can be connected with local colleges and outreach programs that may offer a variety of opportunities for students to advance their critical thinking, work-based skills, and understanding of civic responsibility. Relevant questions that SCs may ask students in identity achievement include: "How can I be of help to you?" "What would you like to know more about?" and "How is the information you seek related to your future goals?"

Managing Anxiety

Exploring one's personal goals (Crocetti et al., 2016) and career exploration in general (Pisarik et al., 2017) is associated with distress and uncertainty. According to Marcia's theory, anxiety is likely to be a prominent issue for students exhibiting identity diffusion, foreclosure, and moratorium. Identity-diffused and identity-foreclosed students may be more likely to avoid the anxiety of career exploration. Identify-diffused students may wish to avoid the topic altogether. Identity-foreclosed students may manage their anxiety by simply adopting their parents' or peers' perspectives of who they are and what they should pursue in terms of a career. Identity-moratorium students may demonstrate elevated levels of anxiety as they undergo self-exploration. When advising students, SCs should look for signs of anxiety and avoidance and help students with managing their anxiety related to their career exploration. SCs should also be concerned about students who exhibit ruminative exploration, which is defined as extensively lingering on the fear of possibly making a bad choice (Negru-Subtirica et al., 2016).

SCs should normalize the experience, affirming the fact that not knowing is normal and essential for self-exploration and that most of their peers are having a similar experience. Additionally, students' ambivalence can be normalized, with SCs suggesting that while thinking about one's future career can be scary, it may also be exciting. Moreover, the SC can explore, from a solution-focused theory approach, strategies that the student has used to effectively manage their anxiety. Finally, the school can introduce mindfulness concepts, having the student engage in some typical introductory mindfulness practices, such as intentional breathing or sensation awareness (Orsillo & Roemer, 2011). Mindfulness practices may be particularly useful for adolescents who exhibit ruminative exploration. Indeed, present-mindfulness has been found to promote the development of identity in the transition to young adulthood (Shirai et al., 2016).

Consultation and Collaboration With Parents and/or Legal Guardians

Marcia (2002) and Erikson (1968) both acknowledge that adolescents' development of an ego identity is related to their caregivers' ability to support their identity exploration. Caregivers who help younger members of the society to grow and develop achieve a sense of generativity, whereas caregivers who fail to effectively support younger generations experience a sense of stagnation (Marcia, 2002, p. 199). ASCA's (2017) position statement regarding advisement indicates that SCs are expected to collaborate with families and/or legal guardians in ensuring that students develop their own academic and career plans. From the perspective of Erikson (1968) and Marcia (2002), by assisting caregivers, including parents, legal guardians, and teachers, in supporting adolescents' identity exploration, SCs are helping caregivers satisfy their psychological need for generativity.

SCs should be sensitive to the likelihood that sociocontextual variables, including family and environmental characteristics, influence the student's identity status and career maturity. Lower levels of family cohesion are associated with career commitment anxiety among college students (Lustig, 2018), while adolescents who are highly attached to their parents are more likely to have a higher level of career maturity (Emmanuelle, 2009). Adolescents tend to prefer that parents allow them to select their career and encourage them to explore various career interests and alternatives (Dietrich & Kracke, 2009).

In contrast, adolescents are likely to avoid career exploration when they perceive their parents as controlling them (Savickas, 2002). Because career activities selected and endorsed by parents tend not to promote their children's career maturity, Lim and You (2019) suggest that parents should assist rather than lead their children's explorations. In doing so, they can provide their adolescent with relevant information and then encourage them to make decisions independently.

With this in mind, SCs should seek to educate parents, either through workshops or literature, about developmentally appropriate ways to engage their child in career exploration. The entrée into adolescence is considered to require a qualitative transformation of the parent-child relationship, involving parents moving from a directive approach to that more of a consultative position (McGoldrick et al., 2016). Whereas in preadolescence, parents provide high structure and information to their children, with adolescence, the parent should be asking more questions of their adolescent, with such general questions as, "What do you think about it?" or "Does that fit with how you see yourself?"

Unfortunately, adults in these adolescents' lives may seek to alleviate both their own and their children's anxiety by encouraging the student to commit to a life/career decision. While deciding about one's career path may alleviate the student's anxiety in the short-term, premature commitment to a career curtails the exploration that is considered necessary for understanding one's values, strengths, limitations, etc. Parents can be made aware of the tendency to wish to minimize their child's anxiety by offering them advice. Furthermore, SCs can encourage parents to identify and manage their emotions in knowing that their child is experiencing anxiety with career decision-making and help them recognize the ways in which they can support their child in learning to manage their anxiety.

Consultation and Collaboration With Teachers

In working with teachers, SCs can use Marcia's (1966, 2007) theory as an overarching framework for using evidence-based strategies to promote students' career development. Verhoeven et al. (2019) conducted a narrative review of the literature regarding teachers' role in facilitating students' sociocultural and personal identity development. Specifically, the following instructional activities were associated with students' identity exploration: exposing students to unfamiliar learning contents, on-site and hands-on activities, encouraging self-reflection through writing and classroom discussions with peers, and supporting students in connecting academic knowledge to their personal lives (Verhoeven et al., 2019). Additionally, supportive school climates have been identified as a contributor to students' identity exploration, with research suggesting that students need to feel secure with their peers and teachers in order to engage in psychological risk-taking.

Educators who have close personal relationships with and compliment their students tend to be seen as effective in helping them with their identity development. Teachers can facilitate peer support by using learning activities that invite mutual encouragement among students and make adolescents aware of their commonalities. Unfortunately, learning activities that facilitate students' identity exploration are currently not well integrated in the formal academic curriculum (Verhoeven et al., 2019). However, Marcia's (1966, 2007) theory can serve as a framework in training teachers in facilitating students' exploration of their identity. We posit that teachers will likely recognize the developmental need for adolescents to explore their academic and career interests and be able to help students identify strategies for managing the anxiety associated with exploration. Moreover, teachers' knowledge of the four identity statuses can help them identify students who are avoiding self- and career exploration.

Influence of Poverty and Race in Identity Exploration

Furthermore, SCs should be sensitive to the contribution of sociocultural variables to adolescents' failure to engage in identity exploration. Students who live in poverty have weaker job-seeking networks (Kneebone & Holmes, 2016), often lack sufficient career information and career development guidance (Turner & Conkel, 2020), and have fewer opportunities to investigate educational and career options (Bloom, 2007). Indeed, a lack of identity exploration among minority students has been linked to teachers' failing to have high expectations of minority students (Verhoeven et al., 2019). Accordingly, Marcia's (2007) theory may be used to help stakeholders understand the need for adolescents to have access to a comprehensive school counseling curriculum that facilitates students' career and personal/social development, which is an ethical mandate of the ASCA (2022).

Moreover, when advising students, SCs should attempt to determine whether a lack of adult support is related to the students' career exploration. In such cases, the SC may help the adolescent identify other persons, such as other family, community members, or teachers, who may serve as a support for managing the anxiety associated with career exploration. Furthermore, SCs may collaborate with stakeholders and community organizations to create school-based programs that promote identity exploration, such as mentorship programs (Hughes et al., 2013).

College Applications

A significant portion of time for high school counselors is devoted to assisting students in the college application process, particularly for districts with a large college-going culture. In assisting students who are applying to college and other postsecondary options, the SC should seek to maintain a focus on promoting students' development and avoid simply serving as a person who processes college applications, as much of such work can be considered clerical and schools may ultimately decide that a master's-level professional position is not necessary for such work. High school counselors should seek to manage their time wisely in regards to college applications. Rather than frequent meetings with individual students to complete college applications, the high school counselor can conduct school counseling lessons in which they teach students the process for applying for college; variables to consider in selecting a college; how to use search engines, such as the College Board and Naviance, to research colleges and scholarships; tips for writing college admissions essays, etc.; and SCs should provide such information to parents through informational sessions. Providing such information through classroom lessons and the school counseling program's website reduces the amount of time spent responding to individual students and parents. However, individual responding to students and parents can never be entirely eliminated, given that many parents and students have considerable anxiety about the next potential chapter of their lives and thus have difficulty processing such information in large group settings. High school counselors can arrange to have recent high school graduates speak to students about the personal/social process they underwent in pursuing postsecondary options and have parents of recent high school graduates speak to parents whose children are currently undergoing the process. There are a number of new technological resources that can assist SCs in effectively managing the time involved with college applications.

Naviance

Naviance (Hobson, n.d.) is a CCR web-based, self-service program that can interface with the school's student information system to allow for ready access to grades and college entrance examination scores (e.g., SAT, ACT). Students are able to access Naviance online to research colleges and careers, manage college applications, construct individualized learning plans, take a career interest inventory, build a résumé, request recommendations form school personnel, request transcripts, research scholarships, etc. Naviance provides SCs with the annual results of the student bodies' college acceptance rates, allowing the SC and student to predict the likelihood of acceptance to a particular college/university based upon previous students' applications. Christian et al. (2017) found that students who logged in to Naviance more frequently had higher application rates. Naviance also interfaces with the Common Application (www.commonapp.org/), which is a free electronic admissions that is accepted by many colleges and universities.

Financial Aid

Part of creating a college-going culture involves helping students and families understand the associated costs of postsecondary education and training. To educate students and parents about financial aid, SCs should conduct lessons and parent information sessions and include this information on the school counseling program's website. Families must be informed that colleges typically assume that students will have some responsibility for financing their education, typically through borrowing loans (Martin, 2013). The student and his or her family should be encouraged to project the potential costs of the education over the students' potential to repay the debt depending upon his or her career aspirations, as student loan debt may impact the student's ability to attend graduate school, purchase a home, or start a family. If the student is determined to enroll in his or her dream school but the financial aid package the school is offering and the family's resources are limited, the family may consider the option of attending a lower-cost school, such as a community college, for two years and then transferring to the student's ideal school. The family should be encouraged to review the College Board's Net Price Calculator (http://netpricecalculator. collegeboard.org/) and the federal government's College Navigator (https://nces.ed.gov/ collegenavigator/) to obtain a sense of the costs of higher education. In the following section, we provide an overview of financial aid so that persons entering the profession have a basic understanding from which they can expand upon with professional experience.

Financial aid may be divided into two categories: need-based and non-need-based (Martin, 2013). Need-based and non-need-based funds may be further subdivided into four types: scholarships, grants, loans, and employment. Most forms of financial aid require the student to complete a FAFSA.

There are several components which are calculated to determine a student's eligibility for financial aid (Martin, 2013). First, the college constructs an estimate of a student's costs for an academic year, and this estimated cost includes tuition and fees, room and board, books, computer, and transportation. Second, the student's expected family contribution

(EFC) is calculated from the demographic and financial information provided by the student in the FAFSA. The student's financial aid is calculated by subtracting the estimated cost of attendance from the expected family contribution. See Box 10.7 for types of federal grants and Box 10.8 for types of federal loans.

Box 10.7   Types of Federal Grants (https://studentaid. ed.gov/sa/types/grants-scholarships)

Pell: Awarded to the neediest students based on EFC. The maximum amount per year is $6,495 as of 2021–2022.

Federal Supplemental Educational Opportunity Gant (FSEOG): Awarded to the neediest students based on EFC. The maximum amount per year is $4,000 as of 2021–2022.

Teacher Education Assistance for College and Higher Education (TEACH): Available for students who are willing to teach in a high-need field (e.g., math, science) at a Title I school after graduation. The maximum amount per year is $4,000 as of 2021–2022.

Box 10.8   Types of Federal Loans (https://studentaid. ed.gov/sa/types/grants-scholarships)

Direct Subsidized: The federal government pays accruing interest (3.73% for the 2021–2022 academic year), while borrowers are enrolled at least half-time.

Direct Unsubsidized: A non-need-based loan. Interest (3.73% for the 2021–2022 academic year) accrues while borrower is enrolled.

PLUS: Borrowed by parents of dependent students to help meet costs not covered by other forms of financial aid. The maximum amount a student may borrow per year is the difference between the student's cost of attendance and other aid received.

College and Career Readiness for Students With Disabilities

SCs seek to promote the CCR of all students, including students with disabilities, whose career development has traditionally received less focus within schools. The Individuals with Disabilities Education Improvement Act (IDEA) of 2004 mandates that students in special education be provided transition services, which include the construction of a transition plan by age 14. While special education teachers typically coordinate Individual Education Plans (IEP), IDEA requires the involvement of related professional when appropriate. ASCA recommends SC participation in transition planning for students with IEPs and 504 plans. However, some studies (e.g., Milsom, 2002) have found that many SCs report not participating in the development of transition plans for students with disabilities. In the following section, we explore how SCs can promote both the CCR of students with disabilities, focusing on how to assist students with disabilities, who may be seeking vocational options following high school, and students who may pursue college.

SCs can assist the IEP team in developing the transition plan by providing up-to-date information about the world of work, matching the students' abilities and interests to career options, encouraging students to broaden their perspectives as a caution against changes in the labor market (Wadsworth et al., 2004). SCs can help students with disabilities increase their awareness of their interests and abilities through short-term job tryout experiences and job shadowing and by examining students' volunteer, leisure, and daily living activities. SCs can help the student and the IEP team identify the students' career values and pursue exploration activities consistent with those values. For example, for a student with a moderate intellectual disability (ID), their interest in being a firefighter may be related to having respect by wearing a uniform and the perceived opportunities to connect with others. Career exploration activities can be designed to incorporate the student's values, having the student train as a fire safety officer, wear a uniform, and conduct fire safety and fire extinguisher checks with school staff. For students with an intellectual disability (ID), the preferred method to assess career interests' and abilities involves an assessment of work behavior; however, there are inventories that are often used, including What I Like to Do Inventory (Meyers et al., 1978) and the Audio-Visual Vocational Preferences (Wilgosh, 1994). When conducting career exploration activities with adolescents with ID, SCs should first teach the steps of decision-making. Instructional activities can also be designed to promote the vocational skills of students with ID (Wadsworth et al., 2004). For example, vocational skills that can transfer to various employment opportunities in clerical and reception jobs may include mechanical skills (e.g., use of office equipment), social skills (e.g., active listening skills), and hygiene (e.g., expected dress and appearance).

Career exploration activities for the elementary- and middle-school levels can prepare students with disabilities to make career choices in young adulthood (Wadsworth et al., 2004). SCs can assist the IEP team relate classroom activities, such as decision-making and social skill development, as vital aspects of career development. SCs may collaborate with teachers to help students with ID to develop career interests and choose from vocational activities. For example, instructional activities may be designed to expose students to various job-related skills (e.g., following directions) and habits (e.g., timeliness). School counseling lessons can expose students with ID to different job-related environments (e.g., working alone vs. in a group) and patterns (e.g., sporadic activity vs. repetitive consistency).

College Readiness of Students With Disabilities

There has been an increase in the number of students with disabilities in the United States who attend postsecondary education. A national survey of students who received special education services in 2000 revealed that 60% enrolled in postsecondary education within eight years of graduating from high school, within two-year postsecondary programs being the most common enrollment option (Dragoo, 2017). Approximately 11% of all undergraduates for the 2011–2012 academic year self-identified as having a learning disability. Federal legislation provisions, such as the transition planning requirement of IDEA (2004) and Section 504 of the Rehabilitation Act of 1973, which requires that postsecondary institutions which receive federal funding provide reasonable accommodations for students with disability, have increased the postsecondary participation of students with disabilities. Despite the increase in college attendance among students with disabilities, they are still less likely to enroll in college (Newman et al., 2010) and graduate from college (e.g., Wagner et al., 2005). The National Joint Committee on Learning Disabilities (NJCLD) asserted "that many students disabilities do not consider postsecondary education options (2- and 4-year colleges and vocational schools) because they are not encouraged, assisted, or prepared to do so" (1994, p. 1).

As advocates for all students, SCs can fulfill vital roles in assisting students with learning disabilities transition to college (Milsom & Hartley, 2005). Milsom and Hartley (2005) recommend that for students with disabilities who are transitioning to postsecondary institutions, SCs can promote development in four areas: (1) knowledge of disability, (2) knowledge of postsecondary support services, (3) knowledge of disability legislation, and (4) ability to self-advocate. *Knowledge of Disability*: SCs can collaborate with special education teachers in helping students obtain knowledge of their disability, providing small-group or individual sessions to help students understand how their skills and abilities relate to potential future careers and college majors. *Knowledge of Postsecondary Support Services*: When choosing a college, students with learning disabilities should obtain information about the specific admission requirements for students with disabilities and the availability and process for obtaining support services. Support services that must be provided by postsecondary institutions under Section 504 include the use of auxiliary aids, such as taped texts, exam readers, and notetakers. *Knowledge of Disability Legislation*: Many students are not closely familiar with the federal legislation concerning students with disabilities and may not realize that the provisions of IDEA do not apply to postsecondary institutions. Rather, students with disabilities are eligible for reasonable accommodations under Section 504 of the Rehabilitation Act. Section 504 only requires postsecondary institutions to provide services for students who request them and who provide appropriate documentation; thus, it is vital that students with disabilities and their families are aware of their legislative rights. *Ability to Self-Advocate*: SCs can work with special educators to help students with disabilities practice self-advocacy skills. Students with disabilities can be instructed in the components of assertive communication, which can then be periodically role-played under the supervision of special educators.

Advisement With Students With Disabilities

Wren and Einhorn (2000) provide suggestions for SCs when conducting advisement with students with disabilities. For students with disabilities that have short attention spans, SCs may schedule shorter sessions, allow frequent breaks, remove distracting objects, provide noiseless objects to hold, or allow students to stand or pace. To increase students' retention of information, SCs can use the beginning and end of sessions to review information, ask a student to clarify his or her understanding of the information provided, decrease sentence complexity and length, and slow the pace of sessions. Students with disabilities often lack self-esteem and efficacy, and SCs can provide students with skills to manage their anxiety and fear related to taking on new risks, such as enrolling in more challenging classes and postsecondary institutions.

Summary

The need exists for SCs to take an active role in students' career and postsecondary planning. By utilizing existing resources and engaging students, parents, teachers, administrators, and community members in the process of planning for a future after high school, students will be more readily equipped to navigate the complex world of work, training, or college life. This chapter contains pertinent information that SCs need to know in order to be in the position to provide appropriate services to students and create a climate of postsecondary readiness in their building. Cultivating a system of resources for students and parents to use as they navigate the plethora of options available will increase the likelihood for career and life success for every student. The resources in this chapter are just a sample of what is continually being offered online for free or a low cost. By creating a school-specific resource portal for students, with information that is most useful to them, SCs may have a better chance of truly supporting all students toward their goals for postsecondary success.

References

American College Testing. (2013). *The condition of college and career readiness.* Author. www.act.org/research/policymakers/cccr13/index.html

American School Counselor Association (2017). *The school counselor and career development.* Author.

American School Counselor Association. (2018). *The school counselor and career and technical education.* Author.

American School Counselor Association. (2019a). *ASCA standards for school counselor preparation programs.* www.schoolcounselor.org/getmedia/573d7c2c-1622-4d25-a5ac-ac74d2e614ca/ASCA-Standards-for-School-Counselor-Preparation-Programs.pdf

American School Counselor Association. (2019b). *The ASCA national model: A framework for school counseling programs* (4th ed.). Author.

An, B. P., & Taylor, J. L. (2015). Are dual enrollment students college ready? Evidence from the Wabash National Study of Liberal Arts Education. *Education Policy Analysis Archives 23*(58). https://doi.org/10.14507/epaa/v23.1781

Association for Career and Technical Education. (n.d.). *What is CTE?* Author. www.acteonline.org/cte/#.VNAWD2jF-N0

Baker, D. B., Gratama, C. A., Brenner, S. C., Gremillion, R., & Peterson, K. M. (2015). *College readiness initiative: AVID and Navigation 101.* The BERC Group. https://core.ac.uk/reader/80510534

Bloom, J. (2007). Misreading social class in the journey towards college: Youth development in urban America. *Teachers College Record, 109*(2), 343–368. https://psycnet.apa.org/record/2007-03098-003

Blosveren, K. (2015). Career clusters at CareerTech VISION: The next step in the career clusters' journey. *Techniques: Connecting Education & Careers, 90*(6), 42–45.

Bryan, J., Farmer-Hinton, R., Rawls, A., & Woods, C. S. (2017). Social capital and college-going culture in high schools: The effects of college expectations and college talk on students' postsecondary attendance. *Professional School Counseling, 21*(1). https://doi.org/10.5330/1096-2409-21.1.95

Bryan, J., Kim, J., & Liu, C. (2020). School counseling college-going culture: Counselors' influence on students' college-going decisions. *Journal of Counseling & Development,* 1–17. https://doi.org/10.1002/jcad.12408

Bryan, J., Moore-Thomas, C., Day-Vines, N. L., & Holcomb-McCoy, C. (2011). School counselors as social capital: The effects of high school college counseling on college application rates. *Journal of Counseling & Development, 89*(2), 190–199. https://doi.org/10.1002/j.1556-6678.2011.tb00077.x

Cabrera, A. F., & La Nasa, S. M. (2001). On the path to college: Three critical tasks facing America's disadvantaged. *Research in Higher Education, 42*(2), 119–149. https://doi.org/10.1023/A:1026520002362

Cerrito, J. A., Trusty, J., & Behun, R. J. (2017). Comparing web-based and traditional career interventions with elementary students: An experimental study. *The Career Development Quarterly, 66*(4), 286–299. https://doi.org/10.1002/cdq.12151

Christian, D., Lawrence, A., & Dampman, N. (2017). Increasing college access through the implementation of Naviance: An exploratory study. *Journal of College Access, 3*(2), 28–44. https://eric.ed.gov/?id=EJ1167422

College Board. (2006). *Creating a college going culture guide*. Author. https://secure-media.colleg-eboard.org/digitalServices/pdf/highered/college-ed-create-college-going-culture.pdf

College Board. (2010). *Eight components of college and career readiness counseling*. National Office for School Counseling Advocacy. Author. http://media.collegeboard.com/digitalServices/pdf/nosca/11b_4416_8_Components_WEB_111107.pdf

Council for the Accreditation of Counseling and Related Educational Programs. (n.d.). *2016 CACREP standards*. www.cacrep.org/for-programs/2016-cacrep-standards/

Crocetti, E. (2017). Identity formation in adolescence: The dynamic of forming and consolidating identity commitments. *Child Development Perspectives, 11*(2), 145–150. https://doi.org/10.1111/cdep.12226

Crocetti, E., Beyers, W., & Cok, F. (2016). Shedding light on the dark side of identity: Introduction the special issue. *Journal of Adolescence, 47*, 104–108. https://doi.org/10.1016/j.adolescence.2016.01.002

Crocetti, E., Rubini, M., & Meeus, W. (2008). Capturing the dynamics of identity formation in various ethnic groups: Development and validation of a three-dimensional model. *Journal of Adolescence, 31*(2), 207–222. https://doi.org/10.1016/j.adolescence.2007.09.002

Deil-Amen, R., & Tevis, T. L. (2010). Circumscribed agency: The relevance of standardized college entrance exams for low-SES high school students. *The Review of Higher Education, 33*, 141–175. https://muse.jhu.edu/article/365582

Dietrich, J., & Kracke, B. (2009). Career-specific parental behaviors in adolescents' development. *Journal of Vocational Behavior, 75*(2), 190–199. https://doi.org/10.1016/j.jvb.2009.03.005

Dimmitt, C., Zyromski, B., & Griffith, C. (2019, March). *Identifying evidence-based school counseling interventions*. Evidence-Based School Counseling Conference.

Dragoo, K. E. (2017). *Students with disabilities graduating from high school and entering postsecondary education: In brief*. Congressional Research Service. https://crsreports.congress.gov

Dynarski, S., & Scott-Clayton, J. (2013). *Financial aid policy: Lessons from research* (No. w18710). National Bureau of Economic Research. https://edpolicy.umich.edu/sites/epi/files/uploads/wp-dynarski-scott-clayton-financial-aid-policy-2013.pdf

Emmanuelle, V. (2009). Inter-relationships among attachment to mother and father, self-esteem, and career indecision. *Journal of Vocational Behavior, 75*(2), 91–99. https://doi.org/10.1016/j.jvb.2009.04.007

Erikson, E. (1968). *Identity: Youth and crisis*. Norton.

Falco, L. D., & Steen, S. (2018). Using-school-based career development activities to support college and career readiness: An integrative review. *Journal of School-Based Counseling Policy and Evaluation, 1*(1), 51–67. https://doi.org/10.25774/v1t4-c816

George-Jackson, C., & Gast, M. J. (2015). Addressing information gaps: Disparities in financial awareness and preparedness on the road to college. *Journal of Student Financial Aid, 44*(3), 3. https://ir.library.louisville.edu/jsfa/vol44/iss3/3

Gibbons, M. M., & Woodside, M. (2014). Addressing the needs of first-generation college students: Lessons learned from adults from low-education families. *Journal of College Counseling, 17*(1), 21–36. https://doi.org/10.1002/j.2161-1882.2014.00045.x

Hardin, E. E., Varghese, F. P., Tran, U. V., & Carlson, A. V. (2006). Anxiety and career exploration: Gender differences in the role of self-construal. *Journal of Vocational Behavior, 69*(2), 346–358. https://doi.org/10.1016/j/jvb.2006.05.002

Hatano, K., Sugimura, K., & Crocetti, E. (2016). Looking at the dark and bright sides of identity formation: New insights from adolescents and emerging adults in Japan. *Journal of Adolescence, 47*, 156–168. https://doi.org/10.1016/j.adolescence.2015.09.008

Hobsons. (n.d.). *Naviance* [Software]. Author. www.naviance.com

Holland, J. L., & Messer, M. A. (2013). *Self-directed Search: Form R* (5th ed.). PAR, Inc.

Hoxby, C., & Turner, S. (2013). Expanding college opportunities for high-achieving, low income students. *Stanford Institute for Economic Policy Research Discussion Paper*, (12–014).

Hughes, K. L., & Karp, M. M. (2004). *School-based career development: A synthesis of the literature*. Institute on Education and the Economy, Columbia University. https://doi.org/10.7916/D8SX6B8G

Hughes, R., Nzekwe, B., & Molyneaux, K. (2013). The single sex debate for girls in science: A comparison between two informal science programs on middle school students' STEM identity formation. *Research in Science Education, 43*(5), 1979–2007. https://doi.org/10.1007/s11165-012-9345-7

Individuals with Disabilities Educaiton Improvement Act of 2004 [IDEA], 20 U.S.C 1400 et seq. (2004).

Johnson, J., & Rochkind, J. (2010). *Can I get a little advice here? How an overstretched high school guidance system is undermining students' college aspirations.* Bill and Melinda Gates Foundation. https://files.eric.ed.gov/fulltext/ED508672.pdf

Jones, T., Bensimon, E. M., McNair, T. B., & Dowd, A. C. (2011). *Using data and inquiry to duild equity-focused college-going cultures.* National College Access Network. https://cdn.ymaws.com/www.ncan.org/resource/resmgr/publications/collegegoingcultures_2011.pdf

Karas, D., Cieciuch, J., Negru, O., & Crocetti, E. (2015). Relationships between identity and well-being in Italian, Polish, and Romanian emerging adults. *Social Indicators Research, 121*(3), 727–743. https://doi.org/10.1007/s11205-014-0668-9

Kneebone, E., & Holmes, N. (2016). *US concentrated poverty in the wake of the great recession.* www.brookings.edu

Knowledgeworks. (2018). *Perosnalized learning and the Every Student Succeeds Act: Mapping emerging trends for personalized learning in state ESSA plans.* https://knowledgeworks.org/resources/personalized-learning-every-student-succeeds-act/

Kolbert, J. B., Hilts, D., Crothers, L. M., & Nice, M. L. (2021). School counselors' use of Marcia's identity status theory for career advisement and consultation and collaboration. *Journal of School Counseling, 19*(21). http://www.jsc.montana.edu/articles/v19n21.pdf

Kroger, J., Martinussen, M., & Marcia, J. (2010). Identity status change during adolescence and young adulthood: A meta-analysis. *Journal of Adolescence, 33*(5), 683–698. https://doi.org/10.1016/j.adolescence.2009.11.002

Kuder, G. F. (2012). *The Kuder career planning system.* Author.

Lim, S. A., & You, S. (2019). Long-term effect of parents' support on adolescents' career maturity. *Journal of Career Development, 46*(1), 48–61. https://doi.org/10.1177/0894845317731866

Long, B. T. (2018). *The college completion landscape: Trends, challenges, and why it matters.* American Enterprise Institute. www.aei.org/spotlight/the-college-completion-landscape/

Lustig, D. (2018). Family-of-origin influence on career thoughts. *The Career Development Quarterly, 66*(2), 149–161. https://doi.org/10.1002/cdq.12129

Malin, J. R., Bragg, D. D., & Hackmann, D. G. (2017). College and career readiness and the Every Student Succeeds Act. *Education Administration Quarterly, 53*(5), 809–838. https://doi.org/10.1177/0013161X17714845

Malkus, N. (2019). *The evolution of career and technical education: 1982–2013.* American Enterprise Institute. www.aei.org/research-products/report/the-evolution-of-career-and-technical-education-1982–2013/

Marcia, J. E. (1966). Development and validation of ego-identity status. *Journal of Personality and Social Psychology, 3*(5), 551–558. https://doi.org/10.1037/h0023281

Marcia, J. E. (2002). Adolescence, identity, and the Bernardone family. *Family, Identity: An International Journal of Theory and Research, 2*(3), 199–209. https://doi.org/10.1207/S1532706XID020301

Marcia, J. E. (2007). *Theory and measure: The identity status interview.* University Press of America.

Martin, J. (2013). Applying the essentials of financial aid to an understanding of financial aid packaging models. In *Fundamentals of college admission counseling* (3rd ed., pp. 80–91). National Association for College Admission Counseling.

Martinez, R. R., Baker, S. B., & Young, T. (2017). Promoting career and college readiness, aspirations, and self-efficacy: Curriculum field test. *The Career Development Quarterly, 65*(2), 173–188. https://doi.org/10.1002/cdq.12090

Mattern, K., Burrus, J., Camara, W., O'Connor, R., Hansen, M. A., Gambrell, J., Casillas, A., & Bobeck, B. (2014). *Broadening the definition of college and career readiness: A holistic approach* (ACT Research Report Series 5). American College Testing. https://files.eric.ed.gov/fulltext/ED555591.pdf

McCharen, B., & High, K. (2010). *Career and technical programs of study and early indicators of retention in the College of Engineering.* Association of Career and Technical Education Research. https://gradebuddy.com/doc/2529198/early-indicators-of-retention-in-the-college-of-engineering/

McGoldrick, M., Carter, B., & Garcia-Preto, N. (2016). *The expanding family life cycle: Individual, family, and social perspectives*. Pearson.

Meeus, W. (2018). The identity status continuum revisited: A comparison of longitudinal findings with Marcia's model and dual cycle models. *European Psychologist, 23*(4), 289. https://doi.org/10.1027/1016-9040/a000339

Meyers, C., Dringard, K., & Zinner, E. (1978). *What I like to do*. Science Research Associates.

Military.com. (2020). *The ASVAB test*. www.military.com/join-armed-forces/asvab

Milsom, A. (2002). Students with disabilities: School counselor involvement and preparation. *Professional School Counseling, 5*(5), 331–338.

Milsom, A., & Hartley, M. T. (2005). Assisting students with learning disabilities transition to college: What school counselors should know. *Professional School Counseling, 8*(5), 436–441. www.jstor.org/stable/42732486

Mobley, C., Sharp, J. L., Hammond, C., Withington, C., & Stipanovic, N. (2017). The influence of career-focused education on student career planning and development: A comparison of CTE and non-CTE students. *Career and Technical Education Research, 42*(1), 57–75. https://doi.org/10.5328/cter42.1.57

Montalto, C. P., Phillips, E. L., McDaniel, A., & Baker, A. R. (2019). College student financial wellness: Student loans and beyond. *Journal of Family and Economic Issues, 40*(1), 3–21. https://doi.org/10.1007/s10834-018-9593-4

Morsunbul, U., Crocetti, E., Cok, F., & Meeus, W. (2014). Brief report: The Utrecht-Management of Identity Commitments Scale (U-MICS): Gender and age measurement invariance and convergent validity of the Turkish version. *Journal of Adolescence, 37*(6), 799–805. https://doi.org/10.1016/j.adolescence.2014.05.008

National Joint Committee on Learning Disabilities. (1994). *Secondary to postsecondary education transition planning for students with learning disabilities: College perspectives on issues affecting learning disabilities: Position papers and statements*. Pro-Ed.

Negru-Subtirica, O., Pop, E. I., Luyck, K., Dezutter, J., & Steger, M. F. (2016). The meaningful identity: A longitudinal look at the interplay between identity and meaning in life in adolescence. *Developmental Psychology, 52*(11), 1926–1936. https://doi.org/10.1037/dev0000176

Newman, L., Wagner, M., Knokey, A. M., Marder, C., Nagle, K., Shaver, D., . . . Schwartinng, M. (2011). *The post-high school outcomes of young adults with disabilities up to 8 years after high school: A report from the National Longitudinal Transition Study-2 (NLTSd)* (NCSER 2011–3005). https://ies.ed.gov/ncser/pubs/20113005/pdf/20113005.pdf

Newman, L., Wagner, R., Cameto, R., Knokey, A. M., & Shaver, D. (2010). *Comparisons across time of the outcomes of youth with disabilities up to 4 years after high school: A report of findings from the National Longitudinal Transition Study-2 (NLTS2)*. SRI International.

Nienhusser, H. K., & Oshio, T. (2017). *Research in Higher Education, 58*(7), 723–745. https://doi.org/10.1007/s11162-017-9447-1

No Child Left Behind Act of 2001, Pub. L. No. 107–110 (2002).

Ohrt, J. H., Lambie, G. W., & Ieva, K. P. (2009). Supporting Latino and African-American students in advanced placement courses: A school counseling program's approach. *Professional School Counseling, 13*(1), 59–63. https://doi.org/10.1177/2156759X0901300104

Orsillo, S. M., & Roemer, L. (2011). *The mindful way through anxiety: Break free from chronic worry and reclaim your life*. The Guilford Press.

Perna, L. W., & Finney, J. E. (2014). *The attainment agenda: State policy leadership in higher education*. Johns Hopkins University Press.

Perry, J. C., Liu, X., & Pabian, Y. (2010). School engagement as a mediator of academic performance among urban youth: The role of career preparation, parental career support, and teacher support. *The Counseling Psychologist, 38*(2), 269–295. https://doi.org/10.1177/0011000009349272

Pew Research Center. (2016). *The state of American jobs: How the shifting economic landscape is reshaping work and society and affecting the way people thinking about the skills and training they need to get ahead*. www.pewsocialtrends.org/2016/10/06/1-changes-in-the-american-workplace

Pisarik, C. T., Rowell, P. C., & Thompson, L. K. (2017). A phenomenological study of career anxiety among college students. *The Career Development Quarterly, 65*(4), 339–352. https://doi.org/10.1002/cdq.12112

Pop, E., Negru-Subtirica, O., Crocetti, E., Opre, A., & Meeus, W. (2016). On the interplay between academic achievement and educational identity: A longitudinal study. *Journal of Adolescence, 47*, 135–144. https://doi.org/10.1016/j.adolescence.2015.11.004

Poynton, T., & Lapan, R. (2017). Aspirations, achievement, and school counselors' impact on the college transition. *Journal of Counseling & Development, 95*(4), 369–377. https://doi.org/10.1002/jcad.12152

Rehabilitation Act of 1973, Section 504, 29 U.S.C 794.

Roderick, M., Coca, V., & Nagaoka, J. (2011). Potholes on the road to college: High school effects in shaping urban students' participation in college application, four-year college enrollment, and college match. *Sociology of Education, 84*(3), 178–211. https://doi.org/10.1177/0038040711411280

Savickas, M. L. (2002). Career construction: A developmental theory of vocational behavior. In D. Brown (Ed.), *Career choice and development* (pp. 149–205). Jossey-Bass.

Schenck, P. M., Anctil, T. M., Smith, C. K., & C. Dahir (2012). Coming full circle: Reoccurring career development trends in schools. *The Career Development Quarterly, 60*(3), 221–230. https://doi.org/10.1002/j.2161-0045.2012.00018.x

Shamsuddin, S. (2016). Taken out of context: Piecing together college guidance information in urban high schools. *Urban Review, 48*(1), 101–122. https://doi.org/10.1007/s11256-015-0347-4

Shirai, T., Nakamura, T., & Katsuma, K. (2016). Identity development in relation to time beliefs in emerging adulthood: A long-term longitudinal study. *Identity, 16*(1), https://doi.org/10.1080/15283488.2015.1121817

Stern, D., Dayton, C., & Raby, M. (2010). *Career academies: A proven strategy to prepare high school students for colleges and careers.* Career Academy Support Network. https://files.eric.ed.gov/fulltext/ED524061.pdf

Stone, III, J. R. (2005). The neglected majority-revisited. *Journal of Career and Technical Education, 21*(2), 67–80.

Sugimura, K., Niwa, T., Takahashi, A., Sugiura, Y., Jinno, M., & Crocetti, E. (2015). Cultural self-construction and identity formation in emerging adulthood: A study on Japanese university students and workers. *Journal of Youth Studies, 18*(10), 1326–1346. https://doi.org/10.1080/13676261.2015.1039964

Turner, S. L., & Conkel, J. L. (2010). Evaluation of a career development skills intervention with adolescents living in an inner city. *Journal of Counseling & Development, 88*(4), 457–465. https://doi.org/10.1002/j.1556-6678.2020.tb00046.x

US Department of Education. (n.d.). *Every student succeeds act (ESSA).* Author. www.ed.gov/essa?src%3Drn

Verhoeven, M., Poorthuis, A., & Volman, M. (2019). The role of school in adolescents' identity development: A literature review. *Educational Psychology Review, 31*(1), 35–63. https://doi.org/10.1007/s10648-018-9457-3

Wadsworth, J., Milsom, A., & Cocco, K. (2004). Career development for adolescents and young adults with mental retardation. *Professional School Counseling, 8*(2), 141–147. www.jstor.org/stable/42732616

Wagner, M., Newman, L., Cameto, R., Garza, N., & Levine, P. (2005). *After high school: A first look at the postschool experiences of youth with disabilities: A report from the National Longitudinal Transition Study-2 (NLTS2).* SRI International. https://files.eric.ed.gov/fulltext/ED494935.pdf

Welton, A. D., & Martinez, M. A. (2014). Coloring the college pathway: A more culturally responsive approach to college readiness and access for students of color in secondary schools. *Urban Review, 46*(2), 197–223. https://doi.org/10.1007/s11256-013-0252-7

Wilgosh, L. (1994). Assessment of vocational preferences for young people with intellectual impairment. *Developmental Disabilities Bulletin, 22*, 63–71.

Wosnik, D., & Zwartjes, J. (2010). *Journey to jobs: Story, lessons, & activities on career choices.* Marco Products.

Wren, C., & Einhorn, J. (2000). *Hanging by a twig: Understanding and counseling adults with learning disabilities and ADD*. Norton & Company.

Yeager, D., & Bundick, M. (2009). The role of purposeful work goals in promoting meaning in life and in schoolwork during adolescence. *Journal of Adolescent Research*, 24(4), 423–452. https://doi.org/10.1177/0743558409336749

Chapter 11

Prevention/Auxiliary Programming

> **Box 11.1   2016 Council for the Accreditation of Counseling and Related Educational Programs (CACREP, n.d.) School Counseling Specialty Area Standards**
>
> 1.e   Assessments specific to P–12 education
> 2.a   School counselor roles as leaders, advocates, and systems change agents in P–12 schools
> 2.d   School counselor roles in school leadership and multidisciplinary teams
> 3.m   Strategies for implementing and coordinating peer intervention programs

---

> **Box 11.2   ASCA (2019) Standards for School Counselor Preparation Programs (ASCA CAEP SPA)**
>
> 3.2   Identify research-based individual counseling, group counseling, and classroom instruction techniques to promote academic achievement, college/career readiness, and social/emotional development for every student.

Traditionally, some of the ways in which SCs have sought to impact the entire student population has been through their implementation and coordination of prevention and peer programs. SCs have long been involved in both prevention and peer programming, as indicated by the American School Counselor Association's (ASCA) position statements on the promotion of safe schools through conflict resolution and bullying/harassment prevention (ASCA, 2016) and peer helping (ASCA, 2021). In this chapter, we review the research regarding the effectiveness of peer mediation and peer support programs, violence and bullying prevention programs, social and emotional learning (SEL) programs, and the SC's role in implementing and coordinating such programs. We discuss emotion-focused therapy (EFT) perspective in promoting emotional intelligence in youth. Finally, we provide an example of an SC's use of consultation and individual counseling to assist a student victim of bullying.

DOI: 10.4324/9781003167730-11

School Violence

SCs have been historically associated with prevention programs that are aimed at reducing school violence. Some have argued that SCs contribute to the academic mission of the school by addressing the social/emotional needs of students, citing Abraham Maslow's hierarchy of needs theory, which posits that physical and psychological safety needs must be satisfied in order for students to attend to the higher-order need of academic learning. Indeed, a longitudinal, meta-analytic study revealed that school violence is one of the strongest predictors of academic achievement and mental health (e.g., Polanin et al., 2021). The term *youth violence* is used to refer to many forms of violence, ranging from acts in which the intention is to cause bodily harm or even death to less-aggressive acts in which the perpetrator's goal is to induce psychological harm (Matjasko et al., 2012). The results of the 2019 National Youth Risk Behavior Survey revealed that among high school students in the past year, approximately 20% reported being a victim of bullying, 8% reported being involved in a fight, and 7% reported being threatened or injured by a weapon (Centers for Disease Control and Prevention, n.d.).

Policy makers' recognition of the substantial role that school violence and school climate have on academic achievement is reflected in the Every Student Succeeds Act (ESSA; US Department of Education, n.d.), which encourages schools to use funds to "develop, implement, and evaluate comprehensive programs and activities that . . . foster and support safe, healthy, supportive and drug-free environments that support academic achievement" (p. 178). Some of the programs explicitly named in legislation include programs for drug and violence prevention, school-based mental health services, bullying and harassment prevention, and relationship-building skills to improve safety and reduce interpersonal violence.

School-Based Violence Prevention Programs

There is considerable variation in the assumptions and nature of school-based violence prevention programs. Some programs focus on tailoring individualized approaches to students who have been identified as being at risk for aggression. Violence prevention programs that are labeled as "universal" involve a curriculum that is provided to all students within a school or grade level. Finally, multiple approach programs seek to involve parents, peers, and/or the community in addition to the school's curriculum (Park-Higgerson et al., 2008). Some violence prevention programs provide instruction regarding the causes of violence and strategies for avoiding violence (Hahn et al., 2007). Such programs assume that students often lack the skills to manage interpersonal conflict without using aggression and provide students with conflict resolution skills, including anger management, active listening, and problem-solving. Other programs assume that aggressive students lack positive self-esteem and teach students prosocial skills and encourage parents and teachers to reinforce students' exhibition of prosocial behaviors. For example, in the elementary-level Peacebuilders Program, students are rewarded for demonstrating behaviors consistent with simple behavioral rules, such as "Praise people" and "Right wrongs." Many violence prevention programs are available commercially and have manuals to increase treatment fidelity.

Effectiveness of School-Based Violence Prevention Programs

Research regarding violence prevention is decidedly mixed. Hahn's et al. (2007) meta-analysis of 53 studies of universal violence prevention programs revealed that such programs reduced violence among children at all grade levels, yielding on average a 15% decrease in the frequency of violence. Interestingly, whereas programs administered by teachers were found to be effective, programs administered by administrators and SCs were not found to be effective. The authors did not speculate about why teacher-led violence prevention programs were found to be more effective than those led by SCs. Perhaps this finding indicates that SCs must receive better preparation for conducting instruction? The results of Park-Higgerson et al.'s (2008) meta-analysis of 26 randomized controlled studies of violence prevention programs differs from that of Hahn et al. (2007) in some important respects. Park-Higgerson et al. (2008) found that programs that focused on at-risk children, in comparison to universal programs, involved students in the fourth grade or higher, and were administered by education specialists, in comparison to teachers, yielded slightly stronger effects in reducing aggression.

School Bullying

Bullying is another form of aggression that is common within schools, and this form of aggression has received considerable attention from school personnel and researchers in the past decade. While school personnel may use the terms *violence* and *bullying* interchangeably, *bullying* is defined as a distinct form of aggression that involves the following three conditions that distinguish it from violence: (1) a person of greater power seeks to harm another, (2) the power imbalance can take a variety of forms, which may include physicality, social popularity, intelligence, socioeconomic status, and race/ethnic status, and (3) the negative actions are repeated (Olweus & Limber, 2010). In summary, bullying typically differs from other forms of violence between students in that the perpetrator has greater power than the victim and the aggressive acts are committed by the perpetrator over a period of time. Bullying behaviors are often categorized by type, including verbal bullying, which includes being made fun of and being called names; physical bullying, which includes being pushed, shoved, tripped, or the destruction of property; and relational bullying, which includes being the subject or rumors, manipulation of a child's friendships, and social exclusion. Cyberbullying involves negative information about a person that is communicated via text or instant messaging, email, posts on social media accounts, pretending to be someone else online, or sending explicit pictures about a person on social media sites (Cyberbullying Research Center, n.d.).

Risk Factors for Bullying Perpetration and Victimization

Cook et al. (2010) conducted a meta-analysis of the predictors of bullying perpetrators, those who are victims, and bully-victims. The study revealed that in comparison to nonviolent peers, perpetrators of bullying are more likely to exhibit externalizing (i.e., defiance, aggression, disruption, and noncompliant responses) and internalizing behaviors (i.e., withdrawn, depressive, anxious, and avoidant responses), a lack of social competence, academic difficulties, negative attitudes and beliefs about self and others, difficulty in resolving problems with others, and experience a family environment high in conflict, a lack of parental monitoring, and negative influence by peers.

Victims of bullying exhibit internalizing and externalizing behaviors, a lack of social skills, negative cognitions about self, difficulties in resolving interpersonal conflicts; come from negative community, family, and school environments; and are rejected and isolated by peers. Bully-victims share many characteristics with victims and perpetrators. Bully-victims are more likely than their peers to demonstrate both externalizing and internalizing behaviors, have negative beliefs about themselves and others, have academic problems, lack social problem-solving skills, and are negatively influenced and rejected by peers. Cook et al. (2010) conclude that the high level of shared predictors support the theory that the three bully status groups have a common etiology.

Social Information Processing (SIP) Models and Aggression

Social information processing (SIP) models are probably the most commonly used theory to explain youth aggression, including for overt violence and bullying. Crick and Dodge (1996) assert that SIP involves five mental steps resulting in a behavioral action. Research generally supports the contention of SIP models that aggressive children exhibit deficits in SIP. Aggressive children register fewer and less-benign social cues, either due to deficits in memory or selective attention (step 1), are more likely to attribute hostile intentions to the actions of others (step 2), are more likely to choose goals that damage relationships with peers (step 3), generate less prosocial responses (step 4), regard aggressive responses more favorably, expect positive outcomes from aggressive behavior, and feel confident in engage in aggression (step 5) (Camodeca & Goossens, 2005).

Proactive vs. Reactive Aggression

Another common distinction used to understand aggression in youth is reactive and proactive aggression (Camodeca & Goossens, 2005). *Reactive aggression* is a defensive response to perceived aggression in others and is accompanied by anger. In contrast, *proactive aggression* is planned, intentional use of aggression to achieve a goal and may invoke pleasure or satisfaction. Camodeca and Goossens's (2005) review of the research indicates that perpetrators of bullying exhibit both reactive and proactive aggression, while bully victims only show reactive aggression. Crick and Dodge (1996) found that reactively aggressive children exhibit hostile attribution bias, meaning, that they tend to misperceive others to have aggressive intent, and thus respond with aggression. Proactively aggressive children regard the use aggression more positively, viewing it as an effective way to achieve goals.

Implications of the SIP Model and Proactive and Reactive Aggression for Counseling

Both SIP models and the distinction between proactive and reactive aggression have implications for working with such students in individual and group counseling (Santone et al., 2020). Reactive and proactive aggressors can be assisted in learning to intentionally examine how they process social events. They can be taught the foundational principle of cognitive-behavioral theory, which is that thoughts have a strong influence upon emotions, sensations, and behaviors. They can be taught to delay their response in order to examine the accuracy of their thoughts. They can be taught to examine their goals in social situations, prosocial ways to obtain status, and to "think through" the likely consequences of their actions. For example, while bullying appears to be a fairly effective way for perpetrators to obtain status in elementary and middle school, the popularity of bullying perpetrators tends to decline in high school.

Effectiveness of Bullying Prevention

Most states have legislation requiring schools to incorporate antibullying policies within their student codes of conduct and implement evidence-based bullying prevention programs.

A recent meta-analytic study revealed that bullying prevention programs reduce school-bullying perpetration by about 19–20% and school-bullying victimization by approximately 15–16% (Gaffney et al., 2019). Gaffney et al.'s (2021) meta-analytic study found that various approaches, including social-ecological approaches which seek to alter environmental conditions that support aggression among youth, are effective in reducing school bullying. Activities that involve informal peer involvement, which typically include whole-class or small-group discussions, cooperative group work, or other types of activities that promote peer interaction, are associated with greater reductions in school bullying than other types of bullying prevention activities. Such informal peer involvement activities do not directly target perpetrators, victims, or bystanders of bullying but appear to be effective in promoting a prosocial classroom and school ethos. The presence of classroom rules and a whole-school approach is more effective than programs which do not include these approaches. Nonpunitive disciplinary methods are associated with greater reductions in bullying. Providing information to parents via leaflets/letters is associated with reductions in bullying, whereas more formal involvement of parents, such as encouraging parents to attend information evenings, is not associated with reductions in bullying. The authors surmised that more formal forms of parent involvement may fail to encourage the participation of parents whose children are involved in bullying. Activities that target victims, which often involve providing victims with cognitive behavioral treatment, are associated with reductions in school bullying. Antibullying activities that appear to be associated with less reductions in bullying include encouraging bystander involvement and teaching socioemotional skills.

Olweus's Bullying Prevention Program (OBPP: Olweus & Limber, 2010)

The OBPP is a comprehensive, school-wide program that seeks to reduce bullying and enhance the school climate through restructuring of the school environment. The program is based on social learning theory in its encouragement of school personnel to assume leadership in fostering a sense of community by modeling and showing interest in students. Other social learning theory tenets include the promotion of adults and, to a more limited degree, students, reducing opportunities and reinforcement for bullying. The OBPP principles suggest that school personnel, and ideally parents, (1) demonstrate warmth and interest in students, (2) establish firm expectations regarding acceptable behavior, (3) use consistent noncorporal consequences for violation of rules, and (4) serve as positive role models for students. These goals and principles are incorporated into school-level (e.g., coordination committee, trainings for staff, conduct survey to determine frequency and location of bullying), classroom-level (e.g., weekly classroom lessons on bullying), individual-level (e.g., increase supervision particularly of problem areas, individual sessions with victims and perpetrators), and community-level components (e.g., increase understanding of the issue and program within the community).

SCs can assume a leadership role in coordinating and implementing such prevention programs as OBPP. SCs should be an essential member of the various planning committees of OBPP, whose responsibilities typically include data coordination, training of staff and parents, implementation of the curriculum for students, enhancing supervision for areas of the school where bullying is found to more likely occur, as indicated by surveying students, educating the larger community, etc. SCs can coordinate the data collection for various aspects of implementing such a program. They can assess students', teachers', and parents' perceptions regarding the frequency of bullying and their perceptions of the need for such a program. SCs also can evaluate the effectiveness of the specific components of the program, assessing the impact of classroom lessons on helping students report bullying, more effectively managing their emotional responses to victimization, including typically rejected/isolated students in socialization, engaging in safe internet behaviors, etc. Furthermore, SCs can work individually with students who continue to bully even after the implementation of the program. Young et al. (2009) provide a description of how the SCs of a middle school assumed leadership in implementing and evaluating a bullying prevention program, which eventually resulted in their principal removing their responsibility for test coordination.

School-Wide Positive Behavioral Interventions and Supports (SWPBIS)

A recent trend in school-based efforts to reduce aggression has been the use of school-wide positive behavioral interventions and supports (SWPBIS). SWPBIS is a prevention-oriented, multitiered framework for the implementation of evidence-based practices with high fidelity to promote academic and social behavior outcomes for all students (Sugai et al., 2011). SWPBIS is based on a behavioral model, which assumes that problematic behaviors are the result of students not understanding the behavioral expectations, lacking the behavioral skill set, and/or receiving environmental reinforcement. Whereas OBPP recommends assigning negative consequences to students who bully (Olweus & Limber, 2010), SWPBIS emphasizes the use of reinforcement to promote prosocial or desirable behaviors and does not recommend the use of punishment to eliminate bullying behaviors (Sugai et al., 2011). However, it should be noted that the nature of consequences used in OBPP, which include firm talks with students who bully, increased supervision, etc., cannot be considered overly punitive.

The tier one level of intervention involves teachers instructing students in how to behave in a respectful, prosocial manner through the acquisition of social skills and character traits, with the expectation that approximately 85–90% of students will respond to the universal level of intervention. At tier two, students who continue to display problematic behaviors are provided with additional support in the form of more intensive skills instruction, enhanced adult monitoring and positive attention, more specific and consistent feedback regarding students' behavioral progress, and additional academic supports if indicated.

Two types of tier three interventions that have received empirical support, and which SCs are often involved in implementing, are the *Behavior Education Program* (BEP) and the *Strong Kids Curriculum Program* (SKCP; Mitchell et al., 2011). In the BEP, also known as check-in/check-out (CICO), the student is issued a daily behavior report card (DBRC) to document behavior aligned with school-wide expectations at tier one. Each morning, the student meets with an adult facilitator, then carries the DBRC to each class and receives feedback and reinforcement from the teacher using a point system. At the end of the school day, the student checks out with the BEP facilitator and takes the form home for a parent's signature. The *Strong Kids* curriculum seeks to promote socioemotional competence. The 12-lesson curriculum includes the topics of identifying feelings in self and others, managing stress and anger, rational thinking, conflict resolution, and goal-setting.

At tier three, students who did not respond to tier one and two interventions receive even more intensive support in the way of individually tailored behavioral modification plans and the use of mental health services, typically in the form of wraparound services. The assumption is that through the support of school and mental health personnel, the student's caregivers can modify the home environment to remove reinforcers associated with the child's aggression.

Students are often identified as in need of tier two and tier three interventions through the use of standardized measurements and assessment procedures. Common assessment screens include office discipline referrals (ODRs), teacher rating scales, and multiple-gate screening systems. The *Systematic Screening for Behavior Disorders* (SSBD) is a highly supported measure for identifying students at risk for internalizing and externalizing behaviors (Lane et al., 2009). The SSBD is a multiple-gated system where students' progress into advanced gates is based upon specific criteria. At gate 1, teachers rank students according to internalizing and externalizing characteristics. The top three students identified with the most concern receive further assessment. At gate 2, the classroom teacher completes teacher-rating scales for the six identified students. Students who receive scores exceeding normal expectations move to gate 3, which involves behavioral observation in academic and social settings.

SCs often have multiple roles to play in the SWPBIS model. They may assist teachers in implementing the universal social skills and character trait curricula at the tier one level or may coordinate the assessment procedures for identifying the necessity of moving students into tier two and three interventions. SCs also may be the primary implementer of social skills training at the tier two and three levels or may coordinate the CICO program. At the tier three level, they may serve as the school liaison that seeks to increase parent involvement and provides the family with referrals for mental health services. The PBIS Center's website (www.pbis.org) has free and downloadable materials, including materials related to bullying prevention.

Peer Helping

Peer helping programs are another type of programming used by schools to increase the school's climate and promote students' socioemotional development. Peer helping can take a variety of forms, including mediation, tutoring, mentoring, and counseling. We will focus on peer mediation, as SCs often coordinate peer mediation programs, and more briefly discuss some peer helping/support and peer tutoring programs.

Box 11.3   ASCA's (2021) Position Statement Regarding the School's Counselor's Role in Implementing Peer Support Programs

School counselors are responsible for determining the needs of the school population and for implementing interventions designed to meet those needs, such as peer support programs. In collaboration with school staff, school counselors:

- Follow the ASCA Ethical Standards for School Counselors as they relate to peer support programs, including safeguarding the welfare of students participating in peer support programs and providing appropriate training and supervision for peer helpers (ASCA, 2022; QPR, 2019).

- Use best practices when developing and implementing peer support programs (Berger et al., 2018).
- Create a selection plan for peer helpers reflecting the diversity of the population to be served.
- Develop a support system for the program that communicates the program's goals and purpose through positive public relations.
- Monitor, assess, and adjust the program and training on a continual basis to meet the assessed needs of the school population the program serves.
- Report results to all stakeholders (e.g., students, teachers, administrators, parents, community).

Reprinted with permission, American School
Counselor Association, www.schoolcounselor.org

Training students to assist their peers can be advantageous for the SC program. Many students would prefer to obtain help from a peer rather than an adult, and this is particularly true for adolescents, as there is research evidence indicating that support from peers is a greater predictor of well-being than support from parents or teachers (Ciarrochi et al., 2017). Peer programs can also extend the outreach of the school counseling program and increase student awareness of the services offered (ASCA, 2021). Box 11.3 identifies responsibilities of SCs in regards to peer helping programs, as indicated in ASCA's (2021) position statement on peer support programs.

Box 11.4

Factors Essential to Making Peer Mediation Work (Skiba & Peterson, 2000).

- *Planning.* Effective peer mediation programs require advance planning, considering such issues as how mediators will be chosen, where and when the mediation will occur, and what types of conflicts peer mediators can address, among others.
- *Training.* The initial training of peer mediators requires 12–15 hours, in which students will learn the basic principles of peer mediation, why conflict occurs, etc. Students will also be taught communication and problem-solving strategies to defuse conflict. Role-playing and active learning help students to move toward solutions for all students involved in conflict.
- *Ongoing Implementation.* Ongoing monitoring of the program is important to its success, including the extent to which mediators are used, the success of the mediators, and how the mediators and their peers view the success of the program. Weekly or biweekly training should be planned for mediators, and peer mediation should be part of a whole-school effort.

Peer Mediation

Peer mediation programs involve training students to conduct mediation with students engaged in conflict. In many peer mediation programs, the trained students conduct formal mediation sessions with peers who either requested the assistance of a mediator or were referred to mediation by a teacher or administrator. Typically, formal mediation sessions involve two trained mediators and the disputants, and there is a school personnel member who has also received peer mediation training who oversees the session. However, peer mediation programs are also used with the presumption that there is a spillover effect, whereby students who are trained in mediation and conflict resolution will utilize these skills with their peers and family members outside of formal mediation sessions. Therefore, SCs hope that the students who participate in the mediation process will obtain conflict resolution skills that they apply in subsequent conflicts.

Box 11.5   Steps of Mediation

• Laying the Ground Rules

"How this works is that both of you will have a chance to explain your concerns, meaning, what is bothering you. While the one person is speaking, the other person is listening, trying to understand how the other person sees the problem. When the person is done talking, the listener will explain what he or she heard the other person saying. Then the listener will have a chance to say how he or she sees things. Once we think we really understand how the other person sees the problem, then we will talk about what it is that we want from each other. Finally, we will talk about ideas on how we can get what we want from each other. Are you each willing to take turns in talking with each other? Another important rule in here is that you must be respectful, meaning, that you will not make nasty comments or put the other person down. Are you willing to be respectful toward each other?"

• Understanding Each Other

It is usually best to have the original complainant start speaking first, since he or she has a clearer idea of what is bothering him or her. The mediators should keep notes to help them identify the students' issues. Once the complainant is finished, a mediator can ask the listener, "Tell Jennifer what you heard her saying just now." Obviously, a potential problem is that the listener interrupts the speaker in an attempt to defend him- or herself. The mediator may remind the listener that he or she will have a turn soon. Or the listener may take the offensive and say something nasty, at which point the mediator can remind him or her about the agreement to be respectful. Once the listener has stated back to the speaker what he or she heard him or her saying, the mediator should ask the speaker, "Do you think the listener heard what you had to say?" If the speaker thinks the listener has not heard him or her, the mediator should ask the speaker to help the listener to better understand him or her by pointing out what the listener left out or where he or she is confused. Only once the speaker feels that he or she has been "heard" should the mediators move on to having the listener talk about how he or she sees it, repeating the process.

• Identifying Wants

An indication that the disputants understand each other is that there is a noticeable reduction in tension and they have little left to share. Next, the mediator should ask the students to talk to each other about what is it that they want. The mediators may have to help the students with identifying their wants, and the mediator can refer to their notes for comments made earlier by the disputants that imply a want. The mediator can summarize the disputants' wants. For example, "Jennifer, what I hear that you want from Amy is that you want Amy to come to you and tell you if she is angry with you, rather than saying things to other people. Is that right?" Then you repeat the process for Jennifer. What would she want the other person to do if she was angry? Where? When? How?

• **Exploring Solutions**

Next, the mediators should identify areas of agreement between the students. For example, "Jennifer and Amy, I hear that both of you want the other to be upfront about disagreements, meaning, if you're angry with each other, you will share it with each other. Is that correct?" The mediators may further explore with the disputants how they plan on carrying out the agreed-upon solution. For example, the mediators may ask them how they want to interact the next time they see each other. For younger (below the age of 14) and concrete-operational students, you may wish to do a more formal brainstorming session in which you write down each suggested solution without evaluation. Once each of the students has identified at least a couple of solutions, you want to have them evaluate each one and ask if they are willing to do that suggested solution. Once they've identified agreed solutions, you have them sign the solution page, as if it were a contract.

Source: Adapted from Kolbert, J. B., and Field, J. E. (2004, June). "The steps of mediation for school counselors." *The Pennsylvania Counselor, LI(5)*, 14–16.

Empirical Support for Peer Mediation

Research suggests that peer mediation benefits both students trained to be peer mediators and the study body as a whole. Peterson and Skiba (2001) concluded from a review of the research literature that peer mediation training increased the self-esteem and academic achievement of peer mediators. Other studies have found that students trained to be peer mediators successfully learned and retained the steps of conflict resolution for up to at least six months (Johnson & Johnson, 1996). From a review of the research literature, Carruthers and Sweeney (1996) concluded that peer mediators experience an increase in their attitudes toward school, and the parents of mediators reported observing an increase in their child's grades and attitudes toward school.

Johnson and Johnson's (2004) meta-analytic study of the efficacy of the *Teaching Students to be Peacemakers Program* (TSP), which includes both conflict resolution and peer mediation, revealed increased academic achievement and long-term retention of academic material and a marked decrease in discipline referrals. Peer mediation also appears to benefit the students who receive peer mediation. Generally, studies indicate that disputants reach agreement 80% to 95% of the time (Carruthers & Sweeney, 1996). However, the most frequent agreement achieved by disputants is to avoid or ignore each other (Johnson & Johnson, 1996).

Cantrell et al. (2007) conducted one of the few longitudinal studies of the effectiveness of a peer mediation program. They found the Peace Pal program had a number of positive benefits for an elementary school. The program yielded a decrease in total out-of-school suspensions for each of the three postprogram years for both Black and White students. Nearly all the disputants reported being satisfied with the results of the peer mediation sessions. Furthermore, the students who were trained as peer mediators demonstrated an increase in knowledge concerning conflict resolution and mediation, and they viewed the program as valuable.

Training/Program Implementation for Peer Mediation

While peer mediation training programs vary, most programs focus on helping students understand the nature of conflict and its causes and teaching peer mediators communication, problem-solving, and negotiation skills (Algozzine et al., 2010). In addition, much of the training in peer mediation programs involves teaching students the mediation process. An example of the steps of mediation can found in Box 11.5.

Implementing a peer mediation program requires considerable planning and resources (Algozzine et al., 2010). Some studies have found that it takes to two to five years before a peer mediation program demonstrates positive results, as both students and teachers gradually accept peer mediation as a legitimate conflict resolution process (e.g., Cameron & Dupuis, 1991). The school must determine which students and staff will receive training, when and where mediation will occur, what the referral process will be, and which types of conflicts mediators will address. SCs often coordinate the peer mediation program and train the peer mediators, given their training in communication skills and focus on social/emotional development. However, it is recommended that SCs collaborate with other school personnel in coordinating the peer mediation program for a variety of reasons. Training teachers to serve as observers of mediations serves to extend the reach of the program and hopefully increase teachers' investment in the program, which is essential for the success of the peer mediation program. Furthermore, involving other, hopefully influential school personnel increases the likelihood that the program transforms the school culture, by not only impacting how students resolve interpersonal conflict, but also by modifying the relationships between students and teachers.

Sellman (2011) concluded from his qualitative examination of nine schools that implemented peer mediation programs in England that successful peer mediation programs resulted in more egalitarian relationships between students and teachers. He also concluded that for programs to be effective, the staff needed to concede ownership of the program to students and permit students to resolve interpersonal conflict through peer mediation in contrast to the traditional response of teachers addressing student conflict through their application of punitive measures.

The training and selection of peer mediators is an ongoing process, as new mediators must be continually identified as the former peer mediators graduate. Day-Vines et al. (1996) recommend that peer mediators vary in terms of academic abilities, gender, and cultural background. Such diversity can increase the perspective-taking of the mediators and possibly increase the students' use of the peer mediation program if they see peer mediators who are similar to themselves. Students should also be selected for their communication and problem-solving skills. The initial training of peer mediators is often a one- to two-day affair, and it is recommended that this training occur after school or on a weekend, to avoid interfering with academic time. In this initial training, peer mediators receive an understanding of conflict, practice active listening skills, learn the steps of mediation, and role-play mediation sessions. Typically, new peer mediators undergo an apprenticeship period in which they observe real mediation sessions conducted by more experienced peer mediators. Teachers who observe the mediations should provide immediate feedback to the peer mediators following sessions, and booster trainings for both the peer mediators and involved teachers are required to increase treatment fidelity.

Peer Helping/Support

In peer helping/support, selected students are trained by school personnel, which often includes SCs, to assist their peers with slight to moderate problems. Peer helping/support programs have been found to enhance the school culture and school connectedness for both mentors and mentees (Voight & Nation, 2016) and increase social contacts for students with disabilities (Asmus et al., 2017). However, McGannon et al. (2005) concluded from a quite-limited literature that peer helpers tend to experience greater benefits from providing support than do the students receiving the support. There are also a number of other concerns with peer helping programs, including how to ensure that the peer helpers maintain the confidentiality of their peers' concerns and do not address issues that are beyond their level of training. SCs are ethically responsible for the welfare of both the helper and the student receiving help, and thus there must be considerable investment in the oversight of the peer helping program and the training of the peer helpers. The training for peer helpers must include an understanding of the role of the helper, active listening skills, helping a peer in the process of problem-solving, and confidentiality and its limitations. Additionally, peer helping programs may consider providing training in understanding aggression and its various forms, including sexual harassment, bullying, dating violence, etc. There are many tasks that can be included in a peer helper program, but a word of caution is to not overwhelm the students with too much information or duties that are developmentally inappropriate. Most peer helpers are dedicated to assisting others and can become easily overwhelmed themselves with other students' life difficulties. Helpers must also be taught how to relate to others' pain.

Peer Tutoring

Leung's (2015) meta-analytic study provided clear evidence that peer tutoring programs have a positive impact on tutees' academic achievement. The effects of peer tutoring were stronger at the secondary level than they were at the elementary level. Peer tutoring was more effective for tutees with higher ability and for tutors with lower ability. Studies which provided tutees with tangible rewards had larger effect sizes than for studies for which tutees were given points as rewards. Studies in which the tutors and tutees were at the same age did not differ from studies in which tutors were older than the tutees. Studies of same-gender dyads exhibited larger effect sizes than studies of mixed-gender dyads. Shorter duration for the tutoring period produced larger effects than studies involving longer tutoring periods. Another meta-analytic study revealed that peer tutoring for mathematics produced greater gains than for peer tutoring for reading or other subjects (Leung, 2019). Although there do not appear to be examples in the research literature that depict SC's involvement with peer tutoring, it would seem that SCs could play a meaningful role in the implementation of peer tutoring, as SCs have the background in training tutors in how to lead within a helping relationship.

Evaluation of Peer Programs

The National Association of Peer Programs (NAPP) has developed a rubric for evaluation and program implementation (Black et al., 2007). Utilizing formative or process data, such as the number of peer helpers, number of interventions, selection process, types of services, and program activities, is helpful in the evaluation of provided services. However, more importantly, coordinators of the peer programs must evaluate the impact of the program in terms of behavioral and/or academic outcomes. Outcome data will include whether the activities and/or program achieved the established goals. Assessments can include perception data with surveys, pre- and postassessments, and opinion data. Utilization of achievement-related data such as school-wide trends in discipline reports or attendance rates may be helpful for demonstrating outcomes. Another method of results data may include achievement data that is specific to topics covered within the program, such as the impact of the program on peer helpers' grade point average or state achievement test scores.

Social and Emotional Learning Programs (SEL)

A common criticism of some violence and bullying prevention programs is that they emphasize the elimination of problematic behaviors. In other words, the criticism is that these programs focus on what students should not be doing rather than instructing in students in prosocial behaviors, meaning, what students should be doing. Some educators have even argued that by focusing on aggression and defining its various forms, etc., such programs actually have the potential for increasing aggression by teaching children who are prone to aggression more sophisticated ways of harming others. Certainly, SWPBIS (Sugai et al., 2011) and violence prevention programs that provide instruction in nonviolent conflict resolution strategies emphasize the acquisition of prosocial behaviors. However, other types of programs aimed at promoting prosocial behavior are programs that involve social and emotional learning (SEL).

SEL has been defined as:

> [The] process through which all young people and adults acquire the knowledge, skills, and attitudes to develop healthy identities, manage emotions and achieve personal and collective goals, feel and show empathy for others, establish and maintain supportive relationships, and make responsible and caring decisions.
>
> (Collaborative for Academic, Social, and Emotional Learning [CASEL], 2021, p. 6)

SEL programs seek to promote students' and adults' development of self-awareness, self-regulation/management, social awareness, relationship skills, and responsible decision-making (see Figure 11.1). CASEL advocates for the use of a systems approach to promote students' SEL, calling for the establishment of equitable learning environments and coordinated practices within schools, classrooms, schools, families, and communities. CASEL has issued a theory of action which asserts that four key elements are necessary for effective implementation of SEL programming (CASEL, n.d.): (1) Schools must *build foundational support and a plan* that informs stakeholders of the benefits of SEL programming and develop a multiyear implementation plan that includes budgeting resources. (2) SEL programming requires *strengthening adults' SEL competencies and capacity* through staff education regarding the empirical support for SEL and best practices and by facilitating a work environment that supports adult SEL

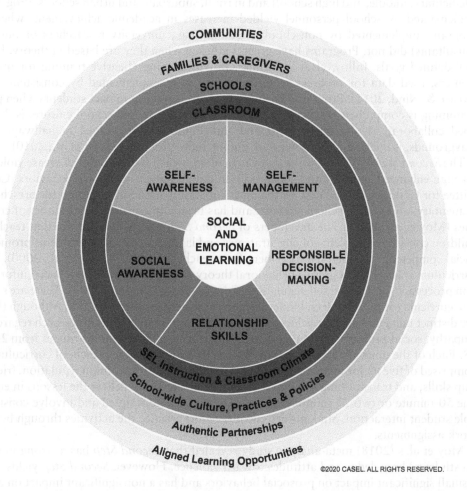

Figure 11.1 © CASEL 2020. Social and Emotional Learning Framework. All rights reserved. www.casel.org.

and cultural competency. (3) *Promoting SEL for students* involves developing standards for socio-emotional learning, applying evidence-based SEL programs, and integrating SEL into all aspects of the school environment, which includes discipline, student supports such as multitiered systems of support. (4) SEL implementation requires *reflection on data for continuous improvement.*

Meta-analytic studies generally have found that SEL programs promote positive student outcomes but that the impact of such programs yields small to moderate effect sizes (Moy et al., 2018). A meta-analysis of 32 SEL programs for secondary school students published between 2004 and 2018 revealed that significant effect sizes were found for each of the five SEL targets, with the largest effects being found for self-awareness and social awareness, and the smallest impact was found for relationship skills (van de Sande et al., 2019). Furthermore, the summary effect for the programs yielded significant positive outcomes for depression, anxiety, aggression, and substance use. A previous meta-analytic study found that SEL programs resulted in an 11-percentile-point gain in academic achievement (Durlak et al., 2011). SEL programs were found to be effective across educational levels (elementary, middle, and high school) and in rural, suburban, and urban schools. Programs implemented by school personnel yielded increases in academic achievement, whereas programs implemented by nonschool personnel (e.g., university researchers or outside consultants) did not. Programs have greater efficacy when they are based in theory, have well-defined goals, follow clear guidelines, provided comprehensive training for implementers, used data for progress monitoring, and were implemented by consistent staff (Weare & Nind, 2011). Programs are more likely to positively impact students when programming is comprehensive, occurs in everyday interaction and school culture, is developed collaboratively by school staff and stakeholders, is reinforced in hallways and playgrounds, is continuously monitored, and includes parents (Horner et al., 2010).

The *Second Step Violence Prevention Curriculum*, which is designed to decrease violence through enhanced empathy and social skills and decreases in aggressive behaviors (Committee for Children, 2011), may be the most commonly used SEL program for preschool, elementary, and middle school students and has been implemented in a number of countries (Moy et al., 2018). The developers of *Second Step Curriculum* believe that teaching children consistent problem-solving strategies and language for social problems promotes social competency through reinforcement from teachers and peers (Frey et al., 2000). The curriculum is based on cognitive behavioral theory, social learning theory, social information processing, and verbal self-regulation (Committee for Children, 2008). There are separate curricula for preschoolers, kindergartners, and students in grades 1–8. Although there are distinct units for each grade level, each unit is based on intervention research regarding empathy, social problem-solving, and anger management. Lesson units ranges from 22 to 28. Each of the units are categorized by themes. For example, the preschool curriculum is comprised of five major units which include learning, empathy, emotion regulation, friendship skills, and transitioning to kindergarten. Trained teachers deliver the lessons in either one 50-minute or two 25-minute sessions. The lessons are scripted and involve considerable student interaction. Students are encouraged to practice the activities through homework assignments.

Moy et al.'s (2018) meta-analytic study revealed that *Second Step* has a strong impact on students' knowledge and attitudes toward violence. However, *Second Step* yields only a small significant impact on prosocial behaviors and has a nonsignificant impact on antisocial behavioral outcomes. *Second Step* has a positive impact on preschool students and has minimal impact for middle school students.

Emotion-Focused Therapy View of Emotional Intelligence

Emotion-focused therapy (EFT) is a modern counseling theory that offers some unique and complex perspectives regarding emotions and emotional intelligence which have deep implications for promoting emotional intelligence in children. Whereas many theories of emotion and counseling emphasize the reduction of emotional intensity, in EFT emotions are viewed as adaptive and require one to experience and reflect upon the emotion in order to understand their meaning and the need(s) associated with the meaning (Greenberg, 2015). According to Greenberg, one of the leading figures in the development of EFT, people must be assisted with developing the language to symbolize their experience rather than seeking to identify and challenge thoughts related to emotions. Emotions are regarded as essential for survival, communication, and problem-solving rather than being viewed as experiences to be eliminated or ignored. Fear indicates that we are in danger, sadness that we have lost something important, and joy informs us that a desirable goal has been achieved. Emotions facilitate decision-making by quickly reducing one's options. Another function of emotions is that they enhance learning, increasing the rapidity of learning by identifying an experience as crucial.

Brain research reveals that emotions and the body are strongly connected. Research has revealed that the limbic system, which is that part of the brain that is shared by all mammals, is responsible for basic emotional processes (LeDoux, 1996). LeDoux discovered that there are two paths for producing emotions: (1) the fast "low" road, in which the amygdala senses danger and conveys emergency distress signals to the body, and the slower "high" road, where the same information is conveyed through the thalamus to the neocortex, which is associated with a more conscious processing. Because the shorter amygdala connection communicates signals more twice as fast as the neocortex pathway, we are quickly oriented to our environment for our survival. These emotional processes occur before our thinking brain is even conscious of them. In some situations, the rapid action of the emotional brain is more adaptive, whereas in other cases, enhanced functioning is associated with integration of emotion and cognition. According to this perspective, preconscious and conscious thought represent two sources of experiencing that they are constantly being integrated to generate our sense of self (Greenberg, 2015). The more conscious-thinking source of experiencing continually reflects upon the experiential, emotional aspect of experiencing. Greenberg (2015) asserts that emotions are adaptively evolved to provide quick indicators of needs. From this perspective, humans are designed to seek out emotions because emotions lead them to pursue needs that assist with survival. People seek to achieve the need associated with the respective emotion. For example, the potential benefit of sadness is that it leads one to reflect upon a need that is lacking, such as wanting closeness with others. Anger and fear provide us with the energy to seek safety. Shame may propel us to improve our competency, or to protect ourselves against criticism.

There are consistent findings regarding research on emotions that have implications for educating youth about emotions. Because much of our emotional experiencing occurs outside of awareness, adults must assist youth in learning to develop the language to identify the emotions associated with physiological sensations (Greenberg, 2015). Adults must help youth develop a rich language to label and differentiate their emotions, as the simple act of labeling an emotion helps decrease emotional intensity (Torre & Lieberman, 2018). A research literature review revealed that the parent-child attachment is consistently related to children's capacity for emotional regulation and coping with stress (Zimmer-Gembeck et al., 2017). Greenberg (2015) asserts that emotions can also be transformed by accessing different emotions. For example, the withdrawal tendencies associated with fear and shame stemming from having been a victim of bullying can be transformed by teaching children to access other underlying emotions, such as one's anger with having been violated. Finally, emotional regulation appears to not only require identification and experiencing of an emotion but also cognitive reflection of the emotional experience (Greenberg, 2015).

Greenberg (2015) recommends that important adults serve as children's emotion coaches. An essential element of emotion coaching is being able to help children process emotions by providing them with language to identify and express their emotions, which helps children integrate emotion and reason. In contrast, some adults tend to invalidate children's emotions by displaying a dismissive attitude, often with the belief that children's emotions are potentially harmful to them and thus should be avoided. Adults encourage children's emotional expression by listening about the events in their lives without passing judgment and by helping them label and process their emotional experiences. With younger children, adults generally need to take a more active role. With an elementary-aged child, the adult might suggest, albeit tentatively, what the child may be feeling. For example, an adult might state, "Juanita, I wonder if you were feeling sad when no one sat with you during free time? Do you think that is right?" With adolescents, adults may assume a less active approach, and rather than giving the child language to identify the emotion, they can use more open-ended questions. For example, the adult might ask a teenager, "So what was going on with you when you heard that Deshawn moved away?"

Adults must also assist youth in learning to transform their emotions. Children frequently avoid their emotions, which often leaves them confused and with a lack of energy to pursue needs and wants. Upon identifying an emotion, adults can help children understand the multifaceted and contradictory emotions for even a single experience. For example, in the case of avoidance of anxiety, children can be assisted to identify how the avoidance of social situations temporarily results in relief, and thus increases the avoidance behavior, but often then results in sadness and loneliness as the child loses out on the opportunity for excitement, achievement, or an opportunity to connect with others. Or an adult may help a child understand that they may be excited about developing a new friendship yet simultaneously scared by the recognition that they may lose that friendship and that there will inevitably be difficulties within that relationship.

Case Study

Josh, a seventh-grade student, is enrolled in the gifted and talented program. During a meeting of Josh's team of teachers, they express concern for Josh's lack of academic motivation and negative peer relations. The teachers report that, despite his intelligence, Josh is failing several of his classes, as he often fails to complete assignments. Furthermore, they note that Josh seems excluded by both the regular education and gifted students and report warning several students who appeared to be making fun of Josh. They refer Josh to you, the SC.

Your first impression upon meeting Josh is that he has some of the physical characteristics associated with children who are frequently bullied. He is short and skinny, he wears glasses, his hair is disheveled, and his clothing is somewhat outdated. Josh states that he really does not understand why he has been asked to come to your office, as he just wants to be left alone. You explain that the teachers are concerned about his grades and the fact that he often seems lonely. Josh quickly retorts that grades are meaningless as school has not taught him anything, and that he couldn't care less about having friends since all the other students in the school are a "bunch of jerks." Despite Josh's reassurance that everything is okay with him, you remain concerned, sensing that he is very unhappy and negative about many aspects of his life.

In your second meeting, you continue to focus on developing rapport with Josh. Although he claims he does not want to change anything about his life, he seems to enjoy meeting with you and readily shares with you his interest in science fiction. Your developing sense of Josh is that he is aware of his intelligence but he is confused and hurt by the rejection by his peers, particularly his fellow gifted students, although he continues to deny any interest in developing friendships. He expresses considerable anger toward his parents, whom he also sees as trying to control him. Josh reports that his father requires him to play basketball in the local recreational league and insists that Josh try out for the school basketball team each year, which so far Josh has failed to make. He expresses having no interest in sports. Josh shares that he has tried to explain to his dad that he just wants to be left alone. Josh grudgingly gives his approval for you to meet with his parents, hoping that this might get him out of having to play sports.

Upon meeting Josh's parents, your impression is that they are very concerned about Josh, taking an active interest in his grades and encouraging him to make friends through requiring him to play sports, which they both report having been heavily involved in during their childhoods. They express considerable concern, reporting that Josh often avoids them and spends most of his time at home in his room, reading science-fiction books. His father shares that upon returning from school one day, Josh seemed furious, stating that he hated himself and all the kids at school. The parents express feeling helpless and generally seem open to suggestions. You affirm the appropriateness of their expectation of wanting Josh to develop social connections. However, you encourage them to grant Josh more latitude in choosing his social activities and suggest discussions with Josh about what types of activities and people with whom he will feel comfortable. The parents decide to continue to require Josh to be socially active but explain to him that he can decide what those activities will be.

You decide to observe Josh in class. You notice that when the teacher asks the students to form into groups to complete a class assignment, Josh sits passively, staring down at his desk, seemingly waiting to be picked. The teacher eventually assigns Josh to a group with two other students who failed to find a group. During the group interaction, Josh frequently makes sarcastic comments about his classmates' suggestions. One of the group mates responds with a sarcastic remark, and Josh responds by withdrawing from the group, pulling a science-fiction book out of his desk.

In your third meeting with Josh, you explore his reactions to your meeting with his parents. Although Josh does not appear pleased that his parents will still require him to be involved in an extracurricular activity, he seems to like the idea that he can select the activity. You ask Josh what activities he has been considering, and he reports that he is unsure. He agrees to your suggestion that he review a list of the school's student clubs and organizations. You indicate that you think Josh's willingness to consider seeking to become involved in an organization is courageous, as it takes strength to consider taking such a risk. Josh admits to feeling somewhat anxious about joining a group. The remainder of the meeting focuses upon what Josh has learned about what works and does not work for him in connecting with other students. Josh is able to identify several of his strengths, including his intelligence and interest in science fiction. You take a risk by sharing that while you genuinely appreciate Josh's intelligence, you wonder if other students might be annoyed or even hurt by his use of sarcasm. Josh appears to accept this perspective, stating that he notices that sometimes people do seem to get annoyed with him.

Over the course of three additional meetings over the course of a month and a half, Josh eventually joins the drama productions club. By the end of the seventh grade, Josh has appeared to make considerable progress. He seems to enjoy coming to school, and his grades have improved. Although he never seems to develop friendships among his gifted and talented peers, he no longer seems upset by their apparent rejection, and thus his need to defend himself through sarcasm dissipates.

Case Study Analysis

Josh shares some of the risk factors common to bully-victims, including negative beliefs about self and others, academic problems, and rejection by peers (Cook et al., 2010), and he can be considered a reactive aggressor rather than a proactive aggressor (e.g., Camodeca & Goossens, 2005). While many children who engage in bullying intentionally seek to harm or embarrass others, Josh appeared to use his sarcastic wit in an attempt to preemptively manage his expectation that he would be rejected.

The SC recognized the discrepancy between Josh's verbal statements that he wanted to be left alone and his actions, which indicated that he enjoyed talking to the SC. The SC effectively developed rapport with Josh before focusing on his parents' and teachers' expectations that he learn to interact more effectively with others. The establishment of rapport appeared to increase Josh's willingness to examine adults' expectations of him and made him more receptive to the SC's feedback for Josh regarding how his sarcasm was perceived by other students. Another factor that likely contributed to the successful outcome was the fact that Josh was highly intelligent and merely needed an opportunity to problem-solve about what had become a fairly emotionally charged issue between him and his parents.

Although the SC only had one in-person consultation with the parents, it most likely made a significant contribution to Josh's successful outcome. When consulting with parents, it is helpful to hypothesize about their strengths and potential areas for improvement. The parents were eager to assist their son and recognized that he needed to develop his social skills. However, the requirement that he attempt to connect with others through sports was developmentally inappropriate, as Josh's parents needed to begin to allow Josh more power and to help Josh identify his strengths and interests. They were unfortunately applying to Josh what had worked for them, namely, learning to connect with others through sports.

It is interesting to note the SC did not explicitly focus upon Josh's experiences with bullying, nor did the SC focus upon Josh's grades. *Provocative victim* is a term that is sometimes used to describe bully-victims, one that seemed to fit Josh. Other students probably did not like being the brunt of Josh's sarcasm and did not see that Josh was attempting to defend himself psychologically. Rather than acquire information about the nature of the bullying incidents Josh had experienced, the SC elected to focus upon helping Josh to learn to reduce his sarcasm and help Josh develop his social niche. The SC intentionally chose not to focus upon Josh's grades because this did not appear to be the most pressing issue to Josh or even his parents.

Summary

Involvement in prevention and peer helping programs offers SCs an avenue for making a broad impact on the school environment. Whereas stakeholders may fail to identify the subtle improvements generated by individual counseling, involvement in prevention and peer helping programs may be a concrete indicator to students, parents, teachers, and administrators that the SC is an integral member of the school staff. As with any activity, SCs must also weigh the positive impact of involvement in such programs with the time and resources they require. This is particularly true for SCs who coordinate such programs, as the time involved in effectively implementing such programs can be substantial. Ideally, SCs should seek to disperse the responsibilities for implementing such programs by adopting a team approach in which there are teachers, parents, and at least one administrator who collaborate in leading the prevention program. A team approach is also probably more likely to infuse the curriculum throughout the school.

References

Algozzine, B., Daunic, A. P., & Smith, S. W. (2010). *Preventing problem behaviors: A handbook of successful of successful prevention strategies* (2nd ed.). Corwin Press.

American School Counselor Association. (2016). *The school counselor and the promotion of safe schools through conflict resolution and bullying/harassment prevention.* Author.

American School Counselor Association. (2019). *ASCA standards for school counselor preparation programs.* www.schoolcounselor.org/getmedia/573d7c2c-1622-4d25-a5ac-ac74d2e614ca/ASCA-Standards-for-School-Counselor-Preparation-Programs.pdf

American School Counselor Association. (2021). *The school counselor and peer support programs.* Author.

Asmus, J. M., Carter, E., W., Moss, C. K., Biggs, E. E., Bolt, D. M., Born, T. L., Bottema-Beutel, K., Brock, M. E., Cattey, G. N., Cooney, M., Fesperman, E. S., Hochman, J. M., Huber, H. B., Lequia, J. L., Lyons, G. L., Vincent, L. B., & Weir, K. (2017). Efficacy and social validity of peer network interventions for high school students with severe disabilities. *American Journal of Intellectual and Developmental Disabilities, 112*(2), 118–137. https://doi.org/10.1352/1944-7558-122.2.118

Berger, J., Black, D. R., & Routson, S. (2018). 2018 revised NAPPP programmatic standards rubric. *Perspectives in Peer Programs, 28*(1), 18–59. http://peerprogramprofessionals.org/uploads/3/4/7/4/34744081/persinpeerprogv28_1_.pdf

Black, D. R., Routson, S., Spight, D. L., Tindall, J. A., & Wegner, C. (2007). NAPP rubric for peer helping programs. *Perspectives in Peer Programs, 20,* 71–92. https://eric.ed.gov/?redir=http%3a%2f%2fwww.peerprogramprofessionals.org%2fpublications%2fpublications%2farchive_ppp

Cameron, J., & Dupuis, A. (1991). Lessons from New Zealand's first school mediation service: Hagley high school 1987–1989. *Australian Dispute Resolution Journal, 2,* 84–92.

Camodeca, M., & Goossens, F. A. (2005). Aggression, social cognitions, anger and sadness in bullies and victims. *Journal of Child Psychology and Psychiatry, 46*(2), 186–197. https://doi.org/10.1111/j.1469-7610.2004.00347.x

Cantrell, R., Parks-Savage, A., & Rehfuss, J. (2007). Reducing levels of elementary school violence with peer mediation. *Professional School Counseling, 10*(5), 475–481. https://doi.org/10.1177/2156759X0701000504

Carruthers, W. L., & Sweeney, B. (1996). Conflict resolution: An examination of the research literature and a model for program evaluation. *The School Counselor, 44*(1), 5–18. www.jstor.org/stable/23897975

Centers for Disease Control and Prevention. (n.d.). *Violence prevention.* www.cdc.gov/violenceprevention/youthviolence/schoolviolence/fastfact.html

Ciarrochi, J., Morin, A. J. S., Sahdra, B. K., Litalien, D., & Parker, P. D. (2017). A longitudinal person-centered perspective on youth social support: Relations with psychological wellbeing. *Developmental Psychology, 53*(6), 1154–1169. https://doi.org/10.1037/dev0000315

Collaborative for Academic, Social, and Emotional Learning. (2021). *10 years of social and emotional learning in U.S. school districts: Elements for long-term sustainability of SEL.* Author. https://casel.org/cdi-ten-year-report/

Collaborative for Academic, Social, and Emotional Learning. (n.d.). *What is the CASEL framework?* Author. https://casel.org/fundamentals-of-sel/what-is-the-casel-framework/

Committee for Children. (2008). *Second Step middle school complete review of research.* Author.

Committee for Children. (2011). *Second Step: A violence prevention curriculum.* Author.

Cook, C. R., Williams, K. R., Guerra, N. G., Kim, T. E., & Sadek, S. (2010). Predictors of bullying and victimization in childhood and adolescence: A meta-analytic investigation. *School Psychology Quarterly, 25*(2), 65–83.

Council for the Accreditation of Counseling and Related Educational Programs. (n.d.). *2016 CACREP standards.* www.cacrep.org/for-programs/2016-cacrep-standards/

Crick, N. R., & Dodge, K. A. (1996). Social information processing theory mechanisms in reactive and proactive aggression. *Child Development, 67*(3), 993–1002. https://doi.org/10.1111/j.1467-8624.1996.tb01778.x

Cyberbullying Research Center. (n.d.). *What is cyberbullying?* https://cyberbullying.org/what-is-cyberbullying

Day-Vines, N., Day-Hairston, B., Carruthers, W., Wall, J., & Lupton-Smith, H. (1996). Conflict resolution: The value of diversity in the recruitment, selection, and training of peer mediators. *School Counselor, 43*(5), 392–410. www.jstor.org/stable/23897830

Durlak, J. A., Weissberg, R. P., Dymnicki, A. B., Taylor, R. D., & Schellinger, K. B. (2011). The impact of enhancing students' social and emotional learning: A meta-analysis of school-based universal interventions. *Child Development*, *82*(1), 405–432. https://doi.org/10.1111/j.1467-8624.2010.01564.x

Frey, K. S., Hirschstein, M. K., & Guzzo, B. A. (2000). Second step: Preventing aggression by promoting social competence. *Journal of Emotional and Behavioral Disorders*, *8*(2), 102–149. https://doi.org/10.1177/106342660000800206

Gaffney, H., Ttofi, M. M., & Farrington, D. P. (2019). Evaluating the effectiveness of school bullying prevention programs: An updated meta-analytical review. *Aggression and Violent Behavior*, *45*, 111–133. https://doi.org/10.1016/j.avb.2018.07.001

Gaffney, H., Ttofi, M. M., & Farrington, D. P. (2021). What works in anti-bullying programs? Analysis of effective intervention components. *Journal of School Psychology*, *85*, 37–56. https://doi.org/10.1016/j.jsp.2020.12.002

Greenberg, L. S. (2015). *Emotion-focused therapy: Coaching clients to work through their feelings* (2nd ed.). American Psychological Association.

Hahn, R., Fuqua-Whitley, D., Wethington, H., Lowy, J., Liberman, A., Crosby, A., Fullilove, M., Johnson, R., Mosicki, E., Price, L., Snyder, S. R., Tuma, F., Cory, S., Stone, G., Mukhopadhaya, K., Chattopadhyay, S., & Dahlberg, L. (2007). *The effectiveness of universal-school based programs for the prevention of violent and aggressive behavior*. Centers for Disease Control and Prevention. www.cdc.gov/mmwr/PDF/rr/rr5607.pdf

Horner, R. H., Sugai, G., & Anderson, C. M. (2010). Examining the evidence base for school-wide positive behavior support. *Focus on Exceptional Children*, *42*(8), 1–14.

Johnson, D. W., & Johnson, R. T. (1996). Conflict resolution and peer mediation programs in elementary and secondary schools: A review of the research. *Review of Educational Research*, *66*(4), 459–506. https://doi.org/10.3102/00346543066004459

Johnson, D. W., & Johnson, R. T. (2004). Implementing the teaching students to be peacemakers program. *Theory Into Practice*, *43*(1), 68–79. https://doi.org/10.1207/s15430421tip4301_9

Kolbert, J. B., & Field, J. E., (2004, June). The steps of mediation for school counselors. *The Pennsylvania Counselor*, *41*(5), 14–16.

Lane, K. L., Little, M. A., Casey, A. M., Lambert, W., Wehby, J., Weisenback, J., & Phillips, A. (2009). A comparison of systematic screening tools for emotional and behavioral disorders. *Journal of Emotional and Behavioral Disorders*, *17*(2), 93–105. https://doi.org/10.1177/1063426608326203

LeDoux, J. E. (1996). *The emotional brain: The mysterious underpinnings of emotional life*. Simon and Schuster.

Leung, K. C. (2015). Preliminary empirical model of crucial determinants of best practice for peer tutoring on academic achievement. *Journal of Educational Psychology*, *107*(2), 558–570. https://doi.org/10.1037/a0037698

Leung, K. C. (2019). An updated meta-analysis on the effect of peer tutoring on tutors' achievement. *School Psychology International*, *40*(2), 200–214. https://doi.org/10.1177/0143034318808832

Matjasko, J. L., Vivolo-Kantor, A. M., Massetti, G. M., Holland, K. M., Holt, M. K., & Cruz, J. D. (2012). A systematic meta-review of evaluations of youth violence prevention programs: Common and divergent findings from 25 years of meta-analyses and systematic reviews. *Aggression and Violent Behavior*, *17*(6), 540–552. https://doi.org/10.1016/j.avb.2012.06.006

McGannon, W., Carey, J., & Dimmitt, C. (2005). *The current status of school counseling outcome research*. Monographs of the Center for School Counseling Outcome Research, 2. https://files.eric.ed.gov/fulltext/ED512567.pdf

Mitchell, B. S., Stormont, M., & Gage, N. A. (2011). Tier two interventions implemented within the context of a tiered prevention framework. *Behavioral Disorders*, *36*(4), 241–261. https://doi.org/10.1177/019874291103600404

Moy, G., Polanin, J. R., McPherson, C., & Phan, T. (2018). International adoption of the *Second Step program*: Moderating variables in treatment effects. *School Psychology International*, *39*(4), 333–359. https://doi.org/10.1177/0143034318783339

Olweus, D., & Limber, S. P. (2010). Bullying in school: Evaluation and dissemination of the Olweus Bullying Prevention Program. *American Journal of Orthopsychiatry, 80*(1), 124–134. https://doi.org/10.1111/j.1939-0025.2010.01015.x

Park-Higgerson, H., Perumean-Chaney, S. E., Bartolucci, A. A., Grimley, D. M., & Singh, K. P. (2008). The evaluation of school-based violence prevention programs: A meta-analysis. *Journal of School Health, 78*(9), 465–479. https://doi.org/10.1111/j.1746-1561.2008.00332.x

Peterson, R. K., & Skiba, R. (2001). Creating school climates that prevent school violence. *Prevention School Failure: Alternative Education for Children and Youth, 44*(3), 122–129. https://doi.org/10.1080/10459880009599794

Polanin, J. R., Espelage, D. L., Grotpeter, J. K., Spinney, E., Ingram, K. M., Valido, A., El Sheik, A., Torgal, C., & Robinson, L. (2021). A meta-analysis of longitudinal partial correlations between school violence and mental health, school performance, and criminal or delinquent acts. *Psychological Bulletin, 147*(2), 115–133. https://doi.org/10.1037/bul0000314

QPR Institute. (2019). *QPR training for youth guidelines: Policies and procedures.* https://qprinstitute.com/uploads/instructor/QPR-Training-for-Youth-Guidelines-2019.pdf

Santone, E., Crothers, L. M., & Kolbert, J. B., & Miravalle, J. (2020). Using social information processing theory to counsel aggressive youth. *Journal of School Counseling, 18*(18). www.jsc.montana.edu/articles/v18n18.pdf

Sellman, E. (2011). Peer mediation services for conflict resolution in schools: What Transformations in activity characterize successful implementation. *British Educational Research Journal, 37*(1), 45–60. https://doi.org/10.1080/01411920903419992

Skiba, R., & Peterson, R. (2000). *Creating a positive climate: Peer mediation.* Safe & Responsive Schools. www.schoolcounselor.org/asca/media/asca/Resource%20Center/Mentoring-Peer%20Mediation/Sample%20Documents/PeerMediation.pdf

Sugai, G., Horner, R., & Algozzine, B. (2011). *Reducing the effectiveness of bullying behavior in schools.* Center on Positive Behavioral Interventions and Supports. www.pbis.org/resource/reducing-the-effectiveness-of-bullying-behavior-in-schools

Torre, J. B., & Lieberman, M. D. (2018). Putting feelings into words: Affect labelling as implicit emotion regulation. *Emotion Review, 10*(2), 116–124. https://doi.org/10.1177/1754073917742706

US Department of Education. (n.d.). *Every student succeeds act (ESSA).* Author. www.ed.gov/essa?src%3Drn

van de Sande, M. C. E., Fekkes, M., Kocken, P. L., Diekstra, R. F. W., Reis, R., & Gravesteijn, C. (2019). Do universal social and emotional learning programs for secondary school students enhance competencies they address? A systematic review. *Psychology in the Schools, 56*(10), 1545–1567. https://doi.org/10.1002/pits.22307

Voight, A., & Nation, M. (2016). Practices for improving secondary school climate: A systematic review of the research literature. *American Journal of Community Psychology, 58*(1–2), 174–191. https://doi.org/10.1002/ajcp.12074

Weare, K., & Nind, M. (2011). *Promoting mental health of children and adolescents through schools and school based interventions.* DataPrev Project: Report of Work Package, 3.

Young, A., Hardy, V., Hamilton, C., Biernessen, K., & Sun, L., & Niebergall, S. (2009). Empowering students: Using data to transform a bullying prevention and intervention program. *Professional School Counseling, 12*(6), 413–420. https://doi.org/10.1177/2156759X0901200616

Zimmer-Gembeck, M. J., Webb, H. J., Pepping, C. A., Swan, K., Merlo, O., Skinner, E. A., Avdagic, E., & Dunbar, M. (2017). Review: Is parent-child attachment a correlate of children's emotion regulation and coping. *International Journal of Behavioral Development, 41*(1), 74–93. https://doi.org/10.1177/0165025415618276

Chapter 12

Helping Students With Exceptionalities

> **Box 12.1   2016 Council for the Accreditation of Counseling and Related Educational Programs (CACREP, n.d.) School Counseling Specialty Area Standards**
>
> 2.d   School counselor roles in school leadership and multidisciplinary teams
> 3.d   Interventions to promote academic development
> 3.e   Use of developmentally appropriate career counseling interventions and assessments
> 3.g   Strategies to facilitate school and postsecondary transitions

> **Box 12.2   ASCA (2019a) Standards for School Counselor Preparation Programs (ASCA CAEP SPA)**
>
> 2.1   Describe established and emerging counseling and educational methods, including but not limited to childhood and adolescent development, learning theories, behavior modification and classroom management, social justice, multiculturalism, group counseling, college/career readiness, and crisis response.
> 7.2   Describe the impact of federal and state laws and regulations, as well as district policies, on schools, students, families, and school counseling practice.

In the *ASCA National Model* (2019b), SCs are encouraged to promote the academic, career, and social/emotional development of all students in accordance with the themes of advocacy and social justice. Historically, SCs' involvement with students with disabilities has depended upon the formal or informal role description of the SC in a particular school or district. However, as the school counseling profession has sought to play a more active role in educational reform, SCs have been encouraged by the American School Counselor Association (ASCA) and Education Trust to identify and address the achievement gaps of all typically disadvantaged groups, including students with disabilities.

Activities provided to children with exceptionalities by SCs often are comprised of the following: (a) delivering counseling support as described in Chapter 6, (b) encouraging

DOI: 10.4324/9781003167730-12

increased family involvement in the child's educational process, such as understanding the nature of the child's disability or exceptionality and the supports and adaptations required for improved school functioning, and (c) consulting and collaborating with other school staff to comprehensively promote the child's success often through 504 plans or individualized education programs (IEPs) and addressing the unique career development needs of students with disabilities.

It is important to note that in its position statement on SCs' role in working with students with disabilities, the ASCA (2016) also cautions SCs to refrain from engaging in any inappropriate *supervisory* responsibilities for children receiving special education services, including oversight regarding the writing or implementation of the IEP, or serving as the formal district representative (i.e., local educational agent; LEA) responsible for fiduciary considerations on behalf of the district. Additionally, although SCs are considered important members of the child study team, they do not singularly make decisions about the child's placement in different educational settings or grade retention.

In order to sort out the best approach for helping students with special needs, it is best to review a few definitions and the responsibilities required by schools. In this way, SCs can feel more sure-footed in the decisions they make and approaches used to engage families. Since 1973, all children—including those with disabilities—have been guaranteed the right to a free and appropriate public education (FAPE; National Center for Learning Disabilities, 2014). *Appropriate* can mean the necessity of an Individualized Education Program (IEP) to adequately meet the students' needs.

Students who do not meet IDEA's eligibility requirements may not receive special education services, although they may qualify to receive accommodations within the general education setting if they meet the conditions set forth by Section 504 of the Vocational Rehabilitation Act of 1973, which requires that students have a "physical or mental impairment which substantially limits one or more major life activities . . . includ[ing] caring for one's self, walking, seeing, hearing, speaking, breathing, working, performing manual tasks, and learning" (US Department of Health and Human Services, n.d.). Conditions for which students typically receive a 504 plan include a temporary (e.g., broken leg) or permanent (e.g., asthma, diabetes, epilepsy) medical condition, emotional disorders (e.g., depression, anxiety, obsessive-compulsive), etc. In summary, for students who do not meet the eligibility requirements for an IEP, schools and parents have the option of considering a 504 plan.

IDEA has gone through several reauthorizations, which has expanded the services required for students with disabilities. For example, in 2017, the US Department of Education specified that in the section 300.114 requirements, educational services are to be provided to students in the least-restrictive environment (LRE) in their home district, included in general education classes to the extent possible (https://sites.ed.gov/idea/regs/b/b/300.114). Service provision for students with IEPs include a highly defined set of parameters, including how they are evaluated (comprehensive evaluation), when they are evaluated (not more than once a year, but at least once every three years at a minimum), who must be consulted, timelines for decisions, access to services that meet their individual needs, LRE, written notification for changes in their placements, timelines for reviewing the IEP progress, annual reviews about the appropriateness of IEP goals, and access to an impartial hearing when there are disputes (DREDF, n.d.) in order to ensure their education program is *individualized*. Accordingly, there are strong sanctions for failing to adhere to special education legal requirements (e.g., district reimbursement for attorney fees, district-funded compensatory education, referral of noncompliant states to the Department of

Justice, and withholding of funds in whole or in part from states, among other options; Wright & Wright, n.d.).

Special Education Overview

Readers are encouraged to consult the US Department of Education IDEA website (https://sites.ed.gov/idea/) for an overview of IDEA and information from the department and its grantees. Another valuable resource is the Federal Register, which publishes notices of IDEA regulations (2006 to the present). Both websites offer answers to questions about IDEA and schools' responsibilities in adhering to the federal regulations associated with the act.

In order to be eligible for special education services, a child must have a disability and demonstrate a need for special education. If a child has a disability but does not demonstrate a need for special education services, he or she is not eligible for special education under IDEA but may be eligible for protections or services under Section 504 of the Rehabilitation Act (Wrightslaw, n.d.).

Box 12.3

What Is a 504 Plan?

"Section 504 is a federal law designed to protect the rights of individuals with disabilities in programs and activities that receive Federal financial assistance from the U.S. Department of Education (ED) . . . the Section 504 regulations require a school district to provide a 'free appropriate public education' (FAPE) to each qualified student with a disability who is in the school district's jurisdiction, regardless of the nature or severity of the disability. Under Section 504, FAPE consists of the provision of regular or special education and related aids and services designed to meet the student's individual educational needs as adequately as the needs of nondisabled students are met" (US Department of Education, n.d.).

Section 504 of the Rehabilitation Act of 1973 Plans

According to the US Department of Health and Human Services, Section 504 of the Rehabilitation Act of 1973 is a national law that protects qualified individuals from discrimination based on their disability (see Box 12.3). Students with disabilities who attend schools receiving federal financial assistance may be eligible to receive accommodations or services under Section 504. In order to receive such protections, a student must have (1) a physical or mental impairment that substantially limits one or more major life activities or (2) a history of such an impairment. Section 504 requires that school districts provide a free, appropriate public education (FAPE) to qualified students in their jurisdictions (see Box 12.3; US Department of Health and Human Services, n.d.).

For example, consider that a fifth-grade student diagnosed with ADHD is earning mostly Bs and few Cs in his classes; his friendships are well-developed. Teachers describe him as "hyper" and complain his homework is often "destroyed" (e.g., folded, crushed, torn, or crumbled) before it is turned in. Upon inspection, his locker is disorganized and jammed with old papers, folders, and projects. In this case, a school child study team may use a

504 plan to help improve the student's organization skills (e.g., clean the locker, teach him how to use shelves or drawers so that materials can be reliably located, teach him how to use an organizer so he can plan for short- and long-term assignments, show him how to manage a backpack to increase its usefulness) in order to help improve the probability of getting homework to and from school in better condition.

Box 12.4   "Dear Colleague" Letter for 504 Eligibility

In 2012, the US Department of Education's (ED) Office for Civil Rights (OCR) issued guidance regarding the effects of the Americans with Disabilities Act Amendments Act of 2008 on public elementary and secondary programs. In the form of a "Dear Colleague" letter, school districts were advised to use an expanded definition of and services for students with disabilities. The recommendation of the letter is that students who traditionally may not have been identified under Section 504 and Title II under ADA should be re-evaluated and tested under a broadened definition (Wright & Wright, 2012).

Given the student's satisfactory grades and adequate social-emotional development, it would be appropriate to argue that while there is a diagnosed disorder (i.e., ADHD), there is no educational need that would render the student eligible for services under IDEA. Indeed, as long as the student continues to develop on this trajectory, a 504 plan would be appropriate. The use of a 504 plan becomes inappropriate when the student's disorder interferes with his education and there becomes a need for special education services. Once his educational outcomes (e.g., social emotional functioning, academic achievement) are negatively impacted, a special education eligibility evaluation must be then initiated. Moreover, when the school is aware the student has a disability and is aware that he is not succeeding, the school is required to seek services to help him benefit from his educational environment; this requirement is called Child Find.

Box 12.5   Child Find (Section 300.111)

(a)   General.

   (1)   The State must have in effect policies and procedures to ensure that—

      (i)   All children with disabilities residing in the State, including children with disabilities who are homeless children or are wards of the State, and children with disabilities attending private schools, regardless of the severity of their disability, and who are in need of special education and related services, are identified, located, and evaluated; and

      (ii)   A practical method is developed and implemented to determine which children are currently receiving needed special education and related services.

(b) Use of term developmental delay. The following provisions apply with respect to implementing the child find requirements of this section:

(1) A State that adopts a definition of developmental delay under Sec. 300.8(b) determines whether the term applies to children aged three through nine, or to a subset of that age range (e.g., ages three through five).

(2) A State may not require an LEA to adopt and use the term developmental delay for any children within its jurisdiction.

(3) If an LEA uses the term developmental delay for children described in Sec. 300.8(b), the LEA must conform to both the State's definition of that term and to the age range that has been adopted by the State.

(4) If a State does not adopt the term developmental delay, an LEA may not independently use that term as a basis for establishing a child's eligibility under this part.

(c) Other children in child find. Child find also must include—

(1) Children who are suspected of being a child with a disability under Sec. 300.8 and in need of special education, even though they are advancing from grade to grade; and

(2) Highly mobile children, including migrant children.

(d) Construction. Nothing in the Act requires that children be classified by their disability so long as each child who has a disability that is listed in Sec. 300.8 and who, by reason of that disability, needs special education and related services is regarded a child with a disability under Part B of the Act (Authority: 20 U.S.C. 1401(3)); 1412(a)(3); U.S. Department of Education, n.d.

Child Find

Child Find is an IDEA mandate to find and identify all students with a disability from birth to 21 years of age (see Box 12.5). This includes all children in the district catchment area, those who attend private or parochial schools, those who are homeless, migrant, immigrant, are wards of the state—everyone. States manage to fulfill this requirement in a variety of ways. Often, infants and toddlers are identified through pediatricians and are referred either to the district's early intervention services or to the relevant agency (e.g., cystic fibrosis foundation), which coordinates services with the district services.

Box 12.6 Using RtI to Determine Learning Disabilities in Individuals with Disabilities Education Improvement Act (IDEA, 2004) Regulations

With regard to identifying children with SLD, the regulations: (1) allow a local educational agency (LEA) to consider a child's response to scientific, research-based intervention as part of the SLD determination process; (2) allow States to use other alternative research-based procedures for determining whether a child has a SLD;

(3) provide that States may not require the use of a severe discrepancy between intellectual ability and achievement to determine whether a child has a SLD; and (4) require a public agency to use the State criteria in determining whether a child has a SLD and discuss the role that response to scientific research-based interventions plays in a comprehensive evaluation process (US Department of Education, 2007).

For other children who are not yet school-age, many districts set up screening procedures several times a year, advertising widely to all community members to bring their children into school or community facilities to ask questions about health concerns, determine if their development is within normal ranges, and by law, identify the presence of a disability. Rotating through each area of development, the child's health, vision, hearing, motor abilities (e.g., gross motor skills, such as walking, running, jumping, and fine motor skills include holding a crayon, closing/opening buttons, using zippers), communication abilities (e.g., listening and comprehension as well as nonverbal and verbal expression), cognitive development (memory, learning, attention), academic (pre-math, pre-reading, pre-writing) skills, social skills, and emotional control are reviewed, and results are compared to criterion-referenced age expectations.

When delays are present, early intervention services are provided to children 3 and younger, usually free of charge or on a sliding scale. When disabilities are present, special education services are required and provided free of charge by the district or agency designated by the district. Note that states have the choice to recognize and support the remediation of childhood delays—problems that are not yet considered a disability—for children between the ages of 3 and 9, or any age grouping therein (e.g., 3 to 5 years, etc.).

The Child Find requirements, to identify students with disabilities, extend throughout the child's educational experience (i.e., until he or she graduates). Furthermore, the requirement extends to all children residing in the district even if they attend a different school (e.g., private, parochial, etc.). Once children are attending school, the teachers, parents, administrators, and counselors monitor child development and progress and should work together to find students with disabilities. When a student at a private school requires a 504 or special education evaluation or services, the public and private schools coordinate in order to meet the child's needs. Some public schools share their professional staff with the private school. Other schools may hire independent or statewide services to be implemented at the private school. However it happens, the home district (i.e., catchment area where the student lives) ensures that each child has access to the same services as those that would be provided in their public school building.

Problems may occur when school personnel fail to understand how to implement the Child Find process, by confusing the requirement to find students with disabilities to mean that every child should be considered for special education services even if the child study team does not believe that the student needs specialized instruction. SCs can help child study teams by reminding them that children who are referred for special education consideration should, by definition, be showing problems and that such a problem cannot be remediated via general education practices or a 504 plan. Stated simply, there is no reason (need) to refer a child for special education eligibility consideration if he or she is not having difficulty or if the difficulty can be resolved with less-intensive and less-intrusive adjustments. SCs can help children and families by guiding them through the school's established evaluation processes (discussed in detail in the following passages). Also, families need to understand some of the limitations of the law; for example, some disabilities (e.g., nonverbal learning disabilities) are not yet recognized. Indeed, prior to 1991, ADHD was not recognized as a disabling condition for which children were eligible to receive special education support (Rabiner, 2006). Yet at that time, families of children with ADHD needed guidance regarding navigating the system in order to receive help.

In summary, it is appropriate for school personnel and parents to request an evaluation for special education for children who appear to be having difficulty, either academically, emotionally, behaviorally, or socially; however, special education services will not be considered necessary unless there is an identified need. If the school identifies such a potential need, this should be communicated to parents in seeking their permission to evaluate their child for eligibility for special education services; indeed, schools must make reasonable efforts to obtain permission from parents for an initial evaluation to determine if a child has a disability. Notably, permission granted by parents for an initial evaluation should not be construed as approval for initial provision of special education services (US Department of Education, 2017b). Alternatively, if parents or caregivers identify a need, they may request that a multidisciplinary evaluation be undertaken by school personnel, which must be completed within 60 days.

IDEA/Special Education Eligibility

In determining whether a child has a disability and is in need of special education and related services, the parents of the child and a team of qualified professionals are convened to do so. The term *qualified professionals* include the child's regular teacher or a regular classroom teacher that is qualified to teach a child of this age and at least one person qualified to complete an individual diagnostic examination of children, which is often a school psychologist but also may be a speech-language pathologist or remedial reading teacher (Federal Register, 2006).

A comprehensive psychoeducational evaluation is typically prepared, which includes information from multiple informants, representing multiple environmental contexts, an observation of the child in the educational setting, and from a test battery that is developed based upon the referral question. Often, tests or measures assessing aptitude, achievement, neurological and executive functioning, behavior, adaptive behavior, and emotional and social development; information from parents; information from teachers and other educational professionals; observations of the student's performance in other contexts; and information about a student's social, cultural, and linguistic background are administered and/or collected. Independent educational evaluations (IEE) paid for and provided by parents to the school also may be accepted, in part or in whole, if deemed appropriate by the child study team. Parents may seek an IEE if they are in disagreement with the school's findings in the comprehensive evaluation; parents may ask the school to pay for the IEE.

The role of the SC is to help the child study team to identify and gather relevant data regarding the child's strengths and why the child is not learning (Ockerman et al., 2012). This may include information about the classroom instruction, previous supports that have been attempted, and where and how progress is made. Also, SCs are an important point of contact for the child to express his or her impressions of the classroom, teacher, instructional materials, etc. Moreover, SCs' connection to the everyday building activities is an invaluable resource to child study teams.

Although the determination of some disabling conditions is relatively straightforward, others may be more difficult to establish, owing to issues of lack of access to instruction, cultural and linguistic differences, poverty, insecure food and housing, and so forth. An example of this is determining the presence of a learning disability, which is the most common referral question for special education services. In 2018–2019, of the 14% of students between the ages of 3 and 21 that received special education services (US Department of Education, n.d.), 33% had a specific learning disability, with 80% to 90% experiencing reading problems (Federal Register, 2006), 19% had speech or language impairments, 15% had other health impairments, while students with autism, developmental delays, intellectual disabilities, and emotional disturbances each accounted for between 5% and 11% of students receiving services under IDEA.

Response to Intervention (RtI)

While learning disabilities traditionally have been identified using an IQ-achievement discrepancy model, critics of this method have cited the problems associated with this model. These include the overidentification of students with learning disabilities, the overrepresentation of children with minority backgrounds in special education, inadequate reliability (including too many false positives and too few true positives), the variability of identification rates in different settings (such as district or regional differences), and a wait-to-fail approach, as the degree of the discrepancy requires time to develop (see Box 12.6; Hughes and Dexter [n.d.], www.rtinetwork.org/learn/research/use-rti-identify-students-learning-disabilities-review-research).

Box 12.7

Did You Know?

One of the reasons the federal government permitted an alternative process for identifying students' eligibility for special education services is the assertion that minority students are overidentified as disabled and disproportionately represented in special education (e.g., Sullivan & Bal, 2013). However, a study found that minority children were less likely than similar English-speaking White children to be identified as disabled and thus receive special education services (Morgan et al., 2015).

As a means of addressing such concerns, an alternative method to identify learning disabilities, the response to intervention (RtI) model to scientific, research-based intervention, was developed in the 1980s and refined by multiple researchers to become the version of the model included in the Individuals with Disabilities Education Improvement Act (2004; Hughes & Dexter, n.d.). RtI is a three-tiered model (Fuchs & Fuchs, 2006), often depicted in the shape of a triangle. At its base, tier one (bottom of the triangle) represents empirically supported interventions designed for all students in a regular education setting. Although these interventions are preventative, approximately 15% of children will require more intensive support in tier two (middle of the triangle) after failing to respond satisfactorily to interventions in tier one. About 5% of students will require even more intensive instruction in tier three (top of the triangle) after failing to respond at tier two. The movement to more intensive intervention is both to select interventions that are tailored to the needs of a specific child and to ensure the evidence for the usefulness of the intervention for that child. Given that fewer children require tier two interventions and fewer yet require tier three interventions, making sure that there is empirical evidence for a specific intervention, and a match of the intervention to the child's needs becomes more complicated. Indeed, some districts argue that tier three is essentially individualized instruction, akin to what is provided in special education programming.

Advocates for RtI assert that the tiered system solves the problems associated with the IQ-achievement discrepancy model mentioned previously (see Box 12.6). Specifically, RtI is designed to prevent learning problems, since all instructional techniques have an established evidence base in a tiered intervention system, which allows for a quick progression to more intensive services given an ongoing need, regardless of disability status. Both models for identifying eligibility for special education require that a student is failing to demonstrate adequate academic progress. The IQ-achievement discrepancy requirement was removed in the 2004 IDEA revision, which ushered in the use of RtI to identify a learning disability. Yet the implementation of these revisions is not uniformly adopted by states, and what is allowed in one state (e.g., relying on RtI data to determine a learning disability) may not be permissible in another. Nevertheless, the evaluation of a child suspected of having a learning disability must include a "variety of assessment tools and strategies and cannot rely on any single procedure as the sole criterion for determining eligibility for special education and related services" (Federal Register, www.federalregister. gov/documents/2006/08/14/06-6656/assistance-to-states-for-the-education-of-children-with-disabilities-and-preschool-grants-for).

The Federal Register indicates that there is evidence to support the use of RtI models to identify children with learning disabilities, including young children and those from minority backgrounds, e.g., "several large-scale implementations in Iowa (the Heartland model; Tilly, 2002); the Minneapolis public schools (Marston, 2003); applications of the Screening to Enhance Equitable Placement (STEEP) model in Mississippi, Louisiana, and Arizona (VanDerHeyden, et al., 2007); and other examples (NASDE, 2005)" (Federal Register, 2006). Furthermore, determining the reasons children have not responded to research-based intervention necessitates a comprehensive evaluation (Federal Register, 2006).

Individualized Education Program (IEP) Teams

After the evaluation is complete, the IEP Team is convened, which includes the parents of the child, at least one regular education teacher (if the child is or may be participating in the regular education environment), at least one special education teacher or provider of the child, a representative of the public agency who is "qualified to provide, or supervise the provision of, specially designed instruction to meet the unique needs of children with disabilities, ii) is knowledgeable about the general education curriculum; and iii) is knowledgeable about the availability of resources of the public agency" (US Department of Education, 2017a), an individual who can interpret the instructional implications of the evaluation results (who may also be the regular education teacher, special education teacher, or representative of the public agency), individuals who have knowledge or special expertise of the child, including personnel of related services, as appropriate, such as the SC, and the child with the disability, whenever appropriate. When the child is of age for transition services, the public agency must invite the child with a disability to attend the IEP Team meeting if the purpose of the meeting is the consideration of postsecondary goals for the child and transition services needed to assist the child in reaching such goals and a representative of any participating agency likely to be responsible for providing or paying for transition services (US Department of Education, 2017b).

The IEP team meets to discuss the child's needs and write the IEP goals, which are tailored to address the child's needs. For example, children with ADHD may need reading help, or children with autism may need counseling support. How and when (but at least annually) feedback on IEP goals is provided should also be established.

IDEA Categories of Eligibility

At present, IDEA recognizes 13 areas of eligibility. Prior to reviewing these in detail, it is important to address some issues that may represent potential points of confusion for child study teams. Special education categories do not always match well with psychological, psychiatric, or developmental disabilities disorders as described by the Diagnostic and Statistical Manual of Mental Disorders—Fifth Edition, Text Revision (DSM-5-TR). Indeed, IDEA categories are designed to be broad and general. Furthermore, because the child study team determines eligibility decisions, a formal diagnosis from the DSM-5-TR is not required.

Although the use of the IDEA areas of eligibility instead of a formal diagnosis from the DSM-5-TR is meant to allow schools flexibility in making determinations for special education services, it can interfere with selecting evidence-based interventions. As discussed previously, many symptoms are associated with numerous disorders; a broad eligibility category is not necessarily helpful to IEP teams in sorting through which interventions are most likely to be effective. Consequently, it is important that SCs encourage IEP teams to be specific in describing the nature of the child's difficulty and insist on clarity in purpose when providing supports.

Developmental Considerations

Children may be identified as eligible for special education at any age between birth and 21 years. However, there are some general timelines to observe. Severe deficits (e.g., autism, intellectual disabilities), developmental delays, and significant health issues are typically noticed very early in the child's development. As discussed previously, pediatricians often notice problems in infants and toddlers. Learning disabilities typically begin to be noticed in children of preschool or elementary school age, when academic requirements increase. In fact, behavior difficulties in an otherwise-unremarkable preschooler—that is, in a child who has met developmental milestones and has no history of abuse or neglect—are more likely an indication of a learning problem than a serious emotional disturbance. Social-emotional disabilities tend to present themselves in middle childhood and adolescence.

There are many reasons that a learning problem could appear later than expected. Perhaps, the support given in the general education classroom was enough to mute the impact of a disability, for example. Unfortunately, it is possible that the diagnosis may have been missed or the child study team was slow to act. Adults working with young children tend to want to wait and see if the children grow out of their difficulties, but this may leave minor problems unattended until they have become major deficits. SCs can support teachers and parents in obtaining needed services, which may or may not include specially designed instruction, as soon as possible. Despite adults' inclination to use a wait-and-see approach, it is well documented that early intervention has the best chance of producing best outcomes. Moreover, children with minimal differences in their skills in comparison to typical age-mates are easier to assist than those with significant differences.

It is also true that children who show significant problems at a younger age tend to have the most difficult time in achieving the performance of their typical peers. Simply put, they do not have the reservoir of skills to fall back on. A good point of comparison is *when* a person experiences depression. If the depressive disorder evidences itself when an individual is 38, his or her coping skills are well-developed, as he or she has likely enjoyed sufficient support over many years and, as such, has more resources to use. If the person is 8, however, he or she has only had a short time to develop coping skills, and the development of subsequent skills are likely to be affected by this event, even if symptoms are controlled relatively quickly. In summary, how quickly adults respond to the child's needs is of utmost importance. SCs can help assure nervous parents and teachers that they are correct in asking for school support as soon as they recognize the presence of a problem in a child.

Direct Services With Children

SCs can support children by helping them understand their disability in a manner that is developmentally appropriate. Children need to know about their symptoms and how to manage them. Most importantly, children need to know that they are not the sum of their disorder. A primary reason for using children-first language is to ensure that adults maintain the perspective that the child has a disability as opposed to viewing the child as disabled. By keeping the disorder or symptoms separate from the child, the child can join with the teacher, parent, or counselor to combat the symptoms. The message, therefore, is, "We are all working together, as a child study team, to manage the symptoms of . . . autism," for example. Relatedly, helping the child to build assertiveness skills so that he or she is comfortable in self-advocacy will not only help the child but also help parents and teachers hear—from the child himself or herself—what is needed. Continued communication is essential for many reasons but most centrally is necessary in consideration of the fact that the child's needs will change as he or she ages.

For example, children with autism have deficits in social interactions. A child with autism who may show limited interest in socializing as an elementary student may become interested in friendships or even dating as an adolescent. While the disorder may interfere with the expression of their social contact, their wants and desires can develop alongside the onset of puberty. Adults can teach the child communication skills, which will increase the likelihood that the child can express his or her changing desires. A change in dating and intimacy interests for a child with autism may alert the child study team to add social skill instruction that includes the differences between friends and people you date (e.g., how to initiate these different relationships, how to pursue a dating interest, actions appropriate between people who date as compared to those between friends, etc.).

Indirect Services With Children

SCs also provide indirect services to children by helping the adults in their lives, with the idea that supported adults are better prepared to effectively help children. When adults are overwhelmed by task demands or have a lack of knowledge or skills in assisting children with disabilities to manage or cope with their symptoms, they often do not have the attention, motivation, or energy level to understand the needs of or assist the child. Furthermore, both adults working with children with disabilities and the children themselves may be angry at having to deal with the disability altogether. Parents can be devastated when they realize their child has a disability. Many feel a sense of loss as they reconcile the realities of the child they have with the child they planned to have. It is not uncommon to find parents in all stages of grief; some are in denial, angry, bargaining, or experiencing feelings of depression, while others accept the disability.

The SC is an essential individual to bridge the gap between school personnel and family members in creating a synergy to allow for a combined effort on behalf of the child (Milsom, 2007). Alongside the parents, the child study team will have a long-term role in supporting the child. Over the years, SCs are often the most consistent child study team member who works with a child; teachers change by grade, while SCs typically are assigned to a whole building of grades. By forecasting the SC's long-standing support for the parents, SCs can help parents move through their grieving more effectively and comfortably.

Teachers can show similar patterns of frustration with children who have disabilities. General education teachers are prepared often to work with children who are developing typically. They may not be as well prepared to work with a child with a disability, although many states are increasing the special education requirements for regular education teacher certification. Given that a child with a disability who has an IEP requires individualization to instruction, teachers often have to modify their teaching practices significantly. There may be numerous students with IEPs in the general education classroom, magnifying the demand on teachers' time and energy. Furthermore, because some teachers may not have training in accommodating students with special needs in the classroom, this lack of knowledge may lead to feelings of inadequacy or humiliation. When teachers are unable to manage the classroom as they planned, feelings of resentment and anger may be outwardly expressed to the class or directly to the child.

SCs can help distressed teachers in many ways. First, providing an empathic ear when teachers need to vent is often helpful. Second, coordinating resources, such as collaborating with special educators, the reading specialist, or the school psychologist in order to assist the general education teacher in his or her own skill development, not only will help with the teacher's immediate frustrations but also will be helpful to future children with disabilities in their classroom. SCs can also contribute to the professional development planning in their building; noticing patterns in teacher and parent needs can determine what type of professional development programming should be delivered. At times, SCs may communicate with principals about the teachers' needs; good principals will find additional ways to support stressed teachers. For example, rotating highly desirable activities (e.g., teaching honors students) or giving a special education teacher a year in general education to refresh his or her energy are all suggestions that counselors can use with administrators to support the whole teaching staff.

IDEA Definitions

All special education categories carry the qualifier that the problem conditions interfere with children's ability to *benefit from their educational environment* (Assistance to States for the Education of Children with Disabilities and Preschool Grants for Children with Disabilities, 2006). Recall the previous discussion about need; children who require special education services need these individualized education programs in order to make satisfactory educational gains. Failing grades are not a requirement for eligibility (Assistance to States for the Education of Children with Disabilities and Preschool Grants for Children with Disabilities, 2006), and poor social-emotional development may comprise the majority of the child's difficulty that is adversely affecting their ability to benefit from their educational environment. Each category is listed in the sections that follow.

Autism

Autism is a developmental disability (Autism Spectrum Disorders; ASD; US Department of Education, 2017d). In contrast to psychiatric disorders, in which symptoms can diminish, autism is considered a lifelong disorder. In some high-functioning individuals, when adequate treatments are provided, symptoms can be well managed. Autism occurs on a spectrum, meaning, that students will vary in the number and severity of their symptoms. Symptoms include poor (verbal and nonverbal) communication skills and social interactions, often evident by the age of 3. Although the DSM-5 requires restrictive/repetitive behaviors for a diagnosis of autism, IDEA only considers these symptoms as sometimes associated. Children on the autism spectrum may demonstrate resistance to changes made in the environment or to their daily routines, as well as unusual responses to sensory experiences (US Department of Education, 2017f).

Because there is such variability in the way in which individuals with ASD behave, this disorder is especially difficult for parents and teachers to accommodate and treat. For youth with severe impairments, their deficits are obvious, and while requiring intensive interventions, most adults trained in evidence-based treatment strategies can readily see behavioral patterns that require interventions. However, for individuals whose symptoms are less severe, adults often find working with these youth to be very frustrating. In some ways, the demands of treatment increase with the child's degree of functioning, because it is less clear where and when a youth with high-functioning autism spectrum disorder (HFA) will fail to understand how to act. Furthermore, it is hard to predict when children with HFA will fail to use a skill set that they already hold; teachers and parents alike will comment, "I know he knows better." Implied in the comment is that they do not understand why the child failed to act appropriately given his or her knowledge.

In addition, because stress can worsen symptoms, a muted deficit in a child with HFA may not be evident until there is an extreme behavioral response. Consider the early adolescent who ran away from the police when they approached to ask him a question about a local robbery. The teenager was not originally suspected of wrongdoing until his response of running away gave the police the impression that he was hiding something. Indeed, it is likely that their loud and hurried approach contributed to his actions; apparently, the police car lights were flashing as they pulled over and used a speaker to call his attention. However, his parents and the youth himself indicated that he knew there was no reason to run away from the police as they are people "here to keep the community safe."

Deaf-Blindness

This category was developed to acknowledge children who simultaneously have hearing and visual impairments and require interventions that are beyond those provided to only the deaf or only the blind—both are separate special education eligibility categories. A hearing impairment is also listed as a disabling condition. This is an example where there is some redundancy in the law, but it is meant to expand care (US Department of Education, 2017g).

Deaf

This is a severe hearing impairment that interferes in processing spoken language. It covers hearing loss that interferes with education; amplification devices are often necessary for the child to benefit from classroom instruction but are not a requirement for qualification (US Department of Education, 2017h).

Developmental Delay

The term *developmental delay*, as described by IDEA, is best understood as below-average development but not yet out of range to a degree that a disability is present. As discussed previously, each state can determine what is meant by a delay in child development that would result in eligibility for services. The IDEA (part C) ensures early intervention services for children from birth to age 3, while IDEA (part B) allows for services for children 3 through 9. Recall that children with disabilities are served through special education. This educational label should not be confused with formal diagnostic terms used to describe developmental disabilities (e.g., autism, intellectual disability; US Department of Education, 2017e).

Emotional Disturbance

Children may also receive special education services for emotional disturbance, which includes one or more of the following: difficulty in learning that cannot be explained by cognitive, sensory, or health reasons, being unable to maintain relationships with teachers or peers, demonstrating inappropriate feelings or behavior in normal circumstances, feeling unhappy or depressed most of the time, or developing fears or physical symptoms in response to personal or school problems (US Department of Education, 2017i). The term also includes schizophrenia. The term does not apply to children who are socially maladjusted, unless it is determined that they have an emotional disturbance (IDEA Amendments of 1999 § 300.7(c)(4)(ii)).

This disability category can be controversial. It includes children with internalizing disorders, such as anxiety, depression, and somatic disorders (where emotional distress is experienced as physical pain), as well as externalizing disorders, such as conduct disorder, oppositional defiant disorder, bipolar disorder, in addition to schizophrenia. However, the criteria for an emotional disturbance are not well defined; they do not match well with DSM-5 descriptions of psychological disorders and, most significantly, require a distinction for individuals who are socially maladjusted. *Social maladjustment* also is not defined.

Hearing Impairment

Hearing impairment is similar to deafness, which is listed prior, but is meant to capture children with transient conditions. That is, permanent hearing loss is not required for a child to be eligible for specially designed instruction for a hearing impairment, as it can be fluctuating, but that adversely affects a child's educational performance (US Department of Education, 2017j).

Intellectual Disability (ID)

An intellectual disability, formerly termed *mental retardation*, refers to an individual of significantly subaverage intellectual functioning *and* adaptive behavior skills, which IDEA notes occurs "in the developmental period" associated with school attendance (US Department of Education, 2017k). Although not required, schools often use the qualifications set by American Association on Intellectual and Developmental Disabilities (AAIDD), which recognizes the variability in symptoms or characteristics associated with individuals with ID.

For example, the AAIDD recognizes that individuals with ID may have some intellectual or adaptive behavior skills (e.g., up to a score of 75) that are above the standard score of

70 that is strictly used by most states. This may represent an appreciation that tailored interventions can increase an individual's skills, that scores can change over time, and that there is some error in any score, as there is no measure that can consistently provide the true score (i.e., standard error of measurement). Using the AAIDD definition is useful because it is the standard most often used by state agencies providing adult care. Essentially, using the same criteria allows for an easier transition from child to adult services.

Multiple Disabilities

Like deaf-blindness, this category is meant to acknowledge children who have several disabilities simultaneously. This category reminds child study teams that addressing only one problem or providing services in only one setting cannot meet the child's multiple needs. The categories of multiple disabilities exclude deaf-blindness, as this condition has its own category (US Department of Education, 2017l).

Orthopedic Impairment

This category is somewhat broad. It includes impairments that are due to genetic conditions, disease, injury, or other concerns and adversely affect a child's educational performance. The impairments may be caused by congenital anomalies, impairments from disease (e.g., poliomyelitis, bone tuberculosis), as well as impairment from other causes, such as cerebral palsy, amputations, and fractures or burns that cause contractures (US Department of Education, 2017m).

Other Health Impairment (OHI)

Often referred to by its initials, OHI, this category includes impairments in "strength, vitality, or alertness," including issues of heightened and underarousal. OHIs include impairments from ADHD in addition to acute and chronic health problems (e.g., asthma, diabetes, epilepsy, a heart condition, hemophilia, lead poisoning, leukemia, nephritis, rheumatic fever, sickle cell anemia, and Tourette syndrome). Although both ADHD and ADD are listed in the description, ADD is not a current term used in the DSM-5-TR. Rather, there are three types of ADHD recognized: ADHD with predominantly hyperactive-impulsive presentation, ADHD with predominantly inattentive presentation, and ADHD combined presentation (US Department of Education, 2017n).

Specific Learning Disability

The federal law defines a *specific learning disability* as:

> a disorder in one or more of the basic psychological processes involved in understanding or in using language, spoken or written, that may manifest itself in the imperfect ability to listen, think, speak, read, write, spell, or to do mathematical calculations, including conditions such as perceptual disabilities, brain injury, minimal brain dysfunction, dyslexia, and developmental aphasia . . . and does not include learning problems that are primarily the result of visual, hearing, or motor disabilities, of intellectual disability, of emotional disturbance, or of environmental, cultural, or economic disadvantage.
>
> (US Department of Education, 2017o)

The essential components of an SLD are that underlying psychological processes result in the imperfect ability to listen, think, speak, read, write, spell, or do mathematical calculations. In practice, this means that students can qualify for a learning disability in the following eight areas:

- Oral expression (explaining thoughts through oral communication)
- Listening comprehension (understanding what is heard)
- Written expression (communicating in writing)
- Basic reading skills (the link between letters and their sounds/phonemes)
- Reading fluency skills (reading words quickly and easily)
- Reading comprehension (understanding what is read)
- Mathematics calculation (the link between math symbol and the action required)
- Mathematics problem-solving (the process of working through a problem to find a solution)

Notably, a learning disability cannot be the result of cultural factors (e.g., the student's background is different than that of the school or larger society; he or she has limited experience in the culture; poor acculturation), environmental factors (e.g., the student has changed schools often, he or she was exposed to traumatic events, he or she is homeless), economic disadvantage (e.g., exposed to poor nutrition, abuse, neglect), or limited English proficiency.

For students whose primary language is not English, a learning disability is not an appropriate diagnosis if their English-language acquisition skills are not sufficient for them to profit from instruction delivered in English. In short, a person cannot be considered disabled just because they are unable to speak English. School psychologists are required to assess a student's basic interpersonal communication skills (BICS, which typically takes about two years to develop) and a student's cognitive academic language proficiency (CALP, which typically takes between five and seven years to acquire) when considering if an English-language learner may qualify for a learning disability. A CALP is required for a student to function effectively in an academic classroom. Obviously, children who are learning English as a second language will often have poor performance in their academic courses until CALP has developed adequately.

The child study team must ensure that student failure to learn was not due to lack of appropriate instruction in reading or math. Furthermore, child study teams must show that prior to the referral, (a) the child received appropriate instruction in the general education settings that was delivered by personnel qualified to teach the subject and (b) that there is documentation that the teacher assessed the student's performance several times over a reasonable period of time. Finally, those results were to be shared with parents before a special education evaluation was initiated.

Speech and Language

This category covers voice disorders (e.g., an inability to produce speech sounds correctly or fluently), which include stuttering and impaired articulation, as well as language impairment (e.g., delayed language acquisition). Language skill acquisition includes similar skills to those listed in the specific learning disabilities section (i.e., understanding and expressing ideas orally and understanding the sounds associated with letters with enough speed that word comprehension is possible). Language skills that are included in this category overlap with the language skills needed for reading. Children who show early speech and language problems who are not treated successfully are also likely to go on to develop reading difficulties when they become school-age (US Department of Education, 2017p).

Traumatic Brain Injury (TBI)

In IDEA, traumatic brain injury (TBI) refers to

> an acquired injury to the brain caused by an external physical force, resulting in total or partial functional disability or psychosocial impairment, or both, that adversely affects a child's educational performance. Traumatic brain injury applies to open or closed head injuries resulting in impairments in one or more areas, such as cognition; language; memory; attention; reasoning; abstract thinking; judgment; problem-solving; sensory, perceptual, and motor abilities; psychosocial behavior; physical functions; information processing; and speech. Traumatic brain injury does not apply to brain injuries that are congenital or degenerative, or to brain injuries induced by birth trauma.
>
> (US Department of Education, 2017q)

There are three specific age ranges in which TBI seems to be particularly common, two of which include school-age children (birth to 5 years of age and 15–24 years of age). Of the 475,000 children who sustain TBIs, approximately 17% to 19% become permanently disabled from their injuries or accidents. Using another way to represent this information, roughly 180 per 100,000 children 15 years or younger experience TBIs, of which 5% to 9% suffer from severe TBIs (ProjectIDEAL, www.projectidealonline.org/v/traumatic-brain-injury/). Because TBIs are relatively common in childhood and some children become moderately or severely injured through TBIs, they are included as a separate IDEA category of eligibility.

Visual Impairment and Blindness

Similar to the hearing impairment category listed previously, visual impairment is meant to capture children with transient conditions and students who have impairment even with visual correction (e.g., eyeglasses, materials that are magnified, large print). Permanent vision loss is not required to be eligible for services (US Department of Education, 2017d).

Transition Services

Advising students for the transition from high school to the world of work or postsecondary education is a core activity for SCs. Although there are some similar needs for all youth, transition planning for special education students (US Department of Education, 2017c) requires that the child study team address a set of specific skills "in preparing for student with a disability for adulthood." The plan must be in place by the time the youth turns 16, and also, the child must participate in its development.

IDEA indicates that transition services refer to a coordinated set of activities for a child with a disability which, first, is supposed to be a results-oriented process focused on improving the child with a disability's academic and functional achievement to assist his or her movement from school to postschool activities. These include postsecondary education, vocational education, integrated employment (including supported employment), continuing and adult education, adult services, independent living, or community participation. The second part of this process is based on consideration of the individual child's needs, strengths, preferences, and interests and includes (a) instruction, (b) related services, (c) community experiences, (d) the development of employment and other post-school adult living objectives, and (e) if appropriate, the acquisition of daily living skills and provision of a functional vocational evaluation. Additionally, transition services for children with disabilities may be considered a part of specially designed instruction, or a related service, if necessary to assist a child with a disability to benefit from special education (US Department of Education, 2017c).

Transition services (US Department of Education, 2017c) should articulate what the child needs to prepare for life after high school. For example, the child's interests and skills in living independently, participating in the community, employment options, career plans, and postsecondary education should be discussed at length and planned for in the activities developed. What academic and functional skills are needed to facilitate the child's transition to postsecondary life? Will the child continue to need services in adulthood? What are the child's strengths? Given the child's strengths, interests, and needs, the IEP should include a statement of the goals and reflect a plan for how instruction, community experiences, and related services (e.g., counseling) can come together to develop the child's employment and daily living skills.

The SC can continue to support parent involvement not only in IEP discussions about career options but also by supporting the changing family dynamics as this important milestone approaches. Like all post–high school experiences, there is a time of adjustment for parents and their children. Parents often face a loss of identity, purpose, and their right to advocate for their coming-of-age child. Although not formally part of a transition plan, there is a requirement for students with IEPs to have an *age of majority* notification. Schools are required to notify the student about the educational rights he or she has, if any, when maturing into adulthood. Furthermore, the parents of students with IEPs also need to be notified of the transfer of educational rights from them to the child. The notification must occur at least one year before the *age of majority* notification. The transfer of parent rights to the child may vary across states, and information regarding this transfer may be accessed here: http://minors.uslegal.com/age-of-majority/. In the case in which the child does not have the ability to provide informed consent (i.e., not competent to act on his or her own behalf), the parents would retain their rights regarding their child.

Box 12.8

Case Study

John, a 12-year-old boy, has been referred to the child study team by his teachers three months into his sixth-grade year. John is receiving mostly "Ds" in his academic subjects, and the teachers report that he frequently does not submit homework assignments and that he often appears "lost" in class. In collecting data regarding John's progress and health history, the child study team reviews documentation that has been provided by John's physician, indicating that John was previously diagnosed with ADHD, predominantly inattentive type. John's student file indicates that in fifth grade, he was provided a 504 plan as a result of his ADHD diagnosis. The accommodations listed in the 504 plan included seating near the front of the classroom, additional time for testing, receiving tests in portions to reduce John's sense of being overwhelmed, and having the teacher check his agenda planner to ensure that John was accurately recording the assignments.

A child study team meeting is scheduled, at which John's parents, his two child study team teachers, a special education teacher, the assistant principal, the SC, and the school psychologist attend. At this meeting, John's mother forcefully demands that her son receive an IEP because he is not succeeding in his academic classes. The school psychologist informs John's parents of the special education process, explaining that a plan of accommodations within a general education setting first must be created and John's response to the accommodations must be evaluated before it can be determined whether a full-scale evaluation should be conducted to determine John's eligibility for special education services. The child study team then decides that a period of intervention in John's classes will be implemented, including some of the successful strategies used previously, self-monitoring techniques to increase John's attention to tasks and improve his work completion, after which the child study team will determine whether the interventions have been successful.

After a six-week intervention period, the child study team determines that John has not made a sufficient rate of progress. The supports provided have not resulted in improved functioning (e.g., academic performance, feelings of being overwhelmed) in the classroom. Also, the child study team suspects that his ADHD diagnosis is significantly interfering with John's ability to benefit from the instruction provided. Consequently, a multidisciplinary evaluation is conducted. At the subsequent feedback session, the school psychologist explains John continues to meet the criteria for a diagnosis of attention-deficit/hyperactivity disorder, predominantly inattentive type, and that his scores on a measurement of emotional functioning indicate that he meets the criteria for an anxiety disorder. Based upon this assessment data, the child study team determines that John qualifies for special education services under the criteria outlined in the Individuals with Disabilities Education Act (IDEA); specifically, he qualifies under the educational category of OHI and ED. Although John's mother agrees that he is not progressing academically, she indicates she has reservations about the conclusions of the child study team. The child study team informs her that she is free to disagree with the conclusions of the child study team; she may express her disagreement in writing with it attached to the report. An additional meeting is scheduled to develop John's Individualized Education Program (IEP), in which the child study team will discuss with John's parents the form, duration, and location of the specially designed instruction that will be used to address John's educational needs.

At the IEP meeting, the child study team suggests that John receive push-in special education services so that he can receive accommodations in real time in the general education classroom, in addition to twice-weekly counseling sessions conducted by the SC. In response to this proposal, John's mother forcefully disagrees, explaining that she knows her son has a learning disability. She demands that the school do more, in particular, that they send John to a special school for students with ADHD. John's father attempts to express a different opinion, but John's mother ignores him. John's mother becomes angry and storms out of the meeting before its conclusion. Her husband sits looking dejected and eventually also leaves the meeting.

Stimulus Questions

1) What should be the next course of action for the SC?
2) How could the SC work to connect with John's parents to reconcile their wishes regarding John's education in light of the proposal made by the child study team?
3) What supplemental support could the SC provide to John's teachers to help him adjust to special education supports delivered in the general education classroom?

Gifted and Talented Students

In addition to helping children with psychological disorders who receive special education services, child study teams also work with children who show other exceptionalities, such as those identified as gifted and talented (GT). Some states require that schools identify and provide differentiated educational programs for GT students, while others do not. Schools manage gifted education in a variety of ways. Because gifted education does not mandate inclusion or the least-restrictive environment (LRE) in the way that special education does, many schools use pullout (exclusion) classes to deliver a curriculum designed for these students. Some districts allow for talent development in specialized schools (e.g., performing arts, engineering, science), while others use online courses. Advanced Placement (AP) classes are common in high school, as are allowing students to take college coursework. However, the most successful GT school programs use differentiated instruction to accelerate student learning of intellectually advanced students alongside their peers.

Box 12.9 American School Counselor Association (ASCA, 2019c) Position on Gifted and Talented Programs

"The professional school counselor delivers a comprehensive school counseling program as an integral component of the school's efforts to meet the academic and developmental needs of all students. Gifted and talented students have unique and diverse needs that are addressed by professional school counselors within the scope of the comprehensive school counseling program and in collaboration with other educators and stakeholders."

Reprinted with permission, American School
Counselor Association, www.schoolcounselor.org

Current research shows that giftedness is not only representative of an IQ of 130 or above (i.e., performing at or better than 98% of the population) but is also about the child's attitude, passion, commitment, and motivation to succeed (Pfeiffer, 2014). In fact, for a child whose skill level exceeds the instruction provided in the standard curriculum, who shows an intense interest in learning a particular topic, and who is able to persist in his or her work effort, enrichment and/or acceleration may be appropriate in either an exclusion or inclusion model.

The issue that SCs need to be sensitive to is the myth that giftedness is a stable trait. In fact, cognitive skills fluctuate as children age, as do their interests and opportunities. When these match well, much success is possible. However, enrichment and/or acceleration in a subject that is not an interest to a child is simply extra work and is not likely to be a positive experience. Furthermore, it is important for children who are gifted to understand that effort, attitude, and persistence matter to life success. Moreover, for youth who were nearly eligible for gifted education services but did not require enrichment or acceleration, retesting should be considered when the child's strengths warrant doing so, as their skills can improve, and when matched with their interest, such students can flourish in accelerated or enrichment programing. SCs should attend to the interests of gifted and very bright students so that they can aid them in finding opportunities to excel. Moreover, opportunities matched with a child's interests provide a sense of accomplishment and support positive social-emotional development (Elijah, 2011).

Kennedy and Farley (2018) assert that the social/emotional needs of GT are not qualitatively different from the needs of regular education students but recommend that SCs be sensitive to issues that may be particularly relevant for GT students. In order to address GT students' elevated risk for perfectionism (e.g., Wang et al., 2012), the authors recommend using approaches that are typically used to manage anxiety. A cognitive behavioral theory (CBT) approach may be used to help GT students identify and modify the dysfunctional thoughts associated with their perfectionism. GT students can be taught test-taking and study skills, as GT students often experience frustration and confusion when first encountering an academic subject that they find to be challenging. Meditation and other relaxation strategies may be taught to GT students to help manage anxiety during test-taking. There is research to suggest that GT students may exhibit asynchronous development (e.g., Cross & Cross, 2015), meaning, that a student is developmentally advanced in some but not all areas. Kennedy and Farley (2018) recommend that GT students be educated about the concept of asynchronous development and that SCs consider using group-counseling interventions to help GT students who experience social difficulties related to their asynchronous development.

Greene (2006) provides interventions for SCs to address the career needs of GT students. GT students are more likely to experience multipotentiality, which refers to the ability for a high level of competency for a variety of tasks. This apparent strength can be problematic for GT students in that it can result in frustration with having to relinquish the intense development of some interests. Multipotentiality is associated with frequent changing of a major focus of study, delayed decision-making, and premature choices (Stewart, 1999). Often, GT students are directed toward prestigious occupations, such as becoming a doctor, lawyer, or engineer. However, GT students should be encouraged to explore their various interests, including their values, life goals, and leisure activities. Also, GT students and their parents should be made aware that a career decision made at the end of high school is merely one of many potential choices.

GT students are also more likely than their nongifted peers to exhibit early career emergence, showing unusually strong talents and intense interest as early as elementary school (Greene, 2006). Too much encouragement from parents and teachers may diminish the child's interest, but requiring diversification may reduce the child's passion. Greene recommends that SCs encourage the parents and teachers of GT students to seek to achieve a balance between encouraging and challenging the child's pursuit of his or her interest while also encouraging the child to engage in novel experiences. The overly perfectionistic GT student may manage his or her anxiety with making the "wrong" career decision by avoiding a decision or acquiescing to an adult (i.e., identity foreclosure; Greene, 2006). Because

GT students often have a heightened sense of sensitivity and commitment to social justice, Greene (2006) recommends that SCs explore with GT students the importance of selecting a career that is compatible with their values and interests, versus focusing strictly on abilities that students may not be necessarily interesting in pursuing.

Summary

SCs today enjoy a supportive role in working with children and families facing significant educational challenges and opportunities. In particular, SCs are in a unique position to maintain a stable relationship with families that feel vulnerable because of a child's difficulty in his or her educational progress. Whether faced with a struggling student, a student with a disability, or a student with an exceptionality, the communication provided by SCs can help parents, teachers, and administrators solve immediate and long-term educational problems, access general education supports (e.g., school-wide antibullying programs), participate in the development of 504 plans (e.g., adjustments, modifications, and/or enrichments to the curriculum), or navigate the special education eligibility process.

References

American School Counselor Association. (2016). *The school counselor and students with disabilities*. www.schoolcounselor.org/asca/media/asca/PositionStatements/PositionStatPositi.pdf

American School Counselor Association. (2019a). *ASCA standards for school counselor preparation programs*. www.schoolcounselor.org/getmedia/573d7c2c-1622-4d25-a5ac-ac74d2e614ca/ASCA-Standards-for-School-Counselor-Preparation-Programs.pdf

American School Counselor Association. (2019b). *The ASCA national model: A framework for for school counseling programs* (4th ed.). Author.

American School Counselor Association. (2019c). *The school counselor and gifted and talented student programs*. www.schoolcounselor.org/asca/media/asca/home/position%20statements/PS_Gifted.pdf

Assistance to States for the Education of Children with Disabilities and Preschool Grants for Children with Disabilities, 34 C.F.R. (2006).

Council for the Accreditation of Counseling and Related Educational Programs. (n.d.). *2016 CACREP standards*. https://www.cacrep.org/for-programs/2016-cacrep-standards/

Cross, J. R., & Cross, T. L. (2015). Clinical and mental health issues in counseling the gifted individual. *Journal of Counseling & Development, 93*(2), 163–172. https://doi.org/10.1002/j.1556-6676.2015.00192.x

Elijah, K. (2011). Meeting the guidance and counseling needs of gifted students in school settings. *Journal of School Counseling, 9*(14). https://files.eric.ed.gov/fulltext/EJ933180.pdf

Federal Register. (2006). *Assistance to states for the education of children with disabilities and preschool grants for children with disabilities*. https://www.federalregister.gov/documents/2006/08/14/06-6656/assistance-to-states-for-the-education-of-children-with-disabilities-and-preschool-grants-for

Fuchs, D., & Fuchs, L. S. (2006). Introduction to response to intervention: What, why, and how valid is it? *Reading Research Quarterly, 41*(1), 93–99.

Greene, M. J. (2006). Helping build lives: Career and life development of gifted and talented students. *Professional School Counseling, 10*(1), 34–42. https://doi.org/10.5330/prsc.10.1.b55j504360m48424

Hughes, C., & Dexter, D. D. (n.d.). *The use of RTI to identify students with learning disabilities: A review of the research*. www.rtinetwork.org/learn/research/use-rti-identify-students-learning-disabilities-review-research

Individuals with Disabilities Education Improvement Act. (2004). Public Law 108–446 (20 U.S.C 1400 *et seq.*).

Kennedy, K., & Farley, J. (2018). Counseling gifted students: School-base considerations and strategies. *International Electronic Journal of Elementary Education, 10*(3). https://doi.org/10.26822/iejee.2018336194

Milsom, A. (2007). Interventions to assist students with disabilities through school transitions. *Professional School Counseling, 10*(3), 273–278. https://doi.org/10.1177/2156759X0701000309

Morgan, P. L., Farkas, G., Hillmeier, M. H., Mattison, R., Maczuga, S., Li, H., & Cook, M. (2015). Minorities are disproportionately underrepresented in special education: Longitudinal evidence across five disability conditions. *Educational Researcher, 44*(5), 278–292. https://doi.org/10.3102/0013189X15591157

National Center for Learning Disabilities. (2014). *What is FAPE, and what can it mean to my child?* www.ncld.org/parents-child-disabilities/ld-rights/what-is-fape-what-can-it-mean-my-child

Ockerman, M. S., Mason, E., & Hollenbeck, A. F. (2012). Integrating RTI with school counseling programs: Being a proactive professional school counselor. *Journal of School Counseling, 10*(15). https://files.eric.ed.gov/fulltext/EJ978870.pdf

Pfeiffer, S. (2014). The emotional cost of prevailing myths about the gifted. *Supporting Emotional Needs of Gifted Learners.* www.sengifted.org/archives/articles/the-emotional-cost-of-prevailing-myths-about-the-gifted

Rabiner, D. (2006). *Educational rights for children with ADHD/ADD.* www.helpforadd.com/educational-rights/

Stewart, J. B. (1999). Career counseling for the academically gifted student. *Canadian Journal of Counseling, 33*(1), 3–12. https://eric.ed.gov/contentdelivery/servlet/ERICServlet?accno=EJ587278

Sullivan, A. L., & Bal, A. (2013). Disproportionately in special education: Effects of individual and school variables on disability risk. *Exceptional Children, 79*(4), 475–494. https://doi.org/10.1177/001440291307900406

US Department of Education. (2007). *Questions and answers on response to intervention (RTI) and early intervening services.* http://idea.ed.gov/explore/view/p/,root,dynamic,QaCorner,8

US Department of Education. (2017a). Sec. 300.300 *Parental consent.* https://sites.ed.gov/idea/regs/b/d/300.300

US Department of Education. (2017b). Sec. 300.321 *IEP team.* https://sites.ed.gov/idea/regs/b/d/300.321

US Department of Education. (2017c). Sec. 300.43 *Transition services.* https://sites.ed.gov/idea/regs/b/a/300.43

US Department of Education. (2017d). Sec. 300.8 *Child with a disability.* https://sites.ed.gov/idea/regs/b/a/300.8

US Department of Education. (2017e). Sec. 300.8 (b) *Statute/regs main.* https://sites.ed.gov/idea/regs/b/a/300.8/b

US Department of Education. (2017f). Sec. 300.8 (c) (1) *Statute/regs main.* https://sites.ed.gov/idea/regs/b/a/300.8/c/1

US Department of Education. (2017g). Sec. 300.8 (c) (2) *Statute/regs main.* https://sites.ed.gov/idea/regs/b/a/300.8/c/2

US Department of Education. (2017h). Sec. 300.8 (c) (3) *Statute/regs main.* https://sites.ed.gov/idea/regs/b/a/300.8/c/3

US Department of Education. (2017i). Sec. 300.8 (c) (4) *Statute/regs main.* https://sites.ed.gov/idea/regs/b/a/300.8/c/4

US Department of Education. (2017j). Sec. 300.8 (c) (5) *Statute/regs main.* https://sites.ed.gov/idea/regs/b/a/300.8/c/5

US Department of Education. (2017k). Sec. 300.8 (c) (6) *Statute/regs main.* https://sites.ed.gov/idea/regs/b/a/300.8/c/6

US Department of Education. (2017l). Sec. 300.8 (c) (7) *Statute/regs main.* https://sites.ed.gov/idea/regs/b/a/300.8/c/7

US Department of Education. (2017m). Sec. 300.8 (c) (8) *Statute/regs main.* https://sites.ed.gov/idea/regs/b/a/300.8/c/8

US Department of Education. (2017n). Sec. 300.8 (c) (9) *Statute/regs main.* https://sites.ed.gov/idea/regs/b/a/300.8/c/9

US Department of Education. (2017o). Sec. 300.8 (c) (10) *Statute/regs main.* https://sites.ed.gov/idea/regs/b/a/300.8/c/10

US Department of Education. (2017p). Sec. 300.8 (c) (11) *Statute/regs main.* https://sites.ed.gov/idea/regs/b/a/300.8/c/11

US Department of Education. (2017q). Sec. 300.8 (c) (12) *Statute/regs main.* https://sites.ed.gov/idea/regs/b/a/300.8/c/12

US Department of Education. (n.d.). Sec. 300.114 *LRE requirements.* www.hhs.gov/sites/default/files/ocr/civilrights/resources/factsheets/504.pdf

US Department of Health and Human Services. (n.d.). *Fact sheet: Your rights under section 504 of the rehabilitation act.* www.hhs.gov/sites/default/files/ocr/civilrights/resources/factsheets/504.pdf

VanDerHeyden, A. M., Witt, J. C., & Gilbertson, D. (2007). A multi-year evaluation of the effects of a Response to Intervention (RTI) model on identification of children for special education. *Journal of School Psychology, 45*(2), 225–256. https://doi.org/10.1016/j.jsp.2006.11.004

Wang, K. T., Fu, C. C., & Rice, K. G. (2012). Perfectionism in gifted students: Moderating effects of goal orientation and contingent self-worth. *School Psychology Quarterly, 27*(2), 96–108. https://doi.org/10.1037/a0029215

Wright, P. W., & Wright, P. D. (2012). *Wrightslaw: Discrimination-Section 504 and ADA.* www.wrightslaw.com/info/sec504.index.htm

Wright, P. W., & Wright, P. D. (n.d.). *Wrightslaw: Back to school on civil rights, part I.* www.wrightslaw.com/law/reports/IDEA_Compliance_1.htm

Wrightslaw. (n.d.). *Eligibility.* www.wrightslaw.com/info/elig.index.htm

Chapter 13

Crisis Management and Trauma Informed Practice

Box 13.1 2016 Council for the Accreditation of Counseling and Related Educational Programs (CACREP, n.d.) School Counseling Specialty Area Standards

2.d School counselor roles in school leadership and multidisciplinary teams

2.e School counselor roles and responsibilities in relation to the school emergency management plans and crises, disasters, and trauma

2.g Characteristics, risk factors, and warning signs of students at risk for mental health and behavioral disorders

2.k Community resources and referral resources

Box 13.2 ASCA (2019a) Standards for School Counselor Preparation Programs (ASCA CAEP SPA)

2.1 Describe established and emerging counseling and educational methods, including but not limited to childhood and adolescent development, learning theories, behavior modification and classroom management, social justice, multiculturalism, group counseling, college/career readiness, and crisis response.

2.3 Demonstrate established and emerging counseling theories and evidence-based techniques that are effective in a school setting, including but not limited to rational emotive behavior therapy, reality therapy, cognitive behavioral therapy, Adlerian, solution-focused brief counseling, person-centered counseling, and family systems.

News reports highlighting school violence have understandably focused our collective attention on the manner in which schools are prepared to help children and their families when unexpected events occur. The very unlikely event of a school shooting as well as the more common acts of school violence, such as childhood bullying, have resulted in the need for school-wide crisis training. Specifically, today's school teams need to be prepared to prevent, intervene, and recover from crisis situations. Common problems in crisis

DOI: 10.4324/9781003167730-13

preparedness are a lack of basic knowledge about how people react and the appropriate timing for the implementation of intervention strategies. While many students and staff feel confident in the fact that their school has a crisis plan, often, they do not know the expected roles for students and staff and when the plan should be implemented, because such plans are not regularly practiced (Olinger Steeves et al., 2017). This chapter provides an overview of the best practices for crisis prevention, intervention, and response and discusses the SCs' role in preventing and managing crises. In the chapter, we also explore SCs' role in suicide intervention and prevention, and trauma-informed education.

What Counts as a Crisis?

A *crisis* often refers to a sudden and unexpected set of events, which is associated with emotional, social, or cognitive instability. In schools, there is a sense of disruption of students' or staffs' feelings of psychological well-being and/or the learning environment (Brock et al., 2009).

A crisis can result from experiencing acts of war and terrorism, disasters (natural or human caused), threated or actual violent injury, or death, among other causes.

Adults and children can experience a variety of symptoms after a crisis event. It is typical for 80–85% of individuals exposed to a crisis incident to show a noticeable symptom within 24 hours; about half of these individuals can continue to be affected for three or more weeks (California Department of Corrections and Rehabilitation, n.d.). Symptom intensity tends to be associated with the severity of the incident, but not always. Symptoms that may be observed in children and adults include:

- Anxiety, fear, and worry about safety of self and others
- Guilt
- Mistrust, withdrawal from others or activities
- Irritability, anger
- Decreased attention and/or concentration
- Increase in impulsivity, risk-taking behavior, hyperactivity
- Over- or underreaction to noises, physical contact, sudden movements
- Heightened difficulty with authority, redirection, or criticism
- Re-experiencing the trauma (e.g., nightmares or disturbing memories)
- Hyperarousal (e.g., sleep disturbance, tendency to be easily startled)
- Avoidance behaviors (e.g., resisting going to places that remind them of the event)
- Emotional numbing (e.g., seeming to have no feeling about the event)

There are four variables that contribute to the experience of traumatization in a crisis: the event predictability, intensity, duration, and consequences (Brock et al., 2009). Although individuals vary in their sensitivities, as a general rule, human-caused, violent events tend to be more traumatizing than natural disasters. It is not uncommon for students to experience drops in academic performance, increases in behavior difficulties, increases in absenteeism and tardiness, and a worsening of previous problems.

There is no right or wrong way for an individual to cope with a crisis event. Most people, including those showing the symptoms identified prior, recover without further difficulty. However, there are some students and staff who will require extra support. It is important for the school team to monitor how people are functioning. At times, schools can be so focused on students that they are slow to notice staff who also require support; it is important to assess and monitor all student and staff responses.

SCs can assist in crisis preparedness by educating parents, students, and staff about typical responses and coping (Crepeau-Hobson et al., 2012). Pamphlets and brochures are an excellent way for students to take home this information. Ensuring educational information is available in the languages spoken by the district's population is essential for good home-school communications.

School Counselor's Role in Crisis Prevention, Intervention, and Response

The American School Counselor Association's (ASCA, 2019b) position statement on safe schools and crisis response states that one way SCs demonstrate leadership is through involvement in safe school initiatives and critical response preparation and intervention. The position statement lists specific crisis prevention and response practices for SCs, which are listed in Figure 13.1.

Fein et al. (2008) identified several implications for SCs in responding to any serious crisis. Fein's (2003) study of school leaders at four schools which experienced a school shooting revealed that SCs often assumed a leadership position in the aftermath of a school shooting, even though they did not necessarily have a formal role in the school's crisis response plan. Fein urged SCs to seek formal roles on the school's crisis response team, given that their training and skill set prepare them for leadership in response to a crisis. Fein (2003) found that in addition to the stress of secondary trauma, SCs reported stress in dealing with the additional responsibilities that interfered with their other duties and the role conflict associated with providing a leadership role in responding to the crisis. He recommended that schools establish coleaders in order to disperse the responsibilities. Fein encouraged SCs and administrators to understand that role ambiguity may occur, as leaders of the crisis response team may outrank an administrator during the implementation

- providing individual and group counseling
- advocating for student safety by recommending school personnel put consistent procedures, communication and policies in place
- providing interventions for students at risk of dropping out or harming self or others
- offering peer mediation training, conflict resolution programs and anti-bullying programs
- supporting student-initiated programs such as Students Against Violence Everywhere
- providing family, faculty and staff education programs
- facilitating open communication between students and caring adults
- defusing critical incidents and providing related stress debriefing
- participating in district and school response team planning and practices and helping ensure students and staff are able to process/understand crisis response drills
- promoting trauma-informed practices
- advocating for restorative justice programs
- partnering with community resources

Figure 13.1 The School Counselor and Safe Schools and Crisis Response.

Source: This excerpt from ASCA's position statement is reprinted here with kind permission.

American School Counselor Association (2019a). *The school counselor and safe schools and crisis response.* www.schoolcounselor.org/asca/media/asca/PositionStatements/PS_SafeSchools.pdf

of a school's response to a crisis. Fein (2003) found that formal school leaders were reluctant to formally pursue help from others, but SCs reported that they often provided informal help to school administrators, allowing an administrator to ventilate feelings. Finally, Fein et al. (2008) encouraged SCs to take care of themselves by limiting their critical response shift to three to four hours and obtain debriefing from a trained personnel member.

What Is a Good Crisis Plan?

The US Department of Education (2013) recommends that schools develop a school Emergency Operations Plan (EOP) addressing the areas of concern before, during, and after an incident. Prevention, mitigation, protection, response, and recovery contexts are described in the Guide for Developing High-Quality School Emergency Operations Plans (US Department of Education, 2013) and are summarized in the sections that follow.

Prevention

Prevention describes the actions taken by a school to avoid an incident occurring. Prevention activities in the school can address targeted or known risks associated with crime or violence, such as bullying, or suicide prevention programs. Programs aimed at increasing school connectedness are associated with violence prevention efforts (Tillery et al., 2013), including responsible reporting of safety concerns (Catalano et al., 2004).

Protection

Protection means the ability to protect students, staff, property, and visitors from hazards or potential threats. School safeguards, such as video monitoring, metal detectors, and surveillance around school entrance and exit areas, are associated with school protection (Reeves et al., 2012).

Mitigation

Mitigation means the capacity to eliminate or reduce the loss of life and property damage by lessening the impact of the emergency. In the school setting, this includes how the buildings are managed (e.g., the setup of monitored entry points, visitor screenings) and maintained (e.g., anchoring large bookshelves to walls, property fencing designating boundaries) (Sorenson et al., 2013; US Department of Education, 2013).

Response

Response refers to the capability to stabilize an emergency situation once it has begun or when it is clear that it cannot be prevented. Response means establishing a safe and secure environment and facilitating recovery. When responding to a crisis, school teams enact their (previously written) emergency management plans in order to ensure the physical and psychological safety of the students and staff.

Recovery

This involves the actions implemented to restore the learning environment. It is important to note that as the school system returns to its typical functioning, the whole school crisis team should be properly debriefed. The implementation team's care needs to be an intentional part of the recovery process (Brock, 2011).

How to Build a Good Crisis Plan

A good crisis plan is developed through dialogues within the school, as well as with the community at large. Various school personnel need to be included in planning meetings, as well as relevant community partners. Diverse cultural and linguistic groups present in the community also need to be present.

School participants for the school safety and school crisis teams should include administrators, teachers, facility staff, mental health professionals (e.g., SCs, psychologists, and social workers), parents, and students; all provide different and important perspectives. Community members should include first responders and community agencies involved in emergency management (e.g., shelters, Red Cross, etc.), community mental health services, spiritual leaders, and immigrant community contacts that can help address the needs of cultural and linguistic groups represented in the building.

The school safety team focuses on identifying potential hazards (e.g., prevention needs relevant to the school's population) as well as known strengths and weaknesses specific to the building that would impact the school's ability to protect or mitigate the impact of an emergency. The school crisis team, which may include some or each of the members of the safety team, focuses on the implementation procedures for mitigating and responding to a crisis. The school crisis team also plans the implementation of the recovery strategies.

The US Department of Education (2013) identifies several assessment strategies to determine the risk and vulnerability that should be considered by the school safety team. The considerations are discussed in the following section.

Site Assessment

This assessment focuses on identifying the risks and vulnerability of the building(s) and the school grounds. It is designed to provide information about potential hazards and areas that are vulnerable as well as identify which areas provide a safe, Americans with Disabilities Act (ADA)–accessible shelter, where students, staff, emergency responders, and volunteers can gather.

Culture and Climate Assessment

This assessment focuses both on the students' and staffs' perceptions of physical safety and psychological well-being in the building. Its purpose is to identify problematic behaviors or practices that would interfere with a healthy school culture (e.g., where students and staff are free to report concerns). For example, a school where bullying is rampant and unaddressed by the school staff would not promote good communications between students or between students and staff. Bullying is also thought to diminish feelings of connectedness between students and their school (Carney et al., 2020). Results from the culture and climate assessment could indicate a need for a bullying prevention program in order to increase students' sense of psychological safety. Results could suggest a need to improve the school's awareness of the different cultural and linguistic populations represented in the district, the coping strategies preferred by different groups, and the resources these groups can bring to support the school's efforts (Heath et al., 2005). Reeves et al. (2011) provide an example of a physical and psychological safety vulnerability assessment.

School Threat Assessment

A threat assessment is used to identify if communications or behaviors exhibited by a student, staff, or other individuals may pose a threat. The purpose of the assessment is to prevent the incident and refer the individual(s) for supports and services, if appropriate. The threat assessment team should include school mental health personnel (e.g., SCs, psychologists, or social workers) with appropriate training in the methods of assessment, school personnel familiar with the individual and the context, as well as relevant community agency personnel (e.g., law enforcement, mental health personnel). Given the need to consider the mental status of the individual at the time of the threat, this team is necessarily different from the school safety team and crisis response teams; however, membership from the crisis response team may overlap. Cornell and Sheras (2006) have developed an evidence-based threat assessment guideline (National Registry of Evidence-Based Programs and Practices [NREPP], 2013) that has been shown to be used effectively by school teams (Strong & Cornell, 2008). It is important to note, however, that some threats may require ongoing assessment and intervention from the school team (Reeves & Brock, 2018).

Capacity Assessment

This assessment identifies the available resources for responding to both evacuation and in-place crisis responses and includes material resources (e.g., equipment and supplies) and staff assets (e.g., who is trained in CPR, who can assist individuals with disabilities, who can assist with various cultural groups, including English-language learners and their families, etc.).

The US Department of Homeland Security (2013) published a document titled *K–12 School Security Checklist* that helps schools assess many of the areas listed prior and includes psychological safety (www.illinois.gov/ready/SiteCollectionDocuments/K-12SchoolSecurityPracticesChecklist.pdf). The National Association of School Psychologists (NASP) provide resources and the rationale for the needed processes and practices to ensure school safety (www.nasponline.org/resources/handouts/Framework_for_Safe_and_Successful_School_Environments.pdf).

How to Prevent a Crisis

SCs play an important role in delivering the support services that can prevent or mitigate a crisis. This is because the SC is often aware of which students and families are in distress and can help school teams direct support services toward those in need. Also, SCs are aware of the cultural and linguistic diversity in the building and can help districts incorporate diversity needs into the programs provided. As such, most SCs are likely to find themselves on the crisis and threat assessment teams charged with addressing the psychological safety of students and staff.

Psychological safety initiatives focus on a person's emotional and physical well-being (Howell et al., 2019; Nickerson et al., 2021). Programs tend to be multitiered, where universal supports are provided to all students, targeted interventions are provided for those who are at risk, and intensive interventions are aimed to those who are experiencing extreme distress. Common multitiered programs, also referred to as multitiered systems of support (MTSS), include:

- Academic support through response to intervention (RtI; see Chapter 12 for a full description)

- Positive behavior support (Positive Behavior Interventions and Supports, n.d.), which uses the RtI model for behavior improvement
- A social-emotional learning curriculum that addresses safety, school climate, and antibullying more directly (Safe and Civil Schools, n.d.)
- Programs aimed at improving home-school partnerships

Durlak and colleagues (2011) conducted a meta-analysis that revealed that schools using evidence-based programs with a high level of fidelity at the universal level of intervention demonstrated a positive impact upon student behavior. The researchers concluded that high expectations for academic success, engaging teaching practices, caring student-teacher relationships, and a safe and orderly classroom environment were essential for effectiveness at the universal level of intervention.

SCs have several roles within the tiered framework of crisis intervention. At the universal level of intervention, SCs can lead home-school partnership activities, support teachers in implementing programs with fidelity, or provide direct instruction on the problem-solving portions of these programs. For the targeted and intensive intervention levels, the SC ensures good communication within team members. Effective communication is necessary because as targeted and intensive interventions are paired and added onto the universal support, those new team members will require a bridge to what has already been done, where the child continues to show challenges and access to how the counselor has approached the parent or guardian. The school's vulnerability assessments and academic and behavioral data should drive the selection of targeted interventions.

Responding to a Crisis as It Happens

Responding to a crisis is a complex matter that requires everyone in the building to know their role and to implement it in coordination. The SC is likely to serve as a conduit between the school crisis team, which is managing the system, and the teachers, who are in more immediate contact with students. The perspective of the school crisis team and the teachers are presented in the following section.

In the Classroom

Well-informed teachers, prepared for clear communications, who are able to remain calm during uncertainty, are key assets in managing a crisis. All school staff require in-service instruction and practice regarding crisis responding. Individual teacher responses need to be understood in the context of the system response.

The first priority in crisis communications is to reassure all children that they are safe. Children require an honest explanation about what is happening. In low-trust school environments, that honesty may need to be explicitly stated: "I will tell you all that I know, as soon as I know it." In linguistically diverse environments, that communication needs to be delivered in a manner that is understood by the children in the class. Explanations need to be developmentally appropriate to best meet the needs of students (National Association of School Psychologists, 2007).

- Elementary children require a brief statement with concrete reassurance about their safety. Teachers should point out locked doors, how the school has practiced fire drills, and how adults are always making sure children are safe (e.g., in the cafeteria, on the playground, on the bus).

- Older elementary and some middle school children will often wonder how the teacher can know if they are really safe. This group needs help sorting reality from fantasy. Teachers can provide reassurances, such as that the school has a safety plan and the police and fire department respond within three minutes when we practice for an emergency situation.
- Middle and high school students often wonder if society is really safe, if a school can really protect anyone. This group should be encouraged to give their suggestions for school safety improvements and prompted to use the strategies in place for responsible reporting of safety concerns. They often need to talk about the differences between gossiping, tattling, and responsible reporting. What are appropriate (e.g., talking with friends and family) and inappropriate (e.g., use of violence, drugs, alcohol) ways to solve problems? Who else in the community is dedicated to helping others: doctors, policeman, faith leaders, etc.? What is the possibility vs. the probability of a violent act at school? Adolescents can be informed that schools are one of the safest places for children and they are safer now than they have been in the last 20 years (Robers et al., 2013).

All children should be encouraged but not forced to talk. Listening to children's thoughts and feelings will help the school crisis team know who may require additional support. Teachers need to be explicitly told that the SC wants to know whom they are concerned about and why; teachers need to know not to wait a couple of weeks to let the counselor or other members of the school crisis team know how the children are responding. Some example statements for teachers in such discussions include:

- Reassuring statements. We are in a safe place. We have followed the plan; everyone (police, fire department, your parents) knows where to come find us when it's time. We are here together; we can help each other while we wait.
- Explanations. The principal has told us there was a fire. The principal has called for help. Help is on the way/already here.
- Listen. Your thoughts are important. Tell me more about how you are thinking/feeling. I can see how you might think of it that way.
- Talk about it. Lots of people have more thoughts or feelings as time goes by; we can talk about that if it comes up for you.

While open communication is encouraged, returning to routines is also important. If students are to remain in their classroom, returning to classroom-like activities may facilitate a sense of normalcy. This does not necessarily mean that the scheduled test should resume as planned during a lockdown, but rather that educational activities can help pass the time and reinforce that the students are safe, the plan is being carried out, and school routines can resume. At times, however, students will be evacuated to another location and teachers may be pressed to be creative. One French teacher employed a French version of Simon Says during an hour outside to help pass the time and keep track of wandering teenagers (Olinger Steeves et al., 2017). To the extent that students and staff know what to do, more rapid recovery is more likely.

At the Building Level

The National Education Association (NEA, n.d.) provides a comprehensive overview, along with checklists, of the types of considerations that need to be addressed when the crisis is happening in the publication *School Crisis Guide: Help and Healing in a Time of Crisis*. As stated, school teams should have roles delegated (who is doing what and when) along with redundant checks to make sure that all the responses are covered during the crisis event. No detail is too small. An excellent resource, the NEA lists nine priorities to complete in the first hour.

In addition to the initial response, the NEA provides a detailed list of the steps/functions that need to be addressed in the first day of the crisis. Included are implementing the established operating procedures as well as communication plans and use of volunteer support. The NEA also provides guidance on how to manage day 2 and the first week of a crisis. SCs may wish to review the *School Crisis Guide: Help and Healing in a Time of Crisis* at the beginning of each school year in order to refresh their knowledge and to participate in discussions about their role on any of the school teams (e.g., school safety, school crisis, threat assessment) as the academic year begins.

Crisis Recovery

The response after the crisis is as important as the response during the event. SCs will find that they are needed to provide support to students and staff as well as to help ensure the delivery of the response plan. Accordingly, the NEA provides a back-to-school checklist that SCs may find helpful to review.

Crisis Preparedness Is Essential

No school can prevent every crisis; some events are simply unstoppable. However, it is clear that schools are required to be prepared for a crisis; the No Child Left Behind (NCLB) legislation requires schools to develop safety and crisis plans (NCLB, 2001), the White House (2013) *Now Is the Time* initiative provides strategies and funding recommendations regarding making schools safer as well as how to increase access to mental health services, and then in 2015, the Every Student Succeeds Act (ESSA; US Department of Education, n.d.) provides funding opportunities for schools and districts to implement key elements of comprehensive school safety, titled the *Framework for Safe and Successful Schools*. This joint statement was developed in collaboration between the American School Counselor Association (ASCA), the National Associations of Elementary and Secondary School Principals, the National Association of School Psychologists (NASP), the National Association of School Resource Officers, and the School Social Work Association of America. Not only has child safety remained a high priority, but there is also an increasing awareness in the need for coordinated best practice action (Cowan et al., 2013). The *Framework for Safe and Successful Schools* can be downloaded for free (www.nasponline. org/Documents/Research%20and%20Policy/Advocacy%20Resources/Framework_for_ Safe_and_Successful_School_Environments.pdf).

Counseling Victims of Trauma

Many students who are exposed to trauma, either as the result of a crisis occurring in a school or community or through other trauma experiences (e.g., victims of sexual, physical, or emotional abuse, witnessing domestic violence, etc.), can benefit from more intensive, ongoing support. A review of evidence-based counseling approaches for treating individual youth exposed to traumatic events found that interventions generally produce positive but modest reductions in posttraumatic stress, depressive symptoms, anxiety symptoms, and externalizing behavior problems (Racco & Vis, 2015; Silverman et al., 2008). There is also a general consensus that cognitive behavioral therapy (CBT) interventions are more effective than non-CBT approaches; trauma-focused cognitive behavioral therapy (TF-CBT) appears to have the most promise (Chipalo, 2021), although more research is needed. Although children show a wide variety of responses to trauma, there appears to be common elements of effective counseling interventions. These common elements include educating youth about the variety of reactions to trauma, providing them with skills to manage anxiety and other emotions, learning to label and process thoughts and emotions associated with trauma, discussing and organizing one's memory of the traumatic event, and problem-solving regarding establishing feeling of safety and identifying relationships that are supportive.

Emotional processing theory (EPT) asserts that following exposure to trauma, it is normal for persons to have a variety of negative cognitive, emotional, and behavioral experiences, including anxiety, hyperarousal, intrusive memories, and nightmares/flashbacks, feelings of guilt and hopelessness, and avoidance behavior (Foa et al., 2007). Usually, these responses decrease gradually as the person processes the trauma and returns to a normal routine, which facilitates a healthy sense of self and a view that the world is generally a safe place, thus weakening the link between the trauma and the initial anxiety (Abramowitz et al., 2019). The majority of persons exposed to trauma recover naturally and fairly quickly from trauma. It has been suggested that for persons who experience posttraumatic stress disorder (PTSD), there is a disruption in the natural recovery process. Persons who develop PTSD do not undergo adaptive processing of the trauma; rather, they consistently avoid reminders of trauma, resist thinking about the event, and take excessive precautions to ensure safety in safe situations. Persons who engage in what are referred to as "safety behaviors" begin to develop the belief that the world is very dangerous and that they are incompetent. As a consequence, thoughts, memories, images, and situations or stimuli that are objectively safe yet which are reminders of the trauma activate fear responses. Furthermore, avoidance and safety behaviors are negatively reinforced because they result in a temporary reduction in anxiety. There are several important implications of the emotional processing theory (EPT) perspective for counseling students who have experienced trauma. Students who have experienced trauma must learn that memories and other reminders of the traumatic event, as well as the anxiety, about this event, are safe and tolerable, although uncomfortable. This happens when people challenge their interpretations that the worlds is always dangerous and that they are consistently incompetent.

There are several cognitive behavioral, school-based interventions for trauma that received empirical support. *Group Cognitive Behavioral Intervention for Trauma in Schools* (CBITS) seeks to reduce symptoms of posttraumatic stress, anxiety, and depression, and in ten weekly group (five to eight students) sessions, each covering one class period, students learn about the symptoms of common reactions to trauma, are gradually encouraged to explore their thoughts and feelings regarding the trauma through writing and/or drawing, receive cognitive (e.g., thought stopping) and coping skills training (e.g., relaxation), and have social skills training (Hoover et al., 2018; Jaycox et al., 2009). *Support for Students Exposed to Trauma* (SSET) is an adapted form of CBITS which is designed to be delivered by paraprofessionals and teachers within classroom and small-group settings. The SSET has been shown to decrease students' levels of PTSD and trauma-related anxiety (Jaycox et al., 2009). The SSET manual can be downloaded for free at the following link: www.rand.org/pubs/technical_reports/2009/RAND_TR675.pdf. CBITS, which is available through Sopris West Publishers, and the SSIT included detailed lessons and worksheets that can be easily implemented in schools. Both SSIT and CBITS have been found to be effective with students of diverse economic, religious, and ethnic/cultural backgrounds and non-English-speaking students.

Trauma-Informed Schools

There is a general consensus that school-delivered trauma counseling should occur in an educational system that is trauma-informed. According to the Substance Abuse and Mental Health Services Administration (SAMHSA, 2014), an organization can only be considered trauma-informed when (a) there is a shared appreciation about what trauma is and how it can affect individuals, (b) the organization recognizes signs and symptoms of trauma rather than interpreting behaviors as acts of willful noncompliance, (c) there is an active resistance to retraumatizing via use of punishments, and instead, (d) there is a successful implementation of trauma-informed policies, procedures, and practices. Specifically, teachers and school staff should be trained to prioritize two issues discussed previously: (a) an emphasis on student's perceptions of physical and psychological safety that is accompanied by (b) supportive adult relationships so that students are then positioned to engage in academic and social-emotional development (Howell et al., 2019). Stated more directly, simply ignoring the impact of trauma toward a business-as-usual approach to schooling is not supportive and is indeed detrimental to children (Rumsey & Milsom, 2019).

To address these priorities, Brunzell et al. (2016) provide a brief how-to for school teams to engage in trauma-informed positive education (TIPE). These recommendations include establishing a rhythm to the classroom by making the schedule known in advance but also by asking when children are in need of brain breaks or physical activities breaks. Students and teachers are encouraged to notice their heart rate, worries, or any other patterns that may be disrupting their learning. Yoga is recommended as a response as it provides a brain and physical activity break that is minimally disruptive to the classroom schedule. Second, promoting self-regulation is supported by asking for students to define their emotional experiences, identify the source, and indicate when and how much they experience distress. Third, mindfulness techniques can be used in response to student needs or as a prevention activity. Mindfulness encourages breathing to support feeling of being present and a grounding in the current experience. Finally, the use of de-escalation is supporting the student's own action in response to stress; it is an educational process designed to promote self-advocacy and self-efficacy skills (Brunzell et al. (2016).

Reinbergs and Fefer (2018) provide examples of trauma-informed school interventions that are integrated throughout MTSS supports.

Suicide Intervention

Suicide is the second leading cause of death among those aged 15 to 24 years (Ivey-Stephenson et al., 2020). Over 18.8% of high school students have seriously considered suicide, and over 8.9% of them attempt suicide (Ivey-Stephenson et al., 2020). ASCA's (2018) position statement indicates that SCs must be aware of the signs of suicidal thoughts and prepare students, staff, colleagues, and parents to recognize warning signs of suicidal behavior. Although long-term suicide risk factors include biological, emotional, and environmental components (Erford, 2013), suicidality may be first indicated by imminent warning signs. One long-term study revealed that among persons under 20 who committed suicide, 49% were known to have self-harmed, 60% shared suicidal ideas with others who communicated suicidal ideas online, including the week before

Table 13.1 Examples of multitiered service delivery options to address trauma in schools. Note: This table was adapted from Reinbergs and Fefer (2018).

Tier	Intervention	Practitioner Support
1	Social emotional learning curriculums (Durlak et al., 2011)	Attitudes Related to Trauma-Informed Care (Baker et al., 2016)
	School-wide positive behavioral interventions and supports (Sugai & Horner, 2009)	Child Trauma Toolkit for Educators (NCTSN, 2008)
	Helping traumatized children learn (Cole et al., 2009, 2013)	Secondary Traumatic Stress: A Fact Sheet for Child-Serving Professionals (NCTSN, 2011)
	Psychological First Aid in Schools (Brymer et al., 2012)	Childhood Adversity Narratives (www.canarratives.org) (Putnam et al., 2015)
2	Cognitive behavioral intervention for trauma in schools (Stein et al., 2003)	Consultations from SMH clinicians NCTSN online professional development (https://learn.nctsn.org)
	Bounce Back (Langley et al., 2015)	
	Support for Students Exposed to Trauma (Jaycox et al., 2009)	
	DBT skills groups (Mazza et al., 2016)	
3	Trauma-focused cognitive behavioral therapy (Cohen et al., 2006, 2012)	Professional quality of life (Stamm, 2010) Employee assistance programs Referrals to outside clinicians

they died, and 60% had recently received mental health services (Rodway et al., 2020a). Previous and recent stresses are associated with suicide among youths, including observing domestic violence, bullying, bereavement, and academic pressures. Youth considering suicide may seek access to lethal means, such as pills or weapons (Erford, 2013). Significant changes in mood, recklessness or aggression, withdrawal from relationships, and increased substance abuse are also important warning signs of suicidal intent (Chesin & Stanley, 2013). Suicidal risk is also greater for persons identified with a number of psychological disorders, including depression, bipolar, anxiety eating, trauma-related, and adjustment disorders (Seligman & Reichenberg, 2012). While SCs should seek to identify potential warning signs of suicide, it should be noted that 30% of adolescents who committed suicide demonstrated no history of suicidal ideas or self-harm, and most youth within this group did not display other risk factors for suicide, such as substance abuse, a mental health diagnosis, recent adverse life events, or reception of mental health services (Rodway et al., 2020b).

A requirement within the *ASCA Ethical Standards for School Counselors* (2022) is that SCs use risk assessments, including for suicide, with caution, and develop an intervention plan prior to conducting a risk assessment. Based upon a meta-analytic review of standardized assessments for suicide, Erford et al. (2018) recommend that standardized assessments should be used in conjunction with an interview, mnemonics (e.g., IS PATH WARM, SLAP, NO HOPE), and evaluation of risk factors to provide a comprehensive assessment of a student's lethality. In situations in which the SC believes that a student poses a significant risk for suicide, the SC should contact the school's mental health liaison and request that he or she come to the school to conduct a formal mental health evaluation. Most school districts have an arrangement with a local community mental health agency to conduct such evaluations.

Box 13.3

IS PATH WARM **Suicide Assessment Mnemonic** (Lester et al., 2011)

Suicidal Ideation	Hopelessness
Substance Abuse	Withdrawing
Purposelessness	Anxiety
Anger	Recklessness
Trapped	Mood change

A standardized assessment for assessing suicide in adolescents that is commonly used by SCs is the Columbia-Suicide Severity Rating Scale (C-SSR; Columbia University, 2014). Administrators read the questions of the C-SSR aloud to a student, asking if they have felt this way in their lifetime or in the past month. The first section of the C-SSR assesses if the student has suicidal ideation. If the student exhibits suicidal ideation, the second section of the C-SSR assesses for the severity of the suicidal ideation. The third section assesses if the student has engaged in suicidal behavior in their lifetime or in the past three months and whether these behaviors were disrupted by the student or others. The final section of the C-SSR involves a brief history of suicide attempts, if relevant. This section asks for the date and a professional assessment of the student's most recent suicide attempt, most lethal suicide attempt, and first suicide attempt. The administrator classifies the lethality of the attempts. If the student responds affirmatively to any item on the suicide ideation section, then they are categorized as having suicide ideation. For the intensity of ideation section, students rate their "lifetime most-severe ideation" and "recent most-severe ideation," which yields an intensity score. If the student responds affirmatively to any item on the suicidal behavior section, then they are classified as having suicidal behavior. There is an online training for the C-SSR that provides certification.

Box 13.4

Short-Term Interventions When Assessing Suicidal Intent (Dollarhide & Saginak, 2016)

1. Remain with the student.
2. Ask direct questions to assess the risk.
3. Encourage the student to identify his or her feelings.
4. Focus on the present vs. the past or the future.
5. Express genuine concern for the student.
6. Encourage the student to identify alternatives to suicide without minimizing the student's concerns.
7. Use active listening skills and accept the student's perspectives unconditionally.
8. Implement your school's crisis plan and notify the crisis team in the building.
9. Contact and inform the student's parents/guardians.
10. Refer the student to a mental health agency.

Suicide Prevention

Most states require high schools to educate all students about suicide and/or provide suicide prevention training to school staff (American Foundation for Suicide Prevention, 2017). School-based suicide prevention programs usually involve one or more of the following three components: screening for early identification of students' suicide risk, gatekeeper training for school staff, or curriculum-based education for students (Singer et al., 2019). Question, Persuade, Refer (QPR; Quinnett, 2013), the most widely used school-based gatekeeper training program, trains teachers and peers to identify warning signs of suicide, provide support to suicidal individuals, and refer suicidal individuals for professional help. A systematic review revealed that QPR programming increases school staff's confidence in dealing with students' suicide-related behaviors but did lead to gatekeepers becoming more active in asking students about suicidal behaviors (Robinson et al., 2013). Signs of Suicide (SOS) is probably the most widely used curriculum-based suicide prevention program, and it also has a student screening component. SOS educates students on the warning signs of suicide, portrays depression as a treatable condition, and encourages students to seek help for themselves and their peers (Schilling et al., 2016). The curricula includes filmed vignettes that model relevant responses to suicidal individuals, testimonials by individuals impacted by suicide, and guided class discussion. Research has revealed that SOS is associated with increased student knowledge and attitudes about suicide and decreased suicide attempts.

Suicide Prevention and Lesbian, Gay, Bisexual, Transgender, and Questioning (LGBTQ) Students

LGBT youth are between two and seven times for more likely than straight youth to attempt suicide (Lytle et al., 2018). Although there are no studies regarding the effectiveness of suicide prevention programs that are specifically designed for LGBTQ youth, LGBTQ students in schools with a gay-straight alliance (GSA) have fewer suicide attempts than those in schools without GSAs, and GSAs have also been found to be associated with less truancy, substance use, and sex with casual partners (Poteat et al., 2013). GSAs are based on a youth empowerment model in which youth assume leadership roles, with adult support, to engage in collaborative efforts to increase school safety and address inequality in schools. They also offer youth peer support to deal with homophobic victimization and parental rejection and opportunities to socialize. ASCA's (2016) position statement regarding LGBTQ youth encourages SCs to advocate for the creation of safe spaces for LGBTQ students, such as GSAs. The Gay, Lesbian & Straight Education Network (GLSEN) provides a free guide for establishing a GSA on their website.

Suicide Postvention

The crisis response and recovery activities detailed earlier are applicable to various types of crises, but it is important to note the response and recovery activities that are implemented should be adapted to the specific form of crisis. Suicide by a student may require modification of the crisis response and recovery, and efforts to decrease the likelihood of subsequent suicide attempts by students have been termed suicide postvention. The goals of school-based suicide postvention efforts are to (1) provide emotional support to survivors, (2) decrease the likelihood of additional imitation or cluster suicides, and (3) assist the school in returning to normal routines (Fineran, 2012). In the following section, we provide a synopsis of Fineran's (2012) review of the literature regarding aspects of crisis response and recovery efforts that are specific to crisis response and recovery regarding a student suicide.

After a Student Dies by Suicide

A meeting before the school with all personnel may be indicated to inform the staff of the incident, provide basic facts while remaining sensitive to the family's privacy, and announce any changes to the school's schedule (Fineran, 2012). School personnel should address the death directly and honestly with students, as ignoring may minimize students' distress. Students should be informed of the death in simultaneous small-group settings rather than making a school-wide announcement. Parents should be notified in a written letter or individual phone calls. An SC should contact the parents/guardians of the deceased child to determine their preferences for disclosure, obtain information on funeral arrangements, inform them of the school's postvention response, identify siblings and friends who may be in need of more intense assistance, and offer support, including references for mental health agencies and survivor support groups. SCs should develop a plan to include SCs from other buildings and external mental health professionals in order to sufficiently staff crisis centers (Fineran, 2012). SCs may need to intentionally pursue students who may be particularly affected by the suicide, given that many students are reluctant to ask for assistance.

SCs should conduct small postvention groups for students who may be potentially at risk following a student's suicide. SCs may find that following the initial shock and denial regarding the student's suicide, students may experience a wide variety of responses, including significant guilt, anger, and cognitive distortions (Fineran, 2012). SCs can emphasize that there is no particularly right way to feeling following a suicide. Survivors should be encouraged to identify and express feelings, learn to distinguish between less-effective and effective coping mechanisms, including how students can obtain assistance from their support network. The leader should encourage students not to focus on the specific student suicide and should discuss suicide in general. Also, students should be encouraged to focus on their memories of the life of the deceased student, as opposed to dwelling on the circumstances surrounding his or her death.

SCs may also consider conducting classroom lessons, particularly if a large segment of the student population appears to be affected by a student's suicide. Research suggests that a suicide curriculum should consist of at least three classes of 40–45 minutes or a semester-long class, as these formats have been shown to decrease suicidal ideation, depression, and hopelessness (Kalafat & Elias, 1994). In contrast, one lesson for suicide prevention has been found to be ineffective (e.g., Kalafat, 2003). The curriculum should focus on protective factors, including social competence, problem-solving, coping strategies, social support, and decision-making, as this type of curriculum has been found to decrease suicidal thoughts and plans (e.g., Evans et al., 1996). In addition, Capuzzi (2009) recommends that students be provided with a realistic understanding of suicide, including the impact upon family and friends, the ability to recognize symptoms in themselves and friends, knowledge of school and community resources, and learning about the myths about suicide. The stress model, which implies that suicide is a normal response to stress, should be avoided as it has been found to be potentially harmful as it appears to "normalize" suicide (e.g., Hayden & Lauer, 2000). Also, media portrayals should be avoided as they appear to glamorize suicide (Kalafat, 2003).

Special Considerations in Suicide Postvention

Memorials

There is disagreement among experts regarding how to honor the deceased student (Fineran, 2012). In general, it is recommended that schools avoid memorial services or shrines within the school as this may encourage students' suicidal ideation. More appropriate memorial activities include a small tribute, such as a yearbook photo, suicide prevention fundraiser, a moment of silence, or creating a memorial scholarship fund.

Media

Only the deceased student's school activities and facts about the suicide should be reported, and speculation about the student's motivation for committing suicide should be avoided (Fineran, 2012). All statements to the media should be approved by the family of the student. To avoid imitation suicides, the method or location of the suicide should not be revealed. The media should be encouraged to emphasize the impact of suicide and provide the contact information of local mental health agencies for those in need.

Ongoing Care

Generally, it is recommended that schools return to the routine schedule as soon as possible, while recognizing that students may take months to years to recover. Attention should be paid to students' emotional status, particularly students who were close to the deceased, have mental health issues, have attempted suicide, or those who are identified by parents and staff. Staff and parents can be encouraged to watch for students who appear disoriented, confused, impatient, sad, inattentive, or disruptive. SCs can monitor attendance patterns and changes in social and academic behavior. It is recommended that close monitoring of students' reactions should be six months following a suicide, and less-intense monitoring should be conducted for one to two years thereafter. Monitoring may include checking in with particularly at-risk students, soliciting the perspectives of staff and parents, and conducting school-wide depression and suicide screenings.

Summary

Being prepared is essential for adequately serving students and in reducing the district's legal risk. If there is a failure to make a good-faith effort to create safe schools, especially if the risk was obvious and foreseeable (Taylor, 2001), the school district may be vulnerable to a lawsuit for negligence (US Department of Education, Office of Safe and Drug-Free Schools, 2007). As such, the call to action regarding crisis preparedness continues. SCs have the training and skill set to significantly contribute to crisis efforts and should seek to assume a formal role and leadership position in preventing and responding to crises, including suicide intervention, and in supporting the development of trauma-informed educational approaches.

References

Abramowitz, J. S., Deacon, B. J., & Whiteside, S. P. H. (2019). *Exposure therapy for anxiety: Principles and practice* (2nd ed.). Guilford Press.

280 Crisis Management and Trauma Informed Practice

American Foundation for Suicide Prevention. (2017). *State laws: Suicide prevention in schools (k-12)*. Author. https://afsp/org/wp-content/uploads/2016/04/Suicide-Prevention-in-Schools-Issue-Brief-1.pdf

American School Counselor Association. (2016). *The school counselor and LGBTQ youth*. Author. www.schoolcounselor.org/asca/media/asca/PositionStatements/PS_LGBTQ.pdf

American School Counselor Association. (2018). *The school counselor and suicide prevention/awareness*. Author.

American School Counselor Association. (2019a). *ASCA standards for school counselor preparation programs*. Author. www.schoolcounselor.org/getmedia/573d7c2c-1622-4d25-a5ac-ac74d2e614ca/ASCA-Standards-for-School-Counselor-Preparation-Programs.pdf

American School Counselor Association. (2019b). *The school counselor and safe schools and crisis response*. Author. www.schoolcounselor.org/asca/media/asca/PositionStatements/PS_SafeSchools.pdf

Baker, C. N., Brown, S. M., Wilcox, P. D., Overstreet, S., & Arora, P. (2016). Development and psychometric evaluation of the Attitudes Related to Trauma-Informed Care (ARTIC) scale. *School Mental Health, 8*(1), 61–76. https://doi.org/10.1007/s12310-015-9161-0

Brock, S. E. (2011). *Crisis intervention and recovery: The roles of school-based mental health professionals* (2nd ed.). National Association of School Psychologists: Primary Author.

Brock, S. E., Nickerson, A. B., Reeves, M. A., Jimerson, S. R., Lieberman, R. A, & Feinberg, T. A. (2009). *School crisis prevention & intervention: The PREPaRE model*. National Association of School Psychologists.

Brunzell, T., Stokes, H., & Waters, L. (2016). Trauma-informed flexible learning: Classrooms that strengthen regulatory abilities. *International Journal of Child, Youth and Family Studies, 7*(2), 218–239. https://doi.org/10.18357/ijcyfs72201615719

Brymer, M., Taylor, M., Escudero, P., Kronenberg, M., Macy, R., Mock, L., Payne, L., Pynoos, R., & Vogel, J. (2012). *Psychological first aid for schools: Field operations guide* (2nd ed). National Child Traumatic Stress Network.

California Department of Corrections and Rehabilitation. (n.d.). *Normal post incident stress symptoms and how to cope with them*. www.cdcr.ca.gov/victim_services/docs/normal_post_incident_stress_symptoms.pdf

Capuzzi, D. (2009). *Suicide prevention in the schools: Guidelines for middle and high school settings* (2nd ed.). American Counseling Association.

Carney, J. V., Kim, I., Bright, D., & Hazler, R. J. (2020). Peer victimization and loneliness: The moderating role of school connectedness by gender. *Journal of School Counseling, 18*(8). https://files.eric.ed.gov/fulltext/EJ1247300.pdf

Catalano, R. F., Oesterle, S., Fleming, C. B., & Hawkins, J. D. (2004). The importance of bonding to school for healthy development: Findings from the Social Development Research Group. *Journal of School Health, 74*, 252–261.

Chesin, M., & Stanley, B. (2013). Risk assessment and psychosocial interventions for suicidal patients. *Bipolar Disorders, 15*(5), 584–593. https://doi.org/10.1111/bdi.12092

Chipalo, E. (2021). Is trauma focused-cognitive behavioral therapy (TF-CBT) effective in reducing trauma symptoms among traumatized refugee children? A systematic review. *Journal of Child Adolescent Trauma, 14*, 545–558. https://doi.org/10.1007/s40653-021-00370-0

Cohen, J. A., Mannarino, A. P., & Deblinger, E. (2006). *Treating trauma and traumatic grief in children and adolescents*. Guilford.

Cohen, J. A., Mannarino, A. P., & Deblinger, E. (Eds.). (2012). *Trauma-focused CBT for children and adolescents: Treatment applications*. Guilford.

Cole, S. F., Eisner, A., Gregory, M., & Ristuccia, J. (2013). *Helping traumatized children learn: Creating and advocating for trauma sensitive schools* (Vol. 2). Massachusetts Advocates for Children. www.unitedforyouth.org/resources/helping-traumatized-children-learn-creating-and-advocating-for-trauma-sensitive-schools

Cole, S. F., O'Brien, J. G., Gadd, M. G., Ristuccia, J., Wallace, D. L., & Gregory, M. (2009). *Helping traumatized children learn: Supportive school environments for children traumatized by family violence* (Vol. 1). Massachusetts Advocates for Children. www.acesdv.org/wp-content/uploads/2014/06/Helping-Traumaitized-Children-Learn.pdf

Columbia University. (2014). *Understanding the C-SSRS*. Author. http://cssrs.columbia.edu/

Cornell, D., & Sheras, P. (2006). *Guidelines for responding to student threats of violence*. Sopris West.

Council for the Accreditation of Counseling and Related Educational Programs. (n.d.). *2016 CACREP standards*. https://www.cacrep.org/for-programs/2016-cacrep-standards/

Cowan, K. C., Vaillancourt, K., Rossen, E., & Pollitt, K. (2013). *A framework for safe and successful schools* [Brief]. National Association of School Psychologists.

Crepeau-Hobson, F., Sievering, K. S., Armstrong, C., & Stonis, J. (2012). A coordinated mental health crisis response: Lessons learned from three Colorado school shootings. *Journal of School Violence, 11*(3), 207–225. https://doi.org/10.1080/15388220.2012.682002

Dollarhide, C. T., & Saginak, K. A. (2016). *Comprehensive school counseling programs: K-12 delivery systems in action* (3rd ed.). Pearson.

Durlak, J. A., Weissberg, R. P., Dymnicki, A. B., Taylor, R. D., & Schellinger, K. B. (2011). The impact of enhancing students' social and emotional learning: A meta-analysis of school-based interventions. *Child Development, 82*(1), 405–432. https://doi.org/10.1111/j.1467-8624.2010.01564.x

Erford, B. T. (2013). *Assessment for counselors* (2nd ed.). Cengage Wadsworth.

Erford, B. T., Jackson, J., Bardhoshi, G., Duncan, K., & Atalay, Z. (2018). Selecting suicide ideation assessment instruments: A meta-analytic review. *Measurement and Evaluation in Counseling and Development, 51*(1), 42–59. https://doi.org/10.1080/07481756.2017.1358062

Evans, W., Smith, M., Hill, G., Albers, E., & Neufeld, J. (1996). Rural adolescent views of risk and protective factors associated with suicide. *Crisis Intervention, 3*, 1–12.

Fein, A. H. (2003). *There and back again: School shootings as experienced by school leaders*. Scarecrow Education.

Fein, A. H., Carlisle, C. S., & Isaacson, N. S. (2008). School shootings and counselor leadership: Four lessons from the field. *Professional School Counseling, 11*(4), 246–252. https://doi.org/10.1177/2156759X0801100405

Fineran, K. R. (2012). Suicide postvention in schools: The role of the school counselor. *Journal of Professional Counseling: Practice, Theory, and Research, 39*(2), 14–28. https://doi.org/10.1080/15566382.2012.12033884

Foa, E. B., Hembree, E., & Rothbaum, B. O. (2007). *Prolonged exposure therapy for PTSD: Emotional processing of traumatic experiences*. Oxford University Press.

Hayden, D. C., & Lauer, P. (2000). Prevalence of suicide programs in schools and roadblocks to implementation. *Suicide and Life-Threatening Behavior, 30*(3), 239–251. https://doi.org/10.1111/j.1943-278X.2000.tb00989.x

Heath, M. A., Sheen, D., Annandale, N., & Lyman, B. (2005). Responding to a crisis. In M. A. Heath & D. Sheen (Eds.), *School-based crisis intervention: Preparing all personnel to assist* (pp. 23–43). Guilford Press.

Hoover, S. A., Sapere, H., Lang, J. M., Nadeem, E., Dean, K. L., & Vona, P. (2018). Statewide implementation of an evidence-based trauma intervention in schools. *School Psychology Quarterly, 33*(1), 44–53. https://doi.org/10.1037/spq0000248

Howell, P. B., Thomas, S., Sweeney, D., & Vanderhaar, J. (2019). Moving beyond schedules, testing and other duties as deemed necessary by the principal: The school counselor's role in trauma informed practices. *Middle School Journal, 50*(4), 26–34. https://doi.org/10.1080/00940771.2019.1650548

Ivey-Stephenson, A. Z., Demissie, Z., Crosby, A. E., Stone, D., Gaylor, E., Wilkins, N., Lowry, R., & Brown, M. (2020). Suicidal ideation and behaviors among high school students: Your risk behavior survey, United States. *MMWR Suppl, 69*(Suppl-1), 47–55. https://doi.org/10.15585/mmwr.su6901a6externalicon

Jaycox, L. H., Langley, A. K., Stein, B. D., Wong, M., Sharma, P., Scott, M., & Schonlau, M. (2009). Support for students exposed to trauma: A pilot study. *School Mental Health, 1*(2), 49–60. https://doi.org/10.1007/s12310-009-9007-8

Kalafat, J. (2003). School approaches to youth suicide prevention. *American Behavioral Scientist, 46*(9), 1211–1223. https://doi.org/10.1177/0002764202250665

Kalafat, J., & Elias, M. (1994). An evaluation of school-based suicide awareness intervention. *Suicide and Life Threatening Behavior, 24*(3), 224–233. https://doi.org/10.1111/j.1943-278X.1994.tb00747.x

Langley, A. K., Gonzalez, A., Sugar, C. A., Solis, D., & Jaycox, L. (2015). BounceBack: Effectiveness of an elementary school-based intervention for multicultural children exposed to traumatic events. *Journal of Consulting and Clinical Psychology*, 83(5), 853–865. https://doi.org/10.1037/ccp0000051

Lester, D. L., McSwain, S., & Gunn III, J. F. (2011). A test of the validity of the *is path warm* signs for suicide. *Psychological Reports*, 108(2). https://doi.org/10.2466/09.12.13.PR0.108.2.402-404

Lytle, M. C., Silenzio, V. M. B., Homan, C. M., Schneider, P., & Caine, E. D. (2018). Suicidal and help-seeking behaviors among youth in an online lesbian, gay, bisexual, transgender, queer, and questioning social network. *Journal of Homosexuality*, 65(13), 1916–1933. https://doi.org/10.1080/00918369.2017.1391552

Mazza, J. J., Dexter-Mazza, E. T., Miller, A. L., Rathus, J. H., & Murphy, H. E. (2016). *DBT skills in schools: Skills training for emotional problem solving for adolescents (DBT STEPS-A)*. Guilford.

National Association of School Psychologists. (2007). Talking to children about violence: Information for parents and educators. *Crisis and School Safety*. www.nasponline.org/resources/handouts/revisedpdfs/talkingviolence.pdf

National Child Traumatic Stress Network (NCTSN). (2008). *Child trauma toolkit for educators*. Author. www.nctsn.org/resources/child-trauma-toolkit-educators

National Child Traumatic Stress Network (NCTSN). (2011). *Secondary traumatic stress: A fact sheet for child-serving professionals*. Author. www.nctsn.org/resources/secondary-traumatic-stress-fact-sheet-child-serving-professionals

National Education Association: Health Information Network. (n.d.). *School crisis guide: Help and healing in a time of crisis*. Author. http://crisisresponse.promoteprevent.org/resources/school-crisis-guide-helping-and-healing-time-crisis

National Registry of Evidence-Based Programs and Practices. (2013). *Virginia student threat assessment guidelines*. www.nrepp.samhsa.gov/ViewIntervention.aspx?id=263

Nickerson, A. B., Randa, R., Jimerson, S., & Guerra, N. G. (2021). Safe places to learn: Advances in school safety research and practice. *School Psychology Review*, 50(2–3), 158–171. https://doi.org/10.1080/2372966X.2021.1871948

No Child Left Behind (NCLB) Act of 2001, Pub. L. No. 107–110, § 115, Stat 4114.

Olinger Steeves, R. M., Metallo, S. A., Byrd, S. M., Erickson, M. R., & Gresham, F. M. (2017). Crisis preparedness in schools: Evaluating staff perspectives and providing recommendations for best practice. *Psychology in the Schools*, 54(6), 563–580. https://doi.org/10.1002/pits.22017

Poteat, V. P., Sinclair, K. O., DiGiovanni, C. D., Koenig, B. W., & Russell, S. T. (2013). Gay-straight alliances are associated with student health: A multischool comparison of LGBTQ and heterosexual youth. *Journal of Research on Adolescence*, 23(2), 319–330. https://doi.org/10.1111/j.1532-7795.2012.00832.x

Putnam, F., Harris, W., Lieberman, A., Putnam, K., & Amaya-Jackson, L. (2015). *Opportunities to change the outcomes of traumatized children: Childhood Adversity Narratives (CAN)*. www.canarratives.org

Quinnett, P. (2013). *QPR gatekeeping training for suicide prevention: The model, rationale, and theory*. Centre for Suicide Prevention.

Racco, A., & Vis, J. A. (2015). Evidence based trauma treatment for children and youth. *Child & Adolescent Social Work Journal*, 32(2), 121–129. https://doi.org/10.1007/s10560-014-0347-3

Reeves, M. A. L., & Brock, S. E. (2018). School behavioral threat assessment and management. *Contemporary School Psychology*, 22(2), 148–162. https://doi.org/10.1007/s40688-017-0158-6

Reeves, M. A. L., Conolly-Wilson, C., Pesce, R., Lazzaro, B., & Brock, S. (2012). Preparing for the comprehensive school crisis response. In S. Brock & S. Jimerson (Eds.), *Best practices in school crisis prevention and intervention* (2nd ed.). National Association of School Psychologists.

Reeves, M. A. L., Nickerson, A. B., Connolly-Wilson, C. N., Susan, M. K., Lazzaro, B. R., Jimerson, S. R., & Pesce, R. C. (2011). *PREPaRE workshop 1: Crisis prevention and preparedness: Comprehensive school safety planning* (2nd ed.). National Association of School Psychologists. https://apps.nasponline.org/professional-development/convention/session-detail.aspx?id=23594

Reinbergs, E. J., & Fefer, S. A. (2018). Addressing trauma in schools: Multitiered service delivery options for practitioners. *Psychology in the Schools*, *55*(3), 250–263. https://doi.org/10.1002/pits.22105

Robers, S., Kemp, J., & Truman, J. (2013). *Indicators of school crime and safety: 2012* (NCES 2013–036/NCJ 241446). National Center for Education Statistics, US Department of Education, and Bureau of Justice Statistics, Office of Justice Programs, US Department of Justice.

Robinson, J., Cox, G., Malone, A., Williamson, M., Baldwin, G., Fletcher, K., & O'Brien, M. (2013). A systematic review of school-based interventions aimed at preventing, treating, and responding to suicide-related behavior in young people. *Crisis*, *34*(3), 164–182. https://doi.org/10.1027/0227-5910/a000168

Rodway, C., Tham, S., Ibrahim, S., Turnbull, P., Kapur, N., & Appleby, L. (2020a). Children and young people who die by suicide: Childhood-related antecedents, gender differences, and service contact. *BJ PsychOpen*, *6*(11).

Rodway, C., Tham, S., Turnbull, P., & Kapur, N., & Appleby, L. (2020b). Suicide in children and young people: Can it happen without warning? *Journal of Affective Disorders*, *275*(1), 307–310. https://doi.org/10.1016/j.jad.2020.06.069

Rumsey, A. D., & Milsom, A. (2019). Supporting school engagement and high school completion through trauma-informed school counseling. *Professional School Counseling*, *22*(1), 1–10. https://doi.org/10.1177/2156759X19867254

Safe and Civil Schools. (n.d.). *Welcome to safe and civil schools*. Author. www.safeandcivilschools.com

Schilling, E. A., Aseltine, R. H., Jr., & James, A. (2016). The SOS suicide prevention program: Further evidence of efficacy and effectiveness. *Prevention Science: The Official Journal of the Society for Prevention Research*, *17*(2). 157–166. https://doi.org/10.1007/s11121-015-0594-3

Seligman, L., & Reichenberg, L. W. (2012). *Theories of counseling and psychotherapy: Systems, strategies and skills* (4th ed.). Prentice-Hall.

Silverman, W. K., Ortiz, C. D., Viswesvaran, C., Burns, B. J., Kolko, D. J., Putnam, F. W., & Amaya-Jackson, L. (2008). Evidence-based psychosocial treatments for children and adolescents exposed to traumatic events. *Journal of Clinical Child & Adolescent Psychology*, *37*(1), 156–183. https://doi.org/10.1080/15374410701818293

Singer, J. B., Erbacher, T. A., & Rosen, P. (2019). School-based suicide prevention: A framework for evidence-based practice. *School Mental Health*, *11*(1), 54–71.

Sorenson, S., Hayes, J. G., & Atlas, R. (2013). Understanding CPTED and situational crimeprevention. In R. Atlas (Ed.), *21st century security and CPTED: Designing for critical infrastructure protection and crime prevention* (pp. 55–78). CRC Press.

Stamm, B. H. (2010). *The concise ProQOL manual*. Proqol.org. https://proqol.org/uploads/ProQOL_Concise_2ndEd_12-2010.pdf

Stein, B. D., Jaycox, L. H., Kataoka, S. H., Wong, M., Tu, W., Elliott, M. N., & Fink, A. (2003). A mental health intervention for schoolchildren exposed to violence: A randomized controlled trial. *JAMA*, *290*(5), 603–611. https://jamanetwork.com/journals/jama/article-abstract/197033

Strong, K., & Cornell, D. (2008). Student threat assessment in Memphis City Schools: A descriptive report. *Behavioral Disorders*, *34*(1), 42–54. https://doi.org/10.1177/019874290803400104

Substance Abuse and Mental Health Services Administration. (2014). *SAMHSA's concept of trauma and guidance for a trauma-informed approach* (SMA14–4884). Author. https://store.samhsa.gov/system/files/sma14-4884.pdf

Sugai, G., & Horner, R. H. (2009). Responsiveness-to-intervention and school-wide positive behavior supports: Integration of multitiered systems approaches. *Exceptionality*, *17*(4), 223–237. https://doi.org/10.1080/09362830903235375

Taylor, K. R. (September, 2001). Student suicide: Could you be held liable? *Principal Leadership*, *2*(1), 74–78. www.nassp.org/portals/0/content/48901.pdf

Tillery, A. D., Varjas, K., Roach, A. T., Kuperminc, G. P., & Meyers, J. (2013). The importance of adult connections in adolescents' sense of school belonging: Implications for schools and practitioners. *Journal of School Violence*, *12*(2), 134–155. https://doi.org/10.1080/15388220.2012.762518

US Department of Education. (2013). *Guide for developing high-quality school emergency operations plans*. Author. www.fema.gov/sites/default/files/2020-07/guide-developing-school-emergency-operations-plans.pdf

US Department of Education. (n.d.). *Every student succeeds act (ESSA)*. Author. www.ed.gov/essa?src%3Drn

US Department of Education, Office of Safe and Drug-Free Schools. (2007). *Practical information on crisis planning: A guide for schools and communities*. Author.

US Department of Homeland Security. (2013). *K-12 school security checklist*. Author. https://cdpsdocs.state.co.us/safeschools/Resources/DHS%20Department%20of%20Homeland%20Security/DHS%20K-12%20School%20Security%20Practices%20Checklist.pdf

The White House. (2013). *Now is the time: The President's plan to protect our children and our communities by reducing gun violence*. Author. www.whitehouse.gov/sites/default/files/docs/wh_now_is_the_time_full.pdf

Chapter 14

Legal and Ethical Concerns in School Counseling

Box 14.1 2016 Council for the Accreditation of Counseling and Related Educational Programs (CACREP, n.d.) School Counseling Specialty Area Standards

2.b School counselor roles in consultation with families, P–12 and postsecondary school personnel, and community agencies

2.g Characteristics, risk factors, and warning signs of students at risk for mental and behavioral disorders

2.n. Legal and ethical considerations specific to school counseling

---

Box 14.2 ASCA (2019a) Standards for School Counselor Preparation Programs (ASCA CAEP SPA)

7.1 Engage in professional behavior that reflects ASCA Ethical Standards for School Counselors and relevant federal and state laws and district policies.

7.2 Describe the impact of federal and state laws and regulations, as well as district policies, on schools, students, families, and school counseling practice.

7.3 Seek consultation and supervision to support ongoing critical reflection in an effort to identify cultural blind spots and prevent ethical lapses.

What do I do if my principal wants me to disclose what I hear during a counseling session? If a parent asks, do I have to tell him or her what his or her child said to me? What and how do I keep my records confidential? When do I call a parent about a child who is cutting?

Unfortunately, there are seldom clear answers to the questions in the preceding paragraph, as the correct response will often depend upon the specifics of the situation. Furthermore, ambiguity in discerning the right answer may be heightened because of the presence of competing principles. For example, the first question regarding the principal's request for disclosure of information provided by a student in a counseling session may involve the maintenance of the school's safety versus the student's right to privacy. The difficulties encountered in ethical decision-making are often referred as "ethical dilemmas."

In order to answer the questions presented in the first paragraph, SCs must be familiar with a variety of sources pertaining to the practice of school counseling. The primary sources that

DOI: 10.4324/9781003167730-14

influence the ethical practice of school counseling include ethical standards, federal and state laws and regulations, case law, and school district policies. In this chapter, we will focus upon what we consider to be the foundational aspects of the *ASCA Ethical Standards for School Counselors* (2022) and discuss laws and regulations associated with these standards. The *ASCA Ethical Standards* (2022) can be downloaded from the ASCA website.

Box 14.3

The primary sources that influence ethical practice include:

- Ethical standards
- Federal and state laws and regulations
- Case law
- School district policies

Negligence and Malpractice

Professionals as a whole seek to practice ethically and in a manner consistent with the law as it benefits consumers and promotes the profession as a whole. Furthermore, SCs want to practice in an ethical manner because they can be found civilly liable if they fail to exercise "due care" in meeting their professional responsibilities (Stone, 2017). While SCs are rarely sued, and in most states employees are protected from personal liability as long as they are not acting in a willful or wanton manner (Euben, 2003), it is important that SCs understand how to decrease the likelihood of being sued.

SCs can be found to be negligent if they "owed a duty," or in other words, failed to act and their failure results in an injury or damage. An example of negligence would be an SC who did not report suspicions of child abuse (Linde, 2007). Most courts have ruled that SCs did not owe a duty to provide accurate academic advice, prevent suicide, or inform parents when their child is considering abortion (Stone, 2017).

SCs are more likely to be accused of malpractice than negligence. *Malpractice* is defined as "professional misconduct or any unreasonable lack of skill in the performance of professional duties" (Lovett, as cited in Hopkins & Anderson, 1990, p. 48). A finding of malpractice requires that a student experienced harm as a result of the SC's lack of skill or appropriate behavior (Linde, 2007). An example of malpractice would be if an SC used what some may consider an invasive counseling technique or theory, such as hypnosis or eye movement desensitization reprocessing (EMDR), when the SC had not received the necessary training for the approach.

Box 14.4

Negligence—failing to act when a student or client is "owed a duty" (a.k.a. failing to act).

Malpractice—professional misconduct or any unreasonable lack of skill in the performance of professional duty (a.k.a. acting in a manner inconsistent with your training).

The standard of practice is used in any court proceeding to determine if the SC's conduct was within accepted practice (Stone, 2017). Often, the testimony of a witness who is considered to be an expert within the profession is used to determine whether or not the professional met the acceptable standard of care. Other sources used by the courts to determine the appropriate standard of care include the SC's involvement and adherence to the requirements of credentialing bodies, the ethical standards of the respective professional organizations, involvement in continuing education, and school board policies. SCs are most likely to experience legal troubles for failing to follow or violating school board policies (Linde, 2007). This highlights the importance for SCs to know the communities they serve. For example, an SC who worked in a district in which there was a large percentage of Latino or Asian American families should understand that encouraging students to follow their career aspirations regardless of their family expectations might conflict with the more communal worldview of the students and their families.

The first thing an SC should do if confronted with a legal action is to contact a lawyer and then inform his or her supervisor (Linde, 2007). The SC should not attempt to resolve the conflict with the student, the student's parents, or the family's lawyer without the advice of a lawyer. Also, the SC should not discuss the case with anyone other than his or her lawyer or supervisor.

Laws, Regulations, and District Policies

As mentioned previously, in addition to ethical standards, SCs must also understand laws, regulations, and school district policies when engaging in ethical decision-making. As we review some of the more important *ASCA Ethical Standards for School Counselors*, we will refer to these other sources that influence the practice of school counseling when pertinent. First, we will provide an overview of these legal sources.

The common law tradition of the US involves the continual emergence of new legislation. Laws that are created by government agencies, such as state departments of education, which are created by state and national legislatures, are referred to as regulatory law (see Figure 14.1).

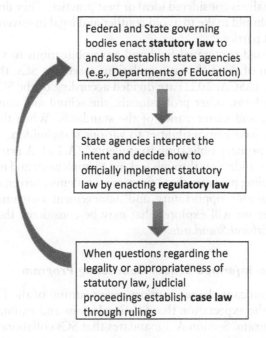

Federal and State governing bodies enact **statutory law** to and also establish state agencies (e.g., Departments of Education)

State agencies interpret the intent and decide how to officially implement statutory law by enacting **regulatory law**

When questions regarding the legality or appropriateness of statutory law, judicial proceedings establish **case law** through rulings

Figure 14.1 Relationship between statutory, regulatory, and case law.

national legislatures to develop what is referred to as regulatory law in order to implement the intent of legal statutes. Case law represents rulings from judicial proceedings that interpret either the legality or intent of statutory laws.

Local school board policies and regulations tend to have more influence than laws upon the day-to-day practice of SCs. For example, school districts may adopt policies regarding the role of SCs, such as if parents should be notified if their child is receiving individual or group counseling, etc. Whereas in larger school districts, they are more likely to have an identified director specifically for the school counseling program and official policies and procedures governing SCs, it is not uncommon for smaller districts to lack policies specific to SCs. Also, in smaller school districts, while administrators may assert that the ethical policies and procedures governing teachers are the same for school counselors, this not necessarily the case. Most SCs adhere to the ethical codes of professional counseling organizations and not professional organizations associated with teaching.

School districts, also, cannot implement policies and procedures that are inconsistent with state laws and regulations (Schmidt, 2013). For example, if a state statute designates communications between a student and their SC to be of a privileged nature (an issue we will discuss later in this chapter), then school districts cannot deny privileged communication status. It is not uncommon for districts and/or administrators to want SCs to engage in practices that may conflict with state laws or ethical standards. School officials may not be aware of regulations specific to school counseling, and thus, SCs must be knowledgeable about the laws, regulations, and ethics that govern the profession and seek to resolve potential conflicts, which usually involves first speaking with an administrator or the supervisor of the school counseling program.

Ethical Standards for School Counselors (ASCA, 2022)

Most SCs abide by the *ASCA Ethical Standards for School Counselors* (2022). The *Ethical Standards for School Counselors*, like most ethical standards, are aspirational in nature, identifying what generally is considered ideal or best practice. They do not always indicate the clear choices SCs should make to avoid conflict and legal involvement and address the needs for the involved parties.

SCs operate in a broad contextual field and have obligations to various stakeholders. Possibly in recognition of the different populations served by SCs, the *Ethical Standards for School Counselors* (ASCA, 2022) are divided according to the SC's responsibilities to students, parents/guardians, other professionals, the school and community, the school counseling profession, and maintenance of the standards. While the *Ethical Standards* acknowledge that SCs have responsibilities to various stakeholders, the standards recognize that SCs "have a primary obligation to students" (A.1.a). A primary way which SCs fulfill this obligation to students is through seeking to implement and maintain a culturally-sensitive school counseling program that "promotes academic, career, and social/emotional development and equitable opportunity and achievement outcomes for all students" (A.3.a). In this chapter we will explore what may be considered the most foundational aspects of the *ASCA Ethical Standards*.

Comprehensive Data-Informed School Counseling Program

Probably the most significant change to most recent edition of the *Ethical Standards for School Counselors* is the expectation that SCs implement and maintain a comprehensive school counseling program. Section A.3 mandates that SCs collaborate with stakeholders and use data in providing students with a comprehensive school counseling program that promotes students' academic, career, and social/emotional development. Section A.4 requires that SCs contribute to a school environment that supports students' postsecondary readiness and seek to identify and address gaps in college and career access. These sections highlight the profession's desire to define best practice as involving working within a comprehensive school counseling program. In other words, the profession is saying that SCs who do not work within a comprehensive school counseling program are not acting ethically. While it seems that the percentage of SCs who work within a school counseling program has increased during the past decade, the authors of a study published as recently as 2017 estimated that SCs' implementation of the *ASCA National Model* was 70% (Fye et al., 2017).

Social Justice Advocacy

A prominent theme within the *ASCA Ethical Standards* is the mandate that SCs are to be committed to promoting equity through invoking systemic change (B.2.d.). As mentioned previously, SCs are responsible for the provision of a comprehensive school counseling program that ensures equitable development for all students (A.3.b). In order to implement and maintain a comprehensive school counseling program, SCs "advocate for a school counseling program free of non-school-counseling assignments" (B.2.c). SCs identify gaps and college and career access and address both intentional and unintentional biases related to college and career counseling (A.4.c.). The preamble of the Ethical Standards states that all students have the right to "a physically and emotionally safe, inclusive and healthy school environment . . . free from abuse, bullying, harassment, discrimination and any other forms of violence."

Confidentiality

The importance of confidentiality to the school counseling profession is highlighted by the fact that there is a separate section devoted to it within the Responsibility to Students section.

Box 14.5

Confidentiality—each person's right to privacy within a counseling relationship.

Confidentiality is considered the most vital aspect of an SC's relationships with students, and yet it is also one of the most difficult ethical issues to negotiate. *Confidentiality* refers to each person's right to privacy within a counseling relationship. It is based upon the ethical principle that the counseling relationship fosters autonomy by providing a secure environment in which students can explore their thoughts, feelings, actions, and goals to develop the insight essential for improving one's decision-making capabilities. The notion is that if students believed that information that they share within a counseling relationship might be communicated to teachers, administrators, or their parents, they would not engage in free exploration.

Although educators like to believe that every child comes to school ready to learn, unfortunately, there are many issues that interfere with children's realization of their academic potential. Assisting a child in managing personal issues in a confidential setting can enable children to actualize their academic potential. One of the most important roles of an SC, who by their training are expected to be more qualified with social-emotional issues than teachers, is to help children manage personal obstacles that interfere with their learning. The SC's training in promoting social/emotional development is an area of expertise that sets these professionals apart from other education professionals.

When initiating a relationship with a student, SCs are expected to obtain informed consent, meaning, that they communicate to the student the purposes, goals, techniques, and procedures of counseling, and the potential limitations of confidentiality (A.2.b), which are

---

Box 14.6

Informed consent—an individual must be deemed competent (e.g., able to make decisions regarding his or her own well-being) and be made aware of the purposes, goals, techniques, and procedures of counseling, as well as the potential limits to confidentiality, before counselors can ethically begin a therapeutic relationship.

---

explained in greater depth later in this chapter. The legal status of minors is highly ambiguous (Stone, 2017). For example, there is considerable variation between states' regulations in regards to when students can drive, marry, engage in sexual relations, enter contracts, and consent to medical services; 18 is commonly considered the legal age of majority unless otherwise specified in state statutes. Minors generally are not able make decisions on their own behalf. Rather, the Supreme Court has ruled that parents have a legal right to make critical decisions about their children (Isaacs & Stone, 1999), and as a consequence, parents are considered to have a legal right to information shared by their children in counseling sessions. Some courts have also ruled that minors cannot legally enter into counseling without parental consent, because it is considered a contractual relationship (Remley & Herlihy, 2013).

State statutes often can provide SCs with some guidance in making a determination of minor status and a child's capacity for informed consent. In some states, there are statutes identifying the age at which children can consent to mental health services without parental permission. For example, in Pennsylvania, at the age of 14, an individual has the right to enter or decline mental health services. Therefore, it can be implied from this statute that in Pennsylvania, students who are at least 14 years old and do not have any cognitive limitations that might impair their reasoning may give informed consent.

Privileged Communication

Whereas confidentiality is an ethical principle, privileged communication is a legal term, meaning, that communication revealed to a professional is protected from having to be revealed in a court of law. State laws vary considerably in regards to privileged communication. In some states, privilege is granted to clients in counseling relationships (Remley & Herlihy, 2013), while in other states, there are specific statutes that provide privilege to communications between a student and a school counselor. The right of privilege may be waived, meaning, that if granted permission by the student/client, the SC is required to share this information in a court proceeding. States vary in regards to whether the right of privilege belongs to the student or the parent. Stone (2013) found that almost half of SCs were not aware if their state granted privilege. Not knowing this important legality can be considered ethical negligence. Courts typically have ruled that communications beyond two people are not privileged (Schmidt, 2013). Thus, the *Ethical Standards* indicate that SCs explain to students that confidentiality is a group norm but cannot be guaranteed (A.7.h.).

Box 14.7

Privileged communication—a legal (not ethical) term indicating which types of conversations and interactions are not required to be revealed in a court of law.

Limitations to Confidentiality

Parents' Rights and Confidentiality

One of the most important limitations to confidentiality is the recognition enunciated in the *Ethical Standards* of "parents'/guardians' legal and inherent rights to be the guiding voice in their children's lives" (A.2.g). Also, court rulings usually are more likely to recognize parents' legal right to information related to their child's counseling (Herlihy & Corey, 2006). Herein lies the essential dilemma. The profession regards confidentiality as the cornerstone of counseling, and yet this principle is not always recognized by courts. SCs must favor parents' rights over the students' rights when students may be a threat to self or others. Most notably, the *Ethical Standards* state that SCs must "[i]nform parents/guardians and/or appropriate authorities when a student poses a serious and foreseeable risk of harm to self or others. . . . Even if the danger appears relatively remote, parents should be notified" (A.9.a.). The *Ethical Standards* indicate that the "students' developmental and chronological age the setting, parental rights and the nature of the harm" are essential factors when considering violating confidentiality and sharing information with parents (A.2.f.).

Serious and Foreseeable Harm to Self and Others

The terms used within the *Ethical Standards* of "serious and foreseeable harm" are not clearly defined within the *Ethical Standards* or by law. *Foreseeable*, as defined by the American Heritage Dictionary (1985), means "to see or know beforehand." Use of the term "foreseeable" means that the behavior in question is in regards to a future and not a past action. In other words, SCs are generally not required to inform parents and/or authorities of actions that have occurred in the past only inasmuch as they may be indicators of the potential for future harm. For example, as surprising as this may sound, in the absence of state statutes or district policies, an SC may not have to break confidentiality in situations in which a student has committed a violent act, stolen property, or used illicit substances unless that data suggests that the student represents a threat to self or other in the future.

Box 14.8

Foreseeable—implies that school counselors are required to break confidentiality only if there are reasons to suggest that the student will be a danger to self or others in the future.

The term "serious" is also not easily defined. While an SC may be concerned about an adolescent's future use of alcohol or drugs, the adolescent's use must rise to the level of "serious harm" in order to justify a breach of confidentiality. Most likely, a high school student who reports that he or she plans to imbibe alcohol or smoke marijuana during a weekend party does not rise to the level of "serious." However, an adolescent who reports that he or she plans to use cocaine or heroin could constitute a situation involving "serious harm," given the potential for single-use lethality with these drugs. Although a future act may be illegal, such as in the case of underage drinking, using cigarettes, shoplifting, prostitution, etc., if it does not necessarily entail serious harm to self or other, school counselors are not required by law to report a crime that has already been committed (Fischer & Sorenson, 1996).

However, the SC must still consider the degree to which the parent should be involved in a situation in which a child is engaging in an illegal act (Stone, 2017). Stone provides the example of a 16-year-old girl who informs her SC that she has shoplifted on a consistent basis. The SC can help the girl understand the potential ramifications of her behavior and may consider referring the girl to a community agency so that she can develop insight regarding her behavior. While the SC may decide to involve the girl's parents in the counseling process, the SC does not necessarily need to reveal that the girl admitted to shoplifting. The best course of action is for the SC to encourage the girl to voluntarily involve her parents in the counseling process, and the SC can offer to meet with the girl and her parents to explore the issue together.

Remley and Herlihy (2013) assert that the most effective way for SCs to justify their ethical decision-making is to act in accordance with the way a reasonable counselor would act in a similar situation. Thus, it can be helpful to know how SCs reason about violating confidentiality when confronted with risk-taking behaviors among students. A national survey found that SCs report being more likely to breach confidentiality when behaviors are more intense (e.g., ranging from a small to large amount of alcohol use) and of greater frequency/duration (e.g., ranging from once several months ago to monthly for several months) (Moyer & Sullivan, 2008). There is considerable agreement among SCs, however, that it is ethical to violate confidentiality when students are engaging in suicidal behaviors, even at the lowest levels of frequency/duration and intensity. SCs were also likely to favor breaching confidentiality for behaviors involving self-mutilation, substance use, and antisocial acts, but the level of agreement for these acts did not reach the level of consistency demonstrated by SCs when asked about reporting students' suicidal behaviors. For sexual behaviors and alcohol use, SCs generally only recommended breaching confidentiality for higher levels of frequency and intensity and were very unlikely to favor breaking confidentiality for any level of smoking.

Many SCs tend to side in favor of parents' rights when assessing a child's risk potential, and this tendency would most likely be supported by many school administrators and courts. However, SCs should remember that the *Ethical Standards* emphasize a student's right to privacy and confidentiality. SCs are urged to remember that they have a special role in helping students. The role of the SC is somewhat different from that of teachers and administrators, who are expected to uphold and maintain school rules and student codes of conduct. The specialized training of SCs provides them with the skills to help students address social/emotional issues that contribute to a student's engagement in self-destructive behaviors and interpersonal violence. In other words, SCs can help some students learn to meet their needs in more effective, socially acceptable ways. If students believe that the SC would breach confidentiality for any sensitive topic, students are likely to cease sharing information that could be vital to the counseling process. The importance of maintaining confidentiality is further supported by the fact that the *Ethical Standards* recommend that SCs consult with appropriate professionals when considering a breach of confidentiality (A.2.h.).

Suicide

The courts have yielded contradictory rulings regarding SC's responsibility in breaching confidentiality in regards to a student's suicidal threats (Stone, 2017). In the case of *Eisel v. Montgomery County Board of Education* (1991), the Maryland Court of Appeals ruled that SCs had a duty to notify the parents of a 13-year-old student named Nicole Eisel, who informed peers that she intended to kill herself. Several of Nicole's friends informed their SC about Nicole's suicidal threats, and their SC informed Nicole's SC. The two SCs questioned Nicole, but she denied making any such threats. The SCs did not inform Nicole's parents or the administrators about the suicidal statements. Soon after, Nicole and a friend committed suicide.

The Maryland Court of Appeals cited the in loco parentis doctrine, which states that educators legally serve in the role of parents. Furthermore, the court ruled that SCs have a special duty to engage in reasonable care to protect a student from harm, defining *reasonable care* to include attempting to prevent a suicide when informed of a student's suicidal intent. Thus, in Maryland, SCs must warn both a parent and administrator of suicidal threats made by a student to an SC. This includes even indirect threats, such as rumors that a student has threatened suicide, regardless of the perceived seriousness of the threat. Since the Eisel ruling, courts in some states have ruled that SCs are liable for failing to notify parents of a student who has written or talked to other about killing themselves, whereas other state courts have yielded opposite rulings (Stone, 2017).

ASCA's (2020) position statement indicates that SCs should inform parents/guardians of any indication/signs of suicidal ideation, unless "the parent/guardian's abuse or neglect is the expressed reason for the student's suicidal ideation." Furthermore, SCs are encouraged to support the district's development of both a formal policy on suicide prevention and the creation of collaborative teams for responding to students who are at risk for suicide.

Sexual Activity and Abortion

The *ASCA Ethical Standards* require that SCs "avoid imposing personal beliefs rooted in one's religion, culture, or ethnicity" (A.1.h). Sexuality is often related to a student's and his or her families' religion and culture. School boards have the right to adopt policies restricting SCs' discussion of specified topics with students, and some school boards have forbidden SCs from discussing sexual activity and abortion (Stone, 2017). In considering whether to breach confidentiality, SCs must be familiar with their state's laws regarding whether minors may seek contraceptive services and obtain an abortion or prenatal care without parental consent.

Box 14.9

Contraceptive Service: 26 states allow minors (12 and older) to obtain contraceptive services without parental consent, while 20 states permit only certain categories of minors.

Sexually Transmitted Infection (STI) Service: All states permit minors to consent to STI services.

Abortion: The majority of states require parental involvement in a minor's abortion.

Prenatal Care: 32 states permit all minors to consent to prenatal care (Guttmacher Institute, 2015).

There is considerable variation between states in regards to the lawful age of consent for sexual activity (Stone, 2017). In some states, it is illegal for two persons under the age of 18 to engage in sexual relations. The age of consent is as young as 14 in some states, and as old as 17 in other states. State statutes regarding the age of consent can be found at www.ageofconsent.com. A related issue is statutory rape, which is defined as an adult who engages in a sexual relationship with a minor. States, again, have different laws regarding the age difference to qualify as statutory rape. To determine if a situation may be defined as statutory rape, SCs can consult with the district's legal counsel or contact Child Protective Services (CPS) or the police department.

Child Abuse and Neglect

Federal law designates all educators as mandated reporters, which requires that they must report suspected abuse or neglect or minors, usually within 24 to 72 hours of first "having reason to suspect." The terms *child abuse* and *neglect* are defined by the Child Abuse Prevention and Treatment Act Reauthorization Act of 2010 (2010) as "any recent act or failure to act on the part of a parent of caretaker which results in death, serious harm, sexual abuse, or exploitation, or an act or failure to act which presents an imminent risk of serious harm" (p. 6). Laws and definitions of child abuse vary across states. Reporters are free from liability for reporting suspected child abuse/neglect, even if a subsequent investigation determines that there is no evidence of abuse/neglect, as long as the report was made without malice, meaning, that the school counselor was not personally motivated to harm the alleged perpetrator (Kenny et al., 2018). Most states have serious penalties for failing to report suspected child abuse/neglect. Mandated reporters are only responsible for reporting suspected abuse to CPS, who conduct the actual investigation if there is a finding of child abuse.

SCs may experience a variety of emotions in reporting suspicions of child abuse and neglect (Tuttle et al., 2019), including fear of repercussions from parents and school officials (Bryant & Milsom, 2005), anxiety that their report would not be investigated (Sikes et al., 2010), and frustration when reports of abuse are not founded (Ricks et al., 2019). Reporting child and sexual abuse is the second leading reason for SCs to attend court (Sikes, 2008). SCs often report feeling frustrated with the lack of information from authorities regarding the investigation of abuse, but due to confidentiality, the reporter is only obligated to be informed of whether there was a finding of abuse (Child Welfare Information Gateway, 2003). Tuttle et al. (2019) recommend that early career SCs use the following steps in reporting suspicions of abuse:

1) Learn and abide by state laws and district/school child abuse reporting policies.
2) Learn and abide by the *ASCA Ethical Standards*.
3) Receive training to identify and recognize signs of child abuse.
4) Identify stakeholders.
5) Develop collaborative partnerships.
6) Provide school-based training.
7) Report child abuse.
8) Follow postreporting procedures.

Duty to Warn

Although the term "duty to warn" is not explicitly stated, the *ASCA Ethical Standards* imply that SCs have a "duty to warn," which means that they must consider breaching a student's confidentiality by warning the intended target if the student poses a danger to others. The basis for the "duty to warn" standard stems from *Tarasoff v. Board of Regents of California* (1976; Stone, 2017). In this case, the client, a graduate student, informed his psychologist that he intended to kill a girl, whose last name was Tarasoff, and who had rejected his advances. The psychologist informed the police, who arrested but then released the client, who, soon after, murdered Tarasoff. The California Supreme Court ruled that the psychologist had a duty not only to protect but also to warn the intended the victim and her parents, as the relationship between a psychologist and parents is special and outweighed the psychologist's obligation to protect the client's privacy.

Since the Tarasoff ruling, some state courts have extended the "duty to warn" standard, while others have limited this obligation (Stone, 2017). Generally, a duty to warn is required in situations where potential victims can be identified. Courts have generally ruled that foreseeability is an essential condition for a duty to warn. If an SC was informed that a child was a potential danger and failed to take action, the SC could be considered negligent.

Duty to Protect

Some courts have ruled that SCs, within the school setting, also have a duty to protect. The case of *Gammon v. Edwardsville Community Unit School District* (1980) illustrates an example in which an SC was ruled to have failed to meet his or her duty to protect a child (Stone, 2017). An eighth-grade student informed her SC that other students told the girl that another girl made physical threats toward her. The SC, who had worked closely with the girl who allegedly had been making threats, conducted an unsuccessful mediation with the two girls. Subsequently, the SC met individually with the student making the threats, warning her that she would be suspended if she engaged in physical aggression. The SC also met privately with the apprehensive student and encouraged her to avoid the girl making the threats. The SC did not inform an administrator or notify the recess supervisors who were supervising the girls later that day. During recess, the aggressor punched the victim, which resulted in a skull fracture that required surgery. The court ruled that the SC violated in loco parentis by failing to attempt to protect the child, and that the SC had sufficient proof of the potential for harm. However, other courts in cases involving similar circumstances, such as in the case of *Sugg vs. Albuquerque Pub. Sch. Dis. (1999)*, have not ruled that an SC has a duty to protect.

Bullying, Dating Violence, and Harassment

SCs report to the administration incidents and threats of bullying, dating violence, and sexual harassment (A.9.e). While SCs often provide services to victims and perpetrators of violence, SCs are required to report discipline issues to the administration.

Box 14.10

Reasons to **ALWAYS** break confidentiality:

- Student is a danger to self (e.g., suicidal thoughts and actions).
- Student is a danger to others → danger must be "foreseeable" and "serious."
- Student reports experiencing abuse or neglect.
- Bullying, dating violence, or sexual harassment.
- Whenever federal or state law, or district policy, mandates reporting.

* Confidentiality regulations vary by state.

Reasons to (strongly) **CONSIDER** breaking confidentiality:

- Drug or alcohol use (especially at elevated rates of intensity and frequency).
- Sexual activity.
- Pregnancy/abortion.

Strategies for Balancing Students' and Parents' Rights

SCs are required to inform students, parents, and other stakeholders regarding the nature of confidentiality of its limitations through "student handbooks; classroom lessons; verbal notification to individual students; and school counseling department websites, brochures, and social media accounts" (A.2.e). Reassuring parents that the SC will definitely contact them at any time they feel their child might be in danger to themselves or others may go a long way to assuage concerns.

When working with individual parents, empathic and nonjudgmental communication can bridge a gap between school personnel, the student, and the parents. Sometimes, allowing parents to vent while validating their concerns may be all that is necessary to quell a conflict. Who better to offer the emotional support needed and be able to provide a forum in which exasperated parents can share their frustrations than the professional school counselor, who has honed those mediation skills?

McCurdy and Murray (2003) suggest using professional judgment for deciding on "appropriate" inclusion of parents. Generally, it is not the SC's job to become "the informant" for the parents. In order to avoid this role, it may be helpful to simply ask the parents what they wish to know. Likewise, asking the child what he or she wants to share has value and may eliminate the problem. When a parent's request for disclosure of his or her child's counseling sessions arises, it may offer a teaching opportunity. This may open the door to a discussion between the parent and SC about the value of the support being offered to the child, while also modeling effective communication. Another effective strategy may be to offer the SC's office as a venue for a discussion between parent and child. SCs can also suggest that the parent directly ask the child about the contents of the counseling sessions because, in many cases, the child wants to share his or her feelings with their parents but lacks the necessary skills. In many ways, confidentiality is not about keeping someone's secrets as much as it is about helping someone learn how to effectively share them (Williams, 2009).

A parent's request to learn about the contents of a counseling session can also be handled by reinforcing to the parent the importance of his or her child's developmental growth that is necessary for independent thinking (Mitchell et al., 2002). The SC's intention is to help the child practice talking about his or her feelings so they can effectively share with his or her parents. This knowledge may help minimize parental skepticism, especially when they understand that the counseling office is a safe place to practice the child's communication skills. Additionally, educating parents about the value of a trusting relationship in the school setting is as important as helping them understand how a breach of confidentiality may harm the child and inhibit his or her willingness to share honestly. This simple information-sharing may mitigate the parent's request to breach confidentiality.

Courts have generally ruled that parents have a right to know the information shared by their child within counseling sessions, but that does not mean that parents have a right to all the information shared by the child. SCs still have a responsibility to serve and protect the students with whom they work, and therefore, SCs need to be mindful of the information shared with the parent that is above and beyond what the parent is asking for, or what the counselor is required to share by law. For example, children may have expressed negative feelings toward a parent, and sharing such information will only increase the tension between the student and his or her parent. When breaking the student's confidentiality in sharing information with the parent, the SC should first seek to only share that information that may be helpful to the parent. The SC may provide suggestions that could improve the parent's relationship with their child. For example, rather than divulge that a student has stated that he or she hates his or her mother, the SC can share ideas about how the parent can hear and understand his or her child's anger.

Confidentiality and School Administration

The *ASCA Ethical Standards* require SCs to inform school officials of activities that "may be potentially disruptive or damaging to the school's mission, personnel, and property while honoring the confidentiality between the student and the school counselor" (B.2.g). Unlike the obligation to inform parents of potential risk-taking behavior, SCs in the vast majority of states are not legally required to breach confidentiality and inform administrators of students' risk-taking behaviors (Glosoff & Pate, 2002). Neither laws nor the *Ethical Standards* provide an operational definition of what may be considered potentially disruptive or damaging behavior. A national survey revealed that SCs thought it was more ethical to reveal private information shared by students to administrators when the behaviors were directly observed versus behaviors that were reported by students, and when the behaviors occurred on school grounds during school hours (Moyer et al., 2012).

Family Education Rights and Privacy Act of 1974 (FERPA)

In regards to maintaining the confidentiality of student records, the *ASCA Ethical*

Box 14.11

Family Educational Rights and Privacy Act of 1974 (FERPA)—federal legislation that describes how all written information, including educational records, should be handled and maintained within schools. It also states that parents must have access to their child's educational records.

Standards require that SCs adhere to school policies and state and federal laws, including the laws within the Family Educational Rights and Privacy Act (FERPA) of 1974. The Family Educational Rights and Privacy Act of 1974 is federal legislation that regulates educational records and outlines how all written information concerning a student must be handled and distributed in order to protect the student and her or his family (Stone, 2017). Ideally, SCs are not responsible for managing educational records, as it is considered an inappropriate duty (ASCA, 2019b), but they should have a deep understanding of FERPA guidelines in order to advocate for students' and parents' rights. The FERPA grants parents of minor students the right to access their child's official school records, which includes cumulative folders, test data, academic reports, attendance and discipline records, health information, family background, etc. Parents' rights to review, seek to amend, and disclose education records are transferred to the student once he or she reaches 18 years of age. However, once a student turns 18, parents may still have access to their child's education record if the child is still financially dependent. The FERPA grants noncustodial parents all the same rights as custodial parents to their child's education record as long as there is not a court order explicitly prohibiting the noncustodial parent's access (Alexander & Alexander, 2009). Stepparents have the same rights as custodial parents if he or she resides in the same residence as the child.

Parents and eligible students have the right to challenge the accuracy of information. If schools refuse to amend an educational record, parents or the eligible student may request a hearing. If the school continues to refuse to amend the educational records, parents or the eligible student may add a statement of disagreement which the school is required to disclose when sharing records with other institutions/persons.

Under FERPA guidelines, schools must have written permission from parents or the eligible student before releasing information from a student's educational record. Universities, military and employment recruiters, and class ring and yearbook companies frequently request directory information. FERPA does permit districts to disseminate "directory information," which includes students' contact information, without consent of the parents of eligible students. If a district elects to make student directory information available, parents have the right of opting their child out of the information dissemination. Schools may use a variety of ways to inform parents of their rights under FERPA, including the student handbook, special letters, emails, etc. If a district decides to make directory information available, they cannot discriminate between groups of requestors. In other words, they cannot provide directory information to one university but deny it to another.

Exceptions Within FERPA

FERPA indicates that educators who have a legitimate educational interest (LEI) may have access to a student's educational records without parental permission. LEI means that a teacher or other school professional may review an educational record for the purposes of performing tasks within the professionals' job descriptions. The information gathered through a record review may be related to a student's educational progress, discipline referrals, or may provide information regarding a service related to the student or to the student's family, such as counseling. SCS have a LEI in performing tasks associated with the position but may not access a student's record out of curiosity. School districts must establish procedures to ensure that school officials, including outside service providers, only access educational records for which they have legitimate educational interests. FERPA allows school officials to disclose information from a student's educational record in an emergency in order to protect the health or safety of students or other individuals. In such situations, school officials may release information and records to appropriate parties, which may include law enforcement, public health officials, and medical personnel.

School Counselor's Notes

Although the varied and demanding requirements of the position do not allow for SCs to engage in extensive note-taking, most SCs maintain case notes (Shea et al., 2018). It is considered best practice for an SC to maintain case notes for some students, either to serve as a memory aid for continuity of services provided or in documenting an SC's decision-making in encountering an ethical dilemma. When the situation arises that requires extensive note-taking, such as for situations involving suicidal threats, self-mutilation, child abuse, etc., case notes must be handled in a thorough and professional manner. Included in these notes are only objective observations and procedures. It is not appropriate to include personal commentary, judgments, or thoughts in these extensive notes. It is wise practice to include in the notes lists of school professionals with whom the SC consulted, what decision was made, and why a decision occurred when documenting a difficult situation. Always consider that a court may subpoena the SC to make his or her notes available.

A distinction is generally made between sole-possession notes and notes that other professionals may access. The criteria for an SC's notes to be considered sole-possession notes are:

1) They serve as memory aids.
2) They are not accessible or shared verbally or in written form with others.
3) They are created solely for the person possessing them.
4) They include only observation and professional opinions. (Stone, 2017)

Box 14.12

Sole-possession notes—a school counselor's case documentation that are brief memory aids intended only for the school counselor and are not added to a student's educational file and, therefore, are not covered under FERPA.

Sole-possession notes are best kept in a personal and secured manner. The notes shall be placed in a locked place when not in use. If an SC's notes are kept on a school-owned computer, they are considered the possession of the school. SCs must also establish and follow a consistent policy for the purging of their notes. For example, the SC may destroy their notes for all students who have graduated from the school or are no longer assigned to the SC. SCs cannot destroy their notes on a discriminate basis (A.13.f). For example, destroying one's notes for a specific child for fear that the notes would reveal sensitive information about the child or call into question the SC's ethical decision is unethical. FERPA designates that "sole-possession records" are not considered educational records, and thus it is important that SCs do not place their sole-possession notes in the student's cumulative file. However, as noted in the *ASCA Ethical Standards*, SC's case notes may be subpoenaed unless there is a specific state statute for privileged communication (A.12.d).

The issue of an SC's case notes becomes more problematic when they are maintained electronically on the district's management system (Shea et al., 2018). Many student management systems provide SCs with opportunities to write notes about students. Shea et al. (2018) recommend that SCs restrict note-taking to either a paper-and-pencil format or only using software programs that advertise as FERPA compliant. The problem with some student information systems is that even if the SC password-protects access to their notes, some school personnel have access to password-protected information. In such a case, the SC's case notes satisfy the criteria as educational records and thus may be subject to parent inspection upon request.

Subpoenas

A survey of SCs revealed that one-third of the respondents reported that they had been asked to testify in court (Stone, 2013). The vast majority of the SC testimony requests concerned custody issues and child abuse. SCs frequently receive subpoenas, and commonly, these subpoenas are either a request for documentation or to testify in court. Upon receiving a subpoena, an SC should contract the school district's lawyer to review his or her options. Lawyers for defendants or plaintiffs frequently submit such subpoenas, but the SC does not necessarily need to comply with the subpoena. In contrast, a subpoena from a judge typically requires compliance.

Case Study

Madison is a highly motivated 13-year-old seventh-grade student who receives mostly "As." Her teachers regard her as the model student, frequently providing assistance to teachers and performing beyond their expectations. The teachers report that Madison is a particularly skilled writer and that she enjoys sharing her "emotionally deep" poetry with them. However, Madison's teachers report that she frequently appears "down" in that she rarely smiles or appears happy, and they have referred Madison to you, the school counselor.

In your first meeting with Madison, you explain that her teachers are concerned that she often seems "down." She readily shares that she often feels rejected by other students, stating, "I just don't get people. I try to be friendly, but they act like I don't exist. What is wrong with me?" In exploring Madison's sadness on a 10-point scale, she reports feeling at about a "3." In response to your question, "Have you ever thought about hurting yourself?" Madison, after some hesitation, says no, but her nonverbal reactions indicate to you that she may have had such thoughts, as she appears uncomfortable but isn't necessarily angry or upset with you asking such questions. You explain to Madison that it is not uncommon for people to think about hurting themselves. You state that you understand that she might feel uncomfortable telling you but that you would like to help her if she is having such thoughts. She states that she does not want to talk about it. You ask her again, but she denies attempting to hurt herself and she changes the subject, complaining that no one likes her. While Madison's thinking in general appears irrational, she readily generates and comprehends abstract thought. Madison agrees to meet with you again in several days.

Madison initiates the second meeting by stating that she recently intentionally scalded herself in the shower, and in previous weeks, she has made scratches on her arm with a needle, which drew blood. When asked if her parents know that she has hurt herself, Madison does not want them to know, believing that her mom would probably say something like, "That is a really stupid thing to do." In the past two weeks, she also reports several incidents where she thought her heart was racing, felt dizzy, and thought, "I'm going to die." When she mentioned one of these episodes to her mother, her mother's response was, "Don't worry about it, it will go away."

You remind Madison that you are obligated to notify those that can help her if she is a threat to herself. You explain that you are concerned about her and want to help. In order to do that, her parents need to know about the problems she is having, because you believe that they know her the best, that they are the ones who are most likely to be able to help her. You inform her that you will be contacting her parents later that day, asking them to meet about some problems that Madison has been having. She declines to be present as she fears that they will be angry at her for sharing her problems with someone outside of the family. You tell Madison that you will tell her parents specifically about her self-injury and possible panic attacks.

When you reach Madison's mother, Mrs. Smith, she seems confused but reluctantly agrees to bring along her husband for a meeting later that day. Mr. and Mrs. Smith readily admit that they are aware of Madison engaging in several incidents of self-injurious behavior during the past year and that Madison's pediatrician encouraged them to seek counseling for her. However, Mr. and Mrs. Smith seem to be strongly united in seeing Madison as "dramatic" and believe that she will "grow out of it." You share with the Smiths what the research literature indicates about some of the potential dangers of self-injury, but this seems to only further harden their position that there is no need for concern. You switch tactics, asking them to identify what would indicate to them that Madison is having a problem, and while they do not identify any specific behaviors, their responses seem to be a bit more thoughtful, suggesting that they are thinking differently about the problem. When asked what they would like Madison to develop at this point in her life, they indicate that they would like her to have more friends. They ask for your help in assisting Madison with making friends, and you agree to include Madison in a social skills group. You also explain that you cannot, however, focus exclusively upon Madison's self-injurious behaviors. You conclude the session by reiterating your concern that Madison is at risk of harming herself, and you provide the parents with the contact information for three mental health agencies in the area which provide counseling services to children and their families.

Over the next several months, you assist Madison in developing friendships. She attends a six-week social skills group, and you meet with her every other week for individual counseling. Madison demonstrates progress in making friends. She develops awareness that she tends to overpursue very popular girls who are not interested in becoming friends with her. She begins to seek out girls and boys who have similar interests and are receptive to being friends with her. Madison also learns skills to manage her anxiety when connecting with peers.

Madison reports that her parents never pursued the referrals you provided them. During your individual counseling sessions, Madison reports being angry and confused with her parents, particularly her mother, whom she describes as suffocating. Through individual counseling, eventually she comes to realize that her mother and father have difficulty hearing about Madison's emotions. She realizes that it is acceptable for her to have strong feelings, including toward her parents, but she concludes that she must be thoughtful about how she manages her emotions in a constructive way, which she does through her poetry, and she must be careful about how she shares her thoughts and feelings with her parents. You occasionally check in with her about her attempts at self-injury, but she appears to be truthful in reporting that she has not acted upon any urges to hurt herself.

Analysis of the Case Study

Madison's presenting problems indicate that she and her family are in need of services that would be more appropriately provided within an agency vs. a school setting, and the SC correctly provided the parents with appropriate referrals (A.5.b). The SC effectively handled breaching confidentiality by informing Madison of the limits of confidentiality, conducting an informal risk assessment, and offering Madison options for how to inform her parents. The fact that Madison's parents are not interested in pursuing a referral, which unfortunately is a fairly common response among parents, presents a dilemma for the SC. The role of the SC dictates that they seek to assist all students and thus are not able to provide long-term counseling. However, the SC also had an ethical obligation to assist Madison, and the SC appeared to achieve an effective compromise in respecting the parents' right to make decisions for Madison while also attempting to assist Madison in at least a more limited fashion.

Summary

Because of the complexity of ethical decision-making when working in a school setting with minors, SCs should utilize a specific ethical decision-making model. Stone's Solutions to Ethical Problems (STEPS) for ethical decision-making have actually been incorporated within the *ASCA Ethical Standards* (F). Consultation with other seasoned professionals is an important and necessary ethical expectation and an important system of support. Reaching out to other professionals for the benefit of your career and the benefit of the children you serve is an ethical mandate. Involvement within the state school counseling professional association can be extremely beneficial, as often SCs who participate in the state professional associations are the most knowledgeable about the regulations within the state. Finally, documenting all steps taken in the ethical decision-making process is essential.

References

Alexander, K., & Alexander, M. D. (2009). *The law of schools, students, teachers in a nutshell* (4th ed.). West Publishing.

American Heritage Dictionary. (1985). *The American Heritage Dictionary* (second college ed.). Houghton Mifflin.

American School Counselor Association. (2019a). *ASCA standards for school counselor preparation programs.* Author. www.schoolcounselor.org/getmedia/573d7c2c-1622-4d25-a5ac-ac74d2e614ca/ASCA-Standards-for-School-Counselor-Preparation-Programs.pdf

American School Counselor Association. (2019b). *The ASCA national model: A framework for school counseling programs* (4th ed.). Author.

American School Counselor Association. (2020). *The school counseling and suicide risk assessment.* Author.

American School Counselor Association. (2022). *The American School Counselor Association ethical standards for school counselors.* Author. https://schoolcounselor.org/About-School-Counseling/ Ethical-Legal-Responsibilities/ASCA-Ethical-Standards-for-School-Counselors-(1)

Bryant, J., & Milsom, A. (2005). Child abuse reporting by school counselors. *Professional School Counseling, 9*(1), 63–71. https://doi.org/10.1177/2156759X0500900106

Child Abuse Prevention and Treatment Act Reauthorization Act of 2010, Pub. L. No. 111–320 (2010). www.congress/gov/vill/111th-congress/senate-bill/3817/text

Child Welfare Information Gateway. (2003). *Child protective services: A guide for caseworkers.* U.S. Department of Health and Human Services, Children's Bureau. www.childwelfare.gove/pubPDFs/ cps.pdf

Council for the Accreditation of Counseling and Related Educational Programs. (n.d.). *2016 CACREP standards.* https://www.cacrep.org/for-programs/2016-cacrep-standards/

Euben, D. (2003). Educational malpractice: Faculty beware? *Academe, 89*(3), 102. https://doi. org/10.2307/40252481

Family Education Rights and Privacy Act, 20 U.S.C. §1232g (1974).

Fischer, L., & Sorenson, P. (1996). *School law for counselors, psychologists, and social workers.* Longman.

Fye, H. J., Miller, L. G., & Rainey, J. S. (2017). Predicting school counselors' supports and challenges when implementing the ASCA National Model. *Professional School Counseling, 21*(1), 1–11. https://doi.10.1177/2156759X18777671

Glosoff, H. L., & Pate, R. H., Jr. (2002). Privacy and confidentiality in school counseling. *Professional School Counseling*, 6(1), 20–27. www.researchgate.net/profile/H-Glosoff/publication/234700799_Privacy_and_Confidentiality_in_School_Counseling/links/0f31753c545050206f000000/Privacy-and-Confidentiality-in-School-Counseling.pdf

Guttmacher Institute. (2015, January). *State policies in brief: An overview of minors' consent law.* www.guttmacher.org/statecenter/spibs/spib_OMCL.pdf

Herlihy, B., & Corey, G. (2006). Confidentiality. In B. Herlihy & G. Corey (Eds.), *American Counseling Association ethical standards casebook* (6th ed., pp. 205–217). American Counseling Association.

Hopkins, B. R., & Anderson, B. S. (1990). *The counselor and the law* (3rd ed.). American Counseling Association.

Isaacs, M. L., & Stone, C. (1999). School counselors and confidentiality: Factors affecting professional choices. *Professional School Counseling*, 2(4), 258–266. www.proquest.com/docview/213243638?pq origsite=gscholar&fromopenview=true

Kenny, M. C., Abreu, R. L., Helpingstine, C., Lopez, A., & Matthews, B. (2018). Counselors' mandated responsibility to report child maltreatment: A review of U.S. Laws. *Journal of Counseling & Development*, 96(4), 372–387. https://doi.10.1002/jcad.12220

Linde, L. E. (2007). Ethical, legal, and professional issues in school counseling. In B. T. Erford (Ed.), *Transforming the school counseling profession* (pp. 51–73). Merrill/Prentice Hall.

McCurdy, K. G., & Murray, K. C. (2003). Confidentiality issues when minor children disclose family secrets in family counseling. *The Family Journal: Counseling and Therapy for Couples and Families*, 11(4), 393–398. https://doi.org/10.1177/1066480703255468

Mitchell, C. W., Disque, J. G., & Robertson, P. (2002). When parents want to know: Responding to parental demands for confidential information. *Professional School Counselor*, 6(2), 156–161. www.jstor.org/stable/42732405

Moyer, M. S., & Sullivan, J. (2008). Student risk-taking behaviors: When do school counselors break confidentiality. *Professional School Counseling*, 11(4), 236–245. https://doi.org/10.1177/2156759X0801100404

Moyer, M. S., Sullivan, J. R., & Growcock, D. (2012). When is it ethical to inform administrators about student risk-taking behaviors? Perceptions of school counselors. *Professional School Counseling*, 15(3), 98–109. https://doi.org/10.5330/PSC.n.2012-15.98

Remley, T. P., Jr., & Herlihy, B. (Eds.). (2013). *Ethical, legal, and professional issues in counseling* (4th ed.). Merrill Prentice Hall.

Ricks, L., Tuttle, M., Land, C., & Chibbaro, J. (2019). Trends and influential factors in child abuse reporting: Implications for early career school counselors. *Journal of School Counseling*, 17(16). www.jsc.montana.edu/articles/v17n16.pdf

Schmidt, J. J. (2013). *Counseling in schools: Comprehensive programs of responsive services for all students* (6th ed.). Pearson.

Shea, M. L., Cinotti, D., & Stone, C. (2018). An examination of school counselors' use of electronic case notes. *Journal of School Counseling*, 16(18). https://eric/ed/gov/contentdelivery/servlet/ERICServlet?accno=EJ1185858

Sikes, A. (2008). A school counselor's guide to reporting child abuse and neglect. *Journal of School Counseling*, 6(25). www.jsc/montana.edu/articles/v6n25.pdf

Sikes, A., Remley, T., Jr., & Hays, D. G. (2010). Experiences of school counselors during and after making suspected child abuse reports. *Journal of School Counseling*, 8(21). www.jsc.montana.edu/articles/v8n21.pdf

Stone, C. (2013). *School counseling principles: Ethics and law* (3rd ed.). American School Counselor Association.

Stone, C. (2017). *School counseling principles: Ethics and law* (4th ed.). American School Counselor Association.

Tuttle, M., Ricks, L., & Taylor, M. (2019). A child abuse reporting framework for early career school counselors. *The Professional Counselor*, 9(3), 238–251. https://doi.org/10.15241/mt.9.3.238

Williams, R. L. (2009, July). *Confidentiality dilemma: Ethical issues in school counseling.* Presented at the annual meeting of American School Counselor Association Conference.

Group Counseling Parent Consent Letter: English-Language Version

August 15, 2022

Dear Parent/Guardian,

Your daughter has shown interest or has been nominated by her teachers to join "Smart-Girl." "Smart-Girl" is an enrichment program designed to teach young girls skills they will need for success during their adolescent years. Girls will discuss issues such as critical thinking, mood management, refusal skills, body image, leadership and bullying, among others. Girls also participate in activities such as role-playing, journal writing, art projects, and many other fun activities.

The "Smart-Girl" group will meet every Thursday from 3:15 p.m. to 4:30 p.m., from September 11, 2014, until November 20, 2014. The groups will be led by Erika Serrano (ELL teacher), Brenda Fritzler (teacher in green pod), and Kris Goen (resource teacher). Matthew McClain, Baker Central School Counselor, will serve as the program manager.

Due to the overwhelming interest and nature of the program, participants must be able to attend most sessions. Former sessions proved to be quite successful, with many of the girls finding it valuable and applicable to their lives. It is our hope that this group will empower our young girls with the knowledge, skills, and confidence to face the challenges of the upcoming years. We hope you will allow your student to participate in this wonderful and exciting group! Please return this permission slip and attached form (portions of the attached form are optional, and information is used by the Smart-Girl program office—no personal information is published) to school no later than **September 5, 2022.** Your daughter will be notified if she is attending this session by Wednesday, September 10, 2022. Our first "Smart-Girl" session will start on September 11, 2022.

If you have any questions regarding "Smart-Girl," you can visit the website www.smart-girl.org, or please feel free to contact Matthew McClain.

Sincerely,
Erika Serrano, Brenda Fritzler, and Kris Goen
Matthew McClain 867–8422 Ext. 44218

* *

_____ **Yes,** I would like my daughter to be a part of the Smart-Girl group at Baker on Thursdays from 3:15 p.m. to 4:30 p.m. I will make sure I have made arrangements for her to walk home or for someone to pick her up at 4:30 p.m. (if transportation is a concern, please contact Mr. McClain).

_____ **No,** I would not like my daughter to be a part of the Smart-Girl group at Baker.

_____   _____
Print Daughter's Name   Parent's Name

_____   _____
Daughter's Signature   Parent's Signature

Group Counseling Parent Consent Letter: Spanish-Language Version

15 de Agosto de 2022

Estimado Padre/Guardián,

Su hija ha mostrado interés o ha sido nombrado por sus maestros para unir "*Smart-Girl*." "Smart-Girl" es un programa de enriquecimiento de diseñó para enseñar chicas jóvenes habilidades que necesitarán para el éxito durante sus años adolescentes. Las chicas discutirán asuntos como pensamiento crítico, gestión de humor, habilidades de negativa, imagen de cuerpo, el liderazgo e intimidar, entre otros. Las chicas también toman parte en actividades como el juego de roles, como escritura de diario, como proyectos de arte, y como muchas otras actividades divertidas.

El grupo de las "Smart-Girl" se encontrará todos los jueves de 3:15 P.M. a 4:30 P.M., del 11 de Septiembre de 2014 hasta el 20 de Noviembre de 2014. "Smart-Girl" no encontrarán sobre interrupción de primavera. Las sesiones serán dirigidas por Erika Serrano (Maestra del ELL), Brenda Friztler (Maestra del equipo Verde), y Kris Goen (Maestra del recursos). Matthew McClain, Consejero de Escuela de Baker Central, servirá como Director de Programa.

Debido al interés y la naturaleza abrumadores del programa, los participantes necesitan asistir la mayoría de las sesiones. Las sesiones anteriores resultaron bastante exitosas con muchas de las chicas que encuentran valioso y aplicable a sus vidas. Es nuestra esperanza que este grupo autorizará a nuestras jóvenes chicas con el conocimiento, las habilidades, y la confianza a encarar los desafíos de los años próximos. ¡Esperamos que permita a su estudiante tomar parte en este grupo maravilloso y emocionante! Regrese por favor este permiso y forma conectada (porciones de la forma conectada son opcionales, y la información es utilizada por la oficina del programa de "Smart-Girl"—ninguna información personal es publicada) al escuela no mas tarde que el 5 de Septiembre de 2022. Su hija será notificada si asiste esta sesión para el Miércoles, 10 de Septiembre de 2022. Nuestra primera sesión de "Smart-Girl" comenzará el Jueves, 11 de Septiembre de 2022.

Si tiene cualquier pregunta con respecto a "Smart-Girl," puede visitar el sitio web *www.smart-girl.org* o sentirse por favor libre contactar a Matthew McClain.

Sinceramente,
Erika Serrano, Brenda Fritzler and Kris Goen
Matthew McClain 867–8422 Ext. 44218

****

_____ **Si,** Quiero que mi hija sea una parte del grupo de "Smart-Girl" en Baker los Jueves de las 3:15 a 4:30 de la tarde. Me aseguraré de que he hecho arreglos para ella que ande a casa o que alguien la recoja a las 4:30 de la tarde (si transporte es una preocupación, contacte por favor a Sr. McClain).

_____ **No,** yo no quiero que mi hija sea una parte del grupo de las "Smart-Girl," en Baker.

Imprima el Nombre de Hija	Imprima el Nombre de Padre

Firma de Hija	Firma de Padre

Index